the
power
of
plants

409. Ranunculus 5. *Matth.*

622. Bugloff. fempervirens. *Ad. L.*

286. Liquiritia. Süßholtz. *M.*

494. Capparis. Kappern. *T.*

Plants are the foundation of all existence,
of humans and animals,
of society and civilization.
To nourish, cure,
delight, and inspire us
they battle constantly with the elements.
And they have launched men
on the most momentous voyages of discovery,
across oceans and continents
and through the inner empires
of the mind.

BRENDAN LEHANE

the power

Plants create most of our
reality and many of our
dreams. They are the
source of our nourishment
and health, pleasures and
ecstasies; they sustain religions, cultures, civilizations. In the end they can
kill us, and return us to the
soil on which they them-
selves feed.

designed by EMIL BÜHRER
and ROBERT TOBLER

f plants

JOHN MURRAY · LONDON

Published by John Murray (Publishers) Ltd.,
Albemarle Street, London, England

ISBN: 0 7195 3443 7

A McGraw-Hill Co-publication

Editor:
FLOYD YEAROUT

Managing Editor:
FRANCINE PEETERS

Picture Acquisition:
EDITH BÜRGLER

Production Manager:
FRANZ GISLER

Graphic Artist:
FRANZ CORAY

Proofreader:
DARYL SHARP

Indexer:
DELIGHT ANSLEY

Jacket Design:
THE GLUSKER GROUP, INC.

Printed by:
POLYGRAPHISCHE GESELLSCHAFT, LAUPEN, SWITZERLAND

Bound by:
LEIGHTON-STRAKER, LONDON, ENGLAND

Composition by:
EDV + FILMSATZ AG, THUN, SWITZERLAND

Photolithography by:
ACTUAL, BIEL, SWITZERLAND

Printed in Switzerland

Wolgemüth.   Origanum.

5

So wil ich dir ein freüdenopffer thün
Das kreütlein wolmüth vil geheime wirküng
erfreüet das geblüt, ist miltz und lungen güt
Also wan Gott üns hilfft, u. lässets wol
so söllen wir dafür ein freüdenopffer br

TABLE OF CONTENTS

The ancients recognized four elements: earth, air, fire, and water. In theory, modern science has clipped and split them into more than a hundred divisions. In substance, the four remain. They are the matter and the force whose constant interplay first brought life into being and continues to sustain it. Behind the face of animated nature, the rhythmical give-and-take of these four—each to and from the other—is an unceasing clockwork.

The sinuous fingers of the sea creep over the land. These rivers and rivulets scrape a veneer of salts and minerals down to the myriad mouths of the ocean. In her turn the sea surrenders moisture to the air. The heat of the solar fire raises a daily draft of mist up to the enveloping atmosphere. Winds transport it in clouds over the earth, periodically shading the land from the glare of the sun, and sprinkling what would otherwise be arid wastes with rain. Thus, by the agency of fire, and through the medium of air, water returns to the mountains and plains, to descend as trickle, stream, torrent, or cascade—progressively enriched by the dissolved surface of the rock.

The first life was lived in the fringes of the sea. From the sea the earliest ancestors of terrestrial plants, animals, and men took their unsteady steps up the shore—the tiny few who could withstand the buffets of wave and current and evade the rigorous grinding of rocks. The people who return year by year to the coast, expose their bodies to the sun and water, and watch the waves lapping or pounding the sand and rocks are revisiting the scene of a miraculous exodus, of the meeting of the four elements, and of the beginnings of all life.

By means of plants, the rays of the sun are transformed into flesh. Alone of all life-forms, plants can not only catch sunlight but—by a unique alchemy—compound it with terrestrial ingredients to make the basic food and substance of all living things. Either directly, or as the base of a pyramid of consumption, the roots, stems, fruits, and

AND THE LORD GOD COMMANDED THE MAN, SAYING,
OF EVERY TREE OF THE GARDEN
THOU MAYEST FREELY EAT:
BUT OF THE TREE OF THE KNOWLEDGE
OF GOOD AND EVIL,
THOU SHALT NOT EAT OF IT: FOR IN
THE DAY THAT THOU EATEST THEREOF
THOU SHALT SURELY DIE.   GENESIS 2: 16–17

flowers of plants sustain the whole of the animal kingdom. Backdrop to our evolution, they attended the vital needs of all our ancestors—marine, amphibian, and primate—as they indispensably supply ours still. No progress in our past, no evolutionary breakthrough, no new organ or cellular extension of our brain was possible without their collusion. In that sense they molded our bodies, faculties, perceptions, tastes. Some of them, with chemical qualities that were able to bend our view of reality, seemed to reveal to us the hidden realms of the spirit.

For all these reasons, whether or not consciously perceived, man's blind search to discover the nature of his maker has always been conditioned by plants. If there were a

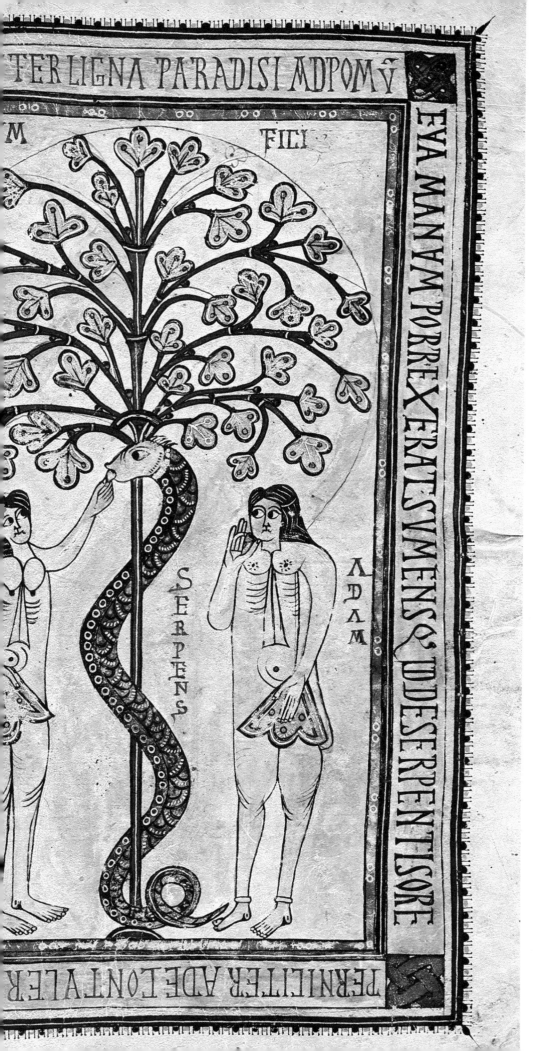

TER LIGNA PARADISI ADPOM꞉ Ꝟ

M

FILI

EVA MANVM PORREXERAT SVMENS Ꝗ UDE SERPENTIS ORE

SERPENS

ADAM

TERNILITER ADE CONTVLER

Opposite top: Adam and Eve, from a woodcut of 1486. *Opposite bottom:* Mushroom god from El Salvador. *Left:* Temptation scene, from the *Codex Vigilanus* at Madrid. *Below:* A seventeenth-century history of the Antilles substitutes the pawpaw for the apple of Paradise.

region where infinite beauty and infinite peace prevailed over the dark and tormented aspects of earthly life, it could not be pictured without plants. In every religion and cosmology, heaven is a garden. If a realm without sin, evil, hatred, and war is thinkable at all, it can be imagined only as a terrain of flowers and fruits set against rich and

gentle greens. Human imaginings of paradise cannot improve on nature's reality.

In most religions, this transcendent role of plants is taken further. The whole universe becomes a tree, its roots the abode of darkness, its earth our earth, its spreading boughs the vault of heaven.

Small wonder, then, that plants not only form the structure of our universe but invade the sphere of morals too. In many faiths, good and evil are mystically embodied in the fruits of a tree. By eating the forbidden fruit man lost his natural innocence and became a sinner. The myth is interpreted in many ways, but one thing is clear: The mind and spirit of man, no less than his body, feed on plants, and are starved without them.

A standard distinction between plants and animals is that the former are static, the latter freely mobile. Yet animals and people are free to roam only within the limits plants allow them, and plants themselves are seldom motionless. They cannot afford to be. Every change in their environment affects them acutely.

All parts of a plant constantly respond to each other and to the conditions around them—to light, warmth, moisture, air pressure, touch, temperature, the position of the sun, and the direction of the wind. Rooted to the spot, they present a picture of rest which is belied by their internal mechanics. Science is still baffled by the series of incredibly complex adjustments that enable a sunflower faithfully to keep its face to the sun, traversing a broad ellipse throughout the hours of light. Nor can botanists fully understand the protective upheavals in, say, a coltsfoot, when sudden rain threatens to swamp the cosmetic gadgetry of scent and color.

This warding off of rain is one of the hiccups of plant life—responses to particular and unpredictable change. Beneath such actions lies the more regular programming, the series of responses to the elemental cycles

All life depends on the green leaf's chlorophyll, which alone can convert sunlight into energy and so powers the whole of organic creation.

Far left: The cross section of a tree shows the rings left by each successive season's growth. *Below:* The mandrake plant, *Mandragora officinarum*, whose substantial roots amass starch for growth, and by their curiously anthropoid shapes feed the imaginations of men.

The aim of conspicuous flowers is always to attract some insect or animal pollinator.

To disperse their seeds some plants wrap them in attractive and nutritious packages.

Bark is the dead covering of an elaborate circulation system, some of whose processes still defy explanation.

In their penetration of the earth to seek water and minerals, roots bypass most hard obstacles, but they can split rock if necessary.

of night and day and the succeeding seasons of each year. Within every seed of a fruit, sometimes within every cell of a leaf, sits the blueprint for the species' survival. The bare stems of a tree in winter, the buds and shoots and flowers of spring, the denser foliage of summer, and the fruitfulness of autumn form a predestined pattern within the gene. Every plant knows what is in general required of it. And there is more, much more, than these outward and visible signs of growth. Beneath the skeletal profiles of winter there is unceasing activity within the earth. Along with routine maintenance goes the construction of the leaves and shoots which must break ground, with unerring timing, when the year's worst privations are over. The shoots emerge primed with a vast store of knowledge—about how tall to grow, at what point to branch, when to leaf, what forms to assume in each of these particulars, down to the last vein on the leaf and the last bristle on its perimeter.

FOEMINA   MARIS

When the launch begins, it is usually part of a general movement that will transform the landscape. Bleak brown hedges, stark black trees, tangles of last year's dead vegetation, the naked dereliction of fields and hills—all warm with a pale suffusion of color. As harbingers of the new scene, catkins tassel the branches and anonymous seed-leaves push up from the expanses of soil. Leaves and buds carpet the ground and clothe the woodland with green. Early blossom patchily sprays the whole.

The movement sends ripples of activity into other forms of life. Animals awaken from their long winter sleep; birds return from their annual exile; and human hearts respond with heightened spirits.

That, at least, is how many of us see it. Perhaps our sentimentality makes more of nature than nature intends. True, it is the purpose of many plants to please—but within strict confines. Most flowers set their seductive sights at one or two particular insects, a butterfly or moth, sometimes a hummingbird. A creature that is exclusive in its visits will more surely pollinate other flowers of the same kind. What to us is beauty or the finest expression of refined emotion is, from the flower's point of view, no more than professional functionalism. The pleasing symmetry of a flytrap's gummy proboscis conceals lethal snares for unwary insects. The pattern of spears protruding from a cactus is both a defense and a device to conserve water. The abstract patterns of orange and chrome yellow on the bark of a sycamore are lichens whose form and color would enable them to survive on the snowcaps of high mountains. The shapes of leaves—long and linear in a lily, complex cut-outs in a chestnut—or of roots or seed-capsules are carefully tailored adaptations to a thousand variations of environment past and present. Beauty is in the eye of the beholder. For the plant, it is an urgent matter of keeping the species going.

Man is more than a beholder. He too must sustain himself and his kind. Beauty is a pleasure, but his first consideration is survival. Whether he eats corn or cabbage, or a cow fed on grass, or a fowl fattened with seed, or a fish plump with the harvest of the

variety with which to sharpen their perception. But their dependence on plants was not less. Throughout recorded history most human settlements have been beside the fields whose produce nourished them.

Cultivated plants gave more than nourish-

WHILE THE EARTH REMAINS
SEEDTIME AND HARVEST
COLD AND HEAT
SUMMER AND WINTER
DAY AND NIGHT
SHALL NOT CEASE

All animals and humans are swung like a pendulum between want and plenty. The pendulum here is the rhythm of the seasons, and its movement is set by the regular cycle of plant life. Myth has enshrined the changes of the seasons in the story of Demeter and her daughter Persephone. The god Hades, enraptured by the girl's beauty, caught her up into his chariot and carried her down to his infernal kingdom. Demeter, the earth mother, forgot her care of plants and growth as she searched day and night for her daughter. When finally she discovered her, the earth had fallen into decay. Green and burgeoning life was replaced by death and dereliction. By a decision of the gods, Hades was made to yield his prisoner for half the year but could keep her for the rest. So Demeter is happily attentive to her duties for the six months of

Above: Inscriptions on the back of a sundial include invocations of tree spirits, as well as magic and religious figures. *Left:* An Indian dance procures good harvests by marrying celestial with earthly rhythms. *Opposite page, top:* A corn dolly, a figure set on corn ricks to keep away spirits. *Right:* Scenes from the harvest through the centuries. *Below:* Cabalistic figure from an early eighteenth century German book on the secrets of nature.

waters, his survival depends—as that of all animals does—on what plants provide. Nowhere are their powers more clearly seen than here. In the days before agriculture, nomads roamed the forests and grasslands, their journeys dictated by the whereabouts of wild foods. If their objective was meat, still the dependence was ultimately on the plants their prey ate. When, after millennia of observation, people put into practice the principles they observed in the plant world and sowed seeds in places of their own choice, their takings increased. As groups they found new freedom, more time, more

ment. They gave spare time, which in turn allowed the development of civilization and

summer, but she still neglects them in winter. When men discovered the secret of the natural cycle, the Olympian bond remained. Farmers were as tied to the seasons as their predecessors. They sowed in spring and harvested in autumn, enjoyed the cornucopia of summer and merely survived the winter on stores. Today's methods have softened the seasonal impact. Preservatives, winter crops, and a world trade that can subsidize one country's winter from a harvest on the other side of the world have blurred what used to be an elemental distinction. Our emotions are not so quick to change. Spring remains a regeneration of the spirit.

all its benefits—and its drawbacks. Riches provoked war. To a starving nation the bulging granaries of another people became an intolerable temptation. The wealth of a settled state aroused the militant jealousy of tribes that still carried on the nomadic ways of pre-agricultural times. From Babylonia to Rome, from Rome to more recent demands for Lebensraum, conquest and imperialism have been resolvable into the need for more food.

Need—and from time to time greed. It was not necessity that drove the explorers of the world at the time of the Renaissance, when against the batterings of wind and wave they forced a route from Europe to the Far

changed the policies of nations, made imperial powers of small countries, turned fishing fleets into colonial navies. The sweet tooth of Europe provoked the giant upheavals of the sugar trade, the transporta-

sparked the rebellion that transformed the colonies of America into the independent United States. History is usually written in terms of kings, politicians, and soldiers. But somewhere behind them, lurking in the wings of the past, lies one plant or another— a most exacting gray eminence.

Less drastic in their consequences have been the medical plants, the sources of thousands of drugs, and the simply decorative plants of our gardens, ballrooms, and festivals. Both kinds have drawn people into jungles, up mountains, or through hazardous routes in the Himalayas, the Alps, and the inland fastnesses of China. Some of those people were killed, others made fortunes. Together

East round the southernmost points of Africa and America. Their aim was spices, and the economic leverage attached to them. Pepper and cloves opened up the world,

tion of millions of Africans to America, the unprecedented enrichment of enterprising shipowners, and a belt of black misery across the Caribbean Sea. Later, a tax on tea

they established a vast, lucrative industry which continues to grow.

Today the stress is on money, not war, and still less on religion. God is said to be out of fashion. We speak of wheat and rice, consumption and hunger, glut and famine, almost as if they were parts of a man-made world, forgetting that it was plants and crops which fashioned us and shaped our bodies, minds, and emotions. It is perhaps the most curious gap in our sacred rituals that plants play so small a part in them. Most churches preserve some relics of plant worship. Christians drink the fruit of the grape and eat the bread from the grain that were once worhiped for their own sakes.

We decorate our churches at the end of the harvest, and we celebrate Christmas with a commercially grown tree (or some synthetic model of one). But we no longer, in our religion, recognize the central and seminal role that plants play in our lives. The reason may be seen in the remoteness of the places where our crops grow from the daily haunts of the people they feed. Our foods come to us disembodied, having lost the savor and suggestion of their natural settings. They arrive in cans and plastic packs, frozen stiff, dehydrated, powdered, blended, or squeezed into most unnatural molds. They take on the artificial aura of their wrappings, seldom retaining a whiff of the soil or climate from which they originate.

14

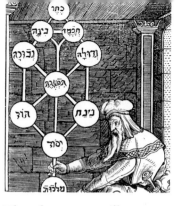

Far left: Astrological signs emanating from a tree in this seventeenth-century engraving show the progression from the earth's minerals—each symbolized by a zodiacal emblem—through plants to the universe.

Left: The Tree of Man's Life, an engraving by John Goddard of 1649, brings together various axioms and adages about the stages of human life.

Below: This Etruscan bowl symbolizes the state of man, between the trees of life and of death. He holds a twig of each.

Life, we are to understand, is a brief gap between birth and extinction.

Top right: The Tree of Life, from the Portae Lucis of Paul Ricci.

Center right: Below the tree of life painted on the wall of an Egyptian tomb (from Thebes, fifteenth century B.C.), people are shown being sprinkled with a heavenly elixir by the earth-mother goddess, settled in the tree's foliage.

Far right: A Tree of Jesse in the Bodleian Library shows Christ's family tree, sprung from the loins of King David.

Right: Yggdrasil, the Scandinavian world tree.

Though we may still preserve an ancestral empathy with those to whom crops and religion were indivisible, we would find it hard to invest the contents of a can with sanctity. It is often hard to think of a processed plant-food ever having come near a seed or leaf.

To our ancestors, the links between food, plants, and gods were self-evident. The land they worked and the food they ate were

both had been downcast by winter. From that recurrent miracle—annual regeneration—came a feeling of awe and respect for nature which it would be difficult to duplicate today.

Awe and mystery are the ingredients of worship, and in addition to the real, material powers of plants over people came attributed spiritual ones. The plants which rose to rescue the human race as scant win-

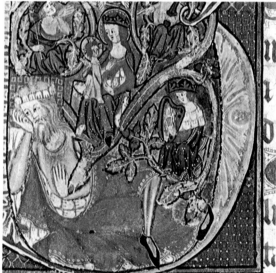

visibly, palpably related. Supermarkets bear fruit the year round, but the fruits and vegetables of the past were seasonal. Mind and body were uplifted by the spring, just as

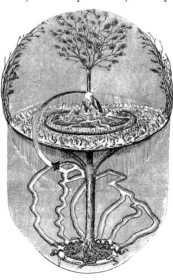

ter stores were exhausted were seen as the gifts of gods, or even at times as the gods themselves. Trees that provided nourishment became trees of life, the source of all existence. And one curious group of plants strengthened this belief in an uncanny manner. Not in all cases related, this group nevertheless contains certain constituents which act on the conscious mind, somehow altering thought processes and the powers of perception. They seem to open doors of awareness normally locked, to reveal vistas otherwise curtained, to raise from deep in the mind feelings of empathy with other people, things, or abstract concepts.

Some of these plants act directly, without any need of preparation. Others require

15

Opposite: Artemisia vulgaris from the seventh-century Viennese edition of Dioscorides.

Overleaf: Watercolor of several flowers by Albrecht Dürer.

a natural process of fermentation to bring out their qualities. Either way, they expose areas within or without the mind which, thus seen, appear for the duration of the plant's effects to answer or annul life's problems. They may induce insight, a feeling of kinship with all creation, ecstasy. Analyzed in the laboratory they are no more than chemicals, able to produce significant changes within our nervous and cerebral systems. Prosaic analysis is not enough to explain their influence, any more than it explains love and other strong emotions. No one speaks of chemicals when he is seeing with the torch of the magic psilocybe mushroom or the peyote cactus. For the powers of some plants over the spirit of man can at times be complete.

There have always been people who hoped to find plants with equally complete powers over the human body. Several have from time to time been put forward as panaceas, cures of all diseases, only to be shown inadequate in some respect. There is no cure-all—none, at least, yet discovered. But plants have always been crucial to our health. For

Above: The figure on the left is that of the German sixteenth-century herbalist Leonhard Fuchs. Beside him stands the Greek father of medicine, Hippocrates. *Below left:* The Greek herbalist Dioscorides receives a mandrake plant from the figure of Heuresis. *Below:* Fifteenth-century woodcut of a medieval pharmacy. *Below right:* Pot containing theriac, a concoction of plant and other substances used to cure various maladies. *Below far right:* 6,000-year-old figure of a shaman from southern Algeria.

What they practiced seemed like magic, but again the magic was plant-derived. Almost all medicines have been found in, or modeled on, the contained juices of plant parts.

That is almost as true today as it was five thousand years ago.

It is true that the herbalists of the past half-filled their work with the most inexcusable mumbo-jumbo; but much of the rest is curiously accurate. New steps in science ak-knowledge that those whose lives are closest to the natural environment often have a knowledge of cures and antidotes which clinical medicine, in its passion for purifying, distilling, and isolating, has for long neglected. As the best hopes for universal health are seen again to depend on nature, researchers trek into the world's most primitive regions to observe and learn the ways of witch-doctors, sorcerers, and shamans, whose knowledge of plants has remained as it always was. Now and again they return with a medicinal treasure, like Prometheus bringing fire from heaven.

Health of mind, religion, poetry, and visions; health of body, medicines, balms, and nourishment—they all, one way or another, stem from plants. Plants supply our needs, provide our pleasures, enrich our leisure. They color, adorn, and frame our

centuries the art of healing was synonymous with a knowledge of the efficacy of plants. Those who specialized in the herbal arts procured a position in society that could rival or even surpass the prestige of kings.

surroundings. They give us our myths and gods, mold our moods, shape the histories of nations. They tap the power of the sun, charging dull matter with life and making our planet unique in the known universe.

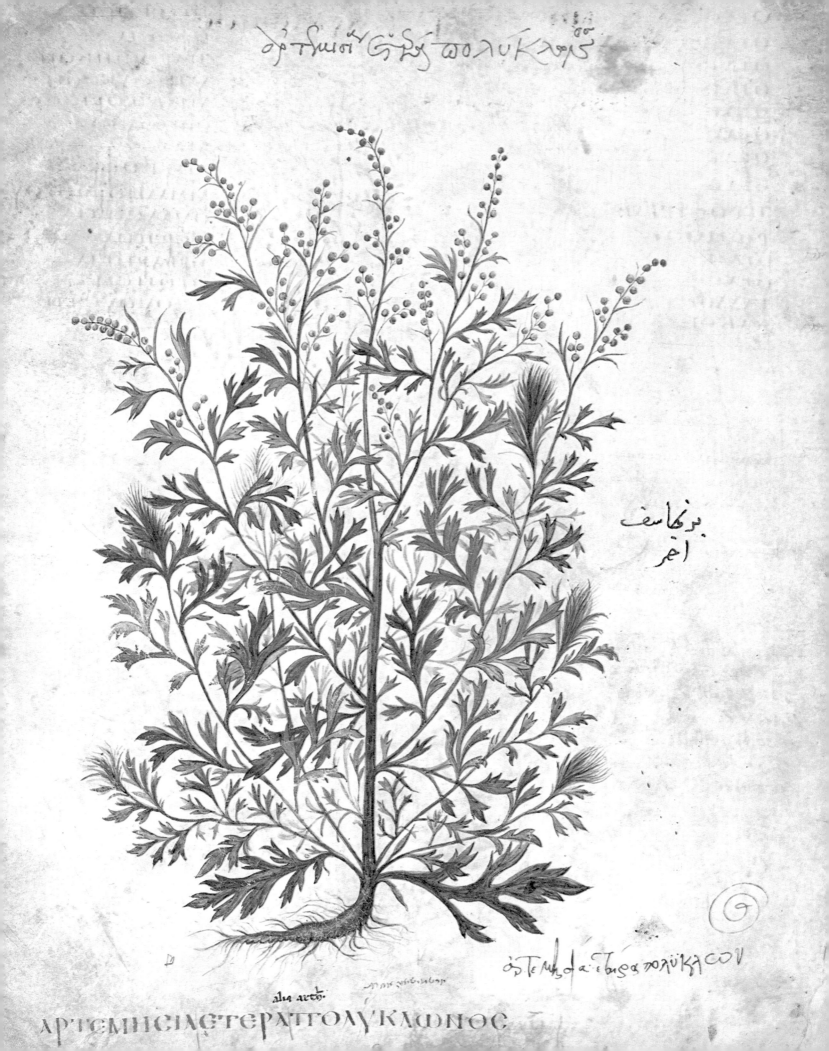

برنجاسف
أحمر

ἀρτεμησία ἑτέρα πολύκλωνος

alia artē.

ΑΡΤΕΜΗΣΙΑΣ ΕΤΕΡΑ ΠΟΛΥΚΛΩΝΟΣ

Behind the fragrance of a violet and the frail beauty of a rose lies the most tenacious life-force in the world: the power of plants to survive. From the momentous day, a billion or so years back, when the first speck of plant protoplasm puffed its first breath of oxygen into some primeval sea, the collective energy of plants has been directed at the colonization of the world. The means of their success has been an almost limitless capacity to change, to assume so many shapes, colors, sizes, and other diversifications that some of them, somewhere, always succeed.

Other plants fail. But in nature even failure is not waste. The fallen tree is leached of goodness by a fungus; the fungus is sucked dry by bacteria; the bacteria decompose into the raw elements of plant growth. Continuing life depends on continuing death and decay. Successful species are fortified by those that fail, and the lottery of gene mutation has spread plants not only through the world's congenial reaches but over bleak tundra, icy wastes, scorched desert. The means they have evolved to survive in different stations are countless.

They imbibe sunlight and make vital power of it. They create life from nonlife and nourish not only themselves but the whole animal creation — many of whom they put to work for their own purposes. They range in size from minute microbe to the world's most massive, tallest creatures. They live to

power to survive

whatever age suits them, be it a matter of hours or five thousand years. They can break rocks, stanch floods, precipitate rain, or knit sand to resist the buffets of the sea. After catastrophes of fire, eruption, hurricane, and avalanche they can rise again, like the phoenix, to retrace their patient progress across the land. To procreate their species they have enslaved whole races of insects. To spread themselves they enlist wind, sea, and animals as porters. No man can garner sunbeams, or commit his offspring to the wind for a journey of a thousand miles. A dandelion can. Science has far to go before it matches the ingenuity of a wayside weed.

THE LIFE CYCLE

Sunrays provide heat and the light energy by which plants synthesize organic foods out of minerals and gases.

Electricity in lightning concentrates nitrates from the air, which rain brings down to the earth.

Some free-living bacteria, especially *Azotobacter,* "fix" nitrogen from the air.

From nitrogen compounds and other minerals, plants form hormones, vitamins, nucleic acids, enzymes, and proteins which are the brickwork of all living tissue. They turn carbon into starches—the energy reserves for themselves and all animals.

Specialized bacteria and fungi cause the decomposition of plant and animal matter, breaking proteins down to form ammonia. Different bacteria help to transform this into nitrates.

The decay of organic matter creates humus, from which bacteria release minerals into the soil. Dead plants and animals, and the latter's droppings, give the soil carbon which may be preserved as potential energy in the form of oil, coal, or gas.

Bacteria on legumes (beans, peas, clover, lupins, and so on) "fix" atmospheric nitrogen to produce nitrates which feed the roots of all plants nearby.

Inorganic nitrogen compounds (chiefly nitrates and ammonium salts), phosphates, potassium, and other useful minerals are present in most soils and in the sea.

Most parts of most plants—flower, fruit, seed, leaf, stem, root, corm, tuber, bark, and hardwood—are liable to provide an animal's food, and so to commence a cycle which will result, after one or more stages, in a new plant.

The dietary interplay between plants and animals in nature is a patternless anarchy from which we have extracted, at some risk, a simplified design. Only one element is constant: the continuous creation by plants of basic food.

This idealized tableau shows sun, air, earth—the lifeless elements on which a line of plants is to perform its skills. Air contains oxygen, carbon dioxide, moisture, and a great deal else; but for every part of all these there are four parts of the gas nitrogen.

Nitrogen, which as the basis of proteins is an essential food for all living things, cannot be absorbed by plants in its simple form. They need it converted into nitrates—compounds which are welded together, or fixed, by bacteria all over the earth and by

certain blue-green algae all over the sea. Fixing takes place in the air, too, through the electric action of lightning. The resultant nitrates are then brought down to the soil by rain. In particular it is carried out by a specialized bacterium which lives

Animals which feed directly on plants expend a lot of energy looking out for and dodging predators, traveling to find food, and (in the case of mammals) operating their multiple digestion systems.

The diet of meat eaters may be from one to about six removes from plants. Of course many animals, including humans, eat both animals and plants; and even committed carnivores like wolves eat the odd leaf or stem.

only on the roots of the legume family (including the clovers). This bacterium while taking sugar from the plant gives it, and all plants nearby, nitrates in return.

Clover is not in the first in-

the plant but only in minute quantities), and colossal amounts of water are also taken in by the roots. The water is needed as a means of conveyance for other nutrients up the plant's long cellu-

stance planted in a pasture to garnish a cow's dull diet. It is put there to enrich the grass with nitrates, and so with protein.

In addition roots ingest phosphates and potassium (both of which are important for making fruit: commercial growers often restrict the nitrate intake of their trees to persuade them to concentrate on fruit production). Other mineral salts, trace elements (elements which are vital for

lar fibers. At the leaf, some of the water will be separated into its constituents, oxygen and hydrogen.

While roots tap the riches of the earth, leaves filter carbon from the air, combining it with hydrogen to make the sugar, starch, and other carbohydrates which comprise the energy stores of living creatures.

Much else is synthesized in the complex factory within a leaf. Then one day, with a

Among the many animals that have essentially plant diets are (1) caddis-fly larvae, (2) bumblebees, (3) earthworms, (4) flies, (5) voles, and (6) kangaroo rats (among the chief plant eaters of the American deserts).

The prime diet of these animals consists of herbivores, such as the animals found in the first column. The groups depicted above are: (1) crayfish, (2) field mice, (3) moles, (4) spiders, (5) skunks, and (6) burrowing owls.

nimals are not influenced by the
stematics of food chains in their
noice of prey. None of these ani-
als would jib at a meal of herbi-
ore. Each, however, is well
dapted to prey on the first-stage
arnivore placed to its left.

cluded in this group of preda-
rs are: (1) eels, (2) stoats, (3)
xes (they will eat almost any
imal they can catch), (4) lizards,
prairie falcons, and (6) gopher
akes.

systems operating at peak, the
mouth of an animal descends
and with a neat tongue-sweep
plucks the delicate mechanism from its stem. A herbi-
vore, no less than a man, is
what he eats, and in time that

same leaf will become the gut,
hide, fat, horn, hoof, muscle,
tooth, and lunging tongue of
its devourer. Cows, gazelles,
rabbits, prairie dogs, and
countless caterpillars are no
more than reworked leaves.
And so, at two, three, four, or
five removes from the original provider, are all predators,
scavengers, and parasites. In
the end, with scriptural inevi-
tability, everything returns to
the soil or the sea, helped on
its way by specialized plants,

APICAL CARNIVORES AND CARRION EATERS

Animals at the head of food
chains, or pyramids, are themselves not without enemies, and
they maintain a healthy suspicion
of humans, among others. Carrion
consumers head pyramids not
through strength, but through a
taste for dead flesh.

This group of carnivores and carrion eaters includes (1) pikes, (2)
tawny owls, (3) golden eagles, (4)
carrion beetles, (5) coyotes, and
(6) peccary, who, though mainly
plant eaters, happily consume
snakes.

the agents of decay. Proteins
are broken into their components: among them ammonia
and other nitrogen com-
pounds. Some of these escape
to the air. Others are sooner
or later fixed by microbes, to

await the pull of a root and
another unpredictable circuit
of nature's tangled supply
lanes.

When an animal dies of accident,
disease, or age, and is not eaten by a
scavenger, the food cycle continues
just the same. Death and decomposition, with their attendant reeks, are
brought about by bacteria eating
dead organic remains and in the
process releasing gases and minerals which will, once again, be the
raw materials of the factory within a
plant. This stage is not only reached
at death. Hair, skin, nails, cara-
paces, teeth, and excrement, continually shed by animals, are as consistently broken down by bacteria,
without which the world would soon
become a museum of sterile waxworks.

If you eat a freshly picked leaf in daylight, some of what you eat will have been part of the sun itself eight minutes before. That is the time it takes for sunlight to reach the earth. Conversion of its energy into food occupies an inconsiderable fraction of a second more. Yet this split-second process is the essential key to all life on earth. It is taking place in every diatom of the oceans and every leaf of every herb, shrub, and tree in the

world, between sunrise and sunset.

Leaves are the main unloading point for the world's new energy supplies derived from the sun. Wind, water, and nowadays atomic power are sources of great energy, but they do not

compare with plant-processed sunlight for continuous effect on living things. Over eons of time, plants have laid down vast energy reserves of coal, lignite, oil, and natural gases. It is estimated that every year plants package potential energy in the form of 150,000,000,000 tons of carbohydrates—all through the agency of photosynthesis.

From an animal point of view, one by-product of photosynthesis—oxygen—is just as important

as the carbohydrates. Without oxygen to combust into energy the food they have stored in their tissues, animals would be as helpless as the Ancient Mariner—thirstily adrift in salt water. If plants were not continuously replenishing the air with oxygen,

The specific sun-trap in a leaf is chlorophyll, a green substance which contains molecules of the silvery-white metal magnesium. This chlorophyll is contained in pellet-shaped granules known as

Carbon dioxide

chloroplasts. While leaves strain, jostle, and twist on their axes to offer the broadest possible surface to the light, chloroplasts likewise adjust to the sunniest position by rolling around the leaf cell. The moment a light impulse strikes one, it begins a series of manufacturing processes. In the same moment, less than one-hundredth of a second later, the series ends. Water (H_2O) drawn up from the roots is split by chlorophyll into its constituents, hydrogen and oxygen. Instantly, carbon dioxide (CO_2), inhaled from the air through minute pores in the leaf's surface, is broken down too, into carbon

and oxygen. A sequence of chemical rearrangements follows, ending in the formation of carbohydrates ($C_6H_{12}O_6$), which are streamed away for storage in various parts of the plant while

some surplus oxygen is released into the air.

Photosynthesis is only part of the function of a leaf. It breathes too. Plants, as much as animals, need to convert their food into requisite energy by means of respiration, the gentle combustion of carbohydrates by oxygen. To do this they exactly reverse, except in one particular, the process of photosynthesis. Carbohydrates ($C_6H_{12}O_6$) are combined with oxygen (O_2) to make carbon dioxide (CO_2), water (H_2O), and energy. The difference is in the form of the energy—no longer light now, but a capacity for physical action.

$$6CO_2 + 6H_2O + \text{light energy} \rightarrow C_6H_{12}O_6 + 6O_2$$
$$\text{carbon dioxide} \quad \text{water} \qquad\qquad\qquad \text{sugar} \qquad \text{oxygen}$$

$$C_6H_{12}O_6 + 6O_2 \rightarrow 6CO_2 + 6H_2O + \text{chemical energy}$$
$$\text{sugar} \quad \text{oxygen} \quad\quad \text{carbon dioxide} \quad \text{water}$$

This magnified cross section of a root shows the fine, hair-like outer structures through which essential moisture and mineral salts pass into the plant.

Water

Mineral salts

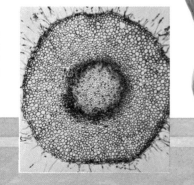

Some of the oxygen used in respiration is the residue of photosynthesis, and some is taken in from the air. More oxygen is used at night, when photosynthesis has to stop for want of sunlight, than by day. All the same, plants' oxygen account with the air is always in credit, supplying enough for all animals as well as themselves.

Oxygen →

Mushrooms (fungi) do not contain chlorophyll and therefore cannot manufacture food from inorganic matter as green plants do. Instead they exist by destroying or changing compounds already built.

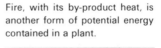

Food containing:
Carbohydrates
– sugar
– starch
Fat
Protein
Vitamins

Fire, with its by-product heat, is another form of potential energy contained in a plant.

the present world supply would be exhausted in under three thousand years. Animals owe to plants not only the food they eat but the air they breathe.

The essential ingredient which enables plants to photosynthesize is the green pigment chlorophyll. Possession of it is part of the standard definition of plants (though about one-tenth of all plant species, including the fungi, lack chlorophyll and are unable to photosynthesize).

Photosynthesis is the root (better say the leaf) of all life forms and functions. It enables plants to reproduce themselves in half a million forms and so to offer us, quite unintentionally, the rich variety which we take for granted on our tables.

The first medium of life had to be water. With no air as it exists today, one prerequisite of life—oxygen—could only be extracted from water. Life, then, began in the seas which had condensed from the vapor and steam of earlier ages. It was the culmination of a process whose origins lay in the mysterious mutations of carbon compounds into amino acids. In time, and in a manner we may never understand, aquatic one-celled bacteria evolved, some of them capable of photosynthesis and therefore classified as plants. Each of these midget organisms gave out tiny oxygen bubbles which escaped

rivers and springs, geysers, and eruptions brought vast quantities of minerals into the sea. Plant life began to proliferate. Half a billion or more years ago, numerous forms of seaweed (or algae) —blue-green, green, red, and brown—abounded round the coasts in depths where they could get enough light.

Plants require no foraging roots in a medium containing all the nourishment they need, though some algae use shoots for the purpose of anchorage. But when plants invaded the land, adapting from sea life to intertidal life to terrestrial life in gradual stages, they put down roots. And

Life in the sea, as on land, is generated by solar energy. Throughout the oceans, which cover four-fifths of the world's surface, free-floating plants, from tiny unicellular diatoms to huge seaweeds, absorb sunlight as a first stage in the complex of marine food chains.

If all the salts in all the seas could be extracted, they would make a bulk some fifteen times greater than that of the continent of Europe above sea level. Originally the seas were saltless. Their present mineral content—on average some 35 parts of salts to 1000 parts of water by weight —has been accumulated from the minute mineral traces swept down by rivers and streams over millions of years. Among these minerals are nutrients essential to sea-plant life. Rivers also bring oxygen to the seas and their animal inhabitants, which need it as much as land animals do. The waste product of animal respiration—carbon dioxide—floats up toward the surface to be used by plants in the process of photosynthesis. And, as on land, dead animals decompose into the chemicals which plants feed on.

from the sea, settled in the atmosphere, and contributed to the buildup of an environment fit for higher plants and animals to live in.

Development within the bacteria themselves was facilitated by enrichment of the originally saltless water. As time passed,

at last, something like 300 million years ago, there were ferns, horsetails, and club mosses permanently settled on the land.

The upper levels of large expanses of the sea teem with plankton, a drifting miscellany of microscopic plants and animals. Plant plankton (1), mainly diatoms, form the basis of all marine food chains.

Diatoms are the main diet of animal plankton (as well as of larger herbivores), which float at all levels of the sea. Among them, the transparent copepods (2) abound in northern waters.

All kinds and sizes of sea creatures, from shrimp to whale, eat animal plankton. Reddish swarms of one kind of copepod, the *Calanus,* form the bulk of the food of the herring (3).

Members of the cod family (4) generally live close to the bottom of the sea, some at depths of 500 to 600 meters. They feed on all kinds of mollusks, crustaceans, and worms; but large cod hunt shoaling fish like the herring. Cod, mackerel, herring, halibut, and squid are all grist to the steely gut of the porbeagle, or mackerel shark (5), which dominates its own food chains and counts only man and parasites as its enemies.

Marsh plants and animals, such as the crab shown eating grass, provide essential nourishment to life in the sea.

The food chain shown at left is not a strict structure and can be broken at any point. For example, the starfish below, in capturing its small prey, has interceded and deprived the cod of its food.

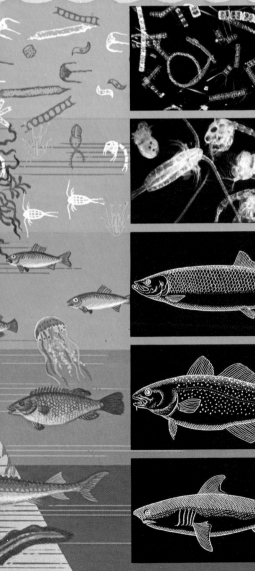

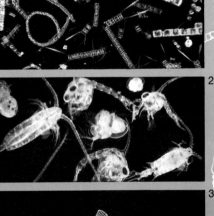

While land plants developed an amazing versatility to cope with the range of conditions they met, those of the sea evolved more gently. Most sea plants still belong to the class of algae, but the submarine gardens they form can look as varied as a glass-house of exotics. Giant brown seaweeds, tethered by suckers fifteen meters down, sprawl for great distances through their dim depths, or tower upward to the surface like the stout mahoganies of an African jungle. Twined around their bulbous foliage like terrestrial lianas and orchids are the smaller brown, green and delicate red algae with fronds like fine membranes, trembling filigree, or thin whip-thongs. Delicate as they seem, these reds can survive at depths of a hundred or more meters, in a darkness which excludes all but violet light. At every level seaweeds support and protect, as land forests do, a teeming population of animals. The grass of the sea is minuscule floating plankton, diatoms of a million shapes that create marine food chains. Seaweeds give an anchorage to mussels and sea mats, sponges and lampreys. In the jungles they form, the invertebrates which evolved with them – octopus, squid, brittle stars, sea squirts, and others – still live out their lives, along with the vertebrate fishes of a later creation.

THE EVOLUTION OF PLANTS

100 MILL. YEARS   75 MILL. YEARS   20 M.Y.   60 MILL. YEARS

BLUE-GREEN ALGAE

Several algae and bacteria existed before Cambrian times. The blue-green alga *(above)*, which still proliferates in wet places, was one of the earliest plant forms.

The chart on these pages represents that period (less than one-eighth of the world's age) within which almost all the important phases of plant evolution occurred. During the Cambrian, Ordovician, and most of the Silurian periods, plants were confined to various classes of primitive algae or seaweeds, and a few simple club mosses and fungi. They inhabited the shallows, depending on bright sunlight and a watery environment. In Silurian times a plant developed —*Psilophyton*—on whose lower

PSILOPHYTES

CLUB MOSSES

FERNS ▲

GIANT HORSETAILS

CAMBRIAN   ORDOVICIAN   SILU-RIAN   DEVONIAN

ALGAE

FUNGI

HORSETAILS

SEED-FERNS

LEPIDODENDRONS ▶

Cambrian fossil remains show a large variety of algae, which in turn supported a great many invertebrate animals. The green alga *(below)* is single-celled, but it tends to form long chains.

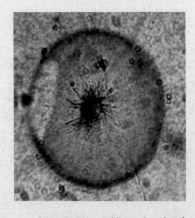

stem grew rootlike hairs, which enabled it to find moisture when the sea left it stranded.

The Devonian era saw a great increase in marine activity. Seaweeds developed the power to photosynthesize at greater depths. Plants consolidated on land too, though they were still confined to swamps. Mosses and liverworts were the first to possess distinct leaves and stems, each with specialized functions. Ferns, horsetails, and club mosses had roots as well, adapting the plants to more efficient absorption of water and minerals from the soil. In contrast to their puny descendants, seldom more than half a meter high, these horsetails and club mosses rose to heights or thirty meters or more, multiplying into luxuriant swampy forests that shaded a surrealist population of amphibians, cum-

By the Silurian period the momentous move from sea to land had taken place. The new surroundings speeded up the rate of mutation and gave rise to a wide range of classes: mosses, liverworts, ferns, horsetails, and club mosses.

MILL. YEARS ▷ 50 MILL. YEARS ▷ 50 MILL. YEARS ▷ 45 MILL. YEARS ▷ 72 MILL. YEARS ▷

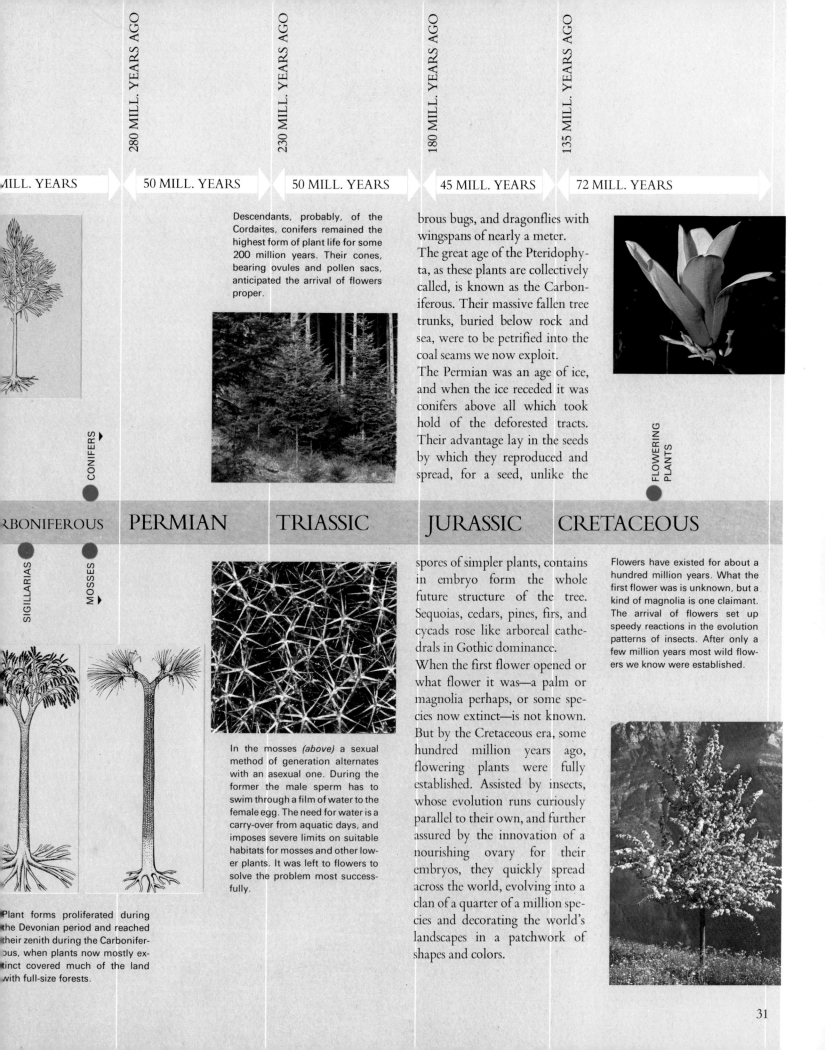

Descendants, probably, of the Cordaites, conifers remained the highest form of plant life for some 200 million years. Their cones, bearing ovules and pollen sacs, anticipated the arrival of flowers proper.

brous bugs, and dragonflies with wingspans of nearly a meter.

The great age of the Pteridophyta, as these plants are collectively called, is known as the Carboniferous. Their massive fallen tree trunks, buried below rock and sea, were to be petrified into the coal seams we now exploit.

The Permian was an age of ice, and when the ice receded it was conifers above all which took hold of the deforested tracts. Their advantage lay in the seeds by which they reproduced and spread, for a seed, unlike the

CONIFERS ▶

FLOWERING PLANTS ▶

RBONIFEROUS **PERMIAN** **TRIASSIC** **JURASSIC** **CRETACEOUS**

SIGILLARIAS

MOSSES ▶

spores of simpler plants, contains in embryo form the whole future structure of the tree. Sequoias, cedars, pines, firs, and cycads rose like arboreal cathedrals in Gothic dominance.

When the first flower opened or what flower it was—a palm or magnolia perhaps, or some species now extinct—is not known. But by the Cretaceous era, some hundred million years ago, flowering plants were fully established. Assisted by insects, whose evolution runs curiously parallel to their own, and further assured by the innovation of a nourishing ovary for their embryos, they quickly spread across the world, evolving into a clan of a quarter of a million species and decorating the world's landscapes in a patchwork of shapes and colors.

Flowers have existed for about a hundred million years. What the first flower was is unknown, but a kind of magnolia is one claimant. The arrival of flowers set up speedy reactions in the evolution patterns of insects. After only a few million years most wild flowers we know were established.

In the mosses *(above)* a sexual method of generation alternates with an asexual one. During the former the male sperm has to swim through a film of water to the female egg. The need for water is a carry-over from aquatic days, and imposes severe limits on suitable habitats for mosses and other lower plants. It was left to flowers to solve the problem most successfully.

Plant forms proliferated during the Devonian period and reached their zenith during the Carboniferous, when plants now mostly extinct covered much of the land with full-size forests.

Fossils are nature's death masks, preserving in minute detail the features of past life—the tracery of a leaf, the tiny pockings of shoot or stem, the condensed bulk of a whole forest. They show us the shape and form of plants that grow no more, and

help to fill in the sprawling jigsaw of evolution. But they are not an open history book. The odds in favor of a plant's survival—its chances of escape from consumption by scavenger, fungus, or bacteria or from the depredations of climate—are so small that only a few organisms have survived intact.

The scenes unveiled by fossils are also likely to be one-sided. Preservation was easier under the sea—where a thin rain of organic particles gradually pressed plants into perfect casts—than on land, where wind, fire, and the oscillations of heat and cold destroyed and dispersed them. So aquatic

(Opposite, left) Reconstructed landscape from the Carboniferous period, showing ferns, extinct horsetails, and early conifers.

(Opposite) The shales associated with Carboniferous coal seams often yield traces of fernlike fronds from the genus *Pecopteris*.

Amber is solidified resin or sap, exuded from the bark of conifers more than 40 million years ago. It sometimes encases *(left)* the perfectly mummified body of a fly or other insect unwary enough to land on it.

A sprig of *Annularia sphenosphyl-loides*, a primitive relative of the calamites, from the upper coal deposits of the Saar *(above)*. A Fossilized frond of the fleshy and extinct *Neuropteris gigantea* *(above, center)*.

The leaf of a Miocene (between 7 and 20 million years ago) flowering plant, showing the intact etching of its veins *(above, right)*.

Bark of the *Lepidodendron*, a fossil tree from Carboniferous times, showing leaf scars *(right, top)*.

The bark of the *Sigillaria davreuxi* —an intact survival through 300 million years *(right, below)*.

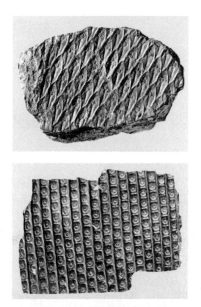

plants made the most common fossils, while those which grew on exposed hillsides are rare. Nevertheless the spur provided a hundred years ago by the theory of evolution, and systematic collation of finds ever since, has built up a record of plant history over the last billion years.

Fossils are not only history. They can be energy too. Where forests grew and died, where seas washed over and infiltrated their prostrate timbers with minerals, and where—over eons of time—millions of grains of rock and microbe corpses floated down to bury them under layers hundreds of meters thick—in such areas pressure and chemical action turned plants into subterranean fields of stone. That stone may now be lignite or coal, which still hides in its carbon blackness both the energy manufactured by the trees' leaves and precise cameos of the primeval forests.

1776

550: The Emperor Justinian crowned at Constantinople. The Roman Empire of the west has teetered, but the Renaissance is a millennium ahead.
800: Charlemagne is crowned emperor of the Franks at Paris, by the Pope. The French monarchy will run for a thousand years, until the Revolution.

1200

The heartwood of a tree is dead. Only the cambium—a paper-thin layer of cells—and several rings of sapwood are alive, providing an ever-lengthening transport system between the roots and the foliage above. Though the cylinder forming the heartwood of a tree has no life, it is the plant's structural mainstay. And it is encapsulated

ample, examination of the wooden poles of thirteenth-century Mexican huts has suggested why a whole area of settlements was abandoned. Rings within

800

550

1066: William the Conqueror lands at Hastings and wins the crown of England. His opponent is killed by an arrow. Efficient musketry is five hundred years away.
1200: Richard Coeur de Lion on crusade. Possession of Jerusalem is still an issue that can uproot thousands of Europeans from their homes. Jerusalem for the Jews is a concept for seven centuries ahead.
1456: Publication of the first printed Bible, by Johann Gutenberg. Printing had first been practiced some sixteen years before.

history—a library of concentric annals.

Every ring represents a year of the tree's life, so any tree's age can be ascertained, through either a core sample of a living tree or the crosscut of one that is felled. Counting may not be easy because lean, dry years leave thin rings, and the rings of a lean decade or century run so close together that they may appear as a blur of brown. Yet even the blur has a story to tell, for it is a climate record whose light on the past may elucidate the weather of the future.

Indications of past weather derived from trees can explain some historical riddles; for ex-

1066

the poles of the outer, newer huts show that the exodus was preceded by years of drought.

The majority of trees, of course, are long-lived if they last two centuries. But the history can sometimes be extended by matching the later rings of long-dead trunks with the earlier rings of living ones and counting back. This principle has been used, among other things, to date dead and desiccated specimens of the oldest living tree, the bristlecone pine.

1456

1776: The Declaration of Independence by the United States of America. The union numbered thirteen states, as opposed to the present fifty.
1891: The German engineer Otto Lilienthal is the first to guide a glider. The era of spacecraft is still confined to the racier brands of fiction.

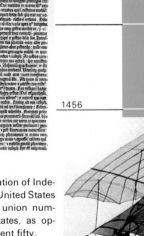
1891

550–1891: the life-span of this *Sequoia giganteum*, from the Kings River Forest near Fresno, California. Not only does it reveal its age by the number of rings in its cross section, but variations in width of rings can tell much about climatic conditions in the past.

In the 1630s Archbishop Ussher of Dublin calculated—and his conclusion found wide acceptance—that the acts of creation described in Genesis took place in the year 4004 B.C. A gnarled old bristlecone pine in Nevada could have set him right, for it grew up among trees that predated the prelate's estimate by several thousand years. It lives still *(right)*, a century short of five thousand years old. It is in fact the oldest living thing in the world, though there is a qualification to be made on that (record claims invite the splitting of hairs). Life of a sort has been preserved far longer in the natural deep-freeze of the Canadian ice. In 1954 seeds of an Arctic lupin were recovered from ice in the Yukon and successfully germinated. Their age, assessed by the radiocarbon method, was about ten thousand years. Without the help of ice (since it kept the lupin seeds not so much alive as in suspended animation) other seeds—notably the lotus—are known to have remained viable for periods of at least a thousand years.

There are, however, plenty of trees older than that. California's giant sequoias *(opposite)*, one of which is a record holder on another score, as the world's most massive living thing, include among their number individuals four thousand and more years old. The revered yews of English churchyards, with their life-spans of a thousand years, are striplings in the field.

PATTERNS OF GROWTH AND MOVEMENT

Plants, unlike animals, continue to grow right up to their last season. Their patterns of growing are different from those of animals, too. Organic growth is concentrated in the tips of roots and stems. (The increase in a tree's girth is growth as well but is due mainly to the accumula-

tion of dead inner tissues.) Most hormones of growth are contained in these tips, which can very in length from a centimeter in the case of common herbs to 25 centimeters in the bounding giant bamboo.

Growing tall is not a standard plant ambition. In the coldest climates ice and wind would soon ruin plants that aspired to large stature, and most of those that thrive there have learned to huddle together in low profile. Even in warmer regions many plants are shy of sunlight and do best under the shade of trees or the taller herbs. All the same, potential for tall growth is a useful asset to most herbs and trees, enabling them to compete with others for a place in the sun.

There are shortcuts to the top. Parasites and epiphytes (which use their hosts for support but do

The coast redwoods *(above), Sequoia sempervirens,* of California include the world's tallest trees, one reaching a height of 110.35 meters.

The parasitic *Rafflesia arnoldii (left)* of Malaya, a vegetable dinosaur whose fetid lank flowers may reach a reported 90 centimeters in diameter.

The inelegant Stinkhorn fungus *(below), Phallus impudicus,* can grow (to about 15 centimeters) and decay in as little as a day.

not tap them for food) have developed several ways—twining, suckering, coiling, hooking—of reaching the treetops without firm stems of their own. Seemingly still plants move in many other ways: opening and closing their petals at particular times of day or night (Linnaeus drew a twenty-four-hour clock to show how different species share out the day and night); bending toward, or away from, light, water, heat, or fulfilling the daylong progress of sunflowers and other plants which follow the sun's course across the sky and bend back in the evening, ready for its next appearance.

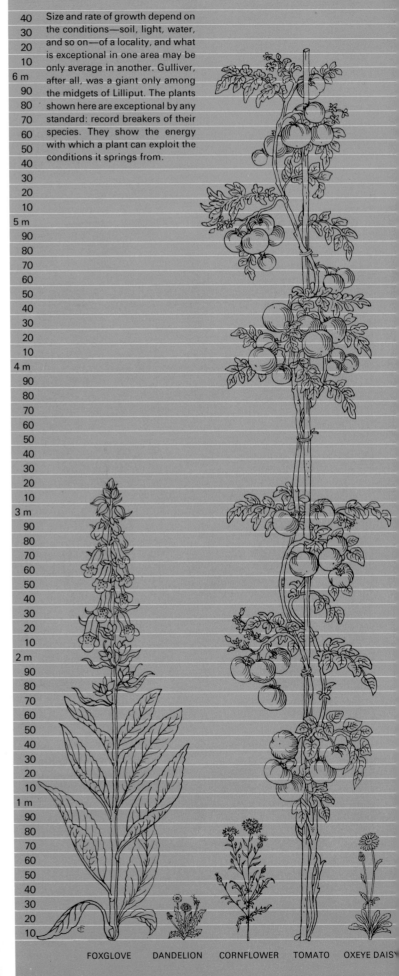

Size and rate of growth depend on the conditions—soil, light, water, and so on—of a locality, and what is exceptional in one area may be only average in another. Gulliver, after all, was a giant only among the midgets of Lilliput. The plants shown here are exceptional by any standard: record breakers of their species. They show the energy with which a plant can exploit the conditions it springs from.

FOXGLOVE   DANDELION   CORNFLOWER   TOMATO   OXEYE DAISY

Some of the giant bamboos *(left)* of Southeast Asia are capable of growing 60 centimeters in a day and as much as 40 meters in one growing season. Each species of bamboo flowers only once in its life, and within that species every plant in the world flowers at the same time; and having flowered and seeded, it dies.

Many plants use the stems of others to carry them up toward the sunlight. To do this they make use of various specialized devices. The hop, *Humulus lupulus (below left)*, is a twiner. It sweeps round in circles up to half a meter diameter in a search for support. When it touches a stem or trunk, or the poles set out by cultivators, the circling continues but contracts to a tight embrace.

Ivy *(top right)* climbs by means of clusters of rootlets growing from its stem. These exude a sticky liquid which secures them fast.

Tendrils are a common means of attachment found in many members of the legume family (peas, vetches, etc.) and in the exotic passion flower *(above left)*.

Hooks and thorns are not only for defense. Many are above all climbing pegs. Cleavers, blackberries, and many of the roses use them in this way, as do the tropical rattans *(above right)* which sprawl for a hundred and more meters across a passive roof of jungle foliage.

PURPLE LOOSESTRIFE   SUNFLOWER   NETTLE   VIOLET   CORN   RIBWORT PLANTAIN

There are limits to plants' success in colonizing the world. They are defied by large tracts of ice and desert, where air and soil alike are too hot, too cold, or too dry for survival to be possible. In general, life and growth can only continue within the limits of 0° and 50 °C, though some minute algae and bacteria can take considerably hotter temperatures and a few lichens some-

and also temperate latitudes, hemmed in by enemies, rivals, and parasites, which give grounds for surprise. By the quirks of evolution, by chance mutations and perfectly natural selection, the arctic lichen has become fitted to its surroundings and could no more cope with the jungle than a fish with dry land. Its living enemies are few: no insects to nibble its foliage, no

stunted, sinuous birches and willows, some of which keep even their trunks below ground so that their treetops look like herbage. For no tree could withstand the razor gusts of circumpolar winds. Lichens and mosses

Crocuses *(above)* are quick to break through winter snow, deriving energy from their thick buried stems, or corms.

The edelweiss *(far left)* is a native of Siberia, brought by the Ice Age to the Swiss Alps where it was naturalized. Its white woolly "petals"—actually leaves—protect it from cold and resist evaporation by the dry mountain air.

Cushion plants like the purple saxifrage *(left)* cluster tightly together to keep out wind and cold, sharing one central taproot.

The Jeffrey pine *(opposite)* spends the winter completely submerged in snow. Each spring it sends up a new, vertical leader-shoot from the nape of its gnarled stem. Then the wind attacks this shoot and bends it over to the horizontal. The process is repeated each year, and what look like branches are in fact a series of leaders frustrated in their high purposes. Without the new growths the tree would soon lie flat and die. It survives by a constant reassertion of the vertical.

what colder. Almost a quarter of the planet's land surface is bare of plant life. It is in the areas fringing these barren extremes that some plants have evolved most ingeniously.

Had they ears, they would be amazed at such praise. To the plant which ekes its water supply from vapor in the air, or snuggles close to others in a cold-resistant cushion, or clings to the sheer face of some windswept rock, it is the commoner plants, the bourgeois denizens of tropical

animals to lop and munch its entire body. It is made to withstand blizzard and permafrost, whereby a few centimeters down the soil is rock-hard with ice throughout the year. The light which the lichen gets—daylong for a few summer months, reduced in winter to unrelieved blackness—and the thin mineral reserves of the rock it clings to in no way reduce its individual chances of survival compared with those of its warmer cousins. Yet that arctic lichen, seen as an

outpost of the great community of plants—a community which first grew and thrived in languid warmth and wet—is testimony to the restless and insatiable progress of plant life across the globe.

In the world's cold extremities— the Arctic, the Antarctic (which is colder), and the peaks of the tallest mountains—plants, if they exist at all, keep their profiles low. In all cases there is a rough line beyond which most trees are not found. Exceptions are certain survive, huddled against rock, able to hibernate under a blanket of ice; and so do some flowering plants, adapted to pack the whole cycle of flowering, pollination, and seed dispersal into six summer weeks, leaving at the end some scattered seeds to repeat the hurried cycle next year. If in these straits you expect a cowed and furtive flora, you must see the snowline of the Alps or Himalayas or the northern reaches of Lapland, Siberia, or Labrador in high summer. Hardly has the snow withdrawn before a rainbow brilliance burgeons out of the soil, attracting squadrons of insects by scent and color to rush through the work of pollination. Grass springs up, so fast that it seems to have lain green and mature all winter under a snowy quilt. And heathers, lings, campanulas, and alpine azaleas spangle tracts which a week or two before were sheets of monotonous white.

The quickest way to experience a polar climate is generally to climb the nearest high mountain. Siberia and Greenland reappear in thin strips on the upper slopes of the Alps (a composite section is depicted here) and Himalayas, and the character of northern Canada exists in facsimile high up the mountains of California. And so, conversely, the plant types on the slopes of a high mountain constitute a kind of index to the broader geography of plants.

This index cannot be exact, however. Every species of plant has a characteristic range or scope, conditioned by the complex interplay of dozens of factors. Alpine peaks and the Siberian tundra may share the same temperature, but they are not swept by the same winds, nor is the Arctic illuminated by the light rays, rich in ultraviolet, present at mountain levels. A large part of Russia's northern steppes is dry cold desert, while the Alps are doused with frequent rains. Soils vary, and the plants' ancestries, and the conditions that shaped their evolution, are different too.

With all that said, important resemblances remain. Plants have conquered the land not in the human way—by an unbending display of force—but by adapting to the conditions they meet through chance mutations. Where the seed of a variant plant happens to come to rest in an environment that suits it, there it thrives. Many of the same genetic features that enabled plants to settle and spread in arctic wastes have fitted them also for more southerly mountain tops.

The link goes further. Each of the four great Ice Ages forced northern plants southward. Many reached the feet of the Alps, where they met and mixed with refugee plants forced down the mountain by cold. The mingling was perpetuated when the ice receded. Some alpine plants moved north; some arctic plants climbed the mountain slopes.

From bottom to top of a mountain there is a steady reduction in the number of plant species and individuals. Again this reflects the global picture. The warmer the climate, the greater on the whole will be the profusion of plants. Plants simply share available resources in a practical way. The lush loam and warmth of a valley give a growing period of half the year. Near the summits growth must be accomplished in the few weeks between the snow's melting and return. So, like their arctic cousins, alpine plants leach the goodness from a broader area and keep each other at arm's length.

A cluster of the cushion-plant *Eritrichium nanum*, "King of the Alps," among lichens, which are also supreme survivors in icy heights.

Androsace glacialis, another ascetic flower drawing its meager nourishment from the screes and moraines of the high Alps.

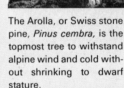

The Arolla, or Swiss stone pine, *Pinus cembra*, is the topmost tree to withstand alpine wind and cold without shrinking to dwarf stature.

Quick-growing and cold-resistant, the larch *(Larix* species) swathes the middle heights of many northern mountain ranges.

Various species of the oak, *Quercus*, dominate huge tracts of the lower, milder mountain slopes.

Essentially a tree of the Mediterranean area, the olive, *Olea europaea*, grows in the warm valleys of the alpine foothills.

3500

3000

2500

2000

1500

1000

500

0

Pioneer plants can gain a foothold, live, and reproduce even on the permanent ice of mountain tops. All such plants belong to primitive classes—algae, lichens, mosses, and liverworts—which faintly tinge their beds of white with greens, browns, and russet yellows. Minute and slow-growing, they live virtually on air.

Where the snow withdraws, for however brief a space, some flowers and grasses survive. Even while skiers slue above them, leaves of the soldanella, gentians, and alpine roses are consuming snow-filtered sunlight and preparing their flower buds for the first day of total exposure. Other plants at these levels—like moss campion and Swiss androsace—have evolved into cushion forms, jointly resisting cold in a hemispherical huddle.

The highest-placed trees are a few prostrate willows, which survive by snaking their stems along the ground. Lower down, dwarf shrubs of bearberry, juniper, spruce, birch, and pine mark the upper limits of the tree-line. Larches sometimes pioneer above them on moraines. Alpine violets, rhododendrons, saxifrages, and many others belong also to these heights.

Conifers are the dominant standing trees of the hypothetical mountain's middle levels. A capacity for quick growth, and the round-the-year activity of their needle leaves, allow them to make more of meager resources than deciduous trees. Among them the Cimbra and Scots pine are the best adapters to high altitudes and arctic cold. Stands of the hardiest deciduous trees—mountain ash, elder, the tiny mountain maple, and other small species—also occur among the upper conifer forests.

Deciduous, broad-leaved trees occupy the lower slopes of the mountain, wherever soil and people allow them to grow. Forests of alder, lime, ash, beech, and chestnut often share boundaries with the evergreen forests above. Among conifers overlapping the lower levels, firs can live on swampy, dry, or rocky soils which defy most other trees. Vegetation of the fertile valleys, rich in alluvial soil, reflects human needs more than natural adaptation. A broad variety of vines and other Mediterranean fruits, hardier cereals and fodder grasses, vegetables, and garden escapees alternate with orchards, meadow broadleaves, and decorative conifers.

43

One useful thing greenhouses do is to protect moisture against evaporation. The *Fenestraria* plant of southwest Africa needs such protection, since the air is very dry. And so, long before people made greenhouses—or even before there were people—it made one of its own. The bulk of the plant stays underground, and only the tips of its fleshy leaves peep above the ground. To look at, these leaf tips could be made of glass: completely transparent, without any chlorophyll. They are proof against the burning powers of the sun, yet able to reflect sunlight through to the buried leaf parts, where the normal business of energy conversion goes on. At

All parts of the foxglove *(above)* contain glycosides, which affect, and in large doses arrest, many animals' heartbeats. Due warning is given by the plant's acrid smell and pungent taste.

Oxalic acid within the leaves of *Rumex* species *(below)* may cause coma and death.

Jungle lianas *(right)* exploit the strength of trees with speedy agility. They climb trunks, dangle their roots to the ground, and sprawl—sometimes for hundreds of feet—across the treetops.

Both monkshood *(below left)* and horsetails *(below right)* contain virulent poisons.

Plants like the stinging nettle *(below, far left)* and poison ivy (not shown here) do their defensive damage on touch, staining the skin with irritant chemicals. The thorn-apple *(continuing left to right)* protects its seeds with thorns but also reserves toxic

the same time these glassy windows prevent leakage of moisture to the air. Thus the plant survives.

Last century the Victorians loved to plant a Mediterranean flower, dittany, in their gardens. Its great appeal was in the way it caught fire. On very hot, dry days it seemed to burst into flame of its own accord. Other-

chemicals within the seed coat. Holly, wild roses, and thistles deter with leaf spikes or sharp thorns. The bristly hairs on the stems of the hemp nettle make climbing difficult for invading insects.

The uncanny *Mimosa pudica (left)*, when touched, begins a slow temporary collapse of leaves and stems; probably as a defense against grazers.

wise a taper held close would cause it to ignite in an engulfing blue flame. What made it more of a conjuring trick was that the plant emerged unscathed. In fact the highly inflammable fumes it discharges are, in its natural setting where small bush fires are common, a useful device. For a sudden mantle of flame, by drawing off much of the plant's warm moisture, cools it so rapidly that it resists the flames. So it too survives.

In fact almost every feature of a plant is a technique of survival: leaves, roots (not all plants have them), shape, color, size, smell, and the infinite complexity of chemical composition. Lianas that hang their roots like bead curtains through tropical glades survive by their technique of climbing. By virtue of the sinewy elastic of their trunks, bamboos and spindly palms can live through the prolonged blasts of hurricanes. An armory of barbs, spikes, thorns, and poisons keeps many plants' enemies at bay. Other pages show some of the means plants use to combat cold, heat, and natural and unnatural disasters, but it would take volumes to describe all the techniques science understands.

Roots of the mangrove *(above)* cannot draw necessary air from their swampy settings. So each root emerges from the ground to form a breathing "knee." Another of the tree's techniques is to retain its long, heavy, pointed seeds until they are ready to germinate. Their weight when they drop rams them into the swamp upright and prevents them being washed away.

There are plenty it does not: plenty of habits and traits whose function it is hard to discern, like some of the strange friendships plants make with insects, or the pale luminescence with which certain fungi and other species glow eerily in the dark.

A barrel cactus flower *(right)* may bloom, depending on the moisture in the air, for a day or a week.

There is water in, under, or over any desert, if only you know how to tap it. Desert plants have collectively evolved a wide range of forms and devices for that purpose. Some plants can live off air, by inhaling the moisture it contains. Some sink deep roots (deeper than those of any other plant) to reach the reservoirs that underlie even the driest regions. Others patiently withhold their flowering or their sprouting until unaccustomed rainfall creates the right conditions for a few days. Others further exploit the rain by filling

each season the sand is painted with a riot of flower color.

Like their alpine relatives, these flowers have to work quickly. In a few brief weeks, before the sun blots the last of the moisture from the soil, they must grow, bud, leaf, flower, conceive, and cast their seeds. Then they die. Only the polymorph cacti and a few other succulents and trees eke out their reserves till the next downpour. Then the seeds left by more ephemeral flowers will spring up for the same hurried life cycle their parents followed.

The sharp spines of the cholla cactus *(right)* do not prevent wrens and other, larger birds from nesting among its stems. It is a familiar sight in the deserts of Mexico and Arizona.

The desert of Arizona responds to winter rains with a rainbow profusion of flowers. A few short weeks later the flowers complete their life cycles, and the desert is dry and dormant again.

out their lean forms to Pickwickian dimensions, storing water inside. To be burglar proof, the cacti and many others set out savagely spiny defenses against the maraudings of coyote or jackrabbit.

Though the aridity of the central Sahara eliminates all life, few of the world's other deserts remain a consistent, lifeless golden brown. Many have a rainy season, though the amounts need to be measured in millimeters. And

Cacti are the fittest plant inhabitants of the desert. There are more than 1500 varieties of them, and some giants—the saguaros—can reach nearly 20 meters in height in a slow growth of some two hundred years. Within these rubbery candelabra several tons of water are stored.

The cacti can cope with almost anything. But humans introduced cattle into Mexico and the southwestern United States, and

the cattle ate the grasses which conceal the young saguaro seedlings from rodents. Other less vulnerable cacti spread through the open spaces, giving homes to wood-rats. More wood-rats meant the eating of more saguaros, and now the species is seriously dwindling. To evolve a defense against the speedy predation which human beings at times release is beyond the powers of even the most adaptable plants.

A desert plant must first acquire water, then keep it. Obtaining it requires either long roots—and some desert plants' systems, creeping nearly 20 meters down, are among the deepest in the world—or the means of collecting spasmodic rain or ephemeral dew, or of simply absorbing the air's moisture.

Grasses like those of the *Aristida* genus can spread their roots to a radius of 20 meters, keeping them close to the soil surface to absorb particles of moisture after the briefest shower of rain. The tamarisk is one of several plants whose leaves secrete a solution of calcium chloride. The chemical attracts and absorbs moisture, which is then fed into the leaf

The central or taproot of the mesquite plant can penetrate to a depth of nearly 20 meters in its search for water *(above left)*.
The pygmy cedar *(above right)* is capable, during a prolonged drought, of living on moisture from the night air alone.

The century plant *(top of page)* has succulent leaves with sunken stomata, or pores, to reduce evaporation of water by the dry desert air. The same device is used by the lofty saguaro cactus *(right)*, enabling it to conserve up to 10 tons of water in its bulbous shoots.

The yucca shares with other desert plants a disdain for seasonal regularity. It flowers when conditions are right, and is prepared to wait ten or more years for this. Leaves sprout from its twigs and photosynthesize, and when the rain stops they fall.

system. Several plants can survive with no other water source than atmospheric moisture.

The most widespread means of conserving water is the quality of succulence, whereby the liquid is stored in a plant's inner tissues and the outer skin is partially sealed against loss through transpiration. Succulent plants tend to locate their stomata—the holes through which carbon dioxide is absorbed and oxygen and water exhaled—in little troughs which are les exposed to drying winds than flat surfaces would be.

Plant growth on the desert sands deflects winds upward. As they rise, the winds deposit sand around the vegetation, making in time a series of scoops *(left)* filled with trees and other plants.

To survive long periods of drought the barrel cactus *(above left)* gorges rain when it comes, swelling to Pickwickian dimensions. The paloverde *(above right)* uses rainy periods for accelerated growth.

49

Floral sex is a proxy affair. The arts of enticement are directed solely at go-betweens (various insects, and some bats and birds). To these intermediaries, flowers offer an enchantment of color, perfume, pollen, and nectar. Sometimes they seem, intentionally, to offer sex itself. What they achieve by this ravishment is the distribution of male pollen among other flowers of the same species. To make sure of it they have intricate techniques to coat

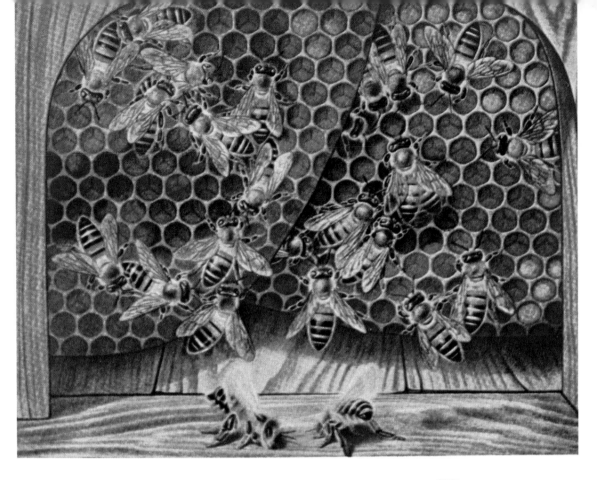

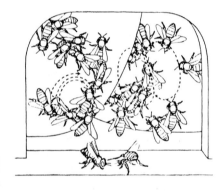

with pollen those parts of the visiting insects most likely to rub against the female organs of other flowers.

Most insect pollinators are specialists, calling on a limited range of plants. This suits the plant because it raises the chance of specific pollination. (One of the many advantages of the industrious hive-bee is that on any outing it always keeps to the same flower species.) Flowers themselves restrict the number of visitors by their shapes. The deep, narrow calyx of honeysuckle, for example, invites only butterflies or moths with long proboscises. Bumblebees can probe deeper than hive-bees; so

Above and left: A worker bee which finds a new nectar or pollen source can accurately direct her co-workers to it on return. A round dance (left, in the picture) indicates a source very close by. The figure-of-eight dance on the right tells, by the size of the angle between vertical and the line of the central run, how the position of the source relates to that of the sun, and also, by the rate at which the bee waggles her abdomen, tells its precise distance.

Right: Certain male bees and wasps are misled by the design, scent, and hairy growths on species of Ophrys orchid into regarding them as female insects, with which they try to mate. The flowers as a result are pollinated.

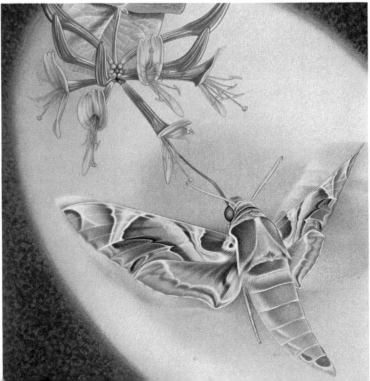

Left: An oleander hawk-moth has a proboscis long enough to reach the nectar of the honeysuckle as it hovers in front of the flower like a hummingbird.

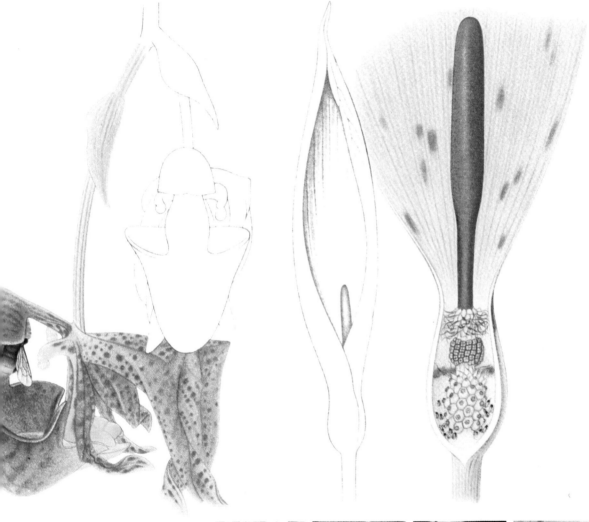

has become in a sense a free-ranging extension of the plant itself. But there are hazards in such mutual fidelity. Neither plant nor insect can spread to an area uncongenial to the other; and if one dies out, the other is also doomed. Fortunately most flowers can be pollinated by at least two carriers, and often several more.

Even the gaudiest flower is a highly functional flirt. What we see as esthetic pattern, shape, and color is usually a complex signpost ideally suited to the senses of the insects involved. The swathes and speckles on a rhododendron petal and the spokes on a speedwell are inviting guidelines for insect callers. Moreover, a flower which seems unadorned to us may present a different picture to insects, since their color spectrum excludes our reds but takes in ultraviolet. The pale wood anemone and the plain yellow buttercup are by no means so chastely pale or plain to an insect's eye. Daubs of ultra-

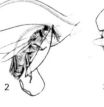

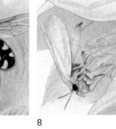

2   3   4   5   6   7   8   9

the nectar of red clover is accessible to the former but generally out of the hive-bee's reach. Evening flowers like night-scented stock, white campion, and evening primroses rely on night-flying moths; and as bright patterns would be wasted in the comparative dark, these flowers announce their presence with strong scents. Daisies and some of their relatives rely on tiny insects to penetrate their minute florets.

Selectivity is carried to extremes when only one kind of insect is capable of pollinating a flower. Each species of fig depends on a single variety of wasp. Only one moth species is capable of pollinating the yucca—so the insect

violet clearly show them where nectar stores lie. Beauty, scent, nectar, and hidden charms are the armory by which plants—unable to move themselves—persuade the animal world to do their moving for them.

Below: The earliest (and still most important) carrier of seeds and spores was the wind. Indeed, many plants have developed wings and streamers to take better advantage of it. Shown above the dandelions are winged nuts of the sycamore and various maples.

Plants bring a debonair extravagance to reproduction and the dispersal of their seeds. In each good season of an oak tree's two-hundred-year life it will produce some 90,000 acorns. A species of Venezuela orchid bears over 3½ million seeds, and one common field mushroom is able to release 16 billion spores to the winds. The air, then, is not as empty as it may seem. For hundreds of meters up it contains a mixed population of pollen, spores, and seeds (and much more besides) wafting to unknown destinations. Some of these passengers—grass or orchid seeds—are so light they need no special support. Others have evolved streamers, wings, and hairy tufts like parachutes for easy elevation by currents.

Where seeds are too heavy for the air, plants resort to ballistics. The pods of gorse, cranesbill, violets, and others scatter their seeds with quite noisy explosions. In each case the two sides of the pod grow at different rates. While moist they hold together, but dried out they split apart and scatter their contents.

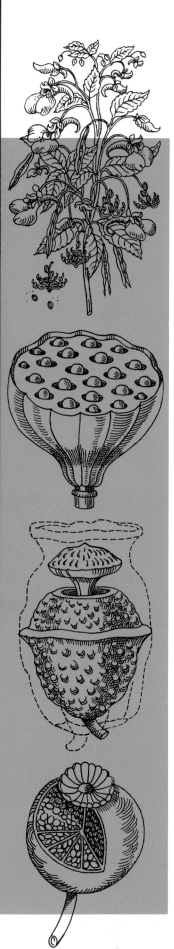

The large illustration opposite shows seeds of the wild clematis, whose hoary tufts covering the hedgerows have earned it in England the name "old man's beard."

Right: So-called vegetative reproduction spreads a species without the use of sexual processes. Plants like the strawberry send runners along the ground which at intervals sink roots and create an independent plant. A parallel process goes on underground in the case of the farmer's hated couch grass (below), as well as in sedges, iris, and Solomon's seal. Tubers, including potatoes, are a variant of this underground dispersal, growing from the base of the parent plant's stem and sending up new shoots from their "eyes." Some plants multiply even more easily. Part of a leaf or twig of a willow tree, for instance, is enough, if it falls on good soil, to develop into a complete plant.

The complex ingenuity of plants in spreading their seeds takes many forms. *(Left, from top to bottom)* The balsam *(Impatiens noli-me-*

tangere) is a waterside flower whose seed pods explode noisily at touch (whence its specific name "don't touch me"), shooting their contents far enough for a good number to be sure of reaching the stream and floating to new positions.
Next is the floating cup of the Egyptian bean, *Nelumbium speciosum.* Its content of ripe nuts germinate in the cup, then break away and insinuate their roots into the mud.
Monkey pots of *Lecythis* species look like knobbly Greek amphorae, complete with lids. Waterlogging after a while expands the neck faster than the lid, and the nuts (much liked by monkeys) spill on to the river bed. Water lilies enclose their seeds in an airy tissue of sponge. The capsule can dawdle downstream for miles before the saturated sponge causes it to sink and settle.

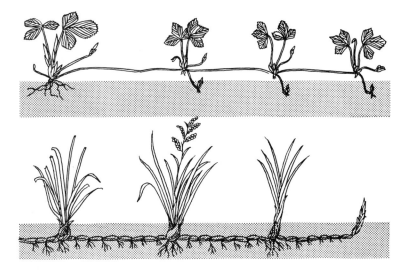

The nutcracker *(left)* swallows nuts and seeds, then regurgitates and buries them for use in winter. Like that other nut hoarder, the squirrel *(below)*, it conveniently forgets most of its caches, giving the seeds a chance to germinate.

Other plants, like the avens and agrimony, have developed hooks which latch on to a passing animal's fur to disperse their seeds.

Water is an important carrier, for a seed dropped by a waterside plant on to a stream or river has a good chance of coming to rest in a wet site that will suit it. Such

journeys call for hardy, nonporous seed cases, as does sea travel. It is the sea which took coconuts thousands of miles to their settlements in the South Pacific.
Animals also serve the colonial ambitions of plants. They swallow berries and nuts, and having digested the nutritious delivery fee they excrete the seeds far

from the parent plant. In other cases hooks, like those of goosegrass or burdock, grapnel, stickseed, or the spiny *Xanthium* (which in South Africa disrupted the breeding of merino sheep by knotting their wool), enable the seeds to hitch a ride on animal fur, hide, and feather by simply clinging on.

THE MONARCH OAK

Oak is synonymous with strength. The Romans had one word for both: *robur,* from which we take both the term robust and the name of northern Europe's commonest oak, *Quercus robur.* Hearts of oak are strong hearts. The oak was the tree of the god-king Zeus. Oaks made ships which rolled back the world's boundaries. Their kingly qualities are attested everywhere. And, like kings, they have to succor and sustain a teeming, raucous, squabbling, greedy, and murderous population.

The tree's strength is prodigious. It can lift hundreds of liters of water from the soil daily. It defies gravity, jutting its branches out horizontally, unlike other trees which lessen the load by sending off branches at narrow upward angles. And in a lifetime of two or three centuries it overproduces acorns by tens of millions. It is this surplus—of flowers, leaves, twigs, bark, heartwood, and roots, as well as acorns—which draws such multitudes to live off and under its dense canopy.

Dependents range in size from root bacteria to the pigs, wild and domestic, which feed on fallen acorns. In Britain alone nearly two thousand species of insect may use the oak as food or shelter. Over two hundred kinds of wasp raise galls on oaks, to nourish their offspring. And each visitor may set in motion an oak-based food chain, attracting bigger insects, spiders, and many kinds of bird and mammal to feed, roost, and sometimes construct or carve out living quarters.

Not only animals benefit. Ivy uses the tree as a ladder to sunlight, mistletoe sucks sap from the ridges of its high branches. Stray ferns and flowers grow from the debris in branch joints. And as old age overtakes the tree, mosses, lichens, and algae veil its limbs in a thickening pall of greys and greens.

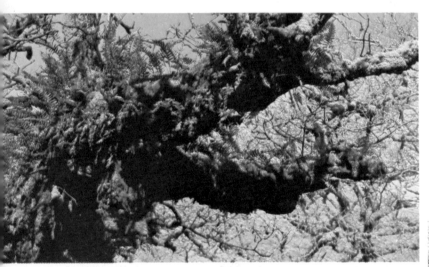

(1) The dapper jay forgets most of the acorns it buries in the ground, giving them a good chance to germinate. Caterpillars of the oak eggar moth (7) create cocoons like silky tents for their pupal phase among the oak leaves that have fed them. (8) The stinkbug, which earns its name from a potent defensive device.

(2) One of the many galls caused by parasitic action on oak trees. Each of those pictured, growing on the underside of an oak leaf, contains and nourishes a gall-wasp larva. (9) The oak leaf wasp or sawfly, whose larval diet is oak leaves. (10 and 11) Two flies in whose life cycle the oak tree assumes importance: *Lasiopticus pyrastri* and *Echinomya pyrastri,* whose larvae live and pupate inside the bodies of certain moths.

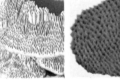

(3) Filaments of the fungus *Daedalea quercina* cause rot inside the oak's heartwood. (4) Oak-loam truffles attract flies, pigs, and not least human gourmets.

(5) The processionary moth's caterpillar, an oak dweller and feeder which travels in comic tandem with its fellows. (6) The radiant underwing moth.

(12) The many insec and inside the oak's attract, among other the spotted woodpe which may also exca nest in a stem rotte fungus.

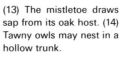

(13) The mistletoe draws sap from its oak host. (14) Tawny owls may nest in a hollow trunk.

(15) The acorn weevil lays its egg inside an acorn for the emergent larva to feed on. (16) Oak-roller moth larvae feed voraciously on oak leaves before dropping to the ground on a silky twine.

(20) The musical katydid grasshopper, with ovipositor like a scimitar, nibbles at oak leaves. (17) As the playground for such a profusion of insects, the oak cannot fail to draw predator spiders. (18 and 19) A cicada, and the skin shed by another during metamorphosis. Large numbers of these insects suck sap from the twigs and leaves of the oak and excrete honeydew, which attracts other insects.

(21) Acorns are a favorite food of squirrels, which lay down surplus stores for the winter. They also devour bark and eggs out of birds' nests. (22) Ants play a large part in woodland life, farming aphids, eating other insects, heaping twigs to make nests, and attracting birds. (23) Damp crannies to live in, and leaves, roots, and fungi to feed on, attract many snails to the base of the oak. (24) Longhorn beetles like *Cerambyx cerdo* eat the wood of the oak, and may hasten the tree's death.

(25) The dazzling beetle *Chrysobotris affinis* feeds off the oak's leaves.

55

TO19527

LIFE AMONG THE ROOTS

When the wind uproots a large tree, a whole universe is rent. If our ears were attuned to the sounds of the soil, the endless jangles, scrapings, crackles, grindings, and tappings of the resident mammals, reptiles, insects, mollusks, crustaceans, arachnids, and annelids might persuade us that there was more peace at a highway intersection than in a forest glade.

Plants in general, and roots in particular, are the cause of much of this activity. Roots creep along the ground—much further than the branches of the tree above them—and deep down into the bedrock in search of water and minerals. Hard rock simply diverts their courses (and in time they break it down by the secretion of acid juices). If they emerge in caves, they simply grow on and down—as much as seven meters in some

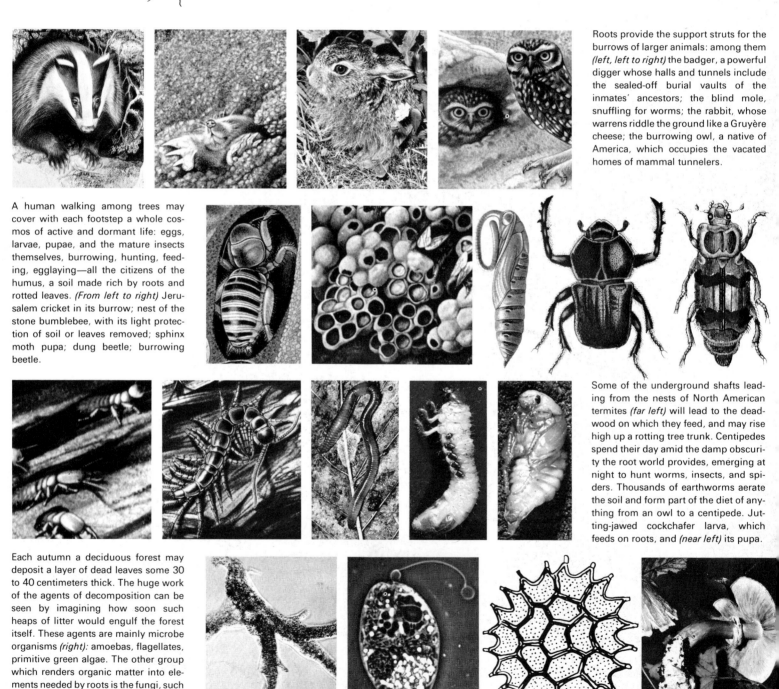

Roots provide the support struts for the burrows of larger animals: among them *(left, left to right)* the badger, a powerful digger whose halls and tunnels include the sealed-off burial vaults of the inmates' ancestors; the blind mole, snuffling for worms; the rabbit, whose warrens riddle the ground like a Gruyère cheese; the burrowing owl, a native of America, which occupies the vacated homes of mammal tunnelers.

A human walking among trees may cover with each footstep a whole cosmos of active and dormant life: eggs, larvae, pupae, and the mature insects themselves, burrowing, hunting, feeding, egglaying—all the citizens of the humus, a soil made rich by roots and rotted leaves. *(From left to right)* Jerusalem cricket in its burrow; nest of the stone bumblebee, with its light protection of soil or leaves removed; sphinx moth pupa; dung beetle; burrowing beetle.

Some of the underground shafts leading from the nests of North American termites *(far left)* will lead to the deadwood on which they feed, and may rise high up a rotting tree trunk. Centipedes spend their day amid the damp obscurity the root world provides, emerging at night to hunt worms, insects, and spiders. Thousands of earthworms aerate the soil and form part of the diet of anything from an owl to a centipede. Jutting-jawed cockchafer larva, which feeds on roots, and *(near left)* its pupa.

Each autumn a deciduous forest may deposit a layer of dead leaves some 30 to 40 centimeters thick. The huge work of the agents of decomposition can be seen by imagining how soon such heaps of litter would engulf the forest itself. These agents are mainly microbe organisms *(right):* amoebas, flagellates, primitive green algae. The other group which renders organic matter into elements needed by roots is the fungi, such as the *Inocybe patouilardii (far right).*

Swiss caves—till they meet and begin to mine the cave floor.

Roots close to the surface attract symbiotic bacteria, which provide them with nitrogen. As reservoirs of moisture, sugars, and chemicals, roots also draw certain fungi, whose hyphae curiously envelop them and suck foods from them, but pass them all they need from the soil.

Other plants grow among the surface roots, enjoying either the shade or the rich humus. And following the plants come the legions of animal species, of which a few representatives appear on these pages.

Soil nutrients are first absorbed by the root hairs, whose composite length—in the case of a big tree—may be over twice the diameter of the earth. Their strength is phenomenal too, for they break into solid rock in their quest for mineral tonics.

The species of tree and the amount of light its leaves let through determine the kinds of flower, moss, fungus, lichen,

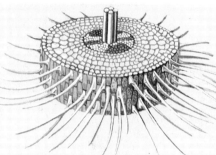

and other plants that grow around its base. These in turn help to condition the nature of the animal population. Some characteristic creatures of a typical temperate forest are the ground snake (1) and several other species; many kinds of snail (2), which use leaf litter as daytime cover; various ants (3) and woodlice (4), whose ability to breathe depends on moist air. Millipedes (5 and 6) feed on decaying plant matter, from which they release useful salts into the soil. Fly eggs and larvae, like that of the greenhead (7), abound in the soil. Most animals introduce parasites like fleas and ticks (8). Among the copious beetle population are the wireworm or click beetle, whose larva (9) feeds destructively on roots; and the wood roach, shown here (10) in pupal form. Roundworms (11) parasitize both plants and animals (including humans). The cicada (12) emerges from one of its many molts on the way to winged maturity.

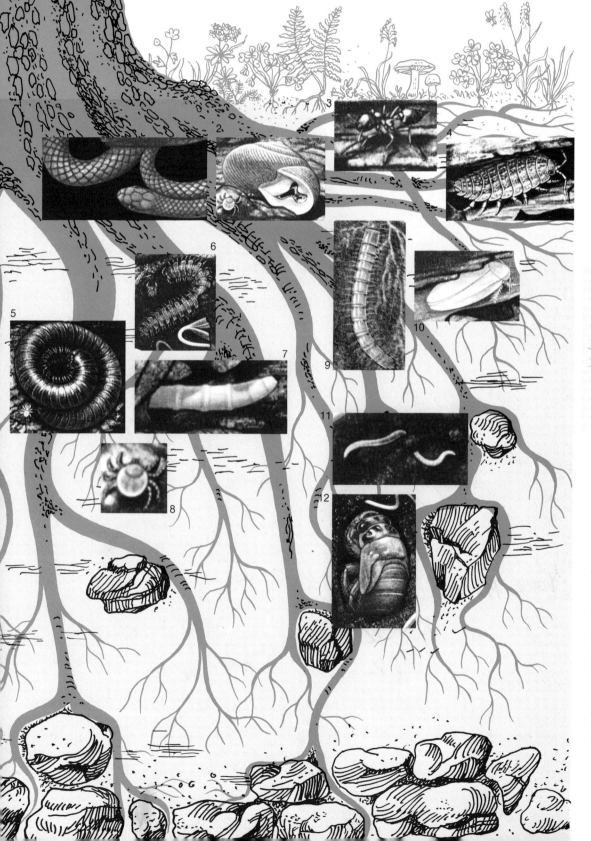

Water fills out plant cells, giving the plant firmness and resilience. Water, broken into its constituents hydrogen and oxygen, makes possible the vital process of photosynthesis. It heaves supplies of nutritious chemicals from roots to all parts of the plant. And most of

Rain falling on bare rock or sand may evaporate in the heat of the sun and be carried off as vapor by the wind. Or it may, if the land slopes, slip downhill as a series of trickles, merge into a torrent, and then rush to the sea. But if there are plants on the land—even a thin covering of grass—some rain will settle in the soil and be absorbed by the roots, drawn up the stem to the leaves, and transpired through them into the atmosphere. In this case the water cycle, though taking longer, will be of greater value. As seasons succeed each other, the level of humus—dead and decomposing organic matter—steadily rises. More plants grow, and their networks of roots, together with the humus, discipline the water flow, absorbing rainfall which might otherwise it, having done its work, is given off as vapor by the leaves.

This upward stream of water is sustained by several different pressures. Osmosis, a process caused by water's natural urge to level the difference between a weak chemical solution (in the soil) and a stronger one (inside the root hairs), draws water into the root system. Transpiration is brought about by a different force: the tendency for water within a leaf to escape to the drier air outside, the result of another watery urge to level differences. But even when the air outside is moist, as on a dewy morning, many plants can maintain a water flow by means of a kind of cellular pressure, forcing drops through glands on the edges of their leaves (as in the strawberry leaf, *left*). (It is the same pressure which causes a newly sawn tree stump to exude water or "bleed".) By these combined techniques a square meter of grass can, in the course of a season, give half a ton of water back to the air.

flush unchecked and useless to the sea. The volume of water transpired by all this vegetation increases, lowering the temperature of the air above. The coolness precipitates rain from other clouds blown into the area (just as cold mountains do). More rain falls. More vegetation thrives. More vapor rises. An acre of corn can transpire a million liters of water in one season; a willow tree 20 thousand liters in a day. It always comes down again, as rain.

It is claimed that almost three-quarters of the rain that falls on land is the result of plant transpiration, only a quarter having been evaporated from the sea. But when deforestation takes place, that tendency reverses. Dry land has no voice to call for water.

The idea of divine resurrection may well have been inspired by plants. They almost always rise again. The worst privations of nature and man are unable to annihilate them. On the contrary, plants obliterate man's most grandiose designs. Colonial settlers felled acres of the mahogany jungles of central Africa and built roads and settlements for the exploitation of the wood there. One or two generations later, the tall mahoganies now

sway again, and it will require a particularly muscular archaeology to uncover any human traces. Like Ozymandias, whole civilizations have died with a boast on their lips—and been erased by moss and grass, herbs and trees, and impenetrable twiners.

Fire is a natural blight, though nowadays cigarettes, matches, and people's bonfires account for more than the natural strikes of lightning, lava, the spontaneous combustion of fermenting vegetation, and blazes produced by the friction of tumbling stones. But for plants fire can also be a boon. When the custodians of Yosemite National Park in California ringed stands of redwood with fire-defying breaks, the huge trees moved into visible decline. Then it was realized that fire is necessary for the redwoods' welfare. Their bark is protection against the heat, so they sustain only slight damage themselves. At the same time fire clears the ground of brushwood and herbage which compete for nutrients with the redwoods' shallow roots. So the foresters reversed their policy, and now, like their counterparts in the acacia stands of west Africa and the teak forests of India, they start fires every few years to clear the tangled undergrowth.

Many plants show an astonishing reluctance to die. Saplings spring vigorously from the stumps of felled trees. The ability was recognized and exploited for centuries by people who coppiced (cut at ground level) willow, hazel, and chestnut for the long poles which would sprout from the stub. (Pollarding follows the same principle, only here amputation takes place higher up the tree, out of reach of browsing animals.) This same power of vigorous recovery causes pruned roses to bloom again and again and beheaded fruit trees to respond with twice

Opposite: Roots of a ceiba tree gradually eclipse a huge Khmer monument at Angkor, Cambodia.

Left: The explosive effect of lightning leaves desolation behind, but new life will sprout among the charred stems.

Below: A young ash tree finds life in a dead trunk.

their original number of branches.

There are plants which have survived the thousands of volts transmitted by a flash of lightning. Every country has its examples: trees scorched and given up for dead a century or more ago whose shattered boles survived and today support a thriving foliage. In sexteenth-century Oaxaca there was a swamp cypress, 500 years old, whose leaves could shade a thousand

people. "This tree," wrote a contemporary, "was strooke with lightning from the toppe to the bottome through the heart." Indians took the flash to be a divine thunderbolt. It hollowed the tree, leaving little more than the bark. Yet the tree still lives, a flourishing symbol of the power to survive even the anger of gods.

And to every beast of the earth,
and to every fowl of the air,
and to every thing that creepeth upon the earth,
wherein there is life,
I have given every green herb for meat:
and it was so.

Genesis I: 30

Trace any particle of any limb, organ, bone, muscle, tissue, nail, or hair of your body to its physical origins, and you come, sooner or later, to plants. Der Mensch ist, was er isst, the Germans pun. Put another way, man is fifty to a hundred kilograms of vegetable matter, chewed, digested, rechewed and redigested perhaps, and possibly again and again, and broken down and built up in new combinations, and finally disposed as the familiar components of the human form.

As man's physique is the artifact of the plant world, so human culture and civilization proceed, as it were, by license from the same source. Before crops were cultivated, people moved in small groups in those places where plants would maintain them, unsettled tenants of vegetable landlords. Even when crop-growing began, the dependence did not disappear. In some ways it increased. Civilizations that grew from that seminal step have always been rooted in and shaped by the produce of their soil. The patterns of our populations are still dictated by the plants that feed them.

For plants have dogged and dominated us at every turn. They have fed us, clothed us, provided our homes and heat. They have caused some of the brightest and some of the darkest chapters of history. They have set us on quests that opened up the world, sparked war, migration, enslavement,

power to sustain

created the wealth and dominion of some nations, and the poverty and subjection of others.

Today it is easy to claim the contrary: to point to our health, our numbers, our longevity, and our achievements; to our computers and flights to the moon and dreams of colonies far beyond; to bouncing pictures off the stratosphere, and probing the mysteries of outer space. But from the power of plants to sustain us we cannot break free. Cut off from them, an Einstein or an astronaut dies as quickly as his Paleolithic forebears, to be reclaimed before long by the fungi and the bacteria from which his vitality sprang.

Pomme de terre ronde blanche
Topinambour
Radis rond
Radis long
Betterave à sucre
Betterave fourragère
Carotte fourragère
Carotte ronde
Carotte demi longue
Navet long
Navet rond
Navet plat
Fève
oireau
Epinard
Salsifis noir
Salsifis blanc
Oseille
Betterave à salade
Oignon pyramidal
Pois mange-tout
Pois droit
Pois serpette
Haricot blanc
Lentille
Cresson
Haricot mange-tout
Oignon rond
Oignon plat
Chou d'York
Céleri
Céleri-rave
Chou-fleur
Chou de Bruxelles
Echalote
Chou cœur-de-bœuf
Chou-rave
Asperge
Ail
Chicorée frisée
Chou de Milan
Mâche
Romaine
Artichaut
Piment long
Scarole
Laitue
Potiron turban
Aubergine longue
Tomate ronde
Piment carré
Melon noir des Carmes
Melon brodé de Tours
Melon à rames
Aubergine ronde
Cornichon
Melon cantaloup
Pastèque
Potiron géant
Tomate ordinaire
Courge à la moelle
Concombre

THE ORIGINS OF AGRICULTURE

The sickle, one of man's earliest inventions, multiplied by several times the amount of corn a man could reap. The farthest left—of bronze with a wooden handle—is from a Swiss lake dwelling. The other is of stone, from Germany. Pots, like this Minoan jar of about 1700 B.C., and basketware were indispensable to the progress of early farming.

It would be curious if, during the quarter of a million years between the emergence of *Homo sapiens* and the first farming successes archaeology credits him with, he did not make some stabs at cultivating plants. His brain was twice as big as that of his nearest hominoid competitors and the same size as our own. A quarter of a million seasonal cycles cannot fail to have made an impression on him. He may have been deterred from acting on his observations by innate conservatism and religious taboos against tampering with nature. The wild larder—of

A rock drawing from Bohus in Sweden shows a Bronze Age plow pulled by two oxen and controlled by a man at the rear. This is an ard, or scratch plow, which is not capable of turning the soil. Turning had to wait for a later invention, the moldboard plow.

plants and animals—was probably adequate for the numbers dependent on it. Mastery of fire and cooking and the invention of axes and pots for carrying had probably eased his life and extended his menu sufficiently to stop him trying more innovations.

Some time before ten thousand

years ago man's curiosity got the better of him. The possibilities that plants seemed to be offering anyone prepared to sink some seeds in the ground and wait for them to grow became overpoweringly tempting. Not just in one place but in several centers round the world, the calculating Cains—settled farmers planting their crops—gradually displaced the easy-going, nomadic Abels. (The implication of that tale shows the moral forces deployed against innovation.)

The breakthrough was probably wrought by a combination of accident and design. Some seeds of wild grains and other plants collected by foraging women (while men hunted) would have been dropped on rubbish heaps and there, in a soil rich in nitrogen, seen to germinate and grow. Once the psychological leap was taken, it would have been a simple matter to collect seed, plant it, and weed out unwanted intruders. It would at the very least have saved walking. In fact it did much more. The moment man took a hand in controlling nature, he embarked on a whole chain of unforeseen reactions. He could count (most years) on a surplus. Sustained surpluses meant more people. His crops, moreover, were at his doorstep—not scattered over the countryside. Close observation now showed him he could plant those seeds whose fruits were easiest to pick (but not readily blown off by the wind), which germinated reliably, and which stored well.

So he was released for the tasks of organizing and government, building better homes, and making better clothes, furniture, art, and sculpture. Settlements grew into villages and towns. The multiplication of mouths to feed became—not the liberation it might first have seemed—but a new kind of tyranny. The goods of one society became the envy of another. But by then it was too late to turn back. Knowledge, which was Adam's curse, had brought civilization, which was Cain's. And plants were instrumental in both.

It was on cereals that the great early civilizations were based: those of Mesopotamia and the eastern Mediterranean, of China, and of the Indus valley. In some areas—Africa, parts of Asia, and the upland settlements of South America—root crops were more important because they grew better there. But the greatest advances were made by peoples who relied on the grass family, which provided not only grain but also, as ordinary grass, the chief fodder of their animals. Grasses were and remain the chief support of civilizations.

The arrival of farming was neither sudden nor simple. Nor, once it had arrived, was its development. This depended, as it still does, on continuous invention: of sickles to harvest the crop and containers to carry it in, pestles to grind the grain, flails to winnow it, and various methods of breaking ground to insert seed and of replacing it as protection against animals and birds. For

ages, long periods of settlement were impossible. Quick exhaustion of topsoil which followed the slash-and-burn clearing of forests compelled communities to move on. Only after the innovation of advanced techniques of plowing (by domestic animals, which in turn necessitated a fairly settled existence) and of fal-

Grain crops were almost certainly the first plants cultivated by man, and emmer (1, pictured in both wild and cultivated forms) may have been the first of these. It and einkorn (2) are thought to have hybridized to make bread-wheats (3 and 4). Oats (5) and rye (6) were weeds of wheatfields till found more suitable than wheat for cold climates. Small-grained millet (7) did better in southerly latitudes.

lowing did man himself put down roots from which successive civilizations have sprung. Exceptions to this were the valleys annually flooded with the diluted soils from lands above. Every year the Nile has brought down the rich silt washed away by Ethiopian monsoons. It is estimated that in seven thousand years of cultivation the Nile valley has benefited from a gift of three hundred times the total area of topsoil of all Europe. No wonder that Egypt rose to early prominence.

Agriculture brought a degree of permanence to early human settlement. Grain was grown beside huts which had been built in the time saved from foraging. With domesticated sheep, cattle, pigs, and goats, a community was sure of a rich diet and the energy for the earliest activities of civilized life: building, making pottery and sculpture, furniture, and elaborate clothing, and evolving social laws and rituals.

Overleaf:
A wall painting from Thebes, dating from 3000 to 3500 years ago, shows some of the range of farming in the Nile valley. Emmer is being reaped in the top panel. The crop being uprooted below is flax, grown in Egypt for its fibers for 6000 years. Next a man and woman respectively plow and sow. Below them are date and doum palms and a kind of fig tree, above several water plants.

The Neolithic farmers who, instead of having casual flirtations with any number of wild plants, wedded themselves to certain staples could not have predicted the course of the marriage. Freed from an obsession with obtaining food, societies broadened their horizon on other fronts. They allotted different functions to different people. Now there were rulers, priests, judges, soldiers, sailors, traders, farmers. In time whole countries were to become specialized, North Africa providing the wheat of the classical world, Greece becoming famous for olives and vines, the Levant for fruits, and nameless countries of the Orient (enveloped in mystery by Arab traders, who thereby were more assured of their

A counter-weighted beam provides leverage for drawing water for the modern Indian *(above)*, as it did for the ancient Egyptian *(right)*.

The plow *(below right)* used fifty years ago on the English Sussex Downs is a bare advance on that used by Romans in North Africa two thousand years ago.

grain-packed silos of early Mesopotamian cultures roused the interest of their neighbors. There was a constant threat from nomadic bands who saw marauding as a preferable alternative to

Persian Gulf, for instance, expanded by breaching the banks of their rivers and irrigating ever wider tracts of land. But in time this constant irrigation drained the soil of all nutrients, and crops

monopoly) for spices and other exotic garnishes.

Yet in all this there was no peace. In offering itself for cultivation, the benign family of grasses had unleashed competition, migrations, and wars on mankind. The

settling down. But the main upheavals were caused by the actions of the farmers themselves, who did not fully understand the natural processes they were exploiting.

Valley settlements round the

failed. In consequence the amassed wealth and manpower of those societies was turned toward grabbing food from other sources. Imperialism was born. In the same way it is possible to explain in part the rise of Greece

and of Rome by their ignorance of the nature of soil. Both Attica and Italy were once fertile, wooded countries. Trees that once precipitated abundant rain and whose roots channeled and held the moisture on hillsides were cut down. Erosion and a drier climate followed. The land became good only for figs, olives, vines. And so, in turn, the Greeks and the Romans looked outward for their basic foods—as both have had to do ever since. The results were empires, but empire is an overstretching of a nation's sinews. For four centuries Rome remained at a peak of power—the long climax of ancient civilization. Then, under pressure from within and without, it crashed. With it tumbled the spirit of inquiry and expansion that had not only dominated the Western world but had made farming more efficient than ever before. For more than a thousand years the plow was to remain subordinate to the sword. With some notable exceptions, monotonous diets and frequent exposure to famine were to be the lot of the majority of people until the eighteenth century, when modern science began to be applied to food growing. Even that has not radically changed the nature of the food we eat. With the exception of sugar-beet and some minor fruits, no food plant grown today is fundamentally different from plants known by people four or more thousand years ago. During most of that time progress was eclipsed by drudgery.

The arduous task of winnowing grain— tossing it into the air for the breeze to blow off light chaff—has only recently been superseded by machinery.

Water was early enlisted to supplement human energy. Windmills, a medieval introduction, are still widely used.

THE MACHINE AGE

Twentieth-century agriculture gradually replaces people with machines. The picture below shows a Wisconsin couple's lush and varied harvest, but their faces reveal the effort involved.

The power of plants to sustain civilizations never changed. The power of men to make use of it did. Rome's demise did not prevent some technical advances: the advent in the sixth century of the moldboard plow, by which heavier earths could be turned and vast tracts of virgin soil claimed by the farmer, and the threefold system of rotation, which by introducing plants of the bean family between the old crop and fallow periods enriched

But in Europe it was the discoveries by Columbus, da Gama, and others that brought the most obvious changes. American maize, potatoes, tomatoes, several beans, fruits, and cocoa became important in the diets of Europeans. American introductions to indigent Africa were nutritionally even more important, still forming the main diet in many areas. Nor were the benefits one-way. From Europe to America went wheat, and

the soil with nitrogen, improved yields, and provided much of the vigor of Charlemagne's empire. A new harness from Asia gradually replaced oxen by the far more efficient horse. The Western medieval society which evolved through these innovations was able to increase and vary its diet by trade, and invaders like the Moorish conquerors of Spain left behind rice, sorghum, sugarcane, and oranges.

from Africa, along with enslaved blacks, went bananas, sugarcane, yams, and other plants.

Still, the world moved slowly. Though agricultural theory blossomed after the Renaissance, it was not till the end of the eighteenth century that a combination of capital, vision, knowledge, the pressure of a prolonged war, and a growing population brought about, in Europe, an agricultural revolution as momen-

tous as the Neolithic. Fertilization, specialization, seed drills, four-crop rotation, selective breeding, and technological advances began to change the world. In the century that followed, increasing knowledge of heredity, plant disease, hybridizing, and mineral nutrition made possible, and were themselves accelerated by, the heady rise in population. But it is the twentieth century that has seen the cumulative results of all this progress, and nowhere more than in the United States.

A hundred years ago the average American farm, with its heavy dependence on human and animal power, produced enough food for five people. Today, production per acre has increased eightfold, and the next decade may see a 50 percent increase over that. A billion acres of land, 5 million tractors, a million combine harvesters are just part of the tools that enable not only Americans but a sizable number of other nationalities to live well. Irrigation projects, new machinery, laboratories, fertilizers, pesticides, and educational schemes proliferate, and even so millions of acres remain to be exploited. No country ever produced so much food in history. Yet even America has this in common with the pygmy picking his day's nuts, leaves, and honey in the forests of the Congo: man is completely dependent on the essential ability of plants to grow and spread.

71

An ideal unit, further idealized in this picture, the village enshrines the principle of communal self-sufficiency. Over it stands the steeple, symbol of spiritual nourishment. All around lie the bodily fuels: plants, or the animals that plants sustain. Herbs, vegetables, fruits, root-crops, and cereals share the clearance with cattle, sheep, goats, and pigs.

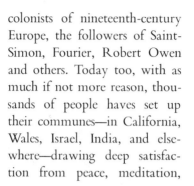

The Westerner preparing his dinner today is likely to be consuming food that was grown in various parts of the world. There is nothing new in this. For five hundred years food has been a main item in the trade of any advanced country. Even in the Middle Ages a nobleman's festive table might display import-

Some monasteries still testify to this arrangement. The chapel served the needs of worship, and living quarters those of sleep, shelter, and study. Beyond them stretch the medicinal garden, the coniger for rabbits, the pond for fish, the park for deer, fields for crops, and surrounding woods, seasonally, for acorn-grubbing

Possibly because an edible plant growing in the earth suggests greater security than the same in a shop window, people have always cherished the idea of direct dependence on the land. Self-sufficiency is an ideal of all ages, not just our own. St. Antony and his deprived colleagues in the desert of Sinai, rejecting the

colonists of nineteenth-century Europe, the followers of Saint-Simon, Fourier, Robert Owen and others. Today too, with as much if not more reason, thousands of people haves set up their communes—in California, Wales, Israel, India, and elsewhere—drawing deep satisfaction from peace, meditation,

ed sea-fish, spices, and fruits. But by and large medieval meals—and clothes and buildings too—were the produce of the surrounding land. The physical shape of a settlement was to a large degree determined by the crops on which the people and their animals lived.

pigs. The system provided a fairly secure sufficiency.
Medieval villages were the lay equivalent. The size and number of these again reflected the amount of locally available food. Many remained largely self-sufficient until well into the present century.

aggressive rootlessness of the Byzantine empire, found that a closeness to the natural order meant closeness to their god too. It is a theme constantly restated: by the Apostolici of twelfth-century France, by lone hermits from biblical times, and by the extraordinary growth of nature-

work, a freedom restrained by the understandable (because visible) dictates of nature, and not least from nature itself and the plant world which supports it.

If high-flying birds had a racial memory, they would recall an extraordinary pattern of evolution over the last ten thousand years, from the time when the northern latitudes thawed back into fertility and the world warmed up. The rate of subsequent changes would have shown marked variations in different regions. In Europe and parts of Asia and North Africa

there would have been slow alterations up to about fifteen hundred years ago, gradual acceleration during the Middle Ages as populations grew, considerable speeding until this century, and the quickest changes of all during the last fifty years. North America would have been slow to move until the last four hundred years, but it would show the most astonishing transformation during the last century. Large areas of the world, particularly in parts of America and Africa, would have consistently displayed the monotonous dark green of woodland, though this would in recent times have been dented and lined by roads, quar-

ries, mines, and hydroelectric schemes.

People are the reason, of course. People who toiled and invented, who cut down forests, reclaimed marsh, fen, and desert, diverted rivers, irrigated whole countries, blasted mountains away, built towns, villages, and isolated houses, and laid out parks and farmland where wilderness had existed before. It was people who selected and sowed the seeds that gave these new faces to the land, and by their scientific researches caused ever better seeds to develop from the plants they grew. There can be no stinting of credit to man.

And yet, no one ever created a plant, any more than a parent creates a baby. In both cases, people are agents in the mysteries of evolutionary change. However amtitious their schemes, they are tied always by what plants allow them to do. However many plants people eliminate by weed killer, plow, fire, or controlled flood, they will never lose their ultimate dependence on the vegetable kingdom.

It is these food plants which have really changed the appearance of the land, even though they have spread where a nature without humans would never have permitted them. The natural vegetation of most temperate, as of most tropical, soils is at some stage trees. Trees are usually the last and lasting phase of plant evolution in any terrain which can support them. What we now know as hedgerow plants were once the fringe decorations of forests, constantly pushed back as the wood colonies advanced. Cereals of the grass family, vegetables, vines, fruits, and various root crops were able to stem this advance when they could enlist men as allies. From then on it has been their demands and preferences which have caused the bird's-eye view to change so drastically.

For centuries the main trend was a reduction: the clearance of huge tracts of forest for the planting, in arbitrary sites, of basic crops. Smallholdings, their boundaries embossed with hedges or engraved with ditches, appeared in distorted patchwork over the areas of population. Then linear terraces appeared along the hillsides of many Mediterranean countries—a pattern that spread with the human taste for wine. Forced enclosures of later times often imposed straight or angular boundaries, but it was our century's machines which brought geometrical precision to the patterns of agriculture, with the straightening of crooked lines and the

merging of small units into land leviathans. The results present that aerial bird with views we might more readily associate with modernistic art galleries.

Ten thousand years ago the last of the four great Ice Ages had receded, leaving bleak and barren deserts in the uplands like that of Judah *(right)*. Since then time and people have transformed the world....

Page 76. A pattern of roads and small fields characterizes the rich farmland of the Vendée, in western France.

Page 77. The rural landscape of York County, Pennsylvania, seems like a crazed abstract from above.

Page 78. Five thousand years after the ice departed, forests had spread to dominate much of the world's temperate zone. But for human incursions, they still would.

Page 79. Low ridges of earth trap water in South Hunan, China, to create paddy fields for the cultivation of rice.

Page 80. Where soil, sun, and drainage allow, large areas of four continents are given over to the vine. This pattern of vineyards is found near Geneva.

Page 81. Orchards of mandarin, or tangerine, interspersed among the rice fields of Kyushu, Japan, typify the geometrical order imposed by people on natural contours.

Page 82. Stands of trees deflect the right-angled regularity of lines made by a harvester in Argentina's pampas.

Page 83. The outer rays of the Star of Enserune, in the Herault department of France, include cereal fields and woodland. Within the circle, segments are given over to maize, sorghum, lucerne, tomatoes, and fruit trees.

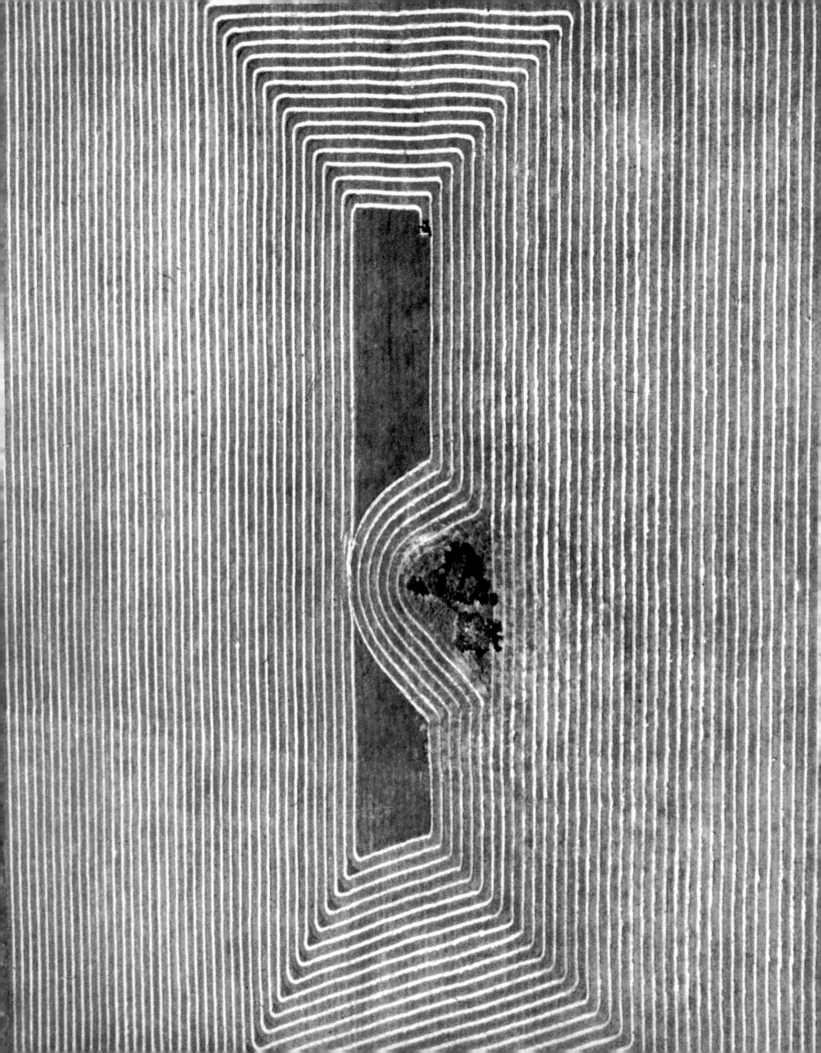

Left: Some plants submit to man's regulation of the world's surface with amazing docility. The water hyacinth, *Eichhornia crassipes,* shown here in the Laguna de Bay, in the Philippines, offers itself as a pasture at man's convenience. It grows and spreads unchecked by any natural enemies, and it has been estimated that the progeny of one of its beautiful pale blue flowers could—if it found the appropriate nutrition in the water—carpet all the seas of the earth within two years. It is the rabbit of the plant kingdom, and its periodic explosions of population cause it to block ports, canals, and other waterways, to conceal buoys and jetties, and foul pumps and ships' propellers. It is not clear why it forms characteristic circles of growth, but wave action may contribute. Though its nutritional value is small, it offers a cheap source of cattle fodder and could be exploited for its cellulose content. More important, it has recently been shown that it can clear waters of many poisonous and polluting substances. Its docility lies in its nomadic potential. Floating without roots in the water, each growth-disk can be pushed or hauled by a single small fishing boat. No land plant is so obliging.

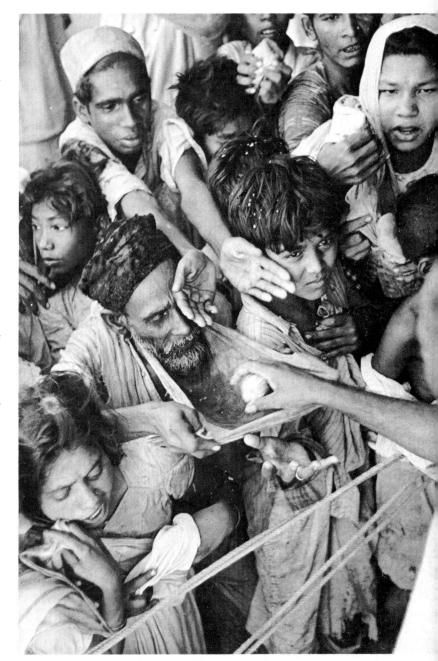

A well-kept, lifelong record could express a person in terms of plants: the total area of grass that fed the cattle that supplied his meat and milk, the tracts of starchy staples which he consumed, the weight of green vegetables, the fruits, legumes, herbs, spices, flavorings, the yeasts and other fungi; all the grapes and cereals that went into the making of his wine, beer, and spirits; the wild plants that nurtured the rabbits, hares, frogs, fish, snails, game-birds, locusts, and other insects which ended their days on his plate. It would, perhaps, make a good topic for a thesis. The quantity and sources of the plants involved would be of interest and might well astonish. Few inhabitants of the developed world do not take for granted a daily menu that draws some of its constituents from at least four continents, harvested and prepared by workers whose language and way of life would be incomprehensible to the consumer. But the main finding would only reinforce what simple logic already shows: that in the last resort people not only depend on plants, they *are* plants whose nature has been changed by the action of substances which themselves derive entirely from plants.

The lengths we go to to acquire the plants we need have formed a significant part of the world's history. Food has been a major motivation for travelers, explorers, and conquerors. Today the world's roads, sea-lanes, and air routes are plied continually by cargoes of crops on their way to those prepared to spend the rewards of their daily work on them. By far the greatest part of the land utilized by people is given over to the growing of food. The control and improvement of plant growing has absorbed more ingenuity and skill, more labor and money than any other human activity. Our reward is an endless range of minutely graded tastes, savors, and consistencies.

PROVIDERS OF OUR DAILY BREAD

A variety of bread grains *(below, left to right):*
1 Emmer, *Triticum dicoccum*
2 Bread-wheat, *Triticum aestivum*
3 Rye, *Secale cereale*
4 Oats, *Avena sativa*
5 Two-rowed barley, *Hordeum distichum*
6 Finger millet, *Eleusine coracana*
7 Sorghum, *Sorghum vulgare*

A late medieval woodcut shows the crowned goddess Ceres presiding over the beneficent crops to which she gave her name.

Opposite page: Before machinery took over, travelers could tell where they were by the particular shapes (which varied from place to place) into which the sheaves of grain were stacked.

Throughout the history of the West, bread has provided more than half—often much more—of the average diet.

Lack of it has whipped up social tornadoes, like the French Revolution. Bread is the staff of life. Some Christians hold that it can be literally changed into Christ's body. In Arabic, the word for it shares a root with the word for life. The person who supplies a family's income is the breadwinner. In recent times both bread and dough have returned as synonyms for money. And in almost all cases bread is a product of the grains of the grass family, which provides us also with most of the fodder of our domestic animals. All flesh is grass, said Isaiah, with more literal truth than he intended.

Basic bread is the result of baking meal which has been mixed with water and kneaded into shape. Almost any meal will do, including that of acorns and chestnuts, but cereals are the main sources. For the early farmers of the Near East their preparation involved considerable effort, since the husks of wild grains clung tightly to the contained kernels and needed a preliminary toasting—on heated stones, in a fire, or by means of a kind of taper—to make them brittle. Even so, the first foods prepared with grain—various gruels and pottages and heavy breads—must have been bothersome to eat, involving a lot of spitting and discomfort.

In due course grains improved, in terms of their convenience to man, simply because people learned to plant seeds of those varieties which suited them best. As later civilization dispersed the original Middle Eastern wheats—emmer and einkorn and the hybrids formed from them—across Europe and North Africa, weed cereals were unavoidably conveyed with the cultivated ones. Some were found to be better suited to the new conditions. In this way barley and oats came to thrive in northern latitudes, and millet and sorghum in the hotter conditions of Africa. But wheat was always in demand, especially after the Egyptians discovered the process of leavening.

This is caused by another group of plants, the single-celled fungi known as yeasts. Always present

1   2   3   4   5   6   7

86

Wisdom, Power and
Goodness meet
In the bounteous field
of wheat.

"The Wheatfield"
Hannah Flagg Gould (1789–1865)

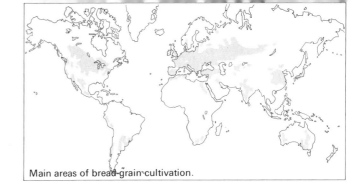
Main areas of bread-grain cultivation.

in the air, they decompose dead organic matter, releasing gases which blow the flour's viscid gluten into millions of miniature balloons. The discovery was perhaps made by accident that when they attack moist dough the subsequent baking produces bread of an infinitely lighter and more palatable consistency than otherwise. (This grain ferment is also the basis of beer.) But not all cereals respond in this way. Bread wheats are the best grain for leavening, and rye follows close behind. Others are better used for one of the huge variety of unleavened breads, gruels, pottages, pasta—or even for the making of spirits. Cereals like oats and barley owe their survival more to hardiness than to bread-making potential.

Up to the eighteenth century more rye bread was eaten in Europe than wheat bread. But when science began to dominate the agriculture of the West it was wheat which spread fastest round the world. It colonized Russia as far as Mongolia, and although it has been present in America since Columbus's time, it was slow to rival the native corn (maize), outside the European colonies, until the nineteenth century.

Then wheat spread with pioneers and by trade through the United States and Canada, Chile, and Argentina. At the same time, European trade and emigration established it in southern Africa and Australia. Now it shares with rice the position of first importance among cereal crops.

Late seventeenth-century engravings from Regensburg show grain arriving for milling, and preparing dough in the bakery.

Though prisoners traditionally live on bread and water, and the poor have often been forced to do the same, there is general agreement with the axiom that you cannot live on bread alone. Bread is seldom the star of a meal. It accompanies, enhances, mops up, fills in, ekes out, or simply provides a nutritious background for the gaudier foods on the table. Till the Middle Ages, slabs of bread, known as trenchers, served as plates for putting things on. In sandwiches, bread is for putting things between. Crumbs are for the birds.

This modesty of bread veils its crucial importance in our diets. It requires only a little cheese and green vegetable to satisfy the body's needs. It contains large quantities of starch and useful amounts of protein, fat, minerals, and vitamins. In some countries, it actually provides more of the protein in an average diet than the protein foods.

fat, fruit, or flavoring, and with or without the process of leavening, bread has assumed a protean range of shapes, tastes, constituents, and decorations, from croissant to crispbread, and pancake to pumpernickel.

Leavening was the most startling development in bread's history. To it we owe many of the most famous regional breads: the brioches and baguettes and croissants of France, the cottage loaves and splits and tins of England, the rich dark rye breads of Germany, with their flavorings of caraway and poppy seeds. Nevertheless leavening did not change everybody's baking habits. Jews still eat an unleavened bread called matzoh during

the Swedes, *smörbrod* by the Danes, pizza in Italy, onion-flavored *non* in Russia, Mexican tortillas, and Indian *papadums*.

Such a vital ingredient of the world's food has achieved in the course of time a more than nutritional significance. It plays its part in religion, reaching apogee in Christianity, where it is held to be transformed into the actual body of Christ. It has also been the object, over the millennia, of the artistic aspirations of the world's bakers. A malleable medium, dough lends itself to a rich diversity of forms, from passable imitations of basketware through the elaborate ornaments of Mexican fiesta bread and Italian Christmas *pan-*

ettone, to the comically biological creations sold in the purlieus of Naples.

In spite of science—the development of new cereals with tougher stalks and bigger yields, the addition of anti-mold agents, emulsifiers, bleaches, and preser-

Round, flat bread, Stone Age.

Bread called *Mitscha* used as a gift at baptisms in one region of Switzerland.

Grittibänz, a typical Swiss pastry served during the Christmas season.

Wedding bread of the type served at the time of Christ.

Yule-bread, Scandinavia, c. 1200.

Bread in the form of the seal of Solomon.

Its importance is reflected in the variety of forms it assumes around the world. From the elemental mixing of flour and water, with varying additions of

the Seder feast of Passover, to celebrate the exodus from Egypt. For many nationalities the flat breads are continued for their own sakes: *lefsers* and *flatbröds* by

vatives—much of the world's baking continues as it always has. Indeed, those countries where the processing of bread has removed it farthest from its orig-

Bowl-bread, late Stone Age.

Egyptian bread, 1200 B.C.

Barley bread, sacrificial, ancient Egypt.

Barley bread, ancient Egypt.

Ring bread, Greece, 580 B.C.

Ring bread, Greece, fifth century B.C.

Roman bread, 200 B.C.

Roman consecration bread, second century.

Round Roman bread, second century.

Roman consecration bread, second century.

Bread with bone symbols, third century.

Egyptian bread, sixth century.

Monastery bread, southern Germany, early Middle Ages.

Bread from southern Germany, ninth century.

Cross bread from southern Germany, twelfth century.

inal form and flavor have in recent years shown a marked swing back to the taste for old-style, unadulterated breads.

Not that bakers were single-minded in the past in providing the best and most nourishing value for money. Many a medieval baker was hanged, imprisoned, or ducked in the village pond for weighting his loaves with a fragment of stone or lead. And the English phrase "a baker's dozen"—meaning thirteen rather than twelve—perpetuates the reputation bakers had for giving short weight and the law introduced to avoid it. Like God's gift of Eden to Adam, the blessings brought to humanity by cereal plants have not been unmixed.

Portion bread, twelfth century.

Cross bread, fifteenth century.

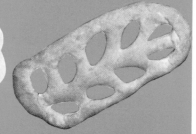
Fougasse bread, southern France.

89

Right: Irrigated rice terraces in the Philippines.

Left, and below far left to far right: A series of eighteenth-century engravings from Chinese paintings shows the stages of rice production: (1) Harrowing helps to mix newly spread water with the sun-dried soil; (2) young nursery plants are bedded out in the paddy

With luck and knowledge, you can make out as much of a country's history from its food as you can a person's character from his or her face. Spain is a good example. Her tomatoes and pimientos are living records of her conquests in America. Her voluminous trade in salted, dried, and otherwise preserved fish dates from the days when she supplied imperial Rome. Olive oil is a legacy of early Middle Eastern settlers. And a taste for various almond-based confections like marzipan and nougat, along with the widespread rearing of sheep for mutton, are among the results of her own conquest by the medieval Moors. Another Moorish gift was rice, which on its arrival in Spain came to the end of a long haul that had brought it halfway round the world. (Much later, it was to move on again, to the United States, where it is grown along the southern coasts and in California; the yield is about one-twelfth of the world's total.) The Arabic Moors had introduced rice to Europe from Persia, now Iran, where it remains one of the most valued items in the national diet. Among the many varieties grown there is the

rare *domsiah,* or black-tailed rice, grown beside the Caspian Sea, which stands in relation to other rices as Caspian caviar to other fish roes. Persia took its original rice from India, and India from Thailand, where the plant was first cultivated between 4000 and 3500 B.C. From Thailand it went both east and west, reaching China some time before 1500 B.C. In spite of its late arrival there, and the fact that rice is now cultivated on five continents, it is China whose history most heavily rests on the plant. It is China, too, whose expanding population has made rice the world's most abundant crop. Of every ten meals consumed in the world today, six will consist to a considerable degree of rice. Although the choice of rices in most Western shops is small—between short- and long-grained, or brown and white (and in parts of America the rare, unrelated wild rice)—the number

rises sharply in the Far East. Marco Polo saw the thirteenth-century shoppers of Hangchow buying rice of various different colors—pink, white, yellow—and of different stages of maturity, and he recorded that at a banquet twelve of the forty separate dishes were rices, each served in a separate bowl and each with its own distinctive, flowerlike fragrance. He was told that there were fifty-four different rice wines, and a great many flat

A rice farmer *(right)* plows a paddy field with his water buffalo. Both the man's hat and mantle are made of rice straw. In addition, his buffalo is probably fed on rice bran. Little of the plant goes to waste.

fields; (3) water level is raised as the plants grow; (4) the harvest is gathered; (5) rice sheaves are stacked; (6) threshing was often carried out on bamboo slats; (7) milling, to remove the outer husks and expose the grain. These methods are still widely employed, since rice does not easily lend itself to modern mechanical techniques. However, sowing from airplanes and the use of combine harvesters are increasingly found in larger areas of cultivation.

Right: Ears of rice, *Oryza sativa.*

Progressive stages *(below)* of the rice plant's growth. Water levels

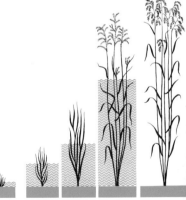

are shown by gray shading. The first plant is a seedling still in the nursery beds. After some six weeks it is transplanted to the fields. Flower panicles begin to develop after a further ten weeks, and seeds ripen eight to ten weeks later. The whole process, from sowing to reaping, takes about six months.

Main areas of rice cultivation.

breads made from rice flour. Today the choice has somewhat decreased, but crops have additional importance as the basis of beer (especially in southern India, where rice is the staple) and of several sweetmeats, as a commercial source of starch, and as animal fodder.

Its primary function, however, is

Similar efforts have kept large parts of India and the Philippines above the breadline, and American-backed research in the Philippines has led to some dramatic recent improvements in the yield and quality of crops. Not all these so-called miracle rices have fulfilled their early promise, however. Some succumbed to

simply to keep a large proportion of the world's inhabitants alive. After World War II an impoverished Japan began a massive program of paddy-field development in order to provide most of its own basic foodstuffs.

pests, some became lumpy and sticky with cooking. But the general success rate has caused some scientists to forecast—what a decade or two ago would have been unthinkable—a world rice surplus by the end of the century.

THE POPCORN LEGACY

The five main varieties of corn—all members of the species *Zea mays (left to right):* Dent, Flint, Flour, Sweet, Popcorn.

Columbus's journey to the Americas in 1492 had the effect of stabbing a sack stuffed full with provisions. Maize (corn), among other produce, spilled out over the Atlantic and into Europe and Africa, providing what soon became a lasting staple for many people who had

tions. First cultivated some seven thousand years ago, probably in New Mexico and Mexico itself, it offered its farmers what must at first have seemed an easy life. Cultivation occupied about fifty days in the year, providing huge surpluses which were traded for other requirements. The rest

European arrival. The importance of corn in these empires was recognized in their religions. It was given the status of a divinity, and even today, under the auspices of the Catholic church, incense is burned in cornfields, and at harvest time cobs are piled in churches for blessing.

The original cultivated plant is thought to have been some kind

corn and their nearest wild relatives. In fact modern corn has left its origins so far behind that the tightly enclosed female seeds (which we eat) are incapable of natural dispersal. In bringing its bounty to people, corn has thrown itself entirely on their mercy. Its post-Columbian history shows it has not done badly by the bargain.

Taos *(above)*, a pueblo near the Rio Grande in New Mexico, where corn has been cultivated since the beginning of American farming.

Personified as the corn god, the plant is shown in a Mexican picture strip *(right)* exposed in turn to each of the seasonal deities.

An American Indian *(right)* boiling a caldron of corn and fish, in an engraving taken from a painting of 1590 by John White, a pioneer settler in Virginia.

An American Indian woman *(far right)* thins corn dough before baking a tortilla.

never tasted it before. True, Queen Isabella was rather bored by it, having her mind more on gold and spices. But Portuguese merchants were soon carrying it to Africa, the Venetians took it through the Mediterranean to Black Sea ports, and within a century it was being grown in Burma and China.

It had already provided the springboard of great civiliza-

might have been free time, but for a succession of tyrannous regimes: Olmec, Maya, Toltec, and Aztec. Monolithic societies developed, still commemorated in the huge pyramids and other public works erected over the three thousand years before

of popcorn. Its wild ancestors seem to have been eliminated, possibly by the browsing of goats and other livestock introduced by Europeans, and there are large gaps between present varieties of

Seized on by European settlers, it spread north and south on the American continent and then abroad, resisted only by very cold climates. Some of its different regional names—Spanish, Sicilian, and Rhodes corn, *grano turco,* Guinea corn, the ear from Portugal—trace its rapid spread from Europe through Africa to the Far East. (In Africa, ironically, it led to an explosion of population which in time supplied the slave trade to America.) It has been said that within a century corn had doubled the food supply of the continents outside America.

Nothing matches its more recent

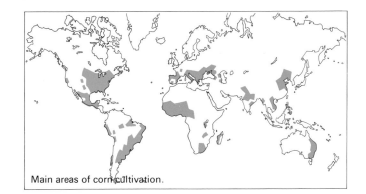

Main areas of corn cultivation.

advances, for it has been the object of the most successful efforts of geneticists. Work began in the 1920s to isolate the qualities in different desirable corn varieties: ease of harvesting, resistance to wind and disease, and high yield. But the inbreeding entailed in these experiments produced in the end enfeebled specimens. It was the discovery that hybridizing with other inbred varieties could restore lost

From early colonial days corn bread has been popular in the United States. The Swiss corn-loaf pictured here *(below left)* is one of many varieties baked in Europe since the introduction of corn from America in the sixteenth century.

vigor that brought about one of the great triumphs of plant breeding. Yields are now three times their previous quantities; this has even caused corn to make headway against its two giant rivals among the cereals, wheat and rice.

Especially in northern Italy and in the south of Switzerland, corn is a popular staple food. It may be prepared in various ways, depending on the rest of the meal. The traditional *polenta* usually is roasted in the open fire *(above)* and then served in crispy slices.

The history of the potato is not without black dramas. Its closest relatives—the deadly nightshade, henbane, and nicotiana—contain some of the most virulent poisons known. On potatoes themselves, green patches signify poisonous alkaloids which are only

First domesticated in the Andes some two thousand years ago, the potato became a staple crop and the object of a local cult, to which numerous potato-shaped vessels bear witness.

made harmless by cooking. In the Andes, where the potato originated, it became an object of veneration, associated with the creator god—the jaguar—and blood rites used to placate it. Later, Spanish conquistadors found it a cheap staple for their gold-mine slaves. But no calamity with which it is linked approaches the great Irish famine of the middle 1840s.

When the potato reached Ireland, some time about 1600, it was readily welcomed as a basic foodstuff. For a century of spasmodic warfare, it proved its worth. Scorched-earth campaigns would have brought a country dependent on visible crops to ruin. The potato, hid-

den below ground, was safe. It was good and nutritious, and the Irish came to grow it to the exclusion of other important crops. By the nineteenth century Ireland was virtually a one-crop state.

The villain of the 1840s was not the potato, but another plant, the fungal potato blight. In 1845 it struck the crops of northern Europe. Ireland was worst hit. Grain prices rocketed, cattle were slaughtered for their meat, milk gave out, and the country was left diseased and starving. A million died, and a million more embarked for America. The Irish vote of the Eastern states is due in no small measure

to the failure of this subterranean provider.

Today the potato is reinstated (though nowhere so exclusively). It is most important to the countries of northern Europe (being the greatest single source

The white, sometimes purplish, flowers *(above left)* of the potato, *Solanum tuberosum;* and *(above)* a wood engraving of the whole plant, showing a separate flower on the left and fruit on the right. This fruit, which resembles a small, unripe tomato, is seldom produced. Underground stems, or rhizomes, swell at their ends to form tubers from which new plants shoot in the spring. These tubers are the potatoes we eat.

A new shoot rises from the "eye" of a potato *(below left)* to form a new plant. Eyes are in reality young buds. Under modern culti-

vation only potatoes grown in areas certified free of disease are used for the propagation of new plants. The rest are consumed. The photograph *(above)* shows potatoes as they lie in the ground. Some are already sending down their own roots to feed the plants which will rise from them.

The drawing *(left)* illustrates the potato's growth. First, a shoot from a seed potato has developed into a young plant. Later it sends out its own underground stems, each of which, if they were collected and allowed to grow, would give rise to another plant in the following season.

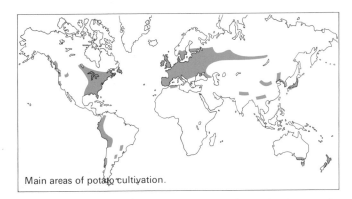

Main areas of potato cultivation.

of vitamin C for the British). But it grows almost anywhere, except low-lying tropical areas. In soups, stews, and pies; as flour, powder, or chips; boiled, fried, baked, steamed, or roasted, it provides more food value per acre than any cereal (though its water content makes it heavy and costly to transport). It also forms the basis of Swedish schnapps, some vodkas, and oth-

Other important tubers are the tropical cassava *(above)* and the sweet potato *(above right)*.

er drinks. Trade figures rate it eighth in the list of the world's most important food plants. Curiously, Europe was slow to recognize its merits. Hemmed in with myth, it was claimed as aphrodisiac, cure of rheumatism, cause of leprosy, deadly poison. The French first thought it a truffle, tasted it, and grew indifferent. The Scots resisted it for two hundred years on the ground that it was not mentioned in the Bible. But by and by its virtues were seen. The researches of Antoine-Auguste

Parmentier brought it to the attention of Louis XVI, in 1787, and led to a craze. The English had accepted it long before, and by the time Antoine Beauvilliers wrote in 1814 of his visit to London, and extolled (along with English *plomb-poutingue,* for example) a dish he called *machepotetesse* as the best way of serving the knobbly tuber, its future was assured.

The potato had a chequered career in France from its introduction in 1540 until the agronomist Antoine-Auguste Parmentier (1737—1813) established its nutritional value and excellence. In the starved 1780s he successfully grew a field of potatoes, having it guarded by day but left open at night—when, as he hoped, curious Parisians stole the crop and were delighted with it.

95

OIL PRODUCERS

Oil permeates our lives like a fifth column. It seems to lead a life of its own, refusing to mix with other liquids, wholly resistant to most of them, but spreading everywhere. A drop on a hand or a cog soon becomes a thin film over the whole object. To people of the past oil seemed positively miraculous. It soothed as an ointment, was a vital and

1

mals. Within the plant they serve to store food for future use, forming an important part of many seeds (the Brazil nut, for instance, is 70 percent oil). There are many different kinds and grades—as many as there are spe-

tasty part of cooking, and preserved the form and features of the dead. Above all it brought light to those who equated light and life. And so it entered the realms of magic.

Apart from fossil oils (which are of different composition, though they derive substantially from ancient plant life), oils come mainly from plants, and to a diminishing extent from ani-

cies of plant, though only in a few does the amount justify extraction.

Oil has an oblique style. It seldom plays the leading role. It garnishes salads, facilitates cooking, permits incompatible elements to run smoothly together. Unobtrusively and invisibly, it makes life easier and nicer. Greeks and Romans rubbed their bodies with it after bathing, and in the evenings their homes were illuminated by the lamps containing it. The source of oil for both uses, the olive, became a chief feature of their economies. Among Old Testament Jews oil was essential in the rituals and liturgies of the temple. The chrism of perfumed oil was used for the consecration of kings—a

1 Coconut oil is obtained from the dried white meat of the fruit (copra) and is used mainly for making soap, of which it is one of the world's main sources.

2 After the seed hairs, or lint, have been removed from the seeds of the cotton plant, a valuable edible oil is pressed from them.

3 Corn oil, obtained from embryos of corn, is used in cooking and margarine manufacture.

4 Apart from its culinary uses (cooking, salads, and margarine), soybean oil is employed in paints, plastics, and other industrial products.

5 Sunflower seeds yield an excellent edible and cooking oil, recently found effective in the treatment of multiple sclerosis.

6 Castor oil from the plant *Ricinus communis* is a well-known purgative.

7 Fat from the Shea butternut *(Butyrospermum)* is much eaten in its native tropical Africa.

8 Nearly half a ripe peanut consits of oil, much of which goes to the making of margarine.

9 The sesame seed provides oil for local consumption in India and the Far East.

10 Wheat germ oil is a particularly rich source of vitamin E, popularly believed to increase virility.

11

11 The oil palm of West Africa and the Far East provides a high proportion of the world's edible oil.

12 Rape seed is a source of colza oil, used to make candles.

13 and 14 Safflower and niger seed supply minor oil crops in India.

15 Poppy seeds provide edible oil but are not worth commercial exploitation.

12

13

14

habit which persists in modern coronations. But Christianity gave oil the symbolic purpose best suited to its mysterious and pervasive qualities, causing it to represent the Holy Ghost, one of the most curious, elusive, yet indispensable elements of the Christian cosmos.

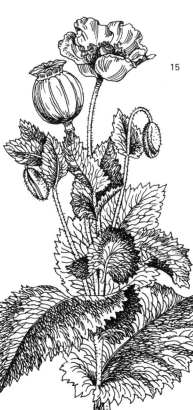
15

Use in cooking heads the list of oil's more mundane functions. Its ability to sustain a higher temperature than water before vaporizing makes possible roasting and all kinds of frying (while in times past boiling oil recommended itself for the exemplary disposal of prisoners). Since a French butter famine in the 1850s stimulated the invention of margarine, vegetable oils have been in increasing demand for its manufacture—a demand that the fear of cholesterol found in animal fats has increased.

Fish canning uses millions of liters of peanut, cottonseed, soybean, olive, and other oils. Oils go into the making of confectionery and many medicines. Apart from human consumption they are important in the making of soap, ointments, candles, paints, varnishes, plastics, putty, glycerine, explosives, oilcloth, patent leather, and linoleum. Because of oil, the paintings of old masters endure, blades keep sharp, we keep clean, and wheels turn smoothly. In a thousand ways, the oil that plants give us lubricates the workaday running of the world.

THE OLIVE

In the Western world, one oil is more highly regarded than all the rest. Like the Parthenon, Pericles, and Plato, the olive stands at the fount of Western civilization. It was the goddess Athene's gift to Athens. Replacing the forests and cereal crops which earlier Greeks had eliminated, its gnarled trunks and subtle greens became, along with vine and fig, the hallmark of the Mediterranean landscape, spreading to Italy and Spain and in due course transported by Spaniards to America.

Its spread was a mixed blessing. Olive roots push downward more than sideways and fail to knit soil together. Erosion exposes rock. One effect is the luminous Hellenic light, reflected by bare white limestone and inspiring poets and painters. Another is poverty, of soil and people.

The classical significance of the olive is matched by its biblical role. It was an olive branch that Noah's dove brought back to the ark. Token of God's reconciliation with man, it has ever since been a symbol of peace. But it offers material benefits too.

It is no facile seducer, like Adam's apple or some gaudy peach. The raw olive has a bitter, desiccating taste, and needs pickling to become palatable. Oil is extracted by a series of pressings of the ripe black fruit. The result of the first pressing is the connoisseur's delight—a golden-yellow oil without any smell.

Olive oil is used for cooking, salads, and canning sardines. Gourmets claim it has, like wine, good and bad years, which by chance coincide with those of Sauternes wines. No sardine, it is said, tastes as good as a 1906, canned in oil from the previous year's Provençal olives.

98

The devotion with which plants seem passively to surrender their whole bodies to the human race is not unlike that of a lover. For our pleasure and nourishment they offer every part of themselves. They present an infinite variety of form, taste, smell, color, and consistency. And if they have their own very pragmatic reasons for doing so—from which all emotions, let alone love itself, are notably absent—the effect is the same. The thousands of plants that

In their various forms—molds, rusts, blights, mushrooms, toadstools—they can poison, cure, and induce visions of incomparable beauty. They can kill, and can consume—quite literally—our houses and our crops. Yet without them the world would long since have become a heap of indestructible garbage. They also provide us (and many animals too) with wholesome food.

But for all this they look so uncanny and behave in such an

There are people who live on them almost exclusively. Charles Darwin found a tribe on Tierra del Fuego which subsisted on mushrooms, fresh or cured, and what little meat they could muster. In the poorer, colder areas of northern Russia, the absence of winter vegetables is made good by fungi pickled or dried in the autumn.

All the same, poisonous fungi have smirched the name of the good ones, and only the anemic cultivated mushrooms are uni-

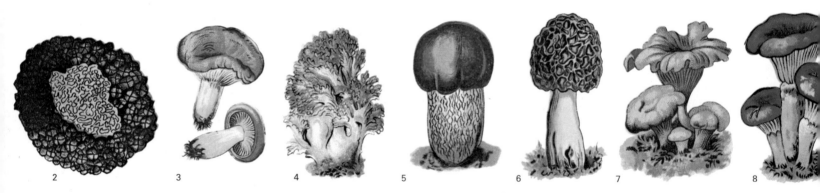

people eat comprise a range of savors far more subtly differentiated than the adjacent notes of a piano. Once we move from the staples—the bricks and mortar of nutrition, to one or more of which every society has committed itself for basic security—we find an Eden of vegetable charms in competition.

No class or family of plants is an exception to this rule. Even those dwarf survivors of the Carboniferous woodland, the horsetails, contrive a passable imitation of asparagus. But the power of plants is nowhere more dramatically manifest than in the fungi.

elusive and capricious manner—lying low for years, then appearing in abundance as aboveground fruiting bodies—that they have been invested, more than most plants, with magical and religious powers.

versally popular. Ethusiasm for wild ones comes and goes like a fashion for hats. A hundred years ago more varieties were sold in the markets of London than in Paris, a situation so thoroughly reversed now as to be scarcely credible. In Europe, where many

species are eaten, precautions in the form of posters, books, and consultant experts appointed in every village are general. It was the same in ancient Rome, where the wealthy employed special collectors. "Good God!" wrote Seneca of the emperor

1 *Boletus aurantiacus*
2 Black truffle, *Tuber melanosporum*
3 *Lactarius volemus*
4 *Ramaria botrytis*
5 *Boletus aureus*
6 Morel, *Morchella esculenta*
7 Chanterelle, *Cantharellus cibarius*
8 *Gomphidius glutinosus*
9 Honey fungus, *Armillaria mellea*
10 *Helvella gigas*

A stem of Brussels sprouts, in shape not unlike a mushroom, packing its enlarged and edible buds close in under a leafy mantle; peanuts in their double shells; and a halved melon, a succulent treasury of seeds—together these represent the range of appearance, taste, and texture of the vegetable kingdom.

Claudius's mushroom foragers, "how many men labor for one

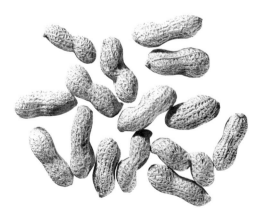

single belly." (In the end, in spite of his care, Claudius succumbed to a dish of *Amanita.*)

Of all the fungi, one has secured itself a place among the aristocrats of the table. Partly because it is difficult to find—calling for a sixth sense found only in pigs, dogs, and a few sensitive people—partly because of its rarity, partly because of alleged aphrodisiac qualities, and largely because it combines refined taste with delicate texture, the truffle is, as Brillat-Savarin called it, the jewel of cookery. "Nobody dares admit," he wrote of Parisians in 1825, "having been present at a meal which did not include a truffled dish." Only one recent development threatens its position among caviar, champagne, oysters, and the few other foods at the apex of gastronomy; and that is the discovery that, by applying special chemicals to oak trees, they can be induced to succor a large population of truffles. Familiarity may yet breed contempt; it has, in the past, with oysters.

By showing the whole range of plant potential, the fungi serve as introduction to the whole range of vegetables and fruits and other plant garnishes, and to the varied responses—greed, lust, snobbery, gratitude, love, and even worship—we greet them with.

101

VEGETABLE BOUNTY

1 Blood-red onion, *Allium cepa*
2 Common onion, *Allium cepa*
3 Sweet pepper, *Capsicum annuum*
4 Tomato, *Lycopersicon esculentum*
5 Avocado pear, *Persea americana*

The food regime in Eden was vegetarian. "To every beast of the earth, and to every fowl of the air, and to every thing that creepeth upon the earth," God told Adam, "I have given every green herb for meat." And when, in a later and corrupt age, Isaiah looked forward to a Utopian future, his vision was of a world in which "the lion shall eat straw with the ox." Every society since has numbered people who shared his views. Even more prevalent than the vegetarian practice is a sneaking idea that an exclusively vegetable diet is somehow better, purer, almost more pious, than one that allows meat. On medical grounds there is little to be said for it. Well chosen, however, plants can provide virtually all the nutrition humans need. And we derive more from our plant foods than nutrition. We get delight of taste, sight, smell, and touch (touch not merely of the hands—tough that is important—but from the contact of tongue and teeth and throat with foods of various consistencies). The selection shown on these pages, small though it is, represents some of the variety of these pleasures.

Inside their satin-smooth coats, onions pack a pungency which brings tears to the eyes and an agreeable savor to the dishes they garnish. Sweet peppers can look

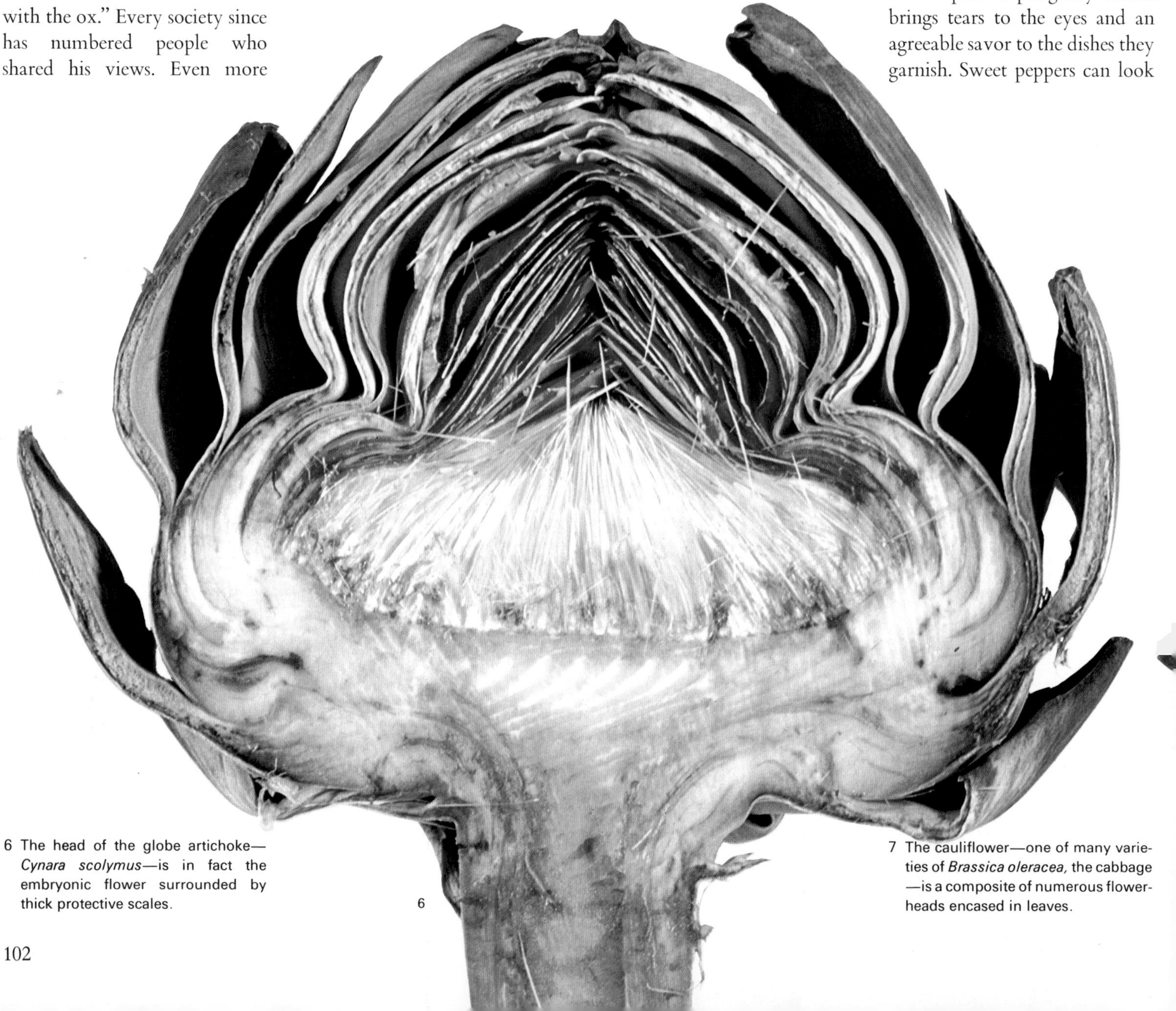

6 The head of the globe artichoke—*Cynara scolymus*—is in fact the embryonic flower surrounded by thick protective scales.

6

7 The cauliflower—one of many varieties of *Brassica oleracea*, the cabbage—is a composite of numerous flowerheads encased in leaves.

102

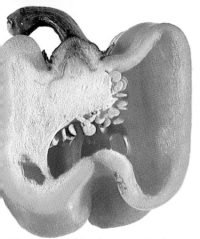

4

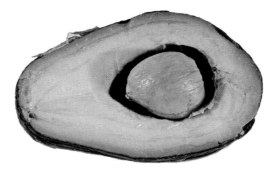

5

like polished leather outside, but bring a distinctive taste and fabric to salads, pickles, and stews. The cheekily bright, innocently fresh tomato was thought to be an aphrodisiac or death-dealer

when the Spanish first brought it from Peru. But the sweet juiciness of its many present varieties —deep yellow to blush-red, tart to full-bodied—has lost all sinister associations. The avocado

pear, another Central American native, offers more protein than any other fruit and can consist of a quarter oil, which gives its lime-green flesh a silky smooth texture. The star of the thistle

family, the artichoke, has evolved from a persistent European weed into the object of a gastronomic ritual: a predatory scraping of its leaflike scales for their basal flesh, followed by the extraction of the bristly center, leads at last to the sweet, soft heart. Cauliflowers have come far from the cabbagey leafiness of their forebears, developing their fleshy floral branchlets into a white, nutty, and nutritious curd.

7

1 Peach, *Prunus persica*
2 Orange, *Citrus sinensis*
3 Lemon, *Citrus limon*
4 Pawpaw, *Carica papaya*
5 Mango, *Mangifera indica*
6 Cherimoya, *Annona cherimolia*
7 Prickly pear, *Opuntia ficus-indica*

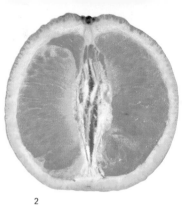

The contents of almost all fruits and vegetables are nine-tenths water. Half the rest is cellulose, a material we are unable to digest. From the remainder we take a little protein, a little starch, some traces of minerals, and vitamins. It is enough. Results of centuries of careful breeding, of turning the power of plants to our own advantage, these fruits are the luscious rewards of civilization. Whatever solid pleasures could be extracted from Paleolithic native to China, is a sensual treat. More peaches are canned than any other fruit, and in total world sales they are exceeded only by apples and oranges. Also originally Chinese, but tarter eating because of their acid content, oranges have taken on a multiplicity of functions. Millions are canned as juice, rich in vitamin C. Millions more go to chutney. The cherimoya, a variety of custard apple, also strays little from its native land, the Central American tropics, where its pineapple flavor makes it valued for drinks and eating.

The abundant seeds of the Persian pomegranate are responsible for its classical associations with fertility and, as a consequence, wealth, also for the messiness involved in eating it. To avoid this, the juice is usually pressed from it for use in wines and con-

life, they never included the sweet thirst-quenching of a watermelon on a hot day, the impalpable softness of a syrupy peach, the rapier assaults on the taste buds of orange or lemon, the bland juiciness of a pear. Nature's candies, encapsulated juleps, they sweeten life with melting refreshment.

From the rosy bloom on its downy skin to the durable wrinkles of its seed, the peach, the making of marmalade. The oils of their skins make flavorings and perfumes. And most of all they are eaten fresh.

Papaws, the melonlike berries of a tropical tree, provide within their succullent raw flesh certain enzymes used medically to help digestion. The same tropical climate suits the mangoes, the most popular fruit in India, though they seldom reach temperate climates in any form but that of

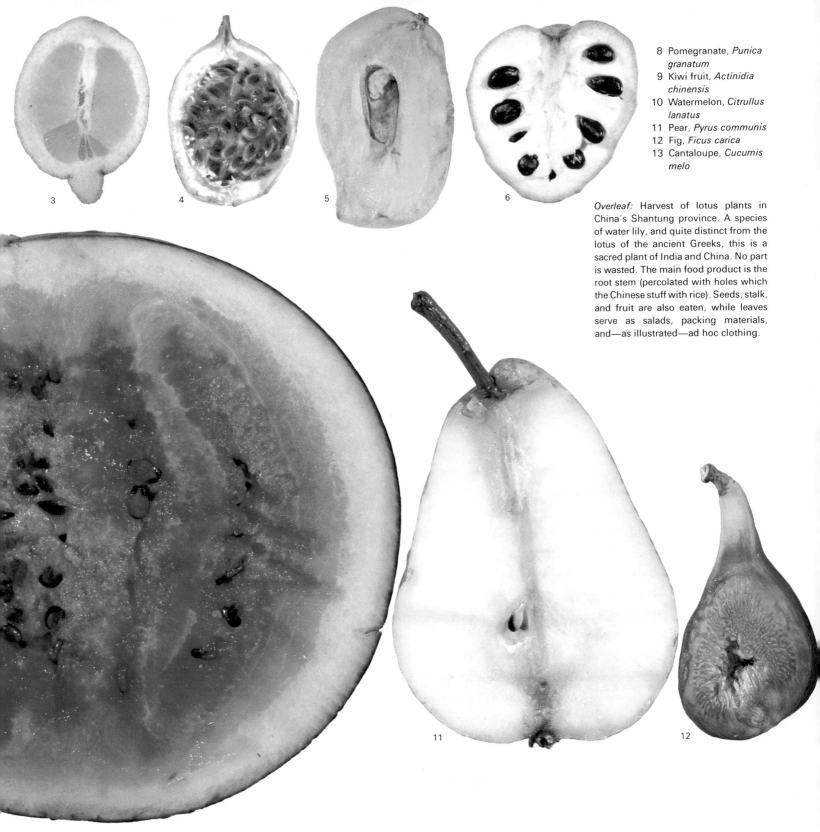

Overleaf: Harvest of lotus plants in China's Shantung province. A species of water lily, and quite distinct from the lotus of the ancient Greeks, this is a sacred plant of India and China. No part is wasted. The main food product is the root stem (percolated with holes which the Chinese stuff with rice). Seeds, stalk, and fruit are also eaten, while leaves serve as salads, packing materials, and—as illustrated—ad hoc clothing.

serves and the scarlet beverage grenadine. Sweet, fleshy, plum-shaped kiwi fruits, or Chinese gooseberries, are mainly grown in New Zealand for home consumption. Sugary relatives of the marrows, squashes, and cucumbers, watermelons are natives of Africa, with a luscious, thirst-quenching consistency appropriate to hot climates. In fact they contain more water than any other fruit—something like 95 percent. Cantaloupes are a scaly-skinned melon variety with orange flesh. Pears do well in temperate climates. Blander, elongated, more perishable versions of the apple, their use is mainly confined to desserts and fruit stews.

Object of cults (and with leaves used for censoring shame), the fig is an ancient Mediterranean fruit, delicious fresh or dried. Drying is carried out by exposure to the sun, during which the fruit's rich sugar content forms a syrupy deposit on the skin, where it acts as an effective preserver.

SAVORY VEGETABLES

For many plants, man is the best evolutionary vehicle. Nothing in nature could have spread wheat, rice, and corn as human cultivators have spread them. These are the spectacular gainers, but there are other plants which have bound man to them, exploiting his tastes, his gluttony, and his passion for security and handing over to him the direction of their evolutionary progress.

This is especially true with vegetables. For reasons not altogether sound, many peoples attach more nutritional importance to vegetables than to fruits. Vegetables are not in fact better than fruits necessarily, but they are important to all diets, containing as they do vitamins and minerals as well as starch, protein, and roughage. They offer a wide gastronomic spectrum, with a variety of savory tastes from bland to fiery, and of textures from crisply fibrous to mushily soft. They may be cooked or eaten raw.

To define "vegetable" is a matter of some difficulty. Beans, peas, and zucchini are vegetables in everyday parlance, but scientifically they are fruits. By legumes, botanists mean members of the pea family, whereas in French the word means vegetables in general. The word's derivation does not help. It is from the Latin *vegetus* and means simply—and perhaps unjustifiably—vigorous. In most of the Western world the word implies plant parts of unsweet taste eaten early in the meal, often with meat.

Exceptions are so numerous that they have, for our purposes, to be overlooked.

Of the vegetables shown here, celery is the latest to be developed, though its wild ancestor was popular with the Romans, who fed it in bulk to animals due for slaughter on the grounds that it improved the taste of the meat. The modern celery plant was bred in Italy around the fifteenth century. Its primary use, as a raw salad, has been enhanced by the technique of blanching which came in during the same period. Blanching—piling up earth against the stems to keep out light, and consequently chlorophyll—tones down the natural pungency, as it does of leeks and chicory.

108

The knobbly excrescences of the ginger root conceal a spicy strength which, dried and ground, is an important ingredient in curries. Primarily a spice, it earns its place here by its high content of starch—about half the whole root. A balmier root is the carrot, beloved of donkeys, rabbits, night guards, and (for the decorative value of its leaves) the courtesans of England's Charles I. Rich in vitamins, it has been popular at least since Roman times.

The bean family, or pulses, are among the oldest plants to be cultivated, and of them the broad bean may be the oldest. Their presence in a garden helps other plants because their roots attract nitrogen-fixing bacteria. Pythagoras banned them from his followers' diets, but he may only have used their name figuratively for politics, dried beans being used for registering election votes. In fact they are rich in protein and starch and are highly nutritious.

Beans are seeds. Zucchini, or courgettes, are technically berries, small and succulent members of the marrow family. Okra and chili peppers are also seeds, stockinged in pods, but the resemblance goes no further. The okra is a hibiscus, the chili a potent member of the capsicum family, a red and red-hot flavoring for stews and curries.

Perhaps the classic vegetables are leaves and leaf stalks, of which the lower photographs present a selection. Their qualities are as varied as their forms. Cabbage packs sixteen times more vegetable oil than leeks; leeks three times as much protein as cabbage. Florence fennel adds to its crispness a gentle aniseed flavor.

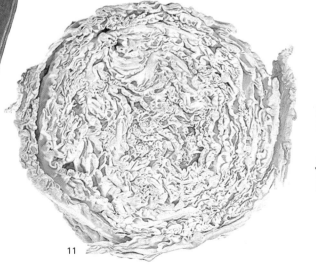

11

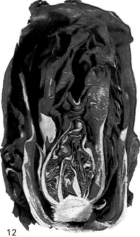

12

9

10

1 Walnut, *Juglans regia*
2 Chestnut, *Castanea sativa*
3 Hazelnut, *Corylus avellana*
4 Brazil nut, *Bertholettia excelsa*
5 Pistachio, *Pistacia vera*
6 Almond, *Prunus amygdalus*
7 Pecan nut, *Carya pecan*

8 Sugar cane, *Saccharum officinarum*
9 Sugar beet, *Beta vulgaris*
10 Sugar maple, *Acer saccharum*
11 Sugar palm, *Arenga sacchifera*

Nuts. Nutshells are famous for containing condensed versions of things like problems and arguments. In nature, most of them hold condensed food—mainly proteins and oils—within their hard, woody cases. They have contributed to human diets since man appeared.

Walnuts (which are technically not nuts, but drupes) are natives of Persia and have been eaten since earliest times. In medieval Europe they were swallowed whole at the end of a meal as a sort of stomach stopper. Chestnuts are poor in protein and oil but rich in starch; ground into flour, especially in Italy, they are used as a cereal substitute. The hazel is widespread through Europe and Asia and is grown in several cultivated forms. The Brazil nut is the richly oily fruit of a tall tree growing in the Amazon valley. Pistachios, like many other nuts, go into the making of confectionery and ice cream, but their winsome green makes them also a favorite dessert.

Almonds are the most widely produced of all nuts, eaten by themselves or as an ingredient of marzipan, macaroons, chocolates, puddings, and candies. A similar gamut of roles attaches to the pecan nut, which is mainly grown in North America.

Sugar plants. The human race's sweet tooth is well catered for by plants. Sugars of one kind or another are present in almost all plant (and animal) tissue, and in addition, until the sixteenth century, most of mankind had ample access to honey. But during the Reformation, especially in northern Europe, honey was dealt an indirect but heavy blow. Suppression of Catholic monasteries meant suppression of their bees, which were kept primarily to provide church candle wax. Sweetness was suddenly at a premium, and the need was answered from Central America. The sugarcane, grown originally in Southeast Asia, had been seeping into Europe since the Crusades, but it was very costly. Its introduction to America opened up opportunities for widespread cultivation. All that was needed was labor.

No crop has ever exerted such diabolical power over human history as sugar has. To expedite its growth, at least twenty mil-

12 Blackberry, *Rubus fruticosus*
13 Strawberry, *Fragaria vesca*
14 Raspberry, *Rubus idaeus*
15 Gooseberry, *Ribes grossularia*
16 Mulberry, *Morus nigra*
17 Juniper, *Juniperus communis*

12

13

14

15

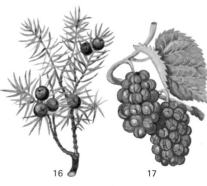

16   17

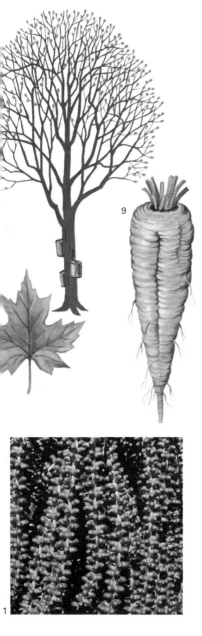

9

1

England's virtual monopoly persuaded Napoleon to bolster the development of sugar beet, scarcely known before. Today the two plants provide almost equal halves of the world's sugar supply, with cane just tipping the balance. Syrups and sugars of regional importance come from the sugar maple of North America and various Indian and African palms.

Berries. Spring is the season of the embryo, summer and autumn the time of the mature seed,

ring to the wild berry, whose taste, despite science, is still unrivaled.) The blackberry readily burgeons wild, but too often suffers the contempt paid to familiar objects. Nevertheless these "best of all bush berries," as André Simon called them, like their cousins the raspberries and the smaller, hardier, and more northerly cloudberries, are important summer fruits for jams, pies, jellies, and canning. Other temperate berries include the gooseberry, one of the earliest to ripen; the luscious mulberry, too

18

19

20

18 Cranberry, *Vaccinium oxycoccus*
19 Blueberry, *Vaccinium corymbosum*
20 Sloe, *Prunus spinosa*

21 Redcurrant, *Ribes rubrum*
22 Cloudberry, *Rubus chamaemorus*

21

22

lion Africans were brought to North American plantations between 1600 and 1850. The triangular trade—of guns and trinkets from Europe to West Africa, slaves thence across the Atlantic, and sugar back to Europe—was a traffic of despair. But it also made fortunes. Half the stately homes of England were built from it.

when fruits and berries spangle the deepening greens of trees and bushes; plumply, colorfully, succulently inviting bird, man, and animal to take their fill.

Of them all, the strawberry is perhaps best loved. "Doubtless God could have made a better berry," wrote Dr. Butler in the sixteenth century, "but doubtless God never did." (He was refer-

perishable for commercial use; the cranberry, best of all for tempering the flavor of strong game; the inconspicuous whortleberry, faintly acid but good with sugar or as jam; and the subtly refreshing redcurrant. The bitter berries of sloe and juniper are mainly used in flavoring liquor, such as gin.

111

MARCO
POLO

Early in the fifth century B.C., that proto-journalist Herodotus reported the method used by Arabians to collect cinnamon bark. They first cut up dead oxen or donkeys into large, heavy joints and placed these near some inaccessible precipices inhabited by certain outsize birds. Then they concealed themselves. Soon the birds flew down and returned to their nests with the hunks of meat, whose prodigious weight broke the nests and brought them tumbling down. Among the fallen debris was cinnamon bark, which the birds had brought from unknown sources. This device was the only way of collecting the bark and was the basis of an important trade.

The account, of course, was colorful make-believe; but it shows the ingenuity used by

Arabs to protect their lucrative monopoly of the spice trade. This they enjoyed for roughly three thousand years, from 1500 B.C. to about 1500 A.D., a period

which included the finest flowering of Islamic culture. Spices made a substantial contribution to the mosques, palaces, and neat white cities of medieval Arabia.

The Romans developed a passion for pepper and other spices, but when the empire went into decline, the spice trade followed suit.

It was the Crusades which revived the craving and the trade. Brought back as souvenirs to western Europe, spices so enhanced the salt meat, dried fish, insipid beans, and bread that made up most winter diets that demand mushroomed. (Spices were also valued ingredients of medicines, perfumes, and love-potions.)

As much as the Arabs, the Venetians benefited from this revival. By the fifteenth century, some 2500 tons of pepper and ginger were annually passing through their hands. It was estimated that their profits, added to those of the Arabs, multiplied by eight the original price paid for the goods in Asia. The other European powers determined to break Venice's hold on the trade. And that is how a small group of plants came to expose the whole world to European ambitions and greed.

Though Aristotle had shown the world was a globe, the knowledge had been lost. Medieval Europe saw it as a disk afloat in a limitless ocean, with the land mass divided by the Mediterranean (the vertical stroke of the T), the Nile, and the Don (together forming the horizontal stroke).

It was the unknown fringes of the world that Renaissance explorers braved for the sake of pepper *(above)* and other treasures. Against them were pitted accepted ideas of geography and rigors like the stormbound Cape of Good Hope *(left)*.

HENRY
THE NAVIGATOR

CHRISTOPHER COLUMBUS

VASCO
DA GAMA

PEDRO CABRAL

FERDINAND MAGELLAN

JAN COEN

Up to this time, screened by Arab middlemen, the Orient had almost totally preserved its mystique. In spite of Marco Polo's travels round the China of Khubla Khan in the thirteenth century, the world beyond the Mediterranean was still an amalgam of fabulous empires, exotic cities, and rare jewels, plants, and animals. Now, spurred by the lure of spices, fortunes, and prestige, the Portuguese began to edge round the coast of Africa to open up a southern sea route to the Indies. At the same time the Spanish, reviving the long-latent idea that the world was round, pushed westward. Within five years of each other, in the 1490s,

Marco Polo's travels round China in the thirteenth century were an inspiration to the voyages of discovery two hundred years later. The first steps toward the east-west sea route round Africa were sponsored by Portugal's Henry the Navigator. Then in 1492 Columbus's landfall in America opened an era of breathtaking discovery. Da Gama rounded the Cape of Good Hope in 1498; Cabral reached Brazil in 1500; and Magellan circumnavigated the globe in 1522. A century later, Dutch administrators, like Coen in Indonesia, were subjecting new continents to old authority.
A fourteenth-century illumination *(below left)* shows the arrival in China of Marco Polo's father and uncle in 1266. *Right:* A meeting of the Seventeen, the first governing body of the Dutch East India Company, in 1602.

But Portugal's position was no more secure than Venice's had been. The Dutch and the English, ignoring the Pope's division of the known world between Spain and Portugal, set up their own East India companies, and other countries followed.

By the late sixteenth century a curious change was taking place. Not only the trade but the taste for spices also was moving to the northerly countries of Europe. Driven by necessity, perhaps, when the markets moved from Venice to Antwerp and Amsterdam, the Italians took to milder diets and lost some of their interest in spices. Leaning more on

In the north, nevertheless, spices drew passionate adherence. Luther grumbled that there were more spices than corn in Germany, and Puritans condemned them, but the trade grew until it reached a peak late in the seventeenth century. By then some of the source plants themselves had been transplanted to Africa and America (and some from America to Africa), and the possibility of a monopoly had disappeared for ever. Pepper is a universal seasoning, and cinnamon, cloves, ginger, nutmeg, and turmeric daily flavor dishes in every country; but the imperial days of spices are over—days when they caused navies to be

the Cape of Good Hope was rounded and America—a grave disappointment at first, owing to its lack of spices—was discovered. But Vasco da Gama's journey

round Africa paid quick dividends. Soon Portuguese ships were plying a regular trade between Europe and the East Indies and collecting vast profits.

their local foods, they developed a simpler, more refined cuisine which moved to France and became the basis of modern gastronomy.

built and hard journeys to be undertaken, and when they revealed India, the Pacific islands, America, and the very shape of the world.

113

ASSORTED SPICES

(1) Nutmegs and mace are respectively the inner kernel and its covering in the fruit of the Indonesian tree *Myristica fragrans,* now also produced in the West Indies. Immensely popular both as a fumigant against plague and for use in cakes, puddings, egg, and cheese dishes, it inspired the creation of pocket graters, often of silver, now collectors' pieces. (2) Mustard (*Brassica* species) is a plant of the cabbage family, whose seeds, pounded with vinegar, wine, and spices, offer a mild to ferocious garnish for meats. (3) Saffron comprises the stigmas of *Crocus sativus,* of which a kilogram contains nearly half a million. Collected by hand to flavor *bouillabaisse, paella,* etc., it is one of the most expensive spices. (4) The seeds of the caraway *(Carum carvi)* give a characteristic, mild flavor to breads and pastries in Austria and Germany especially; also to some cheeses and alcoholic drinks, including *Kümmel.* (5) Coriander (*Coriandrum sativum)* gets its name from the Greek word for a bug, from the foetid smell given off by both plant and bugs when crushed. Once dried, however, the seeds add a rich and complicated flavor, being used in the East—for curries, pilaus, and so on—as much as parsley is in the West. (6) Fennel seeds *(Foeniculum vulgare)* add a slight aniseed flavor to the fish sauces and soups, and the Italian salami, in which they are used. They are also an effective cure of flatulence.

(12) Garlic *(Allium sativum)* was so popular with Roman soldiers that some have claimed it won the Roman empire by driving the enemy away. It allegedly gave great strength: the slave-builders of the Egyptian pyramids were reported to have eaten only garlic and onions. Its popularity as a general flavoring has more recently spread far beyond the Mediterranean countries, to which it was once confined. (13) Chives *(Allium schoenoprasum)* offer a gentler, subtler version of the flavor of onions. In Europe and North America they are used for various salads and cheese and egg dishes. (14) Parsley *(Petroselinum crispum)* is the most commonly used flavoring—perhaps because the easiest to grow—in English-speaking countries. But it is native to the eastern Mediterranean and, like the laurel, was used by the Greeks to crown victorious athletes. Its many varieties are used both for cooking and as garnishes. (15) Mint (*Mentha* species), in its many varieties, has always been popular in all parts of the world. It has an inimitably cleansing and refreshing taste, and has always been valued as a medicine, Gerard noting its curative effect against "beare-worms, sea scorpions, serpents, and (mixed with salt) the bitings of mad dogs." (16) Bay leaves, from the *Laurus nobilis,* stimulate the appetite and are used to flavor numerous savory dishes. Wreaths of the dark, waxy leaves were bestowed on poets in classical times, and the plant was sacred to Apollo. (17) Marjoram *(Origanum majorana)* is one of the nettle family, which provides many culinary herbs. It was cultivated by the Greeks, who believed Aphrodite had created it. To its uses in flavoring meat, fish, soups, etc., it adds a role ·in perfumery and, according to Culpeper, as a deterrent to snakes. Its cousin oregano *(Origanum vulgare),* or wild marjoram, is a popular flavoring in Italian food.

(7) Aniseed *(Pimpinella anisum)* is a member of the Umbellifer family, to which caraway, coriander, dill, fennel, and other flavorings also belong. Oil from its seeds flavors Pernod and other liquors. The seeds themselves are used in curries, cakes, breads (including the German *Anisbrot*), while the leaves are popular potherbs. (8) Cayenne *(Capsicum frutescens)* is both the name of a kind of chili pepper, and of the notorious French penal settlement in French Guiana, where one variety of the plant grows profusely. The Capsicums are a potent tribe which includes paprika. Cayenne is used mostly (and most cautiously) with fish and game dishes. (9) Capers *(Capparis spinosa)* are the unopened flower buds of a spiny Mediterranean shrub, pickled and used with mutton, ham, and many other foods. They are cultivated in France. (10) Cloves are the dried flower buds of a tree, *Eugenia caryophyllus,* found wild in the East Indies and now much cultivated in East Africa. It has been one of the most prized spices since ancient times, credited with healing powers—its analgesic properties still relieve toothache— as well as having the strong flavor it imparts to cakes, fruit stews, and pickles. (11) Ginger, consisting of the dried rhizomes of *Zingiber officinale,* was one of the main inspirers of the spice trade. The Romans ate it in large quantity, and its strong aromatic pungency caused it to be added to almost any dish in medieval Europe. The best ginger now comes from Jamaica.

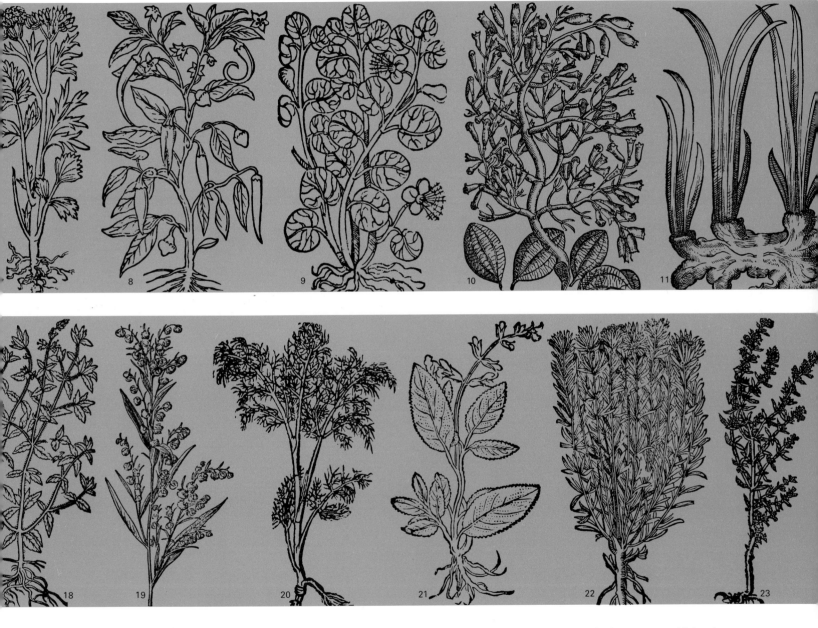

(18) Basil *(Ocimum basilicum)* owes its name to the Greek word for king, and is supposed to have been used in some royal unguent. To the Hindus it is a sacred plant. The reason for these distinctions lies in its many functions, flavoring, preserving, disinfectant, and medicinal. Today it is used in casseroles, salads, and any tomato dish. (19) Tarragon *(Artemisia dracunculus)* has few medicinal attributes (though it is held to alleviate snake-bites). Its high reputation down the ages is due to flavoring properties alone, which is a rare distinction. It enhances salads, chicken, stews, soups, etc. A popular vinegar is based on it, which is used in making true tartare sauce. (20) Dill *(Anethum graveolens)* gives a flavor similar to that of fennel, with which it is easily confused. Its seeds have various uses: against hiccups, flatulence in babies, indigestion. The leaves are used in soups and salads, and for pickling gherkins. (21) Sage *(Salvia officinalis)* has been credited with all manner of healing properties, its botanical name deriving from the Latin for safe, well, and sound. This reputation spread it to every garden in Europe, where it justifies its place, in a cynical age, by its various flavoring functions, particularly with fatty meats and with game. (22) Rosemary *(Rosmarinus officinalis)* has been favored as herb, decoration, talisman, and medicine from classical times. Legend tells that it never grows higher than a man, nor for a longer time than Christ—thirty-three years. Besides numerous culinary uses, it goes into the making of some soaps and cosmetics. (23) Thyme *(Thymus vulgare)* takes its name from the Greek for courage. Its lively taste makes it one of the most widespread potherbs.

THE VITAL NECESSITIES

Vitamins, present in the body in very small quantities, are essential not so much for what they are as for what they make possible. They facilitate the smooth running of the body by their reactions with larger constituents. Most people can subsist without many of them for long periods, but eventually the lack leads to deficiency diseases like pellagra, rickets, scurvy, or beri-beri.

The fuels needed to power the enormous complexities of the human machine are in themselves complex. Today science recognizes forty-five elements and compounds essential for the maintenance of a healthy body. Most people receive these substances—carbohydrates, proteins, fats, vitamins, and minerals—from a diet of both plant and animal matter. But those whom necessity or conviction drives to dispense altogether with animal products can do perfectly well on a purely vegetable diet. Carbohydrates come in plenty from the world's staples, be they grain, root, or fruit. In practice, most protein is derived from animals: a liter of milk, five eggs, or about a hundred grams of meat, fish, or cheese provides the daily requirement, which would otherwise call for the consumption of half a kilo of bread, a kilo of peas, or two kilos of potatoes.

Again, animals are the source of most fats people eat, although the growing preference for plant-based margarine has changed the balance in recent years. Vegetable oils, soybeans, and fruits like the coconut and peanut provide large quantities of fat, and there are traces in most other fruits and vegetables.

The need for carbohydrates, proteins, and fats was well established during the first half of the nineteenth century. It was clear, however, that adequate supplies of them did not eliminate deficiency diseases, and soon another group of vital foods was added. These were the inorganic minerals—salt, iron, calcium, phosphorus, iodine, and some others—each of which has essential specialized work to do in the body.

VITAMIN	SOURCES	FUNCTIONS
A (Retinol)	The pigment carotene, present in carrots, spinach, watercress, and other plants, is converted by the human body into vitamin A. (Fish-liver oils, animal organs, butter)	Important in growing processes, in the protection of surface tissues, and for sight.
B_1 (Thiamine)	Pulse foods (peas, beans, lentils) peanuts, potatoes, whole grains, and many others. (Pork, animal organs, cod's roe, etc.)	Facilitates a steady release of energy from carbohydrates. Stabilizes nerves and appetite.
B_2 (Riboflavin)	Brewer's yeast, whole grains, pulse foods, nuts, and many others. (Animal organs, egg yolks, cheese)	Important in the processes that convert carbohydrates, proteins, and fats into energy.
Niacin	Brewer's yeast, peanuts, rice, bran. (Lean meat, poultry, fish, milk)	Metabolic functions similar to above. Helps maintain skin health.
B_6 (Pyridoxine)	Whole grains, brewer's yeast, wheat germ, pulse foods, green leaves. (Meats, animal organs)	Metabolic functions similar to above. Helps to form antibodies and balance minerals.
Pantothenic acid	Brewer's yeast, pulse foods, whole grains, cereals. (Animal organs, egg yolks)	Helps preserve skin health and produce antibodies. Metabolic functions similar to above.
Folic acid	Green vegetables, pulse foods, many others. (Animal organs)	Aids metabolism of proteins, formation of red blood cells, cell growth and division.
B_{12}	Not present in plants. (Meat, eggs, milk)	Aids blood cell formation and keeps blood cells healthy; also aids energy metabolism.
Biotin	Brewer's yeast, pulse foods, vegetables. (Egg yolks, liver, kidney)	Helps in energy metabolism and in keeping skin healthy.
Choline	Grains, pulse foods. (Egg yolks, liver, etc.)	Important in metabolism of fats and in nerve transmissions.
C	Citrus fruits, rose hips, green peppers, acerola cherries, strawberries, etc.	Essential for maintenance of connective tissues, breakdown of which produces scurvy; for healing wounds and resisting infections.
D	Some mushrooms, e.g. *Boletus edulis*. (Sunlight is an important source, also fish-liver oils, butter, eggs, margarine)	Vital to growth and development of children's bones, hence essential in diet of pregnant women.
E (Tocopherol)	Vegetable oils, wheat germ, green vegetables. (Eggs)	May prevent damage to cell membranes.
K (Phylloquinone)	Cabbage, peas, and other green vegetables. (Negligible amount in some meats)	Important for normal blood clotting.

Minerals play a small but essential part in numerous body processes. The top eight minerals in this list are important constituents of bones, cells, and body fluids, or they are involved in the release of energy from carbohydrates, fats, and proteins. The rest, known as trace elements, are present in minute quantities, but each has a vital role to play. Not all of these functions are yet fully understood.

MINERAL	MAIN SOURCES	FUNCTIONS
Calcium	Green vegetables, bread, dried pulse foods. (Milk and cheese)	Assists growth of bones and teeth, muscle functioning, and blood clotting.
Phosphorus	Almost all foods.	Helps maintain hardness of bones and teeth. Involved in energy metabolism.
Sulfur	Most protein foods.	Important for functioning of tissues and cartilage.
Potassium	Most common foods.	Assists control of body liquids.
Chlorine	Salt, and most foods.	Formation of gastric juices.
Sodium	Salt, and most foods.	Control of body liquids and nerves.
Magnesium	Almost all foods.	Constituent in teeth and bones, and helps normal metabolism.
Iron	Most foods; water, wine, curry powder, iron pots.	Constituent of red blood corpuscles; also involved in energy metabolism.
Fluorine	Drinking water, tea. (Fish bones)	In limited doses, prevents cavities in children's teeth.
Zinc	Almost all foods.	Involved in digestion.
Copper	Nuts, pulse foods, raisins, meat, drinking water.	Formation of red blood cells; constituent of enzymes.
Silicon, nickel, vanadium, tin	Most foods.	Functions unknown, though vanadium helps inhibit cholesterol.
Selenium	Brewer's yeast, whole grains, broccoli.	Helps keep tissue elastic.
Manganese	Most foods.	Activates enzymes involved in synthesis of fats.
Iodine	Vegetables, seafood, drinking water.	Prevents goiter. Helps regulate energy production.
Molybdenum	Pulse foods, whole grains, green vegetables. (Milk, animal organs)	Constituent of some enzymes.
Chromium	Whole grains, brewer's yeast, vegetable oils. (Clams)	Involved in energy metabolism; helps insulin function.
Cobalt	Green vegetables, fruits. (Animal organs, shellfish)	Constituent of vitamin B_{12}; activates some enzymes.
Water	Most foods; all drinks.	Regulates temperature, transports nutrients; constituent of blood, lymph, and other liquids.

Most are present in vegetables, though again animal foods supply most of our minerals.

The last group of essential foods eluded researchers until the present century. Discoveries had been made as early as the eighteenth century that cod-liver oil prevented rickets, citrus juice cured scurvy, and pellagra was cleared up by a nourishing hospital diet. But nobody knew exactly why. At last, researches into the cause of beri-beri in Dutch East India showed that while a diet of polished rice did not prevent the disease, rice with the bran left on it did. The field narrowed, and in 1913 two Americans isolated the nutrient responsible for the cure, which they called vitamin A. Since then more than a dozen other vitamins have been discovered, each essential to good health. Of them all, only one—vitamin B_{12}— occurs naturally only in animal substances. The rest are richly supplied by a varied diet of plant matter. Now, even vitamin B_{12} is produced by forced bacterial fermentation. A vegetarian diet is feasible without any animal products at all, and the power of plants to sustain the human race is (in theory) absolute.

ORIGINS OF STAPLE PLANTS

The map shows the places of origin of the ancestors of many of our most important foods, as well as the nonfood plants tobacco and cotton. In all cases the plants are now grown in large quantities—sometimes as staple foods—far from the areas where they were discovered.

The grape *(Vitis vinifera)* has been cultivated in south-central Asia since Neolithic times, but records suggest that vines are also native to North America.

The wild ancestors of mo ern oats *(Avena sativa)* a hard to locate, since n only do they seem in th time to have given rise

Tracing the origins of plants is a business of endless complexity, aptly graced with the lengthy name of paleoethnobotany. Its methods are any that fill out the contorted ramifications of plants' family trees. (Few humans can trace their descent for more than thirty generations; that would take a plant back no more than thirty years.) There are chance clues like the body of Tollund man, hanged in Denmark some two thousand years ago and thrown into a bog which preserved him well enough for specialists to determine that his last meal consisted of sorrel, barley, and linseed. Elsewhere there are desiccated or charred remains. Techniques of pollen analysis and radiocarbon dating are important. But nothing has provided more illuminating glimpses of plant histories than cytology, the microscopic study of cells. By this means scientists have found how apparently incompatible plants can interbreed to produce new and viable species by freak interplay of their chromosomes. And having found that, they can on occasion recreate the original wild plants from which modern crops have evolved.

The present distribution of crops bears little relation to the original scene. But we can now be sure of the birthplaces of at least some of our food plants.

The prolific family of the cabbage, including cauliflower, kale, Brussels sprouts, and kohlrabi, all sprang from a wild Mediterranean species, *Brassica maritima.*

Tobacco *(Nicotiana tabacum)* is a hybrid of two wild South American plants, and probably originated in Argentina.

The gourd *(Lagenaria siceraria)* was cultivated both in Africa and in Central America in prehistoric times, but seems to have originated in Africa.

the cultivated varietie but farmed oats have al generated weeds. Sou east Europe is genera thought to have been t ancestral home. But sin both the biblical Jews a the Romans knew oa only as weeds, there is tle documentation of th progress.

Beans of the *Phaseolus* genus are natives of South America and were probably first cultivated in Peru around 2500 B.C.

The modern tomato *(Lycopersicon esculentum)* was bred before Columbus arrived, from wild, small-berried Peruvian fruits.

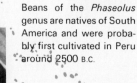

Cultivated now throughout the tropics, cassava *(Manihot esculenta)* originated in South America.

The pineapple *(Ananas comosus)* is one of the South American fruits discovered by Columbus. Its rapid spread thereafter, through Asia and Africa, caused some botanists to regard it till recently as indigenous to these areas.

The potato *(Solanum tuberosum)* has been cultivated in the Andes for two thousand years. Its ancestry lies among scores of wild and hybrid species that grow there.

Maize, or corn *(Zea mays),* is the only cereal crop native to America. Related plants used by aboriginal tribes in Southeast Asia suggest that it may have crossed the Pacific from America long before Columbian times.

Rice (Oryza sativa) is a native of southeastern Asia and has been farmed in China and India for the

Millet (Panicum miliaceum) is only one of a large family of crops which spring from wild ancestors of China, Russia, southeastern Europe, and elsewhere. Originally millet and rice shared the attentions of Chinese farmers, but rice proved the most

rley (Hordeum vulgare d other species) was one the first grains to be ltivated, if not *the* first. ld varieties still grow here it originated, in Asia nor and countries to the st, and traces have been und in the lake dwellings Switzerland. It has giv- rise to several cultivars.

The continuing hybridiza- tion of early grasses of the *Triticum* and *Aegilops* genera in an area that stretched from Syria to Kashmir and southward to Ethiopia was responsible for the development of our bread, macaroni, and oth- er wheats.

Rye *(Secale cereale)* is thought to have originated in Asia Minor and seems to have accompanied wheat in its spread across Europe and Asia, simply as a weed, until its resistance to cold showed it to be a valuable cereal in its own right. It is now a favored crop in northern Russia and in the colder regions of Europe.

Tea *(Thea sinensis)* be- longs to the camellia fami- ly and has been grown in China since prehistoric times. But there are two main categories of the plant—China tea and As- sam tea—and some evi- dence that it originally came from northeast India.

best part of five thousand years. It subsequently came to dominate the agri- culture of countries in Asia, and it is increasingly grown in Europe, Africa, America, and Australia.

useful food. Tropical mil- lets are important staples in Africa and parts of India.

e olive (Olea europaea) ginally grew in those ds which are still most nous for it: Palestine d the countries of the editerranean seaboard.

Fossil records show the coconut *(Cocos nucifera)* as native to southeastern Asia. Its presence in Amer- ica before Europeans ar- rived is most likely explain- ed by the nut's floating across the Pacific.

Oranges and the rest of the *Citrus* tribe stem from southeastern Asia and China (though the lime may be native to India). They are now intensively cultivated in tropical and most subtropical regions throughout the world.

garcane (Saccharum icinarum) first grew in dia and Southeast Asia, ough its cultivation mul- lied in post-Columbian nerica.

Forty or more species of the genus *Coffea*, or cof- fee, are native to a region from East Africa to India. The *arabica* species, which provides most of the world's coffee, originates in Arabia or East Africa.

Pepper *(Piper nigrum),* dis- tinct from peppers of the *Capsicum* genus, is native to India. Close relatives of the plant grow wild in the foothills of the Himalayas and Assam.

The origins of cotton (vari- ous species of the *Gossy- pium* genus) are obscure. Two independent lines of ancestry, one African (though early adopted by India) and one Peruvian, are thought to exist.

SERVING MAN'S NEEDS

The rubber industry is based on the response to wounds of trees rich in latex. Tapping the latex of the *Hevea (left)* stimulates further production by the tree.

The newspaper with the world's largest circulation, Britain's *News of the World,* uses up 15,000 trees in each edition. Thirty trees can go into the making of the cardboard boxes in which the daily requirements of one large supermarket are delivered. Paper products, however, are but one of the chief purposes served by the vast softwood forests of the Northern Hemisphere. The uses of these and other woods—in buildings and furniture, fires, fertilizers, glues, plastics, resins, oils, cork, walking sticks, and Christmas trees—ensure that the average American, for instance, requires about two hundred

clothes (some or all of them cotton, hemp, or kapok), smoking (tobacco or, depending on his regard for the law, other substances), and with a drink (tea, coffee, chocolate, or a plant-based alcoholic drink, maybe) on a table (wood, and resin-polished) beside him. It is unlikely to be long since he washed (with soap) or ate a meal (containing fruits and vegetables).

The hypothetical catalog could go on and on. Yet the portrait is

merely a domestic one. Industrial man depends on plants for oils, fibers, rubber, dyes, gum, wax, and innumerable chemicals. Even synthetics depended originally on a vegetable blueprint.

The word synthetic can mislead, for it conveys an impression of scientists, having filched nature's plans, exploiting them independently of nature. This is not always the case. Plastic, nylon, celluloid, and rayon are chemically produced, but many of the chemicals they consist of are plant extracts. Far from plants losing their importance in human affairs, they are increas-

The forests of Alaska, Canada, the Rocky Mountains, and northern Europe and Asia supply in perpetual rotation the world's enormous appetite for softwoods. In many cases the first stage of transporting the huge crop is by water to downstream riverside sawmills. There it is cut by power-driven saws into planks and beams, kiln-dried, planed, and treated. Then it is sent on to perform any of several thousand functions.

The table below shows a brief selection of the uses to which the world's plants are put.

FIBERS	TIMBER	DYES	RUBBER	GUMS AND RESINS	VARIOUS	ESSENTIAL OILS
About 40 of the 2000 known plant fibers are commercially exploited. Among them, for rope: hemp, abaca, sisal, phormium, cotton, coir. For fabrics: cotton, flax hemp, ramie, jute, kapok. For paper: softwood pulp, esparto grass.	From balsa to lignum vitae, which is eighty times heavier, woods have a multiplicity of uses. Important sources include softwood pines, firs, redwoods, spruce; many different temperate hardwoods; tropical mahoganies, and teak and rosewoods.	Common dyes of ancient and medieval times have largely given way to synthetic coal-tar derivatives. Those still used on a small scale (for clothes, inks, cosmetics, etc.) include indigo, gamboge, henna, lichens, mosses.	In spite of synthetics, tires still take most of the world's natural rubber. The high yield of *Hevea brasiliensis* has displaced most other sources, but Panama rubber, goldenrod, and milkweed are used on a local scale.	Gums are much used in paints, pigments, and confectionery. Gum arabic and gum tragacanth are important sources. Chicle provides the base of chewing gum. Resins are extracted from pines, frankincense, myrrh, storax.	Plant waxes come from carnauba, Brazil palms, esparto grass, and others. Acacia, mangrove, oak, and hemlock barks yield commercial tannin. Two million hectares of cork oak provide the world's cork.	Being volatile, thes release their scen into the air; they a the basis of perfum and flavorings, f example. Importa sources include ger nium, rose, lavende bergamot, storax, ja mine, patchouli, car phor, gardenia.

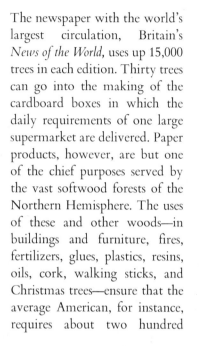

kilograms of wood products a year to maintain his way of living.

For plants' functions in relation to man are by no means confined to feeding. They can house, warm, and clothe us. A few of their uses are exhibited by a person sitting on a chair (part or all wood, probably) in his home (with wooden laths, beams, joists, and furniture), wearing

ing it. In an age which is threatened by energy starvation, plans are advanced for the creation of electricity from seaweeds and fuel gases from the interaction of algae and sewage. Meanwhile, in India, a new kind of cement has been devised for the age of technology; its main constituent is the silica-rich husks of rice.

Jute *(Corchorus capsularis),* shown at left, is mostly grown in Bengal. Its fibers are separated from the stems by retting, that is, moistening them with water in order to season them. The fibers are then softened by the application of kerosene or fish oil (which gives jute a characteristic smell). Strong, coarse, and woody, the fiber is used to make rope, hessian, sacking, and the underlay for carpets and linoleum.

Within the infant rind
of this small flower
Poison hath residence,
and medicine power....

Romeo and Juliet
William Shakespeare

Contentment rests on good food and a well-functioning body. "Few radicals," said Samuel Butler, "have good digestions,"and the claim is borne out by the pain-racked career of choleric Martin Luther. Since good health is largely maintained, and failing health often restored, by the action of plants, we may say that plants have an inordinate influence not only on the body of man, but on his feelings too. From being the source or model of nearly all known medicines, plants have exercised a power over man which has at times equated them with gods.

Gods, and devils too. For the boundaries between opposites often prove narrow. Genius marches with madness, love may turn to hate. And plants, from which derive almost all the known cures of human illness, can be killers as well.

True, what plants contain is for their good, not our harm. Their venom is directed against vegetable rivals and insect invaders (some of which they turn to advantage by consuming) for the legitimate purposes of survival. As such, the venom benefits us. Most poisons used by man kill pests and weeds that afflict our crops. But they are agents also in the darker sides of human activity.

power to heal and kill

The most beautiful bloom may, like some malevolent courtesan of the Medicis, conceal a dagger in her skirts. The florid henbane gloves her poison in petals of soft satin. Hemlock waves its spray of white flowers as innocently as sweet cicely, and the deadly Amanita looks no less inviting than a palatable mushroom. Poisoning has always been the most hated of crimes, for it arrives quietly, arouses no defenses, then strikes repeatedly and with a crescendo of pain. It adds a sinister dimension to their complex characters that plants can dispense agony and death with such passive unconcern.

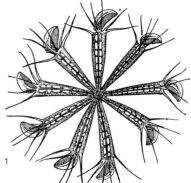

Some plants arm themselves with poisons or prickles as a deterrent and defense. Others live by killing and overtly lure their prey by means of bright colors and tantalizing smells. These are the plant carnivores,

The Australian *Byblis gigantea* uses this method. Its prize trophies, attracted by the sight of gnats and flies, are frogs and lizards.

Some of these carnivorous plants have gained extravagant reputa-

1 The water-trap plant, *Aldrovanda vesiculosa,* floats on the surface of freshwater ponds and slams its caps shut on tiny insects when they step on its trigger hairs.

2 Like the "iron lady" of medieval torture chambers, Venus's-flytrap, *Dionaea muscipula,* native to South Carolina, imprisons and consumes its prey, mainly ants.

3 Venus's-flytrap eating fly.

4 From each of the bubblelike chambers of the bladderwort, *Utricularia vulgaris,* protrudes a featherlike trigger. When sprung, it causes the chamber door to open, suck in the victim, and shut, all within a second.

5 The rank smell of the butterwort, *Pinguicula vulgaris,* attracts

and animal flesh is a necessary part of their diet. Their techniques range from mechanically operated springs and traps to a more passive enticement into a cup of poison. Their victims are mostly insects, which, once caught, are marinated in digestive acids and absorbed into the plant's channels. But there are cases where such a small fry is left struggling on its gummy foothold as bait for bigger victims.

tions. Travelers in the swampy jungles of Mexico and Nicaragua have returned with tales of trees grasping large birds which settle on their boughs, hustling them to the hollow vortex of their trunks, and hours later adding some feathers and dry bones to the accumulating pile on the ground.
Authenticated carnivores keep to a more modest diet. There are hundreds of species, and they

grow in most warm and temperate parts of the world, mainly in boglands where the soil's nitrogen supply needs supplementing. Most are so small we hardly notice them. They blend in with the general prettiness of the moorland scene, and we pass by in ignorance of the glutinous mechanism of springs, tubes, and suckers strangling their improvident prey.

gnats, which are trapped by an oily secretion on the plant's surface. Acids are then released to digest and absorb the insect.

6 The glinting drops on leaves of sundew, *Drosera anglica,* are sticky, catching insects whose struggles stimulate further production of the juice.

7 The Mediterranean *Drosophyllum lusitanicum* also traps passively with gummy secretions.

8 The pitcher plant, *Sarracenia purpurea,* lures insects by smell and the colors on the lips of its cups. Alighting, they slip helplessly to a reservoir of digestive liquids within.

9 The cobra plant, *Darlingtonia californica,* also lures prey by a false promise of nectar.

10 Another pitcher plant, the *Nepenthes hookeriana.*

1 Fly agaric, *Amanita muscaria*, can
produce delirium and breathlessness a few hours after consumption
but is rarely fatal. The poison elements are contained mainly in the
skin of the cap.

2 The death cup, *Amanita phalloides*, kills more people than any

2

other fungus. Not unlike the edible
field mushroom, though often
greenish in color, it produces no
symptoms for several hours—even
as much as two days. If untreated
then, it goes on to produce agonizing convulsions and death.

Nowhere does the legend that
the devil planted poisonous
plants to confuse the unwary
seem so potent as in relation to
the fungi. For every edible species that uplifts the palate there is
a noxious one that may convulse
the whole body. Indeed, it says
much for the good ones that we
continue to risk the most agonizing forms of death in seeking
them out. Descriptions of the
lingering torments produced by
the death cup, *Amanita phalloides*, and others of its tribe
might be expected to deflect
anyone from eating mushrooms.
For it is easy to mistake the death
cup for the most common and
palatable of mushrooms, *Agari-*

lie to it by dying in horrible convulsions. One of the easiest of
fungi to peel is the death cup,
which is held to cause far more
fatalities than any other species
in the world. Another rule states
that a silver spoon dipped into a
cooking pot containing poison
fungi will turn black. Again, it
does not apply to the death cup,
or many others.

Rank smells, evil looks, and a
tendency to change color when
cut are other features claimed to
be warnings. They are worthless.
The ability to identify accurately
is the only sure test, and it is not
acquired easily.

The great likelihood of mistakes
gives poisonous fungi a high

7   8   9   10

cus campestris. We nevertheless
persist—and, in fact, expert identification can eliminate most
risks.

Rules of thumb are not to be
relied on. The most common is
that the skin on the cap of edible
species peels away easily, while
that on poisonous varieties does
not. It is curious that those who
pass on this view do not give the

place in the annals of crime. Both
an emperor and a pope are supposed to have succumbed to
them. The poisoner can always
put the deed down to innocent
confusion.

7 *Russula emetica* attracts with its
scarlet cap and slight honeylike
smell. Like many other poisonous
species, it is made harmless by
cooking. Otherwise it can cause
stomach pains, and diarrhea.

8 The brownish-gray *Rhodophyllus
sinuatus*, which grows from early
summer to autumn in woods, can
damage the liver and sometimes
kills.

9 *Entoloma lividum* is known in
Burgundy as "the great poisoner of
the Côte d'Or."

3 The cap of the "destroying angel," *Amanita virosa*, is often slightly asymmetrical. It is white, and like that of the death cup and fool's mushroom, its cap retains for some hours fragments of the veil which originally covered the whole plant. The painful death it causes led a French botanist to say

4 Some species of *Amanita* are perfectly edible, and one of them—*A. rubescens*—is easily confused with the highly toxic, though seldom fatal variety illustrated here: the panther cap, or *Amanita pantherina*. Both appear in the late summer and autumn, and both have patchy remnants of the veil

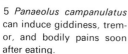

3

4

5

that the luckiest sufferer was the one who did not survive a third day.

remaining for some time on the cap. But the flesh of *A. rubescens* gets reddish spots in time.

5 *Panaeolus campanulatus* can induce giddiness, tremor, and bodily pains soon after eating.

6

6 Paler than the death cup, fool's mushroom, *Amanita verna*, can be even more dangerous in being easily mistaken for an edible mushroom. Gills that stay white and a membranous volva at the base of the stem are the most reliable features to show that it is not a mushroom. With a stem somewhat taller and more slender than that of the death cup, its toxic effects are similar.

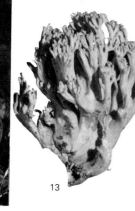

11

12

13

14

15

16

10 Inocybe, *Inocybe patouillardi*, which turns red when touched, quickly causes vomiting, breathlessness, and on rare occasions death.

11 A parasite on rye and other members of the grass family, ergot—*Claviceps purpurea*—can cause convulsions and hallucinations (see page 220).

12 Pleasant eating normally, the inky cap *Coprinus atramentarius* can cause great discomfort and even heart failure if eaten with alcohol.

13 Looking like brushes of pink seaweed, *Clavaria formosa* may cause violent purging.

14 Yellow stainer, *Agaricus xanthodermus*, can be mistaken for the edible horse-mushroom. It may cause vomiting and coma.

17

15 If uncooked, *Gyromitra esculenta* can poison the blood.

16 *Clitocybe dealbata* contains the poisonous element of fly agaric and can cause vertigo, blindness, and delirium.

17 The brown to olive-green *Lactarius blennius* can produce violent stomach convulsions.

POISONOUS PLANTS

The close affinity between cures and poisons meant that the great medieval herbal gardens were also repositories of poisonous plants. Besides, as Livy wrote, kings have always had poisons in readiness "for the uncertainties of fate."

The columbine, *Aquilegia vulgaris*, used to be considered a favorite food of lions. Rubbed on the hand, it gave a lion's courage. It is in fact poisonous, though its poisonous properties have not yet been isolated. Infusions of its seeds are used as medicines in some countries, but they have been claimed to kill small children. All parts of the plant are suspect.

In the country, and in the garden, we walk through a minefield of poisons. Laurel leaves and yew berries, irises, lily-of-the-valley, the leaves and stems of potato and tomato, the demure columbine with its skirts of mauve calico—these and hundreds more can, if eaten, produce effects that range from discomfort to death. Some children, and some adults who aspire to be Thoreaus or noble savages, do eat them, and a few die every year. But most of us learn to avoid them, or we turn the toxic powers of plants to our own advantage. We use them to kill or repel insects and other pests of farm and garden. Hunters and poachers use them to stun or stultify game birds or fish. To a fortunately lessening extent we employ them to get rid of our human enemies. Plant poisons have even been used as the means of legitimate execution. Their role in the history of medicine has been crucial.

None of these uses was arrived at simply. The vegetable kingdom offers an enormous range of poisons. They may be present in flower, seed, leaf, stem, or root. Their quantity varies according to the time of year, the time of day, the soil, and the weather. A dawn killer may be impotent by noon, and a poor soil can restrict the amount of poisonous glycosides or alkaloids present in the plant.

Victims vary too, for it is truly said that one man's meat is another's poison. We see innocuous evidence of this in the action of airborne pollen. To some it is harmless; to others it brings more or less serious attacks of hay fever. Goethe, on a visit to Schiller, was induced to faint by the smell of rotting apples; Schiller himself wrote happily in the fetid atmosphere. Case histories of different allergies show the enormous differences between individual metabolisms. Some gardeners have to wear gloves to hold tomatoes, in order to avoid a rash. Others develop itchy inflammations—even fevers—from contact with primroses. A cup of cocoa can, on occasion, induce colic, and a large dish of beans a heart attack.

The differences between human and animal reactions are far greater. There is, for example, a beetle which lives exclusively on the leaves of the deadly nightshade. Goats happily consume the hemlock which killed Socrates. Conversely, a carrot can kill a white mouse, and there is enough poison in a handful of castor-oil beans to kill over a million guinea pigs.

With all these varieties and eccentricities, it becomes hard to define poison. There are several attested cases of a quantity of water—some three or four liters—killing a child which drank it by leaching the salts from its body. This either makes water (and by analogous arguments sugar, coffee, cabbage, onions, and avocado pears) a poison; or it proves, as some scientists insist, that there is no such thing as a poison. The shades of ten thousand victims of this sinister aspect of the power of plants would stridently disagree.

The innocent-looking flowers and berries of lily-of-the-valley, *Convallaria majalis,* contain cardiac glycosides which are sometimes more potent than those of digitalis. (No part of the plant is free of these.) Consumption can lead to violent pains, dilated pupils, delirium, and a fatal slowing of the heart.

Pain in the stomach, vomiting, convulsions, delirium, and a progressive slowing of the heart are the results of eating berries or leaves of the revered yew tree, *Taxus baccata.* The presence of the tree (once valued for wood for bows) in churchyards has been explained as being due to the remote chance of cattle reaching it there.

Though the tops of its fronds make an agreeable salad, bracken, *Pteridium aquilinum,* contains poisons in all its rts; those in the rhizome, however, are several times more concentrated than elsewhere, and they often bring about eterioration in horses and cattle, especially in high summer.

The alkaloids contained in ragwort, *Senecio jacobaea,* survive for months the death and drying of the plant. As a result, it is often eaten by cattle in the form of hay. It will then slowly destroy the liver and thus kill the animal. Reports of people dying from the same cause have come both from Africa and the West Indies.

It is said that simply stirring a hot drink with the twig of an oleander, *Nerium oleandrum,* has been enough to kill the person who drank it. The root is the most venomous part, and it is often used in India as a means of suicide or to secure abortion. Being both attractive and poisonous to rats, it is left in places they infest.

A method of capital punishment used in ancient Egypt was known as the "penalty of the peach" *(Prunus persica);* it probably involved eating the ground kernels of the fruit. Like those of the cherry, plum, apricot, and even pips of apples and pears, these seeds contain glycosides which break down into cyanide or prussic acid.

The camphor tree, *Cinnamonum cam-ora,* has many practical uses and had more in the days before artificial syn-sis. Its product, camphor, is obtained distillation of the wood of the tree. Its sonous properties are exploited in the manufacture of insecticides. But there are also cases where people working with it have suffered lung damage.

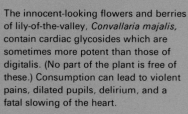

The most poisonous part of meadow saffron, *Colchicum autumnale,* is the underground corm, which can if eaten cause burning sensations from mouth to stomach and lead to death from respiratory failure. It was supposedly one of the plants contained in the venomous brews of Medea, the sorceress.

Like hemlock, the tall waterside water-dropwort, *Oenanthe crocata,* is sometimes mistaken for the more palatable members of the Umbellifer tribe. Cattle are its main victims, but there are plenty of records of humans suffering from it. Its roots in particular are powerfully toxic, but eating any part may lead to rapid death.

The roots are the most poisonous part of yellow jessamine, or *Gelsemium semper virens,* a twining shrub found around the Gulf of Mexico and in the southeastern United States. Its dangers—and consequently benefits—lie in its power of depressing the central nervous system. It is used in treating migraine.

In the past, people smoked the dried stems of old-man's-beard, *Clematis vitalba,* since they gave a good draw and did not burst into flame. It was hazardous, though, since the juice of the plant can cause blistering on the skin and severe pains in the stomach, sometimes leading to death.

A member of the lily family, squill, *Urginea maritima,* contains glycosides which can produce racing of the heart, vomiting, and other symptoms. Its poisonous properties are exploited for killing rats, which eat the plant readily. Related species in Africa cause paralysis and are used for abortions.

Cowbane, *Cicuta virosa,* is a member of the Umbellifer family (which, in spite of several poisonous members, is important in many aspects of gastronomy). All its parts are toxic, perhaps even lethal in a short time. A piece of its root no larger than a walnut is said to be sufficient to kill a cow.

Poison ivy, *Rhus toxicodendron,* produces a virulent itch and inflammation on any part of the body with which it comes in contact. The chemical which causes the reaction is particularly tenacious and will long survive the death and drying of the plant. American Indians have used poison ivy for treating rheumatism.

White bryony, *Bryonia dioica,* has poisonous roots and berries; about forty of the latter could be a lethal quantity. The bulky, tapering roots were used in the Middle Ages as a substitute for mandrake, but the results of consuming it were likely to be acute stomach pains and vomiting.

Lesser celandine, *Ranunculus ficaria,* is a bright and welcome harbinger of spring in temperate climates. Like buttercups, however, and other members of the *Ranunculus* genus, its sap is poisonous, causing skin rashes, burning sensations in the mouth, and (if eaten in quantity) death through intestinal inflammation.

Left and right:
Graceful trails of yellow laburnum, *L. anagyroides,* conceal alkaloids in their seeds which cause more deaths than any other plant in Britain and some other countries. Bark and seeds are equally poisonous, but it is the pods, somewhat resembling those of peas, which mainly attract children.

The leaves and flowers of the common rhododendron, *R. ponticum,* contain a poisonous glycoside which often harms browsing sheep. People are more likely to be affected by honey made from the flower's nectar—a frequent cause of poisoning in Turkey, to which the plant is native. Bees themselves are immune.

Hemlock, *Conium maculatum,* is a tall, attractive Umbellifer, all of whose parts are poisonous. This was one means of capital punishment in ancient Greece—the one suffered by Socrates, among others. Children who use the hollow stems as peashooters are risking a sequence of painful symptoms, and possibly death.

The bark and berries are the principal poisonous parts of *Daphne mezereon,* and its second name derives from a Persian word meaning destroyer of life. Three or four berries will kill a pig, twice that number a human. Its contained glycosides cause a burning sensation in the mouth, and usually deter further consumption.

POWDERS OF INHERITANCE, AND OTHER SUBTLE CONCOCTIONS

Lucrezia Borgia's reputation is of an archetypal poisoner. She was said to be expert with the *annelo della morte,* a ring which pierced the finger of its wearer and injected a poison. She also allegedly applied to gloves and other clothes poisons which killed by touch or fumes. But the tales may be unearned, reflecting the practices not of herself but many contemporaries.

Physical strength is not called for in the administration of poison. What is required is the ability to pick out the right plant—for plant poisons are employed more than animal or mineral—and then, after grinding or other due preparation, to smuggle it into the victim's food or drink.

was no blood, no fighting. Possibly some screams, and agonized spasms, but even these did not necessarily bespeak murder in times when medicine was on the level of superstition, plague and pestilence came and went with no detectable cause, and a dead rat could contaminate the wells.

her husband earned for the potions she used to effect his end the name *poudres de succession,* or powders of inheritance. It casts an interesting light on the Hindu practice of suttee—the compulsory immolation of a wife on the funeral pyre of her husband— that after its introduction the

his wife Agrippina to murder him. Accounts vary—and a considerable amount of scholarship has gone into trying to square them—but it seems that after a choice dish of mushrooms he vomited up all he had eaten. A different dish was prepared, ostensibly as a purge. This con-

Medea *(above)* was the niece of Circe and a devotee of Hecate, goddess of magic. Here she prepares a magic brew for Jason, her lover and leader of the Argonauts. Her skill with herbs and poisons was used against her husband Theseus among others.

Right: The Roman emperor Claudius met his end through a combination of poison and suffocation.

Second right: A coin engraved with portraits of Nero and Agrippina, his mother. Both acquired power by poisoning the opposition.

Henbane, *Hyoscyamus niger.*

Deadly nightshade, *Atropa belladonna.*

Obviously such subterfuge is best carried out in the kitchen— usually the woman's realm. Poisoning is above all the weapon of the woman.

The names of women poisoners ring down through history: Medea, Circe, Locusta, Agrippina, Lucrezia Borgia, the Marquise de Brinvilliers. Poison was subtler than ax or knife. If you prescribed skillfully, there need be no trace of anything but natural death—that is, until the age of forensic medicine. There

Even in modern advanced societies the statistics of detected murders show that poison remains predominantly the province of women. (Undetected murders too are probably, in the main, still the results of poison, and they could perhaps swell the evidence of a sexual bias.) In the past the ease with which a scheming woman could marry for money and then dispose of

life expectancy of males was observed by some to rise dramatically. What point in poisoning, if it amounted to suicide?

Suetonius has recorded the bizarre histories of the Roman emperors who succeeded Augustus. Sexual perversion and a mania for homicide seem almost to have belonged to their genetic makeup. It would be unjust to their powers of invention to claim that they confined themselves to poison as a means of murder. But they used it. Both Claudius and Nero employed a woman of obscure origins but with undoubted pharmaceutical talents as a kind of court poisoner. Her name was Locusta. Having served her apprenticeship under Claudius, she was hired by

tained the poisonous wild gourd, colocynth. Even so he threatened to survive. So, as a last resort, he was suffocated.

Locusta learned by her mistakes. Claudius's stepson and successor, Nero, took her into his confidence. It seems they evinced an academic interest in the arts of poisoning, together watching the deaths of slaves on whom, as on guinea pigs, Locusta's brews

Mithridates VI, king of Pontus in the first century B.C., developed an immunity to poison by swallowing small but increasing quantities from his boyhood on. He survived numerous palace intrigues and died old. He is said to have left an antidote for poisons when he died, which was sold for centuries under the name mithridatum.

were tried. Then Nero turned his attention to his half brother Britannicus, whose claim to the throne was annoyingly better than his own. Locusta prepared a potion. Unluckily it misfired, having a violently emetic effect. In a rage, Nero whipped Locusta with his own hands, then stood by while she concocted the most potent poison known—a mixture, it is thought, of henbane, foxglove, and deadly nightshade.

king of Pontus, Mithridates, scourge of the Roman Empire in the first century B.C., began to eat small quantities of poisonous herbs at a tender age. By the time he came to the throne he was proof against attempts to get rid of him by his enemies at court. A. E. Housman has given him an epitaph in *A Shropshire Lad*:

Eventually, harried from his kingdom by the victorious Romans, he took his own life. Of necessity, he chose to fall on his sword. By the side of his body, Pompey is said to have discovered a list of over fifty ingredients which together made a prophylactic against all poisons. Known as a mithridatum, and varying in composition from time to time, the formula persisted in herbals till the nine-

had done in fact was to help young people understand truth. He died as he had lived, philosophically. "What must I do?" he asked, when handed the lethal cup by his executioner. "Drink, then walk about till your legs feel heavy, then lie down," was the answer. He obeyed. His assembled friends wept, and he reprimanded them for bad manners. Then he lay down. The jailer pinched his foot, but Socrates felt nothing. A little later it was the same with his legs. The numbness progressed. Just before he died, he asked Crito to sacrifice a cock to the god of medicine, Asclepius. It was a thank offering, an acknowledgment that death is a cure for life—and poison, in a sense, a medicine. A moment later he was dead.

Plato's detailed account of these events hardly tallies with other records of the effects of hemlock. It can shake the body with pain before it extinguishes life; and it seems unlikely that even Socrates

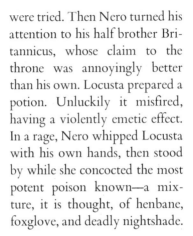

Hemlock, *Conium maculatum*.

Foxglove, *Digitalis purpurea*.

Black hellebore, *Helleborus niger*.

Opium poppy, *Papaver somniferum*.

Pliny, author of the *Natural History* which recorded much of the knowledge of plants, cures, and poisons of the first century A.D.

It killed a trial pig instantly. And that night at dinner it killed Britannicus. Nero explained his death away as due to epilepsy, buried him hurriedly, and gave Locusta a free pardon. She prospered for the rest of his reign, but was quickly done to death at the beginning of the next.

Immunity from poison is not always inborn. It can be acquired. A cunning and resilient

Easy, smiling, seasoned sound,
Sate the king when healths went
round.

They put arsenic in his meat
And stared aghast to watch him eat;
They poured strychnine in his cup
And shook to see him drink it up:
They shook, they stared,
as white's their shirt:
Then it was their poison hurt.
—I tell the tale that I heard told.
Mithridates, he died old.

teenth century. But its origin was almost certainly invented. Mithridates survived not by cure, but by a lifetime of prevention.

Hemlock became famous as a poison through the judicial death of Socrates in 399 B.C. Corrupting youth was his crime. But it was a time when tyranny had succeeded the creative liberalism of fifth-century Athens. What he

Thorn-apple or jimsonweed, *Datura stramonium*, which poisoned several early settlers in America, concealing its venom within an attractive form.

could have disguised his feelings so well. The truth is probably that his fatal draught was mixed with opium, a fact which those who seek release through it would do well to remember.

The goddess Circe was outdone by Odysseus, who learned from Hermes of the antidote for her poison: a scented white flower with a black root, called *moly*.

Plants have been the means of innumerable suicides. The Roman scholar Pliny believed this was nature's purpose. "Wherefore hath our mother the earth brought out poisons," he wrote, "in so great quantity, but that men in distress might make away with themselves?" And he tells of the happy, long-lived inhabitants of Choa, who were accustomed to anticipate fate, before they became infirm or imbecile, with the poppy or hemlock. It was always a way out of disgrace, as the condemned criminals at Nuremberg knew in 1946 when they bit the vials of cyanide concealed in their mouths. It was an escape for disappointed lovers. The poi-

son Romeo swallowed, when he mistook Juliet's temporary coma for death, is supposed to have been aconite, extracted by his mean apothecary from the flowers of monkshood.

There is a legend that a herb growing in Piedmont, Italy, is traditionally used for the relief of suffering by death. It is known as the herb of Mary, and it is employed not by men but birds, which know well its poisonous properties. When their young are captured and put in cages, the parent birds are said to go and pick these herbs and pass them through the bars, knowing that death is preferable to a lifetime of servitude.

Knowledge of the medicinal qualities of herbs is acquired by trial and error. Not infrequently the errors can prove fatal. The herbalist Conrad Gesner was often indisposed as a result of his experiments, and he nearly died after taking a decoction of leopard's-bane. But enthusiastic searches for elixirs by the Chinese (the emperor Chinnung had a glass window fitted to his stomach to be able to study the action of herbs) produced an exceptional list of casualties. No less than six Tang emperors, and many more court officials, are recorded as having died from what were meant to be life-enhancing brews. The tally of criminals—usually appointed as the first testers of new concoctions—can never be known. But the experiences of one palace guard ended happily. He had stolen and drunk a little of a new

Scylla was turned into a sea monster by the enchantress Circe, whose poisonous brews also turned Odysseus' sailors into swine.

elixir which everyone, including the emperor, both believed and wanted to go on believing would be the means of eternal health. His crime was discovered, and he was sentenced to death. But the effect of an elixir, he well knew, was not merely medical. It was supposed to apply to all life's contingencies, and in pointing this out he showed that his own death would invalidate the claims made for the mixture. His ingenuity was rewarded with a reprieve and promotion.

The first poisoners are veiled by layers of magic and witchcraft. Homer tells of the goddess and sorceress Circe, living on an island off the west coast of Italy surrounded by wild beasts—which were in fact men on whom she had worked her herbal magic. When Odysseus came her way with his men, during their long wanderings after the sack of Troy, she prepared a honeyed drink to greet them. In a short while each of them found himself bending forward at the

hips and developing a muscular neck and a flattened snout. By means of herbs, she had turned them into pigs; and it was only by means of a god-given antidote, the mysterious *moly*, that Odysseus himself was restored. Before that, a shepherd called Glaucus had come to Circe, asking her to use her knowledge of plants and cause a nymph, Scylla,

The poisonous upas tree gave rise to legends that its fumes were powerful enough to kill a man.

to return his passionate love for her. Circe, attracted by Glaucus, tried to wean his affection on to herself. She failed, and in her fury went to a bay where the girl often bathed, and to the accompaniment of charms and spells sprinkled "a baneful root" over the water. Scylla duly arrived and went into the water. Looking down, she suddenly noticed what seemed like a pack of wild

The Medici pope Clement VII, whose refusal to allow Henry VIII of England a divorce from Catherine of Aragon hastened the English Reformation, is supposed to have been killed by a plate of poisonous mushrooms or by toxic fumes from a torch held near him.

dogs surrounding her legs. Then to her horror she realized that they *were* her legs. She had become a monster, and monster she stayed until a further change reduced her to rock, twinning with Charybdis as a fatal hazard to ships. Such were the achievements of the earliest poisoners.

As a technology, poisoning has never stood still. It has been transmitted in food and drink, and by means of a small pin concealed in glove, boot, stirrup, or ring. Rings have been made with a chamber for poison since classical times. Hannibal took his own life by swallowing such a draught. But the *annelo della morte* was a Venetian invention of the Middle Ages which worked on a different principle. Among its elaborate ornaments was a projection which, if pressed, released a sharp point inward from the poison chamber to the wearer's finger. It must have satisfied the most subtle malice of Borgia or Medici to be able to kill while clasping, with seeming warmth and smiles, the hand of the victim. Both Cesare and Lucrezia Borgia are said to have used this method, their favorite poison being the fermented decoction of mandrake root. Lucrezia's skills, according to legend, went as far as being able to time the death, by varying the ingredients, up to three

days after the liquid was absorbed, and likewise to be able to vary the agony involved. But history may have been hard on her memory. While the administration of poison has always been easy, accusations of poisoning have been even easier. They could seldom be disproved. Slander could be as insidious a weapon as poison itself.

Imagination or technique continued to progress, and the later Medicis won the same unenviable reputations as had attached to the Borgias. One of them, Pope Clement VII (who in

Catherine de Medici married Henri II of France, and introduced the Italian arts of poison to the French court.

refusing England's Henry VIII a divorce from his first wife accelerated the English Reformation), in time fell a victim to the fashionable crime. He is variously reported as having succumbed

to a plate of lethal mushrooms or to the toxic fumes from a torch carried before him.

His kinswoman Catherine de Medici, in moving to France as the bride of Henri II, won a mixed reputation. On the one hand she is credited with spreading the new Renaissance gastronomy through her adopted land. On the other she was a reputed mistress of the arts of poison. Her most famous victim was Jeanne d'Albret, queen of Navarre and a threat to the reactionary rule of Catherine's family. In a hidden compartment of a glove drawer—and again the account has mythical overtones; Jeanne may well have died of fever—Catherine concealed poppy, hellebore, and belladonna, whose fumes infected the other contents of the drawer. The outcome was as predicted. Jeanne donned her gloves, and three days later she was dead.

It may have been a law passed in the reign of Henry VIII—which enacted that convicted poisoners should be boiled to death—that saved England from the worst excesses of poison mania. From time to time Italy and France suffered from grotesque out-

bursts of poisoning, which seemded to grip society like a fashion in hats. At the center of the most shameless of these was the notorious Marquise de Brinvilliers. With her lover St. Croix she contrived to dispose of her husband, father, two brothers, and several more inside and outside her family, with the aim of augmenting her considerable fortune. St. Croix's promising career was ended when the mask

Madame la Voisin was at the center of what can be described as a fashion for poisoning in Louis XIV's Paris.

The Marquise de Brinvilliers was burned for multiple poisonings in seventeenth-century France.

he used as protection in preparing his noxious potions fell off, and he inhaled some lethal fumes. Inquiries began. A sinister steward of the marquise, while being racked and broken on the

Graham Young, whose sentence to life imprisonment in England in 1972 brought to an end one of the most ruthless poisoning careers in criminal history.

wheel, told all he knew, and she herself was arrested, tried, and burned after a merciful beheading. But criminal trails led this way and that, even to the court of Louis XIV. During sessions which lasted years, a state commission laid charges against 442 people—mostly of high rank—of whom thirty-six were executed and as many banished. Poison, which had for a while seemed the path to the realization of all dreams, went out of vogue.

Plants formed the main armory of poisoners till the end of the eigteenth century. Minerals had been used—arsenic and antimony more than others—and so had animal venoms, but it was not until the nineteenth century that metallic poisons took the lead. Arsenic recurs monotonously in the criminal records of the time. But vegetable poisons cropped up now and then. It was hyoscine—extracted from henbane—which Dr. Crippen used in one of England's most celebrated murders, in 1910.

It was the capture, more than the crime, which caught the public's imagination. Crippen, a qualified doctor selling drugs for a patent medicine company, poisoned his wife, gave out that she had died on holiday in California, and soon after was seen about with a young woman, Ethel Le Neve, who habitually wore the dead woman's jewelry.

North London neighbors were suspicious, and the police were called in. They searched Crippen's house, but nothing untoward was found. Soon after, however, Crippen and Le Neve disappeared. A new police search revealed bits of Mrs. Crippen's body in the cellar, and a warrant was issued.

By this time the refugees were on a steamer bound for Canada. Le Neve was disguised as a boy, and both had registered in the name of Robinson, father and son. Among others, the captain was surprised at the almost amorous attention Mr. Robinson devoted to his boy at the dining table. He had read about the Crippen case, and for the first time in history

Dr. Crippen, whose poisoning of his wife and near-escape to Canada with his mistress created a sensation in England in 1910.

wireless was used to expedite a murder hunt. When they arrived at Quebec, the police greeted them. Later that year, Crippen was tried and hanged in London.

No account of Borgia or Brinvilliers excels in horror the case of Graham Young, an Englishman of twenty-five who was imprisoned, for the second time and for life, in 1972. Born in 1947—his mother died soon after his birth—he had developed unusual tastes by the age of eleven: a devotion to Hitler and black magic, and an active interest in poisons and explosives. His first victims were insects and small mammals. At fourteen, he watched his stepmother writhe in pain before she died of atropine poisoning; he was busy at the same time dosing his sister (who got hallucinations from belladonna), father, and a boy at his school. At the gathering following his stepmother's funeral, he poisoned the drink of a relative of hers. Pride got the better of him. He aired his amazing knowledge, and he was finally arrested, tried, and sent to Broadmoor, an institution for the criminally insane.

Stone walls do not a prison make.... Soon after Young's arrival, a fellow inmate died of

A sprig from the strychnine tree, *Strychnos nux-vomica*, the most important source of this virulent poison.

cyanide poisoning. Laurel bushes (since removed) could have been the source, and there were means of distilling the poison from them. No charges were laid, but there were other rumors that he found belladonna berries and poisoned the institutional cocoa.

Ten years brought him release. He found a job with a chemicals firm, the employees of which were soon afflicted by an epidemic. Young himself seemed immune, but at least eight of his colleagues were acutely ill over a period of months. Two died.

Again Young's expertise gave him away, also his choice, as victims, of people close to him—not, it was said, from malice, but a desire to see the progress of symptoms. His trial in 1972 again revealed his coldly psychopathic character. He claimed equal rating with the Nazis, and asked once whether Madame Tussaud's Waxworks had made approaches to put his image in the Chamber of Horrors. His dream was to have it placed between the figures of Crippen and his greatest hero, the Victorian mass poisoner William Palmer.

A young girl from an East African tribe smells the flowers of *Acokanthera venenata,* which contains the poison *ouabai* and is used both for ordeal trials and hunting.

Blowguns *(below)* are a popular means of firing poison darts. Even a bowstring can make a tell-tale twang as the arrow leaves it. Blowguns are the nearest thing to silent deliverers.

On his last journey to the Orinoco River of South America in 1617, Sir Walter Raleigh was shown a mixture known to the natives of the area as *urari*. He took a speck on his finger and rubbed it, bringing it in contact with a slight but unhealed cut. He promptly fell to the ground, seized with a vertigo that lasted half an hour. Fortunately the type of urari which had entered his bloodstream was weak—used only to kill very small animals.

A selection of elaborately barbed spears used by South American Indians. Each is tailored for a particular prey, as is the viscous poison smeared on the weapon to secure instant death or maiming.

The name urari means "he to whom it comes falls," and a stronger mixture would have killed him instantly.

His and later discoveries about the use of curare, as the poison came to be known, always exercised a powerful fascination on more advanced nations. Arrow poisons seem to be as old as the human race. The word "toxophily"—the art of archery—shows the connection between poison and arrows in sharing a root with the word toxic. The biblical Job laments that "the arrows of the Almighty are within me, the poison whereof drinketh up my spirit." And the Celts, who once occupied the whole of central and western Europe, regularly used arrow poisons. The rediscovery of this ancient technique, in places as far apart as South America, Africa, and Southeast Asia, appealed perhaps to an atavistic streak in Europeans.

Fact and fiction were mingled in the accounts that came back. The fiction was augmented by the secrecy with which natives mixed their lethal brews. Tales were told that the oldest women of a tribe would be set to prepare the poisons in closed huts. If, after two days, the fumes had not killed them, the mixture was taken to be too weak and a new one begun. Some tribes, perhaps truly, were said to put curare under their fingernails, assuring themselves of victory in hand-to-hand fighting by scratching their opponents. Certainly the strength of the venom could be remarkable. Curares are sometimes classified as "one-tree," "two-tree," and so on, the names indicating the distance a monkey hit by a coated arrow might get before it fell dead. The strongest would fell even an elephant within yards of the strike. A

Spanish missionary, seeing a chicken killed instantly, thought the poison would have a great sale in Europe, where game and poultry could be dispatched so quickly that there wuld be no time for their muscles to tense, so causing an unpalatable toughness in the flesh.

Arrow poisons are not used exclusively against animals. They were—and supposedly still are, among primitives—a weapon of war, and several Western explorers who have disappeared without trace in the Matto Grosso are thought to have succumbed to them. They are used against fish and as ordeal poisons—that is, they are administered to those suspected of crimes, who, if innocent, will recover. Those skilled in making them up can vary their toxicity not only to suit the intended prey, but also to secure death or simply paralysis, whichever is desirable. And the weapons used include not only arrows but also blowpipes, darts, and spears.

Below, from left to right:
Strychnos toxifera and other species of *Strychnos* are principal components of the arrow poison curare; the dried root of *Chondodendron tomentosum* has fur-

ther medicinal value as a diurectic and tonic; the poisonous alkaloids contained in the bark of the upas tree, *Antiaris toxica*, make it an important arrow poison.

The plant ingredients are diverse. Some mixtures include the juices of as many as forty or fifty plants, carefully regulated to suit the immediate purpose. This can be made more difficult by the fact that some plants used are more poisonous at certain times of the year than at others.

Besides toxic plants, vegetable gums are also included, to help stick the mixture to the weapon. There will usually be some additional plants put in for purely magical purposes.

The stricken Sir Walter Raleigh had realized that curare might have important uses in the science of pharmacology. But he was to return home to dishonor and death, and little notice was taken of his or other discoveries for over a hundred years. It was not till 1812 that an Englishman, Charles Waterton, learned by experiments on animals that if primary asphyxiation could be prevented, the great benefit of the drug in relaxing muscles and nerves would be of inestimable

Above, from left to right:
Decoctions of the leaves of *Acokanthera venenata* are used both to coat hunting arrows and as an ordeal poison; *Strophanthus hispidus* and related vines contain the drug strophanthin, a

value in surgery. Not long afterward curare was used in treating lockjaw, then in a whole host of ailments from epilepsy to infantile paralysis. Nowadays it is frequently used in the operating room, its dangers completely evaded by the artificial regulation of the patient's breathing.

Curare, as it is medically used, is derived from various species of *Strychnos* and *Chondodendron*. It is not the only arrow poison to have found a new use in medicine. *Strophanthus* species, used

poison that can also be used in heart surgery; the African vine *Strophanthus gratus* yields a glycoside whose action on the heart makes it of benefit both to hunters and to surgeons.

by tribesmen in several parts of Africa and Asia, is the source of a drug, strophanthin, which is used for heart diseases in a similar way to digitalis. For a while, a few years ago, it won headlines as a possible source of cortisone, but procurement proved uneconomical. Species of *Derris, Erythrophleum, Cocculus,* and others have proved to be of medical or commercial importance. In that fall in 1617, Sir Walter had stumbled, indeed, on one of nature's treasure chests.

The calabar bean, or ordeal bean, *Physostigma venenosum,* has been used for centuries in tropical West Africa as an ordeal plant in trials. Those who survive the eating of a few seeds are innocent, those who die are deemed justly punished.

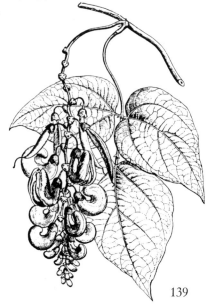

139

LOVE AND HATE
IN THE PLANT KINGDOM

A rose planted beside garlic will generally grow better and bigger, produce more fragrant flowers, and resist more diseases than a rose on its own. But a cabbage or runner bean beside garlic will show signs of acute discontent. Strawberries respond well to the presence of borage but cannot abide a cabbage near them. Their performance will suffer from a gladiolus planted as far as 15 meters away.

Plant likes and dislikes make a complex study. They can be fostered by the compatibility or otherwise of roots, foliage, growth rates and patterns, water usage, mineral usage, or the secretion into the soil of minerals. Any hedgerow will furnish examples of successful partnerships, and sage gardeners make use of many others. Old cottage gardens of Europa and the traditional gardens of Mexico and South America present sights which are not at first aesthetically pleasing to the modern practitioner, trained to think of plants in isolation and to overcome difficulties by the use of sundry chemicals. When a fastidious approach replaces the age-old methods that have gone to make, say, a humble English garden, it does away with nettles and foxgloves on the grounds that they are weeds, and dismisses the lines and clumps of marigold on the grounds that they are vulgar. Yet those three plants have a generally beneficial effect on almost all garden crops. They cheer them up; though of course chemistry, not emotions, is at the bottom of

There are theories that the love of the rose (1) for garlic (2) is based on the yearning of a highly cultivated, inbred plant for one that is scarcely changed from its wild original—a noble savage. It is not yet fully understood why the rose's performance should improve so notably when garlic is planted close to it. It is known, however, that enormous benefit is derived from secretions given out by the garlic's roots (and absorbed by the rose's) which keep away the rose's most harmful pests—greenfly or aphids. And perhaps it is to compete with the garlic that a rose will give out a stronger aroma than it would otherwise.

Strawberries (3) respond well to the presence of borage (4), as they do also to beans (which enrich the soil, as other members of the pea family do, with nitrogen), lettuce, thyme, and nettles. Cabbages, on the other hand, demoralize strawberries and can ruin their crop. Borage has always been associated with health and good cheer; Pliny called it *Euphrosinum* for that reason, and Gerard wrote that its flowers were used in salads "to exhilerate and make the minde glad." Cooks made use of them "for the comfort of the heart, to drive away sorrow, and increase the joy of the minde."

Tomato plants (5) are helped by the presence of stinging nettles (6), which are all too often destroyed to suit the gardener's ideas of tidiness. Nettles secrete formic acid and various minerals into the soil, which together protect the tomato against disease and supposedly improve the flavor of the fruit. Nettles benefit many other plants too, including herbs like marjoram, sage, and angelica, and most soft fruits. Moreover, cut and dried nettles used with stored fruits in the winter prolong their life and maintain their flavor better.

Chamomiles (7) have a special effect on other plants: They can cure them of their depressions and lethargy. More curious, if they stay around too long, the patient will probably suffer a relapse. So in the past chamomile was used as a kind of mobile medical unit by gardeners, who would transplant it close to an ailing plant, but carefully remove it after a short period. With cabbage (8), however, the bond can be a lasting one. Cabbages are particular in their choice of bedmates, but with chamomile their pleasure—as that of the gardener—remains unabated.

The benefits that foxglove (9) can confer on other plants can carry on beyond the grave; for when picked flowers begin to ail in their vases, a decoction of foxglove leaves added to the water will often revive them. On the ground, their stimulant and disease-resistant qualities make them close friends of fruit trees, tomatoes, and potatoes (10). The latter two are not easily satisfied. They cannot abide each other, though they belong to the same family. Plants of the pea family, as well as strawberries and marigolds, are good friends of the potato.

Nasturtiums (18), allowed to grow up apple and other fruit trees, can help to keep away aphids.

If it is true that the chemical structure of plants evolved as a means of defense against insects and other predators, the rue (17) can be said to be a leader in the evolutionary race. Both its smell and taste are extremely bitter, but planted by the windows and doors of houses plagued with flies it acts as a useful deterrent. Although it dislikes the company of many plants, it is fond of the fig tree, which can temper its rankness.

it. Secretions from the marigold kill nematode worms in the soil, and nematodes are great devourers of roots. Nettles and foxgloves pour valuable minerals into the earth and can act as tonics if planted beside ailing plants. Carefully controlled, they do nothing but good.

One of the ways in which garlic serves its rose neighbor is by emitting fumes which deter

in parts of England as rat's-bane, and there are plenty of other "banes" which indicate by their names their deterrent effects on the animal world: fleabane, henbane, wolf's-bane—even leopard's-bane, which, besides in addition to chasing leopards away, can help with other pests. As Turner wrote in his herbal, this plant "layd to a scorpione makyth hyr utterly amased and Num."

11 13 15

12 14 16

Chrysanthemum cinerariifolium (11), grown commercially in East Africa, provides the insecticide pyrethrum. Dried and hung indoors, the flowers of fleabane (12) deter fleas by an aroma which is not unpleasant to man. The roots of varieties of derris (13), grown in Malaysia, yield a chemical, rotenone, widely used as an insecticide. Henbane (14) is a

danger to most birds and mammals. The waste tobacco (15) from cigarette manufacture is used in the making of insecticides. Wolfs-bane (16) is a deterrent not only to wolves; the poison aconite it contains is deadly to many species, but its pesticide purposes died with the retreat of the wolf from most of Europe.

aphids, and similar powers underlie many other close partnerships. Nasturtiums repel aphids too. Ants keep well away from lupins; and fiercer pests like moles and rats can be discouraged—by repute at least—by caper spurge and chervil respectively. Chervil has been known

Extracts from hundreds of different plants have been brought into home, garden, and farm as a result of their powers to repel or kill insects and other pests. Even though synthetic, chlorinated compounds are used more and more, pyrethrum, derris, and tobacco are still widely employed.

THE PHARMACY OF NATURE

In ancient and medieval times the mandrake, *Mandragora officinarum*, pictured here in a copper engraving of 1719, was credited with numerous magic and healing powers. It has recently been reinstated as useful in the treatment of asthma, coughs, and hay fever. Deadly nightshade, *Atropa belladonna (below)*, according to Gerard, "bringeth

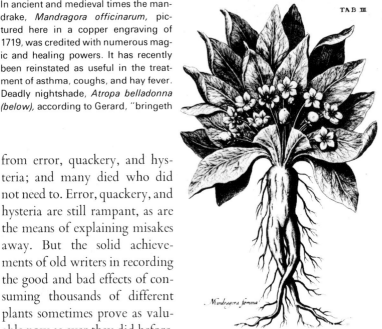

such as have eaten thereof into a deep sleep, whereof many have died." Like many poisons it also has medical value, in the treatment of eye ailments, cramps, and other complaints. Lady's mantle, *Alchemilla mollis (right)*, is an ancient and modern healer of wounds and cuts, with several other beneficent effects.

Today's smooth, multicolored, cellulose-coated medicinal pills seem a far cry from the teeming variety of plant life. Indeed, most properties of modern medicine and the institutions connected with it—hospitals white-painted, their long angular passages polished to gleam, and reeking of disinfectant—present a stark contrast to nature. The word clinical is sometimes used in the sense of unnatural or sterile.

Nevertheless, the dependence of medical science on nature remains strong, as it always has

from error, quackery, and hysteria; and many died who did not need to. Error, quackery, and hysteria are still rampant, as are the means of explaining mistakes away. But the solid achievements of old writers in recording the good and bad effects of consuming thousands of different plants sometimes prove as valuable now as ever they did before. For nature has not changed. Great pharmaceutical companies still comb more backward territories for witch doctors' nostrums, hoping for discoveries that will match those other

The great advantage of science is that it can reproduce the chemicals found in plants in more accurate and reliable dosages. A plant's ingredients vary in quantity from season to season, day to day, even hour to hour. A leaf which at other times might provide a cure could now provide an overdose. The laboratory rectifies these anomalies. Though light, age, and innate volatility can have adverse effects, the medicine in the bottle will have exactly the same effect next week as it would today; and it may be unchanged in a year or more.

However, these advantages of science are not unqualified. The scientist's concern is to match a symptom or a disease with a chemical antidote. Where our ancestors would have concocted a tea, perhaps, from the relevant part of a plant, the chemist first isolates the substance known to act on the ailment and leaves aside all the rest. This purified chemical is now given to, say, a patient with a bad kidney. It is swallowed, and some finds its way to the kidney, where it performs its allotted task and passes on. Meanwhile the rest of the

dose will have traveled in other directions—to the brain, maybe, or heart or lung or skin. Here its effects may not be so beneficial. The side effects of purified and concentrated chemicals can be alarming and even harmful. Rashes, dizziness, fainting, palpitations, blurred vision, diarrhea, and prolonged depression can all stem from a drug which cannot in the nature of things confine itself to one allotted task.

It is here that old-fashioned methods can sometimes prove superior. Those plant constituents which the laboratory rejects may modify the side effects by exerting some form of control over the main principle. Both digitalis and rauwolfia have been shown in recent years to benefit from the balancing action of the chemicals which accompany them in the plant. Numerous other cases are being considered. Not for the first time, nature is shown to have most of the answers.

The danger in science, in other words, is that it is inclined to leave its origins behind. Having isolated its chemicals, it prefers to play what has been described as molecular roulette, while ignoring the lessons which plants themselves, and those who for centuries have written about them, are able to teach.

It is true, of course, that plants are as they are for their own good reasons, and not for ours. The power to cure a headache, or human flatulence or carbuncles or palpitations, was not a consideration during the long course of

been. Often enough these plastic-seeming pills contain extracts of plants or synthetic versions of them—for plants have provided the blueprint for most modern medicines. Though appearances go against the claim, the development of medicine from the earliest times is a continuous one. The practices of the past suffered

plant-based boons: quinine and morphine (a still unsurpassed painkiller), tranquilizing rauwolfia, the anesthetic curare, and emetine, unrivaled as a cure for amoebic dysentery. Cancer, the mysteries of heart disease, and the morbid decline activated by multiple sclerosis may all in time be mastered by plants.

plant evolution. It is equally true, however, that humans evolved in a plant environment and were shaped and conditioned by it. The species of man which alone survives—*Homo sapiens*—was partly enabled to do so by the fact that plants could supply so many of people's needs, including those that arose when they were ill. Plants shaped people—in the last analysis we are recycled plant matter—and having done so they did not resign their responsibility. They followed up their success by providing a natural pharmacy. They offered people minerals and salts which gave resistance to disease, strength to tissues, and help in the regulation of the nervous system. They offered glycosides, which were broken down by fermentation and produced sugar and various other compounds important to the workings of their hearts and bloodstreams. Some improve their circulation, others can cure rheumatism and reduce fevers and pain (salicylic acid, contained in willow bark and violets, is the glycosidal forerunner of aspirin). Tannins, by precipitating proteins in certain parts of the body, aid recovery by preventing the passage of harmful bacteria. Alkaloids can have beneficial effects on the nerves, acids may be useful laxatives, plant mucilage can revive the healthy workings of the intestines. Even the lowest forms of plant life can be vital in curing viral diseases. Penicillin is only one—no doubt the most famous—of these antibiotics.

As in so many other fields of human activity, a sharp change has occurred in medical practice in the last two hundred years; and it sometimes seems that the progress made since the change began is as great as that made in all the millennia before. When one considers individuals, however, this is patently not the case. The mind of the average citizen of an advanced Western society may contain echoes of herbal lore, and fainter echoes—remaining from schooldays—of the principles on which one's body works. The knowledge of medi-

The flower heads of arnica, *A. montana*, make a tincture used in compresses for bruises and skin inflammations.

cine, however, is for practical purposes confined to one indispensable piece of information: the way to the doctor's office. Modern people have, by and large, renounced their familiarity with medicine, entrusting it all to a few professionals. All we

have to do is to describe the symptoms. In return we receive a boxed or bottled concoction, and in due course we are cured. But in the process of this surrender to the specialists we have lost something. Our ignorance would profoundly surprise our ancestors.

Kipling put it well, listing the names of old medical herbs:
Vervain, dittany, call-me-to-you,
Cowslip, melilot, rose-of-the-sun—
Anything green that grew out
*   of the mould*
Was an excellent herb to our
*   fathers of old.*

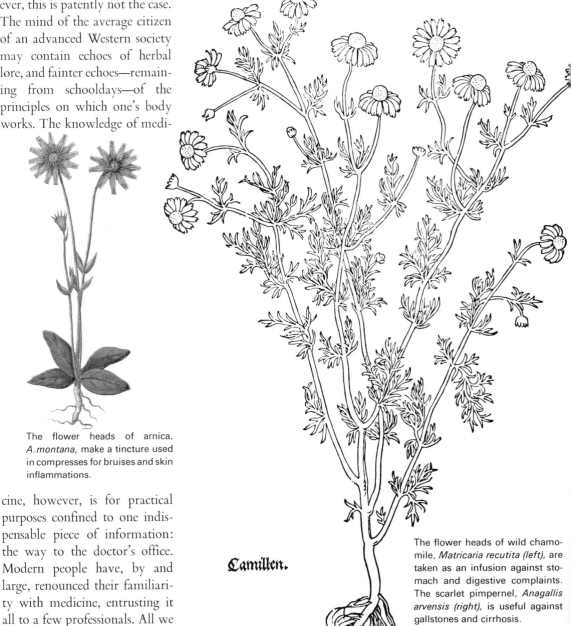

Camillen.

The flower heads of wild chamomile, *Matricaria recutita (left)*, are taken as an infusion against stomach and digestive complaints. The scarlet pimpernel, *Anagallis arvensis (right)*, is useful against gallstones and cirrhosis.

144

Aloes, *Aloe vera* (1), yields from its leaves a drug used in treating intestinal worms, for example. From the leaves and pods of cassia, *C. acutifolia* (2), comes the laxative senna. Alkaloids contained in stalks of *Ephedra sinica* (3) help to raise blood pressure. *Cinchona officinalis* (4) bark combats fevers, notably malaria.

The extraordinary richness—with all their local varieties—of plant names tells us much about the common medical knowledge of past times. In their paths and hedges, woods and meadows, country people recognized the medicine chest that God had given them. All the higher plants had a place in this. Each one of them held a key to some ailment, either in its natural state or after distillation, or mixed with others. In Europe in 1500 every plant had been distilled and its effects tested and broadcast. The centuries had built up, and continued to accumulate, a vast fund of information, much of which was never even written down because there was no need. Communities passed it on verbally. Even today it is not entirely lost, and most people can recall some fragment of lore which, though unrecorded, has been effective

enough to survive so far the scientific revolution. Near where I write there is an old, unlettered herdsman who, when a cow falls ill, dutifully doses it with the antibiotics the professionals recommend. Having thus mollified the gods of science, he

proceeds to the real business of curing the beast, offering it ancient concoctions of valerian, tansy, or St. John's-wort. He is never in doubt about which treatment effects recovery.

He also, it is true, takes a bucket of the cow's milk and flings the contents against a wall while muttering some arcane spell. And herein lies the disadvantage of much ancient and traditional theory: it is glutted with magic and superstition, and much dogma that is irrelevant if not downright dangerous. Many of the Renaissance herbalists regurgitated information they had read in Pliny or Dioscorides without bothering to test their claims, thus preserving a proportion of mumbo-jumbo which cast a suspicious light over all the rest of their findings. Take celandine, advises Banckes's herbal, "and draw out the juice thereof and meddle it with white wine and anoint the visage therewith, and it shall do away with freckles of the visage." Many a hopeful maiden has followed the instructions only to be greeted, when she looked in the glass, by a face as speckled as when she began. "Whoever is deaf," the *Hortus Sanitatis* asserts, "should take the milk of a woman who nurses a boy ten or twelve weeks old and put this with the juice of the houseleek and then drip three or four drops into the ear soothingly. The hearing will come back without fail." It is to be regretted that anyone who goes to the not inconsiderable trouble of procuring these ingredients will remain

as deaf as if he had not bothered at all.

Such lapses give herbal lore a bad name. The result is neglect. Most of the great herbals lie in libraries, unprinted since the fifteenth or sixteenth century. Even information of unquestionable worth is reduced to a mean chemistry in the laboratory, shorn of all the peripheral benefits the whole plant might have conferred. Not that it always did. Synthetic aspirin, for example, is more effective than the salicylic acid derived directly from the willow. But undoubtedly science has too hastily scuttled the accumulated findings of the past, tested through centuries of use with a thoroughness that no laboratory program can now afford.

For speed is of the essence today. Driven by a thirst for profits, the great pharmaceutical companies vie with each other to be first with some new cure. Thousands of years of testing on people are replaced by a few months of experiments on rats, guinea pigs, or rhesus monkeys. Long-term effects cannot be known. Mistakes, when they come, come on a tragically large scale. Meanwhile acreages of wild flowers grow, bloom, and die natural deaths, their offers refused, their powers to heal ignored.

There are signs of change. If the proliferation of literature on a

subject is anything to go by, interest in herbal remedies is mounting to a peak, corresponding with a mounting disillusion in the protective, profit-making industry of orthodox drugs. In Russia and other Eastern states, where commercialism is subject to more checks than in the West, far more notice is taken by public and scientists alike of the possible benefits of the plant world. Nobody there questions the efficacy of the time-honored panacea, ginseng. Even Russian cosmonauts are supplied with it on their journeys into space. But in spite of a growing following in the West, the medical establishment has till recently ignored it, as it has a host of other herbal remedies. A cure that grows in the backyard is not going to increase anybody's dividends.

The attitude is changing. It has been, almost imperceptibly, for years. Perhaps the discovery of penicillin was a turning point, when it was seen that a simple mold could do more—incalculably more—than all the king's horses and all the king's men. It may be that science, somewhat chastened after its bumptious, self-confident adolescence, will turn again to the shamans and witch doctors, the herbalists and old wives and all the others who have refused to see a whole branch of learning die—and in doing so will find its own, and our, salvation.

145

PLANTS THAT HEAL AND KILL

ACONITE, *Aconitum napellus*

This central European plant, its deep blue flowers shaped—as one of its English names suggests—like a monk's hood, is a dangerous poison, and in spite of its medical uses it is not recommended for the amateur herbalist. The whole plant, above and below ground, contains the alkaloid aconitine. Acting on the central nervous system, this is used medicinally as a pain reliever. It is also effective in reducing fevers and in treating complaints of the respiratory tract. Tinctures can be applied externally for the relief of rheumatic and other pains.

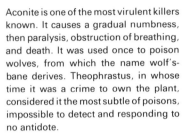

Aconite is one of the most virulent killers known. It causes a gradual numbness, then paralysis, obstruction of breathing, and death. It was used once to poison wolves, from which the name wolf's-bane derives. Theophrastus, in whose time it was a crime to own the plant, considered it the most subtle of poisons, impossible to detect and responding to no antidote.

BLACK HELLEBORE, *Helleborus niger*

The glycosides contained in all parts of this pretty plant are highly active and can have a dramatic effect on the rhythm of the heart and on the amount of blood circulating in the arteries. It can also be used as a diuretic or purge, but again under strict control. The supposed discoverer of its powers, the Greek prophet Melampus, used to prescribe the milk of goats which had eaten hellebore—on the grounds that the intermediate stage toned down its toxic qualities. In the past a decoction was applied as a poultice to children with lice. But even external application is very dangerous.

Solon, the Athenian lawgiver, is said to have poured quantities of hellebore into the water supply of a town his army was besieging, thus poisoning the inhabitants into surrender. The symptoms of hellebore poisoning are violent purging and palpitations, followed by delirium, and often death. Most victims nowadays are livestock.

FOXGLOVE, *Digitalis purpurea*

William Withering in 1775 noticed that local people used the foxglove as an antidote to dropsy—in other words as a powerful purge—but in such complicated mixtures that nobody knew any more which element was responsible for the cure. He was able after long investigations to single out the leaves of this tall and colorful plant. Brewed in regulated quantities, they acted on the kidneys to increase the flow of urine. But it was only later discovered that digitalis's effect is mainly on the heart, increasing its efficiency and reducing congestion in the veins; thus it is one of the most vital plant-based drugs.

Digitalis slows down the heartbeat, enabling each stroke to be fully effective in its pumping functions. But an overdose of the drug will slow the heart too much and finally stop it. Readily available in temperate countries, it has often been used by criminal poisoners. Accidents are rare, however, because of its bitter taste.

HENBANE, *Hyoscyamus niger*

The leaves of henbane usually contain more active alkaloids than other parts, but this can vary with the season (as it does with other plants), and at times the seeds and tubers can be very potent. Oil of henbane—an extract of the leaves—is used as an external balm for aches and pains in limbs. In the past a mixture containing the seeds has been made into cigarettes and smoked to relieve toothache. It has also been used to counteract spasms of the urinary tract. Its components and effects are similar to those of belladonna (below), though generally milder.

Pliny associated henbane with death, saying that it was used in funeral meals and scattered over tombs. A baby suckled at the breast of a woman who had consumed any henbane would be seized by violent convulsions. Nowadays the main danger seems to lie in the ease with which its roots can be confused with the edible ones of chicory or parsnip.

DEADLY NIGHTSHADE, *Atropa belladonna*

The *bella donna* of this plant's scientific name is one whose pupils have been dilated by a solution of the plant's juices. This is a traditional use for the plant in Spain. It also makes atropine (the responsible alkaloid), indispensable in eye surgery. Taken internally, this can accelerate the heartbeat, but its main use is in preventing spasms of the stomach and inhibiting the production of saliva and of mucus in the lungs. All these properties make it of value in the operating theater.

In modest quantities belladonna can induce hallucinations and deep sleep. It was used by the Scots under Macbeth to stupefy the Danes, with whom they were negotiating: the drugging was quickly followed by massacre. Children are sometimes attracted by its berries and have been killed by eating them.

STRYCHNINE TREE, *Strychnos nux-vomica*

This tree, which grows in India and Southeast Asia, produces berries whose seeds contain the alkaloids strychnine and brucine. In minute quantities, strychnine stimulates the nervous system. It has commonly been used as a tonic and as an ingredient of laxatives. In India and the Far East the seeds have been consumed for centuries—and with apparent immunity to their toxic effects—as a prophylactic against snakebites and cholera. Strychnine has no part in modern orthodox medicine, however.

Frequently used as a poison by criminals, strychnine can cause an extremely painful death, involving cramps, convulsions, and intense feelings of fear. It is still a primary method of destroying moles and other garden pests. Those using it as such should realize that the animal's death involves no less agony than a human's would.

THORN APPLE, *Datura stramonium*

The alkaloid daturine and others contained in the thorn apple cause symptoms similar to but milder than those brought about by belladonna. In the past the leaves and seeds of the plant were used to make emetic teas—on the same principle as that observed by people with hangovers, that a small dose of the drink that caused the hangover will drive the symptoms away. Thorn apple has also been employed as a decoction to be inhaled by those suffering from asthma. But the treatment can aggravate bronchitis, and it is seldom followed nowadays.

The plant is sometimes called Jamestown weed, or jimson weed, since it was found in such abundance in the area of that early American community. Its attractive berries were a lure for children and claimed many victims. Among its effects are delirium and hallucinations; it is one of the plants claimed to have inspired the Delphic oracle. Larger doses cause coma and death.

ERGOT, *Claviceps purpurea*

A fungus which grows as a parasite on rye and some other cereal crops, ergot can stimulate involuntary muscles in the human body, and it also interferes with the production and distribution of adrenaline. Consumed whole, its many alkaloids and other constituents can have unpredictable effects. But purified, extracted alkaloids have important medical uses. Ergometrine acts mainly on the muscles of the uterus, contracting them and so helping to prevent blood loss after childbirth. Ergotamine constricts small blood vessels in the head and counteracts migraine.

Ergot has claimed a high toll of victims, most of whom have eaten rye bread infected with the fungus. It causes hallucinations, convulsions, and mental derangement with no predictable pattern. Its ability to constrict blood vessels has also led to cases of gangrene. (See also pages 220–223.)

RAUWOLFIA, *Rauwolfia serpentina*

The root of this shrub, which grows commonly from India to Indonesia, contains several alkaloids, of which one, reserpine, has brought great benefits to local people for centuries. It is in fact one of nature's most effective tranquilizers, reducing blood pressure, slowing the heartbeat, and inducing a persistent calm in nervous or psychotic patients. Rediscovery of its virtues has led to a great increase in cultivation in recent years, for reserpine is in great demand in the West. Mental illness, high blood pressure, and insomnia have all responded well.

Congestion of the nose, lethargy, stomach disorders, and increase in weight are among the possible side effects of rauwolfia. Continued high doses lead to a variety of troublesome symptoms, including deep depressions. Its power to kill is more commonly evinced in suicide than in unsought death.

STROPHANTHUS, *Strophanthus hispidus*

Like several related species, this South African shrub contains the alkaloid strophanthine, which causes similar reactions in the heart to those brought about by digitalis. One of its disadvantages is that it cannot effectively be taken orally. The plant also contains cortisone, and the vast expense involved in collecting this from animal sources led to high hopes, a few years ago, that strophanthus would be a cheaper substitute. The quantities it contains, however, were shown to be too variable for commercial exploitation.

The poisonous properties of strophanthus have caused it to be used for centuries as an arrow poison, its toxic effects on birds and small mammals being quick and thorough. Seeds are steeped in water, and the resultant liquid is mixed with adhesive substances and applied to the points of weapons.

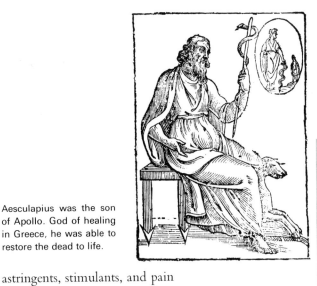

Aesculapius was the son of Apollo. God of healing in Greece, he was able to restore the dead to life.

Shadrafa *(above)* was credited by the Phoenicians with power over evil and disease. The Japanese Buddha *(above, right)* is shown holding a healing fruit in his hand.

In this Chinese painting *(below)* an old sage in the foreground hands a peach—symbol of longevity—to a child.

In 1963 archaeologists opened the grave of a Neanderthal man who had been buried in a cave near Shanidar in Iraq some sixty thousand years ago. Examination of the dust in which the bones lay indicated that he had been buried among flowers, and scholars were surprised to see such early manifestations of people's aesthetic sense. More than ten years later, analysis of the pollen of these flowers showed that almost all the plant species were of medicinal value. It seems almost certain that many thousands of years before the development of farming or any kind of civilization nomadic and primitive people had a considerable knowledge of plant medicine. The plants found in the Shanidar grave were diuretics, emetics, astringents, stimulants, and pain relievers; and they included ephedra, used more and more nowadays as a stimulant.

At this time and for long afterwards, knowledge of plants must have been almost synonymous with expertise in cures. Later on, when the religions of which we have records emerged, gods credited with healing powers always had strong associations with the vegetable kingdom. The cult of Aesculapius, the Greek god of healing, was symbolized by the image of a serpent; and the serpent, a symbol of renovation, was credited with the power of discovering healing plants as it

Called the father of medicine, Hippocrates lived and taught in Greece in the fifth century B.C.

An Assyrian priest holds a medicinal plant, possibly mandrake, in his hand.

Shen-Nung *(above),* emperor of China from 2838 to 2698 B.C., was supposed to have invented farming and begun the practice of herbalism.

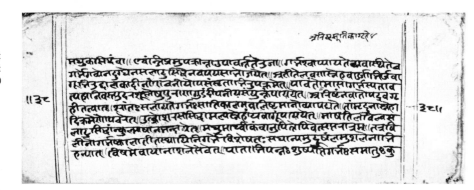

Tscharaka-samhita is the title of the first written medical document from India. It has been given a date as early as 1000 B.C.

sidled among the undergrowth. There were other aspects to ancient medicine: sympathetic, contagious, and imitative magic, the influence of rulers on their subjects' health, the influence of the dead, and the power of charms, amulets, and incantations. But the power of plants was central. It brought physicians close to rulers in prestige. Sometimes they became identical. Solomon was respected because he knew the plants

the unjustified hope of curing his very severe scrofula. And yet healing by plants was based in reality. When medical principles came to be written down—by the followers of Hippocrates and later Greek practitioners—a body of information about plants was recorded which, after much pruning and addition, remains relevant in the modern national pharmacopoeias, and even more so in less orthodox collections.

emperor Shen-Nung, is supposed to have predated Hippocrates by more than two thousand years, precepts and principles share enough ground with those of the West to suggest some common ancestry.

What all of them were striving for was some microcosmic formula that would explain the whole workings of the human body—or indeed of the universe. So arose the doctrine of the elements, by which all matter could

male, active, and light—and the further classification into *kyo* and *jitsu*, the constitutionally frail and the vitally active. In each of these systems, plant cures would be dictated by the predominant humor or principle of the patient. So plants themselves became subject to the same divisions.

This Egyptian relief from Echet-Aton dates from the fourteenth century B.C. and shows a queen holding a mandragora plant.

The oldest handwritten medical document comes from Sumer; it lay buried for four thousand years under the city ruins of Nippur.

Discovered in 1873 in Thebes, the Ebers papyrus contained the tenets of Egyptian medicine from the time of the pharaohs.

The Atharwa-Veda preserves the medical notions and treatments practiced in India after the invasions of the Aryans.

"from the cedar tree that is in Lebanon even unto the hyssop that springeth out of the wall." Witch doctors, shamans, and priests owed their standing to plants, and to the peculiar rites and beliefs associated with gathering and processing them. The obfuscations of ritual persisted, even in advanced societies, to recent times; Dr. Johnson, when a small boy, was taken to be touched by Queen Anne, in

What was true of the Greeks was true also of people in general, and particularly of that extended family known as the Indo-European. Many customs of the West, many prescriptions and individual plants and general medical doctrines too complicated to allow of spontaneous discovery, are shared by the Greek herbals and Eastern works like the Sanskrit Vedas. In China too, where the father of medicine, the

be explained as one of five basic substances, and the theory of the humors. People, according to this, were a combination of four disparate principles: blood, phlegm, choler, and melancholy. And the proportions of these humors within an individual determined his or her personality. The theory was paralleled in China by the division into *yin* and *yang*—the first being female, passive, and dark, the second

The search for unifying formulas went farther. Symptoms of human disease became linked with the outward forms of plants in the doctrine of signatures (see pages 152–153). And the belief arose that it was not beyond man to discover or concoct a plant that would cure all ailments by combining in itself all principles. Much ancient and medieval thought was given up to the search for a panacea.

By attaching a dog to the desired mandrake *(above)*, a m
could sacrifice the animal's life and save his own.

"Death," wrote Bacon, "is the cure of all diseases," but there have been many who looked for a less drastic panacea. One of the oldest human beliefs is that nature provides—if only we can find it—some substance that encapsulates all living principles and that has within its power the means to cure all ills. Panacea means literally a universal remedy, but it was also the name given to a daughter of Aesculapius, the Greek god of medicine. The search was for a divine element contained within a worldly substance. It was the motive that drove the long, vain lucubrations of the alchemists, though their concern was mainly with metals: the conversion of baser elements into gold, which supposedly contained godly powers.

Several plants and combinations of plants have for varying periods been credited with this supernatural power. Even today the idea is not entirely dead. The root of ginseng, for long highly regarded in the Orient, has recently swept over the West, accompanied by dramatic claims which many are all too eager to believe. The nineteenth century was the heyday for tinctures, lotions, cordials, and electuaries sold under labels that made the most extravagant claims for their powers—from improving the function of all bodily organs to a substantial prolonging of human life. Wanting to believe in them, people bought them up in vast quantities. When ingredients like laudanum or cannabis produced quick illusions of an

almost other-worldly well-being, the customer was more than satisfied. Time and sometimes addiction told him how hollow the claims had been.

From time to time snakeroot, or rauwolfia, has been elevated to the status of panacea in India. An eighteenth-century physician wrote that it was an antidote against all known poisons, it abated anxiety, fear, and pain, it

brought relief if applied externally, it allayed fever and vomiting when drunk in solution, and it improved the texture of skin and the clarity of eyes. (He also pointed out that the mongoose, when about to engage in combat with a venomous snake, eats some leaves of snakeroot to provide temporary immunity.)

Every country has its own examples. In England plants that flower on St. John's Day, June 24, are credited with unlimited healing powers derived from the saint himself. St. John's-wort itself is sometimes known as tutsan, a corrupted version of the French *toute saine*. All-heal is the common name for the plant *Valeria-*

A seventeenth-century woodcut *(left)* shows the first of the great herbalists, Dioscorides, receiving a mandrake plant from the goddess of discovery. No plant has ever acquired a more complicated body of lore to add to its undoubted healing and narcotic properties. Many of these legends spring from the shape of its roots, which sometimes suggest a human form. Growing the roots in molds, or sculpting them after they were picked, increased the likeness. By these means, too, male or female attributes could be added to the figures, and the differentiation undoubtedly added to the plant's reputation as an aphrodisiac. The woodcut *(above)* from the *Hortus Sanitatis* of 1498 shows a female root.

A saxon herbal shows the d
attached to the mandrake
succeeded in uprooting.

A sixteenth-century Chinese book on healing plants shows the ginseng plant *(above)*. Various representations of the mandrake root *(right)* show evidence of carving and bending into required shapes.

An uprooted mandrake *(above)* with a dead dog lying beside it. A male mandrake is depicted on the right.

With limited medical powers, and shaped like a female torso, the huge seeds of *Lodoicea maldivica* were credited with all kinds of magical capabilities.

na officinalis, and its medical attributes are endless. (Like rauwolfia, it has special appeal for an animal: cats are said to dig up its roots, roll on them, and gnaw them to pieces in an ecstasy of delight.) At other times and places mistletoe (which could ward off evil spirits as well as more material threats), yarrow, woundwort, and sage have been exalted to panacea status. Even

over all other plants, and the writer of a twelfth-century bestiary noted that it could "cure every infirmity except death." Above all it was an aphrodisiac, but the enjoyment of its pleasures was accompanied by grave risks. For the root of the mandrake was supposed from its shape to be a hominoid imp which, when pulled from the ground, uttered a shriek that

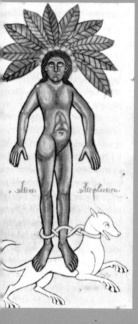

A thirteenth-century illustration from the Bodleian Library, Oxford, shows the same dog-mandrake theme.

Two lifelike mandrakes from an ancient manuscript preserved in the National Library at Naples.

In this mandrake drawing blossoms and fruits are added to the usual leaves topping the root.

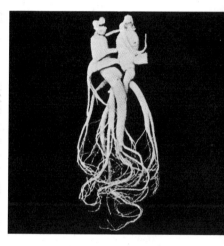

Ginseng roots, also regarded as a panacea, assume forms not unlike those of mandrake.

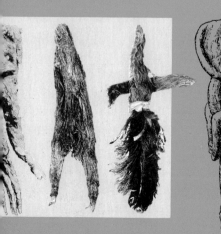

tea held the stage for a short time, but the lofty claims made for it in the seventeenth century probably owed more to advertising skills in its promoters than to the intrinsic virtues of the leaf. Perhaps no plant has been more widely praised than the mandrake. The curious story of Leah, Rachel, and Reuben in the Book of Genesis makes it a cure for barrenness. In Assyria it was held to ward off plague. It could induce sleep, relief from pain, hair on a bald head. The Abbess Hildegard accorded it dominion

would bring madness or death to whoever heard it. Theophrastus suggested one way of avoiding this fate, involving a complicated ritual of anointment, drawing magic circles, and facing west during the main tug. More common was to secure the plant to a dog by means of string, and leave the animal to haul it out. In spite of the dangers, mandrake was in hearty demand well beyond the Middle Ages, and several root substitutes were sold by dishonest apothecaries who could not procure the real thing.

151

It is not impossible, with a generous use of the imagination, to see a resemblance between blood and the juice of the pomegranate, or between the shape of the heart and that of the leaf of wood sorrel, or between the color and form of the leaves of hepatica and those of a human liver. Into such likenesses the medieval mind, intent on discovering the unifying principles of the whole of nature, delighted in reading profound significance. The belief gained ground that in creating the plants God had marked on each one a clue to

its medical properties. Thus, the pomegranate was good for blood diseases, the wood sorrel would relieve heart trouble, and hepatica could be relied on to cure all liver ailments. The theory had its enemies, but it was supported by many writers all over Europe. As late as the seventennth century, the English herbalist William Turner could claim that "God

hath imprinted upon the Plants, Herbs, and Flowers, as it were in Hieroglyphicks, the very signature of their Vertues." Even John Ray, whose work established him as one of the pioneers of modern scientific botany, could not entirely dismiss this doctrine of signatures. "I will not deny," he wrote, "but that the noxious and malignant plants do, many of them, discover something of their nature by the sad and melancholic visage of their leaves, flowers, or fruits." He added that a further dispensation of Providence was that wherever a disease was endemic there could be found a cure for it among the native plants. God, it would seem, had made human life rather like a parlor game, and

added to the enjoyment by a liberal sprinkling of clues.

The proponents of the theory were ingenious to the point of obscurity. No part of the body was without its corresponding herb. The long necks of Canter-

As well as the close ties between parts of the body and plants, medieval pharmacists often considered the influence of the heavenly bodies on both. These could sometimes be ascertained by the shape of the leaf. The horse-shoe plant *(far left)* comes under the moon's influence. The human body *(left)* is shown with its zodiacal correspondences. Sea fennel *(above)* derives its powers from Mercury's influence.

bury bells made them suitable for diseases of the throat. The silky threads of the maidenhair fern made the plant an ideal antidote to baldness. Anything wrong with the head could be put right by walnuts. For, according to William Cole, "Wall-nuts have the perfect signature of the head: the outer husk or green covering, repre-

While some plants healed diseases of those body parts which they resembled, others were supposed to cure bites and stings of animals which seemed to be mimicked by their leaves or stems. So the bite of the scorpion, according to the faulty logic of Giambattista della Porta, was neutralized by heliotrope, cumin, or Scorpiura (right).

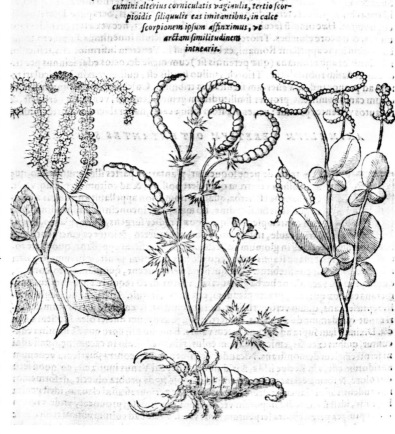

sent the *Pericranium,* or outward skin of the skull, whereon the hair groweth, and therefore salt made of those husks or barks, are exceeding good for wounds of the head. The inner wooddy shell hath the signature of the skull, and the little yellow skin, or peel, that covereth the kernell of the hard *Meninga* and *Pia-mater,* which are the thin scarfes that envelope the brain. The kernel hath the very figure of the brain, and therefore it is very profitable for the brain, and resists poysons....''

Hound's-tongue leaves (1) were variously reported as cures for illnesses in dogs or as antidotes against dog bites. The arrangement of seeds in the pod of the *Malus punicus* (2) sufficiently resembled human teeth to be prescribed for toothache. Chamomile (3) was one of many among the daisy family whose round flowers suggested to della Porta a remedy for eye diseases. Various roots and leaves were taken by their hairy texture to be cures for baldness; in the martagon lily (4), it was the stamens.

to work cures, but those which looked like the causes of distress—scorpions and poisonous snakes, for instance—were also claimed to do so. Moreover, it was clear that God had not been thorough in applying the scheme. Herbs of undoubted medicinal qualities sometimes could not be compared, by any stretch of the imagination, with the limbs or organs they could heal. The herbalists were well up to such objections. In His infinite wisdom, one of them explained, God had left these blanks in the puzzle in order to exercise people's skill in matching them. Another thought God's concern was conservationist: there would be such a run on some plants if their properties were indicated by signatures, that there would soon be none left.

The doctrine of signatures eventually died. It is a backwater in the history of medicine. But it left behind some curious and lively testimonies to the determination of men to find meaning and system in their environment.

Sometimes the links were tenuous. The spathe and spadix of the cuckoo-pint, which elsewhere have been likened to a phallus or to the head of a nobleman within a ruff, were said to represent a baby in its cradle. So mothers were advised to place the plant beside their infant offspring for protection. Long-lived perennials were said to add years to the lives of those who consumed them. And the saxifrage, noted for its ability to penetrate and crack rocks with its tenacious roots, was prescribed for those suffering from kidney or bladder stones. The little oil glands on the leaves of St. John's-wort, which when held up to the light look like holes, made the plant suitable for those who had suistained cuts or wounds which pierced the skin.

The most active advocates of the theory had to admit that it had its drawbacks. The logic of many examples was evidently faulty, for not only were plants which resembled body parts supposed

Cafia folutiua cornicula affert nigra, intorta, & quodammodo rugofa , vt caprarum cornibus non parum conueniant : propinatur ægris cum caprino fero , propter fimiles proprietates,& renes à calculo expurgat. Confimilis facultatis filiqua priori congener, quum nigras & falcatasferat filiquas. Anagyris fimili modo contortas habet filiquas: fi partus mortuus hæret, & fecundæ morentur , d ficulter parturientibus adalligantur, ita vt à partu ftatim auferantur : quod quidem capræ fecunda efficit ex Plinio. Hedy fa-

Della Porta's passion for visual association caused him to invest almost all the larger plants with sympathetic connections. He studiously classified these various connections according to disease, animal, planet, or parts of the body. Here he has collected plants in which there are suggestions of the horns of stag, bull, unicorn, and ram.

As human knowledge increases, the ability of any individual to grasp more than a fraction of it becomes less. A good scholar of the seventeenth century might easily have read all the books ever published in his own language, and a great many in others. Today, the output of, say, the English presses in one week would be more than anyone could—not to say would want to—read in a lifetime. The modern botanist might devote years to the study of one species, or to some tiny internal process or structure of plants, while on a walk in the country he or she might be hard put to give a name

Dioscorides was a physician of the first century A.D. whose writings on medical plants strongly influenced medieval herbalists.

to more than a handful of wild flowers. What is true for the botanist applies eqully to the modern medical researcher. A hundred years ago, however, each would have had a more comprehensive command of the general subject, though he would

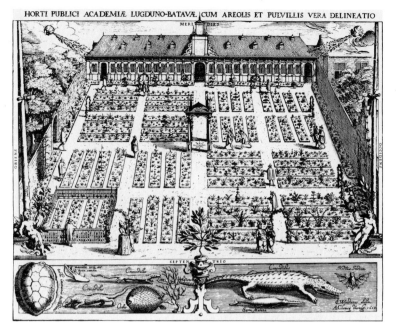

HORTI PUBLICI ACADEMIÆ LUGDUNO-BATAVÆ CUM AREOLIS ET PULVILLIS VERA DELINEATIO

The botanic garden at Leyden *(left)* as it was in 1610.

forfeit the specialist knowledge he can boast now. Two hundred years ago he would certainly have added to his accomplishments in botany or medicine a useful acquaintance with Latin, Greek, art, philosophy, literature, and music. A century farther back, the distinctions themselves would begin to blur. People in the Renaissance straddled all known disciplines. Classifications we recognize today did not exist. In particular, botany was medicine, and medicine botany. It was impossible to heal by profession without a knowledge of plants; and the desire to study plants for their own sake was

the characteristics of known plants. Their success and fame was in large part due to the fifteenth-century invention and spread of printing. The medium of the printed word had awakened a new appetite for knowledge throughout the civilized world, a demand that was generously fed by the rediscovery of classical learning and attitudes.

the work of medieval Arab writers to the Greeks themselves.
At the source of this tradition stands the almost legendary figure of Hippocrates, a Greek born in 460 B.C. who lived, some say, for over a hundred years. The works attributed to him make mention of hundreds of plants, with their healing properties. Aristotle and his follower

expanded on the findings of his predecessors with far more scientific caution than his fanciful contemporary Pliny. Hundreds of copies of Dioscorides survive from late classical times. The work of Galen in the next century, though important in the history of medicine, was, with respect to plants, little more than a rehash of Dioscorides.
After the barbarian invasions and breakup of the old Roman Empire, the pivot of civilization moved east. A succession of Arab physicians—including Razis, Albucasis, and Avicenna (to use their Westernized names)—fostered the works of the Greeks,

A physician, probably the Arab Ibn Botlan, known as Albucasis.

Half genius, half charlatan—the Swiss physician Paracelsus (1493–1541).

Hieronymus Bock, known as Tragus (1498–1554), one of the first great herbalists.

The Italian Pietro Andrea Mattioli (1501–1577), author of the *Commentaries.*

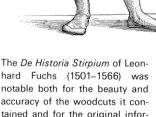

born from the study of their medicinal powers.
The most remarkable scholars in this hybrid field were the herbalists, men whose researches out of doors and in libraries enabled them to compile massive, and often beautiful, tomes listing all

For a thousand years and more the written achievement of Greeks and Romans had been safely preserved in the monasteries and in the universities of the Arabs. So it is not surprising that the traditions of the herbalists can be traced back through

Theophrastus extended the knowledge of the variety, structure, and uses of plants. But the work that most influenced the Renaissance herbalists was that of Dioscorides, a physician of Cilicia, who lived in the first century A.D. He collected and

The *De Historia Stirpium* of Leonhard Fuchs (1501–1566) was notable both for the beauty and accuracy of the woodcuts it contained and for the original information discovered by the author.

spread them round the Mediterranean with the conquests of the Saracens, and added their own discoveries and inventions—notably that of distilling—to the sum of botanical knowledge.

Even in the West the great medical schools of the Middle Ages owed their distinction to Arabs and to Arabic scholarship. Yet throughout all these centuries, observation and empirical techniques were in short supply. When Europe breathed the fresh air of the Renaissance after the stifling dogmatism of the Middle Ages, it was once again to Dioscorides that she turned. The first productions of the golden age of

herbals were little more than translations or adaptations of the work of that seminal figure.

Some of the greatest names among herbalists owe their fame more to their predecessors—and their artists—than to their own researches. Otto Brunfels picked from the writings of classical and medieval authors, and from those of his Italian contemporaries. He scarcely deserves the title some of his countrymen have given him—one of the founders of modern botany. But he was discriminating enough to choose the painter Hans Weiditz to illustrate his herbal, the *Herbarum Vivae Eicones*, and "living

Marco Polo *(left)* was the earliest European traveler to bring back information about plants from the Orient. The influx of exotic herbs—many of them medicinal—after the opening of the world's sea routes before and after 1500 stimulated the work of many of the great herbalists.

testantism of Luther. Bock's work is suffused with piety. He begins his herbal: "Having read

everythin there is to read [a modest enough claim at the time], I see clearly that the Almighty God and Creator is and always will be the foremost gardener, cultivator, and planter." He makes God, Adam, Cain, and Abel the first botanists, and acknowledges his debt

Above, from left to right:
Jacques D'Aléchamps (1513–1588) collected plants in the neighborhood of Lyon and published a description of over a thousand in his *Historia Generalis Plantarum*. Konrad Gesner (1515–1565) was the first to classify plants under their different methods of propagation. Rembert Dodoens (1517–1585), known as Dodocus, published his herbal *Cruydeboeck* in his native Flemish in 1554.

portraits" is what Weiditz, a friend of Dürer, made of his subjects. He painted nature as he saw it, with its blemishes as well as its glories, and his woodcuts represent one of the high peaks of that craft.

Like Brunfels, Hieronymus Bock and Leonhard Fuchs were natives of south Germany and early converts to the defiant pro-

COCOXOCHITL   GENGIOVO.   DATVRA.

Examples of plants described and illustrated by sixteenth-century explorers *(right)* include the first depiction of a dahlia from Mexico, by F. Hernandez, and two illustrations by C. Acosta—a ginger plant in flower and the narcotic thorn apple.

to them, as he does with more justification to the Greeks.

Bock's editor had, nevertheless, unashamedly made copies from the illustrations of Fuchs's works, as the latter had from Brunfels. There was in fact a certain anarchy in this period, most works being full of plagiarism,

An example of the contribution to European medicine of South American discoveries is seen in the Badianus manuscript *(left)*, a herbal compiled by two Mexican physicians at Santa Cruz in 1552. It describes healing plants used by the Aztecs.

inaccuracy, old myth, and the unsubstantiated claims of contemporaries. In particular, both classical and contemporary plants would get wrong names, for minds were not trained to the classification by genus and species current today. (The first attempts to classify—by Bauhin and others—are the real roots of modern botany.) To add to the confusion, this was the great age of discoveries. Specimens and drawings were arriving in Europe constantly from America, the Levant, and the Far East.

There were moreover the grotesque theories of men like Paracelsus to waylay the infant science. The doctrine of signatures, theories of planetary influence, and conventional magic and superstition were reflected in herbal works for more than a century after these first compilations.

They appear in the work of Mattioli, an extravagant Italian, and ambitious scholar whose tireless bragging won him a 30,000-copy edition of his commentary on Dioscorides as well as appointments as physician at several

fed the imagination too, dramatizing mundane objects with hidden powers. Finally, presumably, they affected the health of Europe, though perhaps not as much as their endless attributions of healing qualities to an ever-increasing number of plants would suggest.

Later in the sixteenth century a new generation of herbalists appeared. Some of their lives read like picaresque novels, for Europe was in the grip of the Counter-Reformation, and Flanders, then a center of learning, was subject to the periodic brutalities of the Catholic Spanish. Nevertheless, men like Dodoens

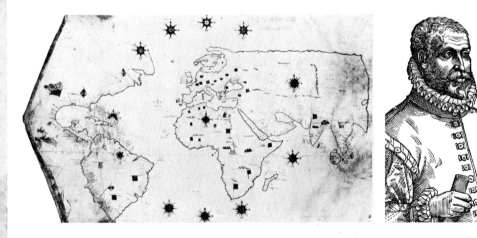

More than anything else, plants lured Europeans to explore the world, and so stimulated the development of cartography. Girolamo da Verrazzano drew the first moderately realistic world map *(above)* in 1529.

A detail of Verrazzano's map shows an angel, placed beside the Caribbean Sea, holding a plant; this symbolized the herbal treasures awaiting travelers to the Americas.

European courts. Educated Europe was avid for these publications. They were attractive in themselves and they strongly influenced the Renaissance garden, particularly the herbal gardens, which acted as private dispensaries—aromatic, perpetually offering blooms, and laid out with paths and box hedges dividing the orderly beds. The books

Above, from left to right:
Charles de l'Écluse (1526–1609), or Clusius, described plants he had seen on travels from the Pyrenees to the Carpathians. Joachim Camerarius (1543–1598) founded a botanical garden at Nuremberg, and published a distinguished herbal in 1590. The Flemish botanist Mathias de l'Obel, or Lobelius (1538–1616), practiced as a physician at Delft and in England, and compiled an important herbal.

Right: Two masterpieces of plant representation from the herbals: a pasque-flower drawn by Hans Weiditz (whose work has been mistaken for that of Dürer) for the herbal of Otto Brunfels, and a depiction of a *Canna indica* for the *Hortus Eystettensis* of Basilius Besler, 1613.

(whose material was beautifully illustrated by the inventive Plantin press at Antwerp), L'Obel, and l'Écluse forged ahead with their work, traveling to find new species or to avoid persecution, studying or teaching at the great universities of France, Flanders, Switzerland, and Germany, meeting and exchanging information, and sometimes losing all their possessions at the hands of a religiously motivated army.

Of these three, L'Écluse was the most progressive. Sunflower, convolvulus, cocoa, potato, tomato, zinnia, dahlia, and hundreds of other new plants were swelling the lists of known spe-duced plants to Europe which had not been known, at least for centuries. The fritillary plants he brought back from Constantinople created a fashion in the gardens of Germany. And he reintroduced some species of *Ranunculus,* unknown since Roman times. Losing and gaining fortunes, indefatigably traveling, losing relatives in religious purges, patronized by aristocrats in various countries of Europe, a master of seven languages, and finally professor at the University of Leyden, L'Écluse epitomized the sensitive and rumbustious poles of the Renaissance individual.

Pierre Quethe (born 1519).

Andrea Cesalpino (1519–1603) advanced the classification of plants.

Caspard Bauhin (1560–1626) invented the binomial classification.

John Parkinson (1567–1660), an apothecary, wrote the *Paradisus Terrestris.*

Nicholas Culpeper (16 1664) wrote a still popular bal.

cies, and a reliable system of classification was becoming urgent. L'Écluse failed to find the criteria of a lasting system, basing his divisions on external characteristics; but in this he was at least more perceptive than those who had gone before. He also intro-

Mathias de l'Obel, or Lobelius—all these plant collectors continued the tradition of the schoolmen in Latinizing their names for professional purposes—was another who suffered from the ructions in the Low Countries, but he collected and described quantities of plants in what is now Belgium. He also classified ten varieties of rose. Politics drove him to England, where he spent the later years of his life, becoming royal botanist at the court of James I. England had had its full complement of her-balists, whose language and conceits remain alive and evocative to the present day, but they had plagiarized without shame and added only notes on their own observations to the findings of others. The cleric William Turner, during a lifetime which

Canna Indica rubra.

being most fit for English bodies." That was in 1649. As even the title shows, Culpeper had lost little of the superstitions and illusions of the past. But change was imminent.

Botany and medicine were heading for a divorce. Each one was too extensive to allow men time to study the other in any profound sense. With Linnaeus the breach is complete. All the same, men have continued to study plants in order to find antidotes to disease. True, from now on they limited their attention to smaller horizons, like William Withering, who spent years matching digitalis extracted

on Linné, or Linnae-
07–1778), founder of
n botany.

Albrecht von Haller (1708–1777) of Bern, botanist and physiologist.

William Withering (1741–1779) revealed the value of digitalis.

Samuel Hahnemann (1755–1843) was the originator of homeopathy.

Friedrich Sertürner (1783–1841) isolated morphine from opium.

spanned most of the religious *volte-faces* of the Tudors, produced first a short work listing "The names of Herbes in Greke, Latin, Englishe, Duche and French wyth the commune names that Herbaries and Apotecaries use," and later a herbal

which earned him the label of father of English botany. John Gerard, Nicholas Culpeper, and John Parkinson produced works which made much use of their Continental models, but displayed an ebullience of style and thought which has helped them

survive. Culpeper described 369 medicinal herbs in what he called a "Compleat Method of Physick whereby a man may preserve his body in health; or cure himself being sick, for threepence charge, with such things onely as grow in England, they

from foxglove to certain disorders in the human body, or Fleming, who found something akin to a panacea in the fungal penicillin. But the period during which the study of plants united all the major branches of learning was by necessity short.

Whether techniques arise to suit the needs of great art or great art follows the independent invention of these techniques is an unsolved argument. Certainly the distinction of many of the earlier, and best, herbals lies in their use of the woodcut. And the woodcut, though examples of crude engraving—even on metal—exist from earlier times, was essentially an invention of the fifteenth century. It made possible the finesse with which many of the earliest examples of printing were illustrated. Not least, it endowed the herbals with high artistic quality, bringing to thousands of homes a technical excellence which has seldom been surpassed in the whole record of best sellers. Enormous skill was needed by the artists who prepared woodcuts. A black-line picture, either original or copied from a painting or drawing, was penned onto the flat wood. Then the wood on either side of all the lines was cut away, leaving only the lines themselves exposed to the inked roller of the press. (The use of gouges as well as knives to produce the *white*-line engravings of such masters as Bewick was a much later invention.) In the execution of simple drawings and outlines this process was not a greatly demanding one. But when it was applied to the detailed and sensitive creations of a Renaissance master, to lifelike curves and swathes and lines of varying thickness, it called for supreme artistry.

The pasqueflower shown on

page 158, executed by Hans Weiditz for the herbal of Otto Brunfels, shows an example of this technique which has never been surpassed. The flagging leaves and the slight droop of the petals on the left seem to invite the spectator to water the page in order to revive the plant. In another illustration Weiditz depicts the teasel. His choice of specimen here was a far more forlorn example than the pasque-flower. The leaves hang limply, and one of the stems is broken off. It is just such a teasel as one might see after drought and parasites have done their worst. Yet Weiditz, in reproducing what he saw in minute particular, with a minimum use of imagination, evinces a more emotional response than his contemporary Albrecht Meyer, whose drawings illustrated the herbal of Leonhard Fuchs. Meyer's teasel decorates this page. It is a proud, upright, almost idealized example of the species. It indicates a genius which has more appeal to the pure botanist, for as one of them—Agnes Arber—has written: "The drawing which is ideal from the standpoint of systematic botany avoids the accidental peculiarities of any individual specimen, seeking rather to portray the characters fully typical for the species." Nevertheless, Meyer's creations are less involving. One does not, as with Weiditz, feel the weather or the season in which the plant is growing. For even in this early period of plant illustration two tradi-

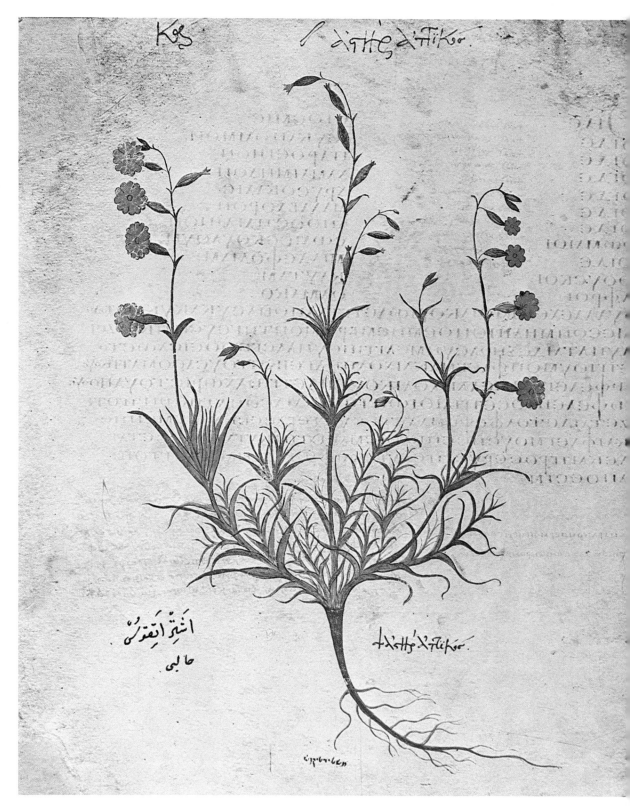

tions are being born: pure, clean, instructive botanical art, and a more sensual, involving style, in which the individual is given prominence over the species.

There was no such distinction in the work of earlier generations. The Renaissance seems in some respects to have come at the end of a thousand years of blindness. It is often hard enough to identify the plants drawn in medieval manuscripts without trying to allocate them to a style or grade their sensitivities. But we can only see these matters in retrospect, and after five hundred years of post-Renaissance progress. The anatomical sketches of a master artist—Leonardo, say, or Michelangelo or Stubbs—indi-

cate what has now become a commonplace: that to depict a living thing accurately one must understand both its internal and external workings. In the Middle Ages this principle was unknown. Probably nobody wanted to know it. It would have been an intrusion into the province of God to dissect and analyze his creatures. Furthermore, it is nowadays becoming

increasingly clear that many of the biological discoveries of the future will be made in objects that commonly surround us. Less is known about the housefly than the duck-billed platypus, about daisies than exotic orchids. If familiarity does not breed contempt, it can muffle the desire for objective observation. It took exploration and discovery to waken the appetite for precise knowledge and portrayal. While Europe remained locked away from other continents, people looked inward if they looked at all. Symbol, image, and allegory flourished at the expense of physical reality. Reflecting this attitude, the earliest herbals are decorated not by pictures of plants,

but by stylized, patterned interpretations of them. Taken on their own terms, they are objects of enchanting beauty.

Equally removed from reality were the descriptions which often accompanied these drawings. Without even the slightest regard for the differences between fact and fiction, the compilations of the Middle Ages transmitted a body of lore, superstition, legend, magic, and moral tales from the ancient world to that of the Renaissance. In the process it added or adapted material of its own, especially in giving a Christian significance to the accounts of the heathen. So the vervain shown on this page (from the

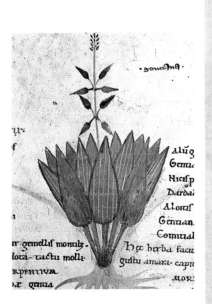

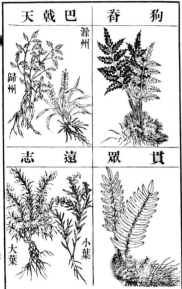

A thirteenth-century English illuminated manuscript *(above)* shows the snake-repelling powers of vervain.

Illustration of the herb dill *(below left)* from the Bodleian herbal of 1100. Plant *(below)* from a fifteenth-century Persian manuscript in the Topkapi Museum, Istanbul.

Overleaf: Plant illustrations from the Viennese manuscript known as the *Wiener Dioskurides.* On the left, wild teasel, whose roots are credited by the author with power against ulcers and warts. On the right, dog's mercury; a decoction of leaves of the male plant favors conception of a boy, those of the female plant a girl.

A fifteenth-century Italian miniature *(below)* illustrates the legend that Charlemagne was shown a thistle which would halt the spread of plague.

thirteenth century, a period in which strictly botanical art reached its nadir) has beside it a cameo of a man killing a snake. The author is not so much concerned with its vermifuge properties as with its power of repelling that allegorical serpent, the devil; and the picture of the carline thistle *(above)* illustrates the legend that Charlemagne's troops were stricken with plague during one campaign. An angel appeared to the emperor and told him that the plant on which his next arrow alighted would halt the disease's progress. And so, of course, it came to pass.

† Τῶν ἀκανθῶν τῶν καυλοῦ δὲ
ἐς αὐτ τηλὸν, ἀγαθω σ̣εῖς·
καὶ φύλλ̣α μᾷ ἐπ̣ε̣ῖ δεῖλια̣ω̣ς. Κατὰ̣ Ραχον Ι̣ο̣π̣ύ
ὅτ πομ κ̣η̣ ἀ καν̣θα̣ δ̣ι̣ω̣· καὶ ὁ ζ̣ρχε̣ ὁ π̣ι̣ λ̣ω̣ι̣ω̣
τῆς ρα̣ λ̣ε̣ω̣ς· ἑ̣ο̣τ ιπ̣α Ἀκανθω δὲ Ταῖς φ̣ύ̣λ̣ν̣σ̣
ἀπο φύ̣ς̣ δα λ̣α̣ π̣ι̣ τ̣ο̣ν̣ ὅμ̣ βρ̣ω̣ν̣ κα̣ εἶ τ̣οὐ δ̣ ῥ̣ό̣ς̣ω̣
φ̣ύ̣λ̣α̣ τ̣ῆ̣ς̣ρ̣ε̣ τ̣ι̣ τ̣ο̣δ̣λ̣α̣· ὅ̣ λ̣κ̣ καὶ Τὸ ὄ̣ν̣ο̣μ̣α̣ ἔ̣τ̣
κ̣ι̣ολι· ὁ Ἀ̣π̣ὸ̣ κ̣ δὲ τοῦς καυλ̣ κατὰ Ἴκα̣ο̣̣̣ε̣ν̣
α̣ἱ̣ π̣ρ̣ο φύ̣σ̣ι̣· Κε φα λὴ, μ̣ια, ἐσ̣ικε̣ι̣α, ἑ̣ ῆ̣μ̣ε̣ς̣
ζ̣ω̣ο̣μ̣η̣κ̣ο̣ δ̣ ἀ̣κ̣α̣ν̣θ̣ω̣ δ̣λ̣· ξηρ̣δ̣ν̣ θ̣ύ̣ο̣υ̣σ̣δ̣ε̣·
λ̣ά̣κ̣η̣· ἑ̣ ρα̣ δ̣ὲ̣ Καὶ ὁ̣κ̣ λ̣η̣κ̣ι̣α̣, κ̣ η̣μ̣α̣ τ̣ο̣π̣ρ̣
τ̣η̣ν̣ σ̣τ̣ε̣ε̣ω̣ρ̣ι̣ω̣· Ἱ̣ ε̣ἶ̣τ̣α̣ δ̣ὲ̣ τ̣α̣ύ̣τ̣η̣ς̣ ὅ̣ν̣
ο̣ἶ̣μ̣α̣ σ̣φ̣ε̣ τ̣η̣ε̣ ι̣σ̣α̣ κ̣α̣ὶ̣ Κ̣ο̣ π̣η̣σ̣α̣, Κ̣ω̣
ρ̣ω̣τ̣ῆ̣ς̣ λ̣α̣β̣ο̣ῦ̣σ̣α̣ π̣α̣ι̣ ρ̣ο̣σ̣ Τ̣α̣τ̣ τ̣ι̣ δ̣λ̣κ̣
τ̣υ̣λ̣ι̣ω̣ρ̣α̣ δ̣α̣ι̣λ̣α̣ω̣· Κ̣α̣ι̣ ο̣υ̣ ρ̣ι̣τ̣α̣σ̣, ε̣ἱ̣
τ̣ι̣ ο̣δ̣υ̣τ̣ε̣ω̣· Κ̣α̣ι̣ ὅ̣τ̣ι̣ τ̣ι̣ θ̣ρ̣α̣τ̣η̣, δ̣δ̣ς̣
π̣α̣λ̣· α̣π̣ο̣τ̣ι̣ θ̣ε̣α̣δ̣ δ̣ ρ̣ε̣λ̣ι̣, τ̣ς̣
λ̣α̣λ̣κ̣ η̣υ̣ π̣υ̣ξ̣ι̣ο̣ς̣ τ̣ο̣ φ̣ μ̣α̣κ̣
φ̣α̣σ̣ι̣δ̣ε̣· μ̣ι̣ῆ̣ρ̣μ̣ι̣κ̣ι̣ω̣ν̣ Κ̣α̣ι̣ λ̣
Κ̣ρ̣α̣χ̣ο̣ρ̣δ̣ο̣σ̣α̣ν̣ α̣ὐ̣τ̣ο̣, δ̣ρ̣λ̣ι̣μ̣α̣ς̣ ῆ̣ν̣ε̣ε̣
ο̣ι̣σ̣ε̣ ν̣ τ̣ι̣ Κ̣ε̣φ̣α̣λ̣η̣ ο̣κ̣ω̣ λ̣η̣κ̣ο̣θ̣,
δ̣ἐ̣ς̣ ο̣κ̣υ̣τ̣ι̣σ̣η̣ σ̣υ̣ δ̣ε̣χ̣ο̣μ̣ν̣ι̣· Κ̣α̣ι̣
π̣ε̣ε̣ ι̣α̣π̣τ̣ο̣μ̣β̣ν̣ο̣ι̣δ̣α̣μ̣λ̣α̣, ι̣ε̣σ̣
β̣ε̣α̣ γ̣ο̣π̣ι̣, ι̣σ̣ο̣ρ̣ο̣ῦ̣ν̣τ̣ε̣ Τ̣ε̣τ̣α̣ρ̣τ̣α̣τ̣ι̣ς̣
ἡ̣ ζ̣α̣π̣δ̣ά̣ν̣ †

ΛΙΝΟΖΩϹΤΙϹ ΘΗΛΕΙΑ
ΛΙΝΟΖΩϹΤΙϹ ΑΡΡΗΝ
ΟΙ ΔΕ ΘΗΛΥΓΟΝΟΝ
ΟΙ ΔΕ ΠΑΡΘΕΝΙΟΝ
ΟΙ ΔΕ ΕΡΜΟΥ ΒΟΤΑΝΗ
ΟΙ ΔΕ ΑΡΓΙΟΝ
ΟΙ ΔΕ ΧΡΥϹΙΤΙϹ
ΑΙΓΥΠΤΙΟΙ ΑΜΟΦΩ
ΡΩΜΑΙΟΙ ΕΡΒΑ ΜΕΡΚΟΥΡΙΑΛΙϹ
ΟΙ ΔΕ ΜΕΡΚΟΥΡΙΑΛΙϹ ΦΗΜΙΝΑ
ΑΦΡΟΙ ΛΕΟΥΜΕϹ

The sixteenth century saw the full effect of Renaissance attitudes on the depiction of plants. Leonardo's pen drawing of 1505–1506, from the Windsor collection, brings great restraint and accuracy to the portrayal of two species of anemone.

"Behold how much it exceedeth to use medicine of efficacy natural by god ordained than wicked words or charms of efficacy unnatural by the devil invented." The words are those of Laurence Andrew, translator of Jerome of Brunswick's *Book of Distillation* in 1527. They show the new spirit of skepticism which was to grow from now on among the writers on botany. Just as the Protestants of the period viewed with distaste and disbelief the agglomeration of myth and fancy which had over the centuries obscured the central tenets of Christianity, so herbalists like Bauhin, Dodoens, Turner, and Bock—most of them also Protestants—rejected the

gullibility of their predecessors. Nature needed no gilding.

From the medical point of view, this change of attitude was overdue. Other branches of medicine were taking huge leaps forward. This was the period during which Leonardo, Michelangelo, Raphael, and Dürer were using the scalpel to ascertain the internal structure of the human body. Leonardo in particular was able, even at this early stage, to demonstrate the ventricles of the

brain, or the uterus containing the fetus and its membranes. Vesalius was advancing the science of anatomy at a faster rate than anyone before or since. One of the herbalists, Andrea Cesalpino, was himself an anatomist of repute; and it has been claimed that his observations on the heart and circulation of the blood anticipated the more widely known discoveries of William Harvey.

But herbalism could not easily

An illustration from the *Neu Kreuterbuch* by Hiernonymus Bock, first published in 1546.

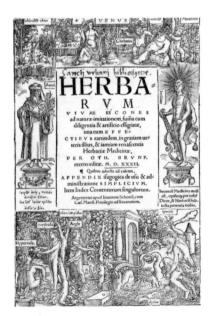

The frontispiece of the *Herbarum* by Otto Brunfels, published after 1530.

Sonnaw oder vnser Frawen mantel.

Hans Weiditz was the artist responsible for this and other drawings in the herbal of Otto Brunfels.

166

A watercolor *(left)* by Hans Weiditz of viper's bugloss, *Echium vulgare*. Watercolors like this served as models for the woodcuts used in Brunfels's herbal.

A watercolor *(left)* of the valerian, *Valeriana rubia,* by Jacob Ligozzi (1547–1626), designed for Ulisse Aldrovandi's *Istoria Naturale.*

Albrecht Dürer's study of the columbine, *Aquilegia vulgaris (below),* in a natural setting of grass, dated 1526.

throw aside the tales it had accumulated over two thousand and more years. It was to be a long time before science could test the efficacy of different plants by reference to the chemicals their parts contained. In the minds of most people superstition died hard. Both these factors assured the preservation of beliefs which would have been better smothered. Even an astute and straight-cut writer like Turner could reproduce a fair amount of nonsense, as when he instructed that, when somebody had taken an overdose of opium, "if the pacient be too much slepi put stynkynge thynges unto hys nose to waken hym therewith." No amount of experience could per-

suade herbalists that the mandrake root was not a perfect anesthetic, and Dodoens was simply repeating what all his fellows said when he claimed

A woodcut of the cotton plant, *Gossypium herbaceum,* from the Czech edition of 1562 of Mattiolus's herbal.

One of the fifteen hundred or so illustrations *(below)* left unpublished at his death by Konrad Gesner.

The first printed illustration of tobacco *(below)* to appear in an English book— the "Joyful Newes out of the newe

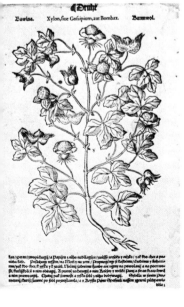

founde Worlde" by Nicolas Monardes, published in 1570.

that "the wine in which the root of mandrake has been steeped or boiled causes sleep and assuages all pain, for which reason men give it to those they intend to cut, saw, or burn, in any part of their bodies, because they shall feel no pain." Any surgeon of the time with experience of incisions, amputations, or cauterizing would have been able to correct this belief. But it continued well into the seventeenth century.

The illustrators of the herbals were ill served by such utterances. It is true that the art of the woodcut declined during the lat-

167

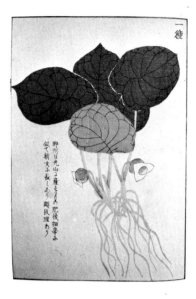

Japanese text in tategaki on the illustration:

Illustration of the Japanese *Asarum* or *Asarabica (left),* a plant with many medicinal properties contained in its roots, taken from one of the rare colored copies of *Honzo Zufu* by Iwasaki Tsunemasa (1830).

Striking likenesses *(below)* of a nasturtium and daisies by Basil Besler, 1613. The smell of nasturtium is referred to in the plant's name, which means in Latin "twisted nose."

er half of the sixteenth century and was out of fashion during the seventeenth. But metal engraving and etching arrived to take its place—arts which, unlike woodcuts, resulted in the printing of the cut-out designs (which were filled with ink) while the uncut parts of the metal surface were wiped clean and left no impression on the paper. Oil painters, too, and watercolorists continued to improve their techniques, and there is little in the record of flower painting to match the best products created

Drawing of the quinquina *(below, left)* from the *Flora Peruviana et Chilensis* published in Madrid, 1798–1802.

A red pepper in flower *(below),* painted by Maria Sybille Merian in 1726.

The rhubarb plant *(bottom),* as shown and glorified in the work of A. Muntig in 1698.

Bellis Sylvestris minor flor mixtis.

Bellis minor fl...

Nasturtium Indicum.

during the seventeenth century. By this time, however, the interests involved were realigning. Pure botany was going its own way, toward the watershed investigations of Linnaeus and microscopic analysis, which for two hundred years was to be led by the English. Art increasingly served the garden lover or horticulturalist. Still lifes and horticultural publications occupied the labors of the best artists. Between the two, herbalism foundered. The national pharmacopoeias, beginning in the seventeenth century and in some ways the natural heirs of the herbals, were not concerned with art. They were moreover more analytical than the herbals had been, preoccupied with precise measures and as much with metallic or animal derivatives as with plants. To some extent plants were becoming, in the minds of many, a debased coin-

The foxglove *(left),* as shown in the *Flora Londinensis* of 1777–1798 by William Curtis. The same picture was used by William Withering as the frontispiece to his book *The Foxglove and its Medical Uses.*

age. Orthodox medicine viewed them askance, lumped them in with old wives' tales, and put its faith in the science of the laboratory.

This process accelerated when scientists developed the means of isolating the active constituents of certain plants. For nobody was concerned in the laboratory with the whole shape of the plant, or with identifying it in the field, or with the colossal variety of plants—each with its different properties—that could be found both in the wild and in the garden. Even today when many scientists are prepared, in the face of recent work on drugs drawn from plants all over the world, to admit that plant chemicals may have more effect on health than even the herbalists dreamed of, the herbalist is still a fringe practitioner. The supply of herbal material has never dried up; indeed, in terms of numbers it has probably never been so popular as now. All the same, there must be few people who, with a headache to cure, will prepare a decoction of willow bark when a bottle of aspirin is at hand.

The golden age of the herbalists was a phenomenon that can never recur. In the field of medicine there could never again be such a harmonious matching of need, art, knowledge, and verve; of the aspirations of the healer, the gardener, the lover of flowers, and the lover of painting. The many publications that have appeared and continue to appear, advocating tisanes and electuaries, decoctions and infusions, though they have dispensed with much of the

The caper spurge *(above),* drawn by John Miller in 1777 for his book *Illustratio Systematis Sexualis Linnaei.*

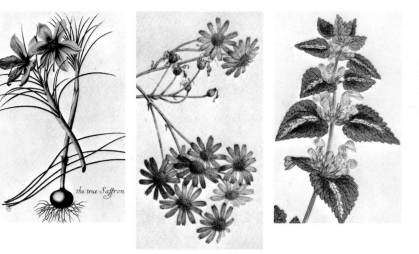

Saffron, cineraria, and spotted dead nettle, as shown in late eighteenth- or early nineteenth-century works *(above).*

matter of the herbals have added little new. To drink a peppermint tea today, in order to sleep sounder, is to drink a toast to a gallery of Renaissance masters who eloquently recorded the kindnesses done to man by the same plants.

1 *Capsella bursa-pastoris,* shepherd's purse, with heart-shaped pods.

2 *Inula helenium,* elecampane, a perennial of the daisy family.

3 *Primula officinalis* or *P. veris,* the yellow cowslip.

4 *Viola riviniana,* the common violet, with unscented flowers.

5 *Galium odoratum,* woodruff, a fragrant inhabitant of woodland.

6 *Allium sativum,* garlic, crucial to gastronomy as well as medicine.

7 *Pimpinella saxifraga,* burnet saxifrage, with its flower umbels.

8 *Hypericum perforatum,* St.John's-wort, with translucent petal spots.

18 *Tanacetum vulgare,* tansy, named from the Greek for immortality.

19 *Coriandrum sativum,* coriander, with innumerable flavoring uses.

20 *Verbena officinalis,* vervain, able to repel snakes and lizards.

21 *Sempervivum tectorum,* houseleek, an ornament of rock and roof.

22 *Equisetum palustre,* marsh horsetail, one of the most ancient plants.

23 *Potentilla erecta,* common tormentil, hardy relative of the strawberry.

24 *Calendula officinalis,* garden marigold, a boon to plants and men.

25 *Fumaria occidentalis,* fumitory, named from the smoky scent.

26 *Urtica dioica,* stinging nettle, which brings relief as well as pain.

9 *Carum carvi,* caraway, provider of an aromatic oil in its seeds.

10 *Gentiana lutea,* great yellow gentian, which favors high places.

11 *Galium verum,* lady's bedstraw, sometimes known as cheese rennet.

12 *Plantago lanceolata,* ribwort plantain, common throughout Europe.

13 *Artemisia absinthium,* wormwood, named after the goddess of chastity.

14 *Tussilago farfara,* coltsfoot, a splash of color in late winter.

15 *Menyanthes trifoliata,* buckbean, growing in fens and shallows.

16 *Alchemilla vulgaris,* lady's mantle, its leaves exuding water drops.

17 *Centaureum erythraea,* common centaury, a herb of chalky areas.

27 *Marrubium vulgare,* white horehound, an ancient cough remedy.

28 *Pimpinella anisum,* aniseed, a flavoring known universally.

29 *Agrimonia eupatoria,* hemp agrimony, yielder of a yellow dye.

30 *Rosmarinus officinalis,* rosemary, a classic and ancient herb.

31 *Melissa officinalis,* balm, whose flower is a favorite among bees.

32 *Hyssopus officinalis,* hyssop, another culinary herb.

33 *Agropyron repens,* couchgrass, a hated weed that can heal.

34 *Origanum vulgare,* marjoram, aromatic, flavorsome, and medicinal.

171

Those who look to nature for their medicine should not blind themselves to the benefits conferred by science. In some ways science has without any doubt improved on natural powers. A flower that blooms in June is not available in January (unless it is dried, distilled, or deep-frozen). Appropriate chemicals are not evenly distributed throughout each plant, or each root, and quantities may even vary with different times of day. A bottle from the pharmacist, however,

Yellow archangel.
This nerve stimulant is mentioned under number 51 in the following list.

comes with a guarantee of its contents.

All the same, many healing plants go to waste which could be used with advantage, and in some cases a greater advantage than a pharmaceutical preparation will provide. There is room here to list only a few which are used by many to this day. Dosage and other instructions should be sought in one of the manuals which abound in every country. It should always be remembered that some conditions, including those listed on these pages, are often no more than symptoms of more serious diseases.

ASTHMA has numerous causes, including psychological ones. Celandine, valerian, fennel, stramonium cigarettes, or an infusion of hyssop, elder flowers, and licorice root may help.

BLADDER TROUBLES may refer to muscle weakness or inflammation. The latter is best cleared by antibiotics. Partial relief from cowberry, birch, chamomile, alder buckthorn.

BOILS can be relieved by compresses of thyme, marjoram, nasturtium, or sanicle, or by scarlet pimpernel infusions.

BURNS. Minor cases respond best to an application of cold water, as well as raw potatoes and onions. Tannin-rich drugs help.

COLDS are best treated by a day or two in bed. Relief of congestion and other symptoms can be obtained from yarrow, peppermint, thyme, or marjoram infusions.

CONSTIPATION is sometimes cured by a reduction of starchy foods. Take molasses, prunes, alder buckthorn, monk's rhubarb, fennel, licorice.

COUGHS. Hyssop, elder blossom, and elecampine teas can alleviate coughing. Also the liquid from an onion sweated in brown sugar.

DANDRUFF is a problem originating inside the skin, not on the surface; but rosemary or eucalyptus shampoo may reduce the condition.

DIARRHEA may be a sign of more serious problems, but it sometimes responds to an infusion of blackberry root or raspberry leaves or plants rich in tannin, e.g. oak bark.

EYE INFLAMMATIONS may respond to frequent baths of water. Honey, castor oil, or lotions of eyebright, chamomile, fennel, and rue may get rid of the symptoms.

FATIGUE, if it indicates no more than a mildly run-down state, responds to tonics: yeast tablets, rose hips, agrimony, peppermint, marjoram.

FEVERS call for rest and warmth. A mixed infusion of honey, yarrow, blackcurrant, thyme, hyssop, and licorice root can reduce temperature.

FLATULENCE, if an isolated condition, responds to charcoal biscuits, tincture of cardamom, caraway, fennel, garlic, yarrow, etc.

GOUT may be helped by colchicum preparations (which must be made professionally: the plant is poisonous), hyssop, juniper, birch.

HEADACHE is brought about by many different causes. Lavender, mint, rosemary, chamomile, poppy may reduce the pain.

INSOMNIA is not easily cured by simple herbs, but an infusion of peppermint, valerian, hops, aniseed, or fennel, taken before retiring, can make sleep deeper.

MOUTH INFLAMMATIONS can be healed by washes of oak bark, herb robert, tormentilla, and thyme.

NERVOUS CONDITIONS may respond to the tonics mentioned under fatigue; an infusion of hops or valerian is recommended.

RHEUMATISM and arthritis are a universal bane. It is important to keep regular habits. Bee stings, rolling in nettles, and the external application of cuckoopint and rosemary bring relief.

THROAT TROUBLES are the most important indicator of troubles elsewhere in the body. Sage, thyme, chamomile, and origanum are used to overcome them.

VOMITING may be prevented by infusions of peppermint, spearmint, centaury, chamomile, etc.

WOUNDS need applications of lotions or pulps. These may be based on St. John's-wort, herb robert, comfrey, sanicle, and many others.

Plants listed here are illustrated on pages 170–171 and 174–175.

1 SHEPHERD'S PURSE
The dried flower-head is used in infusions to control blood flow by constricting veins. Helps contractions of womb at childbirth.

2 ELECAMPINE
Roots and rhizomes stimulate gastric juices and the appetite. Also used as diuretic and bronchial expectorant.

3 COWSLIP
Made into tisane, both flowers and rhizomes are good for catarrh. Also diuretic and laxative.

4 VIOLET
Flowers and stem, infused, act to allay fevers and relieve rheumatism. Also diuretic, and expectorant for catarrh.

5 WOODRUFF
Infusion of the whole herb makes a tonic used for nervous problems, depression, and fevers.

6 GARLIC
Bulb contains antibiotic substances. Useful in diarrhea and other stomach troubles, and against worms in children; also for bronchial congestion.

7 BURNET SAXIFRAGE
Root is active against dropsy as a diuretic, while infusion can be applied to cuts.

8 ST. JOHN'S-WORT
An infusion of flowers, leaves, or stems (best picked when plant is in flower) can soothe and heal some stomach disorders, and mixed with olive oil makes an external balm for cuts and wounds.

9 CARAWAY
The seeds crushed and boiled in water can give instant help in cases of flatulence, stomachache, or poor digestion.

10 YELLOW GENTIAN
Infusions from the ground root stimulate appetite and improve digestion.

11 LADY'S BEDSTRAW
Infusion of the whole plant (except roots) will alleviate some stomach disorders and act as diuretic and cleanser of kidneys and bladder.

12 RIBWORT PLANTAIN
Leaves infused, and left boiling for some minutes, help with bronchitis. Seeds can clear diarrhea.

13 WORMWOOD
Leaves and stem in infusion stimulate appetite and soothe stomach pains. Also get rid of worms, but too large a dose is dangerous.

Ginseng, *Panax ginseng,* has been esteemed in China for four thousand years. Now, with its close relative *P. quinquefolium,* it has swept across the West with a dramatic array of attributes, not all strictly genuine. It does seem to be a potent stimulant of the nervous system, delaying mental and physical fatigue, and some reports suggest that it combats several virulent germs.

14 COLTSFOOT
Tea drunk for poor skin condition and during chills. Lotion helps to heal cuts.

15 BUCKBEAN
Tea improves digestion, stimulates appetite, and may help reduce fever.

16 LADY'S MANTLE
Tisane from the leaves checks diarrhea and excessive menstruation. Recommended as a regular tonic during menopause.

17 CENTAURY
All parts of the plant except roots act in a tisane as a tonic, and stimulate appetite and digestion.

18 TANSY
Dosage must be most carefully regulated as the plant contains poisons. It has uses in stimulating circulation and as worm-killer.

19 CORIANDER
Raw leaves or seeds soothe indigestion and stomach pains.

20 VERVAIN
Recommended since ancient times as a reducer of fevers and calmer of nervous disorders. It may also be applied externally to sores and ulcers.

21 HOUSELEEK
Pulped, it can be applied to the skin as a balm for rashes and inflammations, stings, etc. Internally helps to get rid of worms.

22 HORSETAIL
Tisane is used as a diuretic, and is said to strengthen the lungs in pulmonary tuberculosis. Externally applied, helps to heal wounds.

23 TORMENTIL
Decoction of rhizome good for diarrhea and excessive menstruation. Externally applied to sunburn and inflammations.

24 MARIGOLD
Flower-heads made into a tisane are used in jaundice. It can also heal cuts and wounds if applied externally.

25 FUMITORY
Infusion of the leaves and flowers used as a remedy in most liver complaints, including jaundice. Also alleviates general stomach troubles.

26 STINGING NETTLE
All parts of the plant act as a tonic in infusions. The stings applied externally can relieve rheumatic pains.

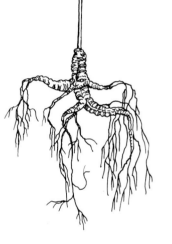

27 HOREHOUND
The whole plant (preferably when in flower) can be used in a tisane to stimulate appetite and to soothe bronchitis.

28 ANISEED
Dried seeds, chewed or in a tisane, are used against flatulence and constipation.

29 HEMP AGRIMONY
Infusion of the whole plant helps sore throats and ulcerated mouths; also good against diarrhea and kidney complaints.

30 ROSEMARY
Leaves pounded and made into ointment are used against headaches, rheumatism, migraine, etc.

31 BALM
Aptly named for its soothing effects in stomach disorders and nervous complaints. Infusion of leaves is used.

32 HYSSOP
Infusion made from whole aboveground plant is a tonic, stimulating appetite and helping allay bronchitis, flatulence, and diarrhea.

33 COUCHGRASS
Decoction of the chopped-up rhizome is used in kidney and bladder complaints. People are usually more concerned to banish couchgrass than make use of it.

34 MARJORAM
Infusion of whole plant soothes inflammations and sores of throat and mouth; also useful against coughs and diarrhea.

35 HOLLYHOCK
As a tisane, the dried flowers help stomach conditions as a purgative; also used as mouthwash.

36 WHITE DEAD NETTLE
Tisane made from whole plant is applied externally to bruises, burns, and cuts. Internally, helps relieve constipation and diarrhea.

37 GROUND IVY
An infusion is a useful tonic. It used to be applied to eyes, especially of animals, to clear inflammations.

38 ELDER
Flowers and leaves, in a tisane, bring relief to colds and chills and other fevers, and help alleviate rheumatism.

39 ICELAND MOSS
Tisane is used to clear catarrh and to stimulate poor appetite.

40 ANGELICA
Roots and rhizomes go into a tisane used as a general tonic for the nervous system and as a stimulant for appetite and digestion.

41 HOLLY
Tisane made from leaves acts as diuretic and helps dispel fever and allay coughing in colds and bronchitis.

42 BLACKCURRANT
Fruit is rich in vitamin C and can be used as tonic, as a soother during colds, and to dispel sores in mouth or throat.

43 BLACKTHORN
Infusion of flowers is used to reduce fever, constipation, and disorders of the blood. Fruit, boiled and with sweetener added, is a tonic.

44 MISTLETOE
Contains toxic substances and should not be used without advice. It is employed in the reduction of high blood pressure and of certain tumors.

45 WALNUT
A tisane of the leaves is taken internally to help bad skin conditions. It is a reputed aid in destroying worms.

46 DANDELION
An infusion made from the ground root, in the manner of coffee, is used as a diuretic and prugative; stimulates appetite and digestion.

47 VALERIAN
The roots and rhizomes, boiled in an infusion, are good for nervous disorders and reputedly for palpitations and insomnia.

48 JUNIPER
A tisane made from fruit or wood is a diuretic and a stimulant of appetite. Lotions are applied externally to bruises and cuts; also used to relieve rheumatism.

49 YARROW
Tea made from flowers and leaves allays flatulence and other stomach disorders; applied externally, it is good for cuts and wounds.

50 PEPPERMINT
Whole plant, especially leaves, taken in unboiled infusion against liver complaints, flatulence, and digestive disorders.

51 YELLOW ARCHANGEL
Infusion of the flowers is said to stimulate the nerves. It may improve wan complexions.

52 LUNGWORT
As a tisane, the whole plant is used in disorders of the respiratory tract, also as a diuretic.

53 WILD CHAMOMILE
Flower heads in a tisane relieve stomach upsets, nausea, diarrhea, etc., and are applied externally to sores and inflammations.

54 MALLOW
Decoction made from leaves is applied to boils, sores, and abscesses.

55 THYME
A good external application for cuts and wounds. Also taken as an infusion against stomach disorders and whooping cough.

56 BARBERRY
A decoction or infusion of the woody stems is used as a tonic, purgative, and relief for some stomach disorders.

57 STEMLESS THISTLE
A tisane made from the root is used to relieve bronchitis; also acts as a diuretic.

35 *Althaea rosea,* hollyhock, a useful familiar of cottage gardens.

36 *Lamium album,* white dead nettle, a splash of cream in hedgerows.

37 *Glechoma hederacea,* ground ivy, a creeper flowering in spring.

38 *Sambucus nigra,* elder, yielding wine from both flowers and fruit.

39 *Cetraria islandica,* Iceland moss, a lichen with commercial uses.

40 *Angelica archangelica,* garden angelica, whose stem is often candied.

46 *Taraxacum officinale,* dandelion, with nutritious leaves and roots.

47 *Valeriana officinalis,* valerian, credited with diverse healing powers.

48 *Juniperus communis,* juniper, whose berries go to flavor gin.

49 *Achillea millefolium,* yarrow, with curing powers that helped Achilles.

50 *Mentha piperita,* peppermint, a strongly aromatic kitchen herb.

41 *Ilex aquifolium,* holly, a tree or shrub rich in myths.

42 *Ribes nigrum,* blackcurrant, whose sweet berry is vitamin-rich.

43 *Prunus spinosa,* blackthorn, whose white blossoms herald spring.

44 *Viscum album,* mistletoe, a parasite of oak and apple trees.

45 *Juglans regia,* walnut, valued both for its wood and its nuts.

41

42

43

44

45

52

53

54

55

56

51 *Galeobdolon luteum,* yellow arch-angel, basis of a cordial.

52 *Pulmonaria officinalis,* lungwort, promoted by the doctrine of signatures.

53 *Matricaria recutita,* wild chamomile, a pungent colonist of waste ground.

54 *Malva sylvestris,* common mallow, whose flowers illuminate autumn.

55 *Thymus serpyllum,* wild thyme, a favorite odoriferous herb.

56 *Berberis vulgaris,* barberry, a shrub that makes decorative hedges.

57 *Carlina acaulis,* stemless thistle, common in mountain regions.

57

175

In April 1977 a man was dying in a London hospital. In spite of the best available medical attention, the wound left by an operation on his kidney refused to heal. Then a doctor remembered that in parts of Africa the pawpaw fruit is used by local tribes as a kind of poultice for deep cuts. Anything was worth trying. A distinguished grocer was able to supply the fruit, and instead of the usual serums and bottles and hypodermic syringes and catheters, a big round and juicy squash was conveyed along the more. And some of the greatest hopes for the future of medicine rest on the success with which plants are already coping with maladies resulting from modern life-styles. Stress, cancer, coronary disease, sclerosis, ulcers, rheumatism, and several more torments that seem to be accelerated by the pace and rhythms of advanced societies have in some cases already been shown to succumb to the power of plants which were around for millions of years before the ailment was heard of.

hospital's immaculate corridors. In the operating theater it was dissected and applied to the man's side. Three days later he was restored to health.

Plants are still indispensable to the business of healing. But more than that, they can still produce surprises. The pawpaw is one example, but there are many

Rauwolfia serpentina (above left) has been known for centuries in India as a tranquilizer. The discovery by the West that it reduced high blood pressure led to a vast demand, which deprived India of her usual supplies until the government banned exports.

Oil from the seeds of sunflowers *(above)* supplies linoleic acid to sufferers from multiple sclerosis, sometimes delaying its progress.

Tension, stress, neurosis, and nervous breakdown become increasingly common under the strains imposed by modern society. But help is at hand for those who suffer. Plants like valerian, hops, garlic, mistletoe, and hawthorn can soothe nerves now as they have for centuries. Recent introductions from the Orient, such as ginseng, ephedra, and rauwolfia, are helping doctors to tackle various aspects of psychological stress in more natural and lasting ways than some of the scientific techniques, which have often produced harmful side effects.

Foxglove *(left)* is an important weapon against the growing menace of heart disease.

The licorice plant, *Glycyrrhiza glabra,* is an example. Its root, whose habit of growing deep into the soil makes it difficult to harvest, has nevertheless been used for centuries as a confection and a soother of various internal pains. Then in the 1940s, by a combination of luck and diligent inquiry, a Dutch doctor, F.E. Revers, noticed that patients with activated peptic ulcers recovered more quickly if they took pills that had long been marketed by a local druggist but never analyzed thoroughly in the laboratory. His own researches showed that the pills contained a substantial proportion of licorice. The discovery was of great value, but it did not go far enough, for while licorice could now be regularly prescribed for ulcers of the higher sections of the stomach, it did not seem to affect those of the duodenum,

which most often afflict those who live under high stress. Now came one of those desirable unions—the marriage of old practices and modern research. X-rays showed that the duodenum remained quite unaffected because the active ingredients in the licorice were always absorbed by the upper intestines before they had time to reach any further. So a coating of gelatin was added, carefully timed to dissolve only after the few hours taken for the mixture to reach the duodenum. And the plant won an honored place in the armory of medicine against one of the scourges of modern life.

Cancer's toll is often so heavy that it almost seems a natural and inescapable balancing of life's good things with pain and evil—or a permanent retribution for original sin. Yet it too may be defeated by the power of

plants. In some respects it already shows signs of yielding. To be sure, the process is a slow one. In the last twenty years well over a third of a million chemical compounds have been screened for anticancer properties, and of these only a couple of dozen show promise. One of them, *vincristine,* comes from a pretty pink member of the periwinkle family, *Vinca rosea,* which has for some time been used in the treatment of diabetes. As often happens, vague reports of other advantages led to the discovery of its potential in cancer. It was found in the laboratory to kill rats by destroying their white blood cells. Leukemia, or cancer of the blood, on the other hand, kills by producing too many such cells. *Vinca* has now risen to paramount importance in combating various forms of malignant tumor.

Cannabis *(far left)* can arrest glaucoma, which recently threatened two million Americans with blindness.

Periwinkle *(left)*, *Vinca rosea,* is increasingly used to tackle leukemia.

Among the benefits of ephedra *(right)* is the raising of blood pressure and relief of asthma.

Too much tea-drinking turns noses red, but that is not the reason why Mormons and others ban the leaf. It is rather because tea, like coffee, stimulates the mind, trespassing—however softly—on that inner part of man which is seen as his private, inalienable core. What some people prohibit, however, most others enjoy as a mild fillip in the day's routine, drinking—without obvious decline—some hundred thousand cups of one or the other beverage in a lifetime. Certainly these and other plant-based drinks have a hold on us, a hold which has had its effect on history. But most of us could break it without grief. If this were the limit of plants' powers over the human mind, they would pass without comment.

There is more. Some plant stimulants burnish the emotions, giving joy, merriment, wonder, and nostalgia a greater intensity. Some appear to quicken the wits, or sharpen desire, or enhance sensual pleasure. Some bring drowsy forgetfulness, sleep, visions. In a field of opium poppies lie a

power to alter
consciousness

million dreams, and as many perceptions of another world.

These amiable charms hide a harsher core. When plants insinuate their enchantments into the human mind, they secure their advance with steel battens. Pleasure is replaced by chains, obsession, an enslavement which the years strengthen. At times it is no longer bearable, and then it kills. Many plants bring mundane blessings. A few go farther. They seem to offer a glimpse of paradise. But we have enough tormented testimony to know that a mirage of heaven may curtain the gateway to hell.

The black holes of the universe are regions in which the physical laws so far framed by science seem not to apply. There are equivalent mysteries nearer home. Many of the workings of the brain remain inscrutable, for

though we can predict its reactions to many phenomena, we cannot follow the machinery which produces such reactions. Just as almost all our knowledge of astronomy has come by deduction—for our direct experience is limited to a handful of journeys in our immediate periphery—so most of what we know about the brain has been gathered indirectly. Knowledge, memory, emotion, and what are sometimes regarded as transcen-

The *curandeiro* of Brazil *(far left)* is in magical union with gods and plants. Most Latin American families brew drugs from plants, like this one from Paraguay *(center left)*.

Al-Hasan Ibn-al-Sabbah *(left)* organized a campaign of political violence in the twelfth century, using hashish to inspire his men—the assassins.

dental feelings are still kept locked, for most of the time, in this impenetrable casket. Research may ultimately resolve them into a file of chemical formulas—many scientists, at least, would like to think so. But facets may persist which do not lend themselves to such analysis.

Certain plants can be brought into this argument. These are the hallucinogens—plants with constituents which change human perception into a faculty which seems quite remote from normal, mundane observation. Plainly, we no longer believe that plants can contain divine powers. When we eat a plant, or drink an infusion made from it, we are taking in substances which have a chemical effect on—among other things—the physical complexities of our brains. Some of these chemicals have not been isolated, and the means whereby they act on the brain are seldom thoroughly understood. It seems that the process is often the negative one of suppressing some neural reactions so that others are highlighted in a way which can affect the subject's emotional state. Intoxication by alcohol is an example.

Hallucinogens may be subject to the same rules. But their effects are usually more interesting and dramatic than those of other drugs, and more ambitious claims have been made on their behalf. The spiritual and theological aspects of religions may well have been born out of the powers of these plants. The magic mushrooms of Mexico, the soma of ancient India, and the *Amanita muscaria* which was, some claim, crucial to the religions which went before and perhaps gave rise to aspects of Christianity—all these were not only aids to worship but, in themselves, objects of worship.

Intensive research into these plants over the last two decades, and into their use among primitive peoples, has stressed that much ritual, lore, and behavior is still influenced, in a way which earlier observers failed to notice, by insights and visions vouchsafed by consumption of the

Alcohol is one of the most ancient and widespread stimulants. Its influence is shown in Jordaens' *Das Fest des Bohnenkönigs (above)*.

Withdrawal from morphine addiction can bring mental and physical torment to the patient *(right)*.

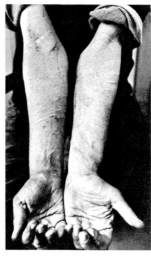

The arms of a heroine addict *(above)* show merely the surface symptoms of the effects of this drug.

plants. And it has indicated that much religion, ritual, and lore in advanced societies stems from similar consumption—with its consequent insights and visions—in the forgotten past.

What research is in no position to do is to distinguish true vision from illusion, or to tell whether a drug which seems like the door of perception of heaven and hell is in fact simply tampering with the brain's storehouse of fact and association. When Aldous Huxley took mescaline, he had his

own theory about the effects, a theory derived from the writings of the French philosopher Henri Bergson. This claimed that all of us are potentially in contact with every person, object, and vibration in the whole universe. Consequently we need a brain and

The most potent gift of the plant world to the religions and rituals of northern Eurasia has been the *Amanita muscaria,* much used by shamans, or priests, to induce transcendental states. A shaman of the Finno-Ugrian religion is seen here uttering incantations to a drumbeat.

nervous system not to apprehend what is happening elsewhere but to cut down the intake of perceptions, which would swamp our existence if not controlled. The brain does not transmit consciousness. It rations it.

Anything which enables us to bypass this custodian—according to Huxley—exposes us to the universal awareness, which Huxley calls the mind-at-large. Some people are born with an ability to go beyond these doors of perception. Others acquire the means of doing so by spiritual exercises. Others, he felt, are enabled to do so by drugs like mescaline. The chemical action of these drugs was to reduce the supply of sugar to the brain. As a result, "mind-at-large seeps past the no longer watertight valve." Then anything may happen. "In some cases there may be extrasensory perceptions. Other persons discover a world of vision-

ary beauty. To others again is revealed the glory, the infinite value and meaningfulness of naked existence."

Huxley is an ingenious, erudite protagonist, but many find him hard to accept for all that. Opposite to his view is one that might be called the evolutionary attitude, an opinion which keeps the experiences induced by drugs closely within the confines of the material world. It is based on the faculty of association, an instinct which perhaps receives less attention than is its due. An infant makes a great effort to put names to objects and derives obvious pleasure from success (the satisfaction may partly derive from rewarding looks or sounds from its parents, but it comes to the same thing: pleasure from association). Many human aspirations—to devise systems, codify, classify, relate—come from this same associative instinct. Some-

how, drugs ease the flow of ideas within the brain and strengthen —if only for a short while—this civilizing power of association. They may help to lead people toward the richer associations of poetry, art, and mysticism. The history of their use, and the value placed on them by different ages and cultures, suggests that they have always done so to a remarkable extent. Indeed, there is no area of the inhabited world in which plants have not made it possible to alter the state of human consciousness to such an extent that people feel they have actually departed from the tiresome realities of the workaday world. Whether they do in fact is a question that cannot yet be answered.

The subject is in ferment. Thirty years ago few people thought of Mexico's magic mushrooms as anything but symbolic totems. Explorers and missionaries trav-

eled and stayed among jungle peoples of South America or Africa or Indonesia, and blessed the state of innocence which they enjoyed. The primitive, they thought, needed no extra stimulus to lead his nobly savage life. Alcohol and tobacco were the luggage of civilized races, anodynes which, taken in moderation, eased their task of governing the world.

True, there were some who saw that even primitives could enjoy a drink, a chew, or a smoke— tobacco after all was a habit learned from the American Indian. And now and again perceptive travelers noted the use of mysterious drugs to aid tribal rituals, without appreciating their dramatic powers or proliferation. Then, following the researches of men like Louis Lewin, and more recently Richard Evans Schultes and fellow anthoropologists, moun-

The fly agaric, or *Amanita muscaria,* in nature, art, and religion. *Far left:* The mushroom is shown growing naturally. It contains toxic alkaloids which can induce a state of frenzy. *Second left:* The fresco at Plaincourault in France, which may represent the mushroom as a tree of life. *Second from right:* As the seat for a gnome or dwarf, the mushroom enjoys permanent popularity in gardens; it is here depicted on a Bavarian postcard. *Left:* A Maya sculpture of a mushroom god, dating from 300 A.D., is probably derived from *Psilocybe,* the hallucinogenic "magic mushroom."

By means of repetitive drumming and the ingestion of *Amanita muscaria,* the Siberian shaman is enabled to ascend to the spirit world above or the abode of the dead below. The drawing *(left)* shows the shamanistic cosmology, which is closely related to the shape of a tree. The shaman above works himself into a state of ecstasy, wearing the prized costume

tains of evidence accumulated concerning the abundance of hallucinogenic plants, their occurrence throughout the world, and

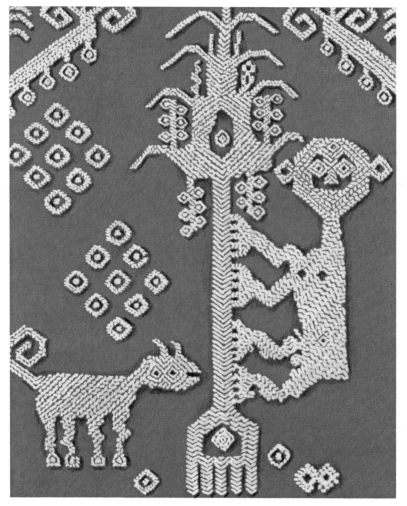

which he alone is allowed to put on. The primitive drawing *(top right)* shows a shaman riding on a bear while summoning the spirit world with his drum.

An Indonesian fabric *(above)* shows the shaman's ascent of the world tree.

the vital part they play in many, if not most religions. Far from the European monopolizing the potent stimulants, he was left far behind by many races, and particularly those of Central and

The central support of the shaman's tent was a birch tree, reputed protection against witches.

The witch with the most celebrated powers of divination was the woman of Endor *(below)*, consulted by Saul on the eve of the battle of Gilboa. She summoned the spirit of the dead Samuel to tell Saul of his impending defeat.

South America (though this may be because intensive research by United States scientists has been directed, so far, more at its neighboring states than those of other continents).

Recent theories have brought at least one European—or more strictly north Eurasian—plant into greater prominence. This is the fungus *Amanita muscaria,* whose white-flecked red cap makes it every child's idea of the toadstool. It is still common enough in northern Europe and across the vastnesses of Siberia, but before the wholesale felling of forests it would have been far more so. According to an amateur, but very serious, dedicated, and learned scholar, R. Gordon Wasson, this fungus is Europe's own magic mushroom. Important to the religions of the Nordic and Russian tribes, it may also have been the divine ambrosia of the Greek gods and their predecessors, the secret element in the mysteries of Eleusis and other towns, bestowing powers of prophecy and visions on those who ate it. Even elements of Christianity may have grown from it—notably the eating of the body of the god, the god being the mushroom itself. In comparison with this, the tea that Wesley encouraged his audiences to drink, to foster an atmosphere of religious fervor—and for which he was strongly criticized by sober citizens—pales into insignificance.

There is a further historic phenomenon which until recently was thought to be based more on imagination than on chemistry, but which research is showing was largely inspired by the consumption of plants. Witchcraft has usually been looked on as an isolated phase of European development, a mania that afflicted a continent emerging from the Middle Ages. It was seen as a Satanic reaction to Christianity of the most dogmatic kind, an aberration of women oppressed by an essentially patriarchal religion.

It was all these things, but it was more. There are good reasons to believe that it was in fact living folklore—a case of ancient rituals carrying on persistently in spite of society's disapproval. The plants and animals which went into the potions familiar to readers of the more gruesome children's stories were not simply quoted as picturesque details. They were potent drugs, containing poisonous and hallucinogenic alkaloids which were able to change the state of consciousness. Witches were alleged to fly through the night on broomsticks. Apart from its sexual symbolism, a broomstick is a plant, or a collection of plants. And flying through the air is an experience which many who are subjected to hallucinogens feel they undergo. In fact, a modern word for a drug experience is a "trip." People today go on trips by means of LSD! Witches went on trips by means of mandrake, deadly nightshade, hemlock, henbane, and other plants. They smeared their bodies with concoctions of these plants—atro-pine and other alkaloids can be absorbed through the skin—and lay down in an excited trance.

In 1902 a German researcher, steeped in the written accounts of Italian and other late medieval witches, followed this procedure. The plants he used were deadly nightshade, thorn apple, and henbane, in the proportions described in a seventeenth-century document. He and some colleagues rubbed the mixture into their bodies, then "fell into a twenty-four-hour sleep in which they dreamed of wild rides, frenzied dancing, and other weird adventures of the type connected with medieval orgies." More recently an expert on poisons, Gustav Schenk, reported his feelings after inhaling the smoke given off by burning henbane seeds. He was possessed by high excitement, but also felt permeated by "a peculiar sense of wellbeing connected with the crazy sensation that my feet were

A recurrent theme in many hallucinations past and present is the appearance of wild animals. Reports by patients who have taken hallucinogenic drugs under clinical conditions often refer to large birds or monstrous beasts. Some of these visions obviously arise from the subject's cultural conditioning. *Pace* Bergson and Huxley, nobody who has lived an isolated life in South America will see, for instance, an elephant in these wild dreams—unless he has often heard stories of elephants or seen pictures of them in books. Moreover it is not uncommon for the subject to imagine that he himself is turned into a bird or animal. Experiences of this kind induce people to think that by means of drugs they transcend the confines of their own bodies and spirits and reach a state of empathy with the whole of nature. "I moved as a tiger," wrote a patient whose visions had been affected by harmaline, an extract of *Peganum harmala*, "in the jungle, joyously, feeling the ground under my feet, feeling my power. My chest grew larger. I then approached an animal, any animal. I only saw its neck, and then experienced what a tiger feels when looking at its prey."

Whether the assumptions in such accounts are right or wrong, the descriptions go far toward explaining a curious deviation from witchcraft: lycanthropy, or the identifying of man with wolf. It is a kind of madness which recurs from time to time in history, and even today it is a

growing lighter, expanding and breaking loose from my body ... at the same time I experienced an intoxicating sensation of flying. The frightening certainty that my end was near through the dissolution of my body was counterblanced by an animal joy in flight." Carlos Castaneda, author of *The Teachings of Don Juan* and other accounts of his psychedelic experiences under the tuition of a Yaqui Indian shaman, tells of similar feelings after rubbing ointment of the thorn apple into his body: "I looked down and saw Don Juan sitting below me, way below me ... I saw the dark sky above me and the clouds going by me. I jerked my body so I could look down. I saw the dark mass of the mountains. My speed was extraordinary."

Such are likely to have been the experiences of the witches of the Middle Ages. Their knowledge of plants had been handed down secretly from the times when infusions and ointments were used more openly and universally in the quest for religious sensation. But it seems that they did not always choose their avocation. Witch-hunts like those at Salem, Massachusetts, in 1692, or in Saxony not long before, have often puzzled historians in that they seemed to be quite unconnected with any general tendency to practice witchcraft. Considerable evidence has been amassed to show that the cause was a recurrent blight among peoples and communities who depended on rye for their bread. This blight was the fungus ergot, a parasite which attacks the ears of rye and poisons anyone who eats the grain. Symptoms include many that would be confused by fundamentalists with witchcraft, and to counter the argument that in a community suffering from ergot poisoning both sexes and all ages would behave in a maniacal manner it is claimed that women and children are more susceptible to ergots than men.

condition recognized by pathology. Quite simply, people imagine themselves to be wolves. They walk on all fours, howl, long for raw flesh—including human—and go to antisocial lengths to acquire it. In the past the condition has affected groups of people—Herodotus speaks of a class known as the Neuri who by their sorcery converted themselves, once a year, into wolves. References to werewolves in European literature (the story of Red Riding Hood is a tame, children's version) point to frequent visitations of this mania. Some accounts refer, not to the human assuming animal form,

centuries, during which some hundreds of people were executed in different parts of Europe for practicing lycanthropy. Both the treatises and some preserved confessions refer often to the use of ointments to bring on the condition. Plants familiar to students of witchcraft are mentioned again and again: deadly nightshade, henbane, thorn apple, and others of the notorious potato family, as well as aconite, cannabis, and opium. The illusions and visions obtained may have little or nothing to do with the plants themselves. We can no more believe that plants possess diabolic powers than we can agree with

A medieval carving from Morlaix in Brittany shows a witch pounding a toxic brew with her pestle and mortar.

There is an old German tradition that mistletoe *(below, far left)* enables a man to see ghosts and to compel them to talk. The mandrake *(second from left)* was an ingredient of witches' brews and a magic charm with evil powers.

witch's state of mind. They were her tools. She was alleged to use them in her magic spells, to make potions, charms, and poisons for people and animals. Her knowledge of herbs was as great as the pharmacist's, but she used them for different ends, to harm and manipulate rather than heal. It is not surprising, considering the periodic persecutions, that she kept her arts secret, and that consequently the place of plants in her armory has been overlooked. Images of clay and wax, stuck with pins to ensure the subject's death; verbal formulas and charms; dances, amulets, talismans—all these were part of her

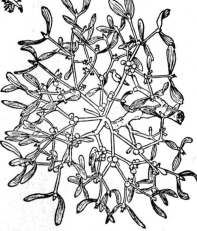

but to the human spirit leaving its own body, apparently lifeless, to take up temporary abode in that of a wolf, its *Doppelgänger*. The theme is inextricably mixed with that of witchcraft, as indeed are some of the attempts to explain it. Treatises were already being written on the subject in the sixteenth and seventeenth

the Mexican peasants that their mushrooms contain the divinity (though many of us come close to it when we take the bread and wine of Christian communion). But that plants can—more often than is generally realized—oil the doors to these personal, perverted hells is beyond question. Plants not only created the

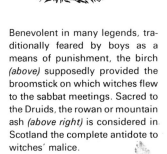

Benevolent in many legends, traditionally feared by boys as a means of punishment, the birch *(above)* supposedly provided the broomstick on which witches flew to the sabbat meetings. Sacred to the Druids, the rowan or mountain ash *(above right)* is considered in Scotland the complete antidote to witches' malice.

equipment, but it must have been chemicals administered to those she wanted to affect which were the basis of her powers. Perhaps we are apt to overlook the affects of suggestion. In an age of greater faith, faith no doubt moved mountains. And perhaps those whose faith was in the powers of darkness could also

With an eroticism unnecessary to his subject, but much in favor with those who depicted it, an unknown fifteenth-century Flemish painter has shown a young witch *(left)* preparing a magic philter. *Below:* With sinister use of the technique of chiaroscuro, this painting shows a familiar theme of witchcraft—a potion being prepared under the devil's supervision.

achieve much by it. When we consider the range of plants made use of in witchcraft, it is hard not to think that faith of a kind played a very large part, for many of the herbs credited with exotic powers prove on analysis to have none. This is nowhere clearer than in one of the off-shoots of witchcraft, a comparatively harmless field in which witches with time on their hands might earn a dishonest penny: love potions.

The quest for means to intensify and prolong sexual pleasure is one that has absorbed almost as much energy and ingenuity as the search for food. The problem is perhaps more marked in back-ward societies where wealth tends to come with age and a man who can afford a dowry is long past his sexual prime. Polygamous societies aggravate the problem acutely. There are still parts of Africa where men will pay any price for an aphrodisiac, forgetting that the last they bought had no effect whatever. Scientists say that no pharmacological agent has yet been found which directly increases an individual's capacity and susceptibility. Some reserve their judgment

A nineteenth-century etching *(above)* shows a maiden and a goat-footed satyr—symbol of lechery—enhacing their revels by draughts of wine.

on the bark of the yohimbee tree, *Pausinystalia yohimba,* found in the Cameroons, but other claimants—and a worldwide list

would fill pages—have all been discredited. Mental and physical health are important, and a plant which improves these may be said indirectly to influence sexual performance. Dr. Henry Kissinger has said that power is the best aphrodisiac he knows. Others assert that sex itself is. Plainly it is often a matter of the individual metabolism. There are those who cannot make love sober, and others who cannot when drunk. There are many who

swear to the aphrodisiac powers of cannabis, others who find it takes away both potency and desire.

Hope springs eternal in the human breast, and a high proportion of that hope has gone toward plants. For want of real powers, they have been credited with magical ones, and here the power of suggestion is paramount. The roots of the orchid sometimes resemble testicles, *ergo* the roots of orchids are sexual

stimulants. (The word "orchid" comes in fact from the Greek for testicle.) The roots of the mandrake can look like naked men and women. They are consequently aphrodisiacs, though the same logic—a parallel to the doctrine of signatures—makes them cures for sterility in the story of Rachel, Leah, and Jacob. The smell of meadow rue—*Thalictrum flavum*—is like the smell of human sperm. The leaf of pennywort—*Umbilicus rupestris*—re-

Tomatoes were considered aphrodisiac by the Indians of South America; they were first known in Europe as "apples of love."

The poisonous berry of the potato plant was a popular ingredient of love potions in the seventeenth century.

Thorn apple *(left),* deadly nightshade *(above),* and black nightshade *(right)* were all credited with stimulant power.

In the fifteent-century woodcut *(far left)*, food, wine, nudity, and bathing are all love-stimulants brought together in Italian Renaissance *bagnios*. *Left:* Burne-Jones's painting of the Hesperides guarding the apple tree with its gifts of immortality and fertility.

The story of Lot and his two daughters, told in Genesis, is distorted in the lusty painting by Lucas Cranach *(below)*. In the original version wine was only an indirect aphrodisiac. It put Lot into a heavy sleep during which, on successive nights, his two daughters lay with him.

LOVE-IN-IDLENESS

Yseult's mother brewed a certain wine for three years. She planned that King Mark of Cornwall should drink it and remain constantly in love with her daughter. By mistake and innocently, Tristan drank the draught. Chroniclers and Richard Wagner have made the sequel famous, but the original brew is a mystery. Another one is better known. In Shakespeare's *A Midsummer Night's Dream*, Oberon sends Puck to fetch a flower—"And maidens call it love in idleness....The juice of it on sleeping eyelids laid, Will make or man or woman madly dote Upon the next live creature that it sees." The upshot is far from Wagnerian. Oberon's queen Titania awakes after the tincture has been dropped on her eyes to see an ass's head on a fool's shoulders—prelude to lively comedy. Love-in-idleness is the wild pansy, *Viola tricolor*.

SERAGLIO PASTILLES

Available until the nineteenth century in Paris, these aromatic lozenges were claimed to be infallible exciters to venery. The ingredients were listed as "bole Tuccinum, musk, ambergris, aloes-wood, red and yellow sanders *(Pterocarpus santalinus)*, mastic, sweet-flag *(Calamus aromaticus)*, galanga, cinnamon, rhubarb, Indian myrobalan, absinthe, and some powdered precious stones." Fortunately for the purveyors, clients were unlikely to return with a complaint that they had failed.

ORIENTAL ARTS

In the East, much use has reportedly been made of external applications. Persian *m'yaujung*—a mixture of ground pepper, pulped nettles, and oil—and the Hindu's *kewaunch*—a bean-pod—provoked a libidinous itching and swelling in the parts to which they were applied (which seldom varied). Insects and spices achieved the same purposes. In southern India, gratifying results were obtained from straddling a shrub known as the milk-hedge. Men of courage were known to induce a bee to sting them.

THE INFALLIBLE PHILTER

"As for herbs and philtres, I could never skill of them," boasts Lucretia, the creation of the Italian Aretino; "the sole philtre that I ever used was kissing and embracing, by which alone I made men rave like beasts stupefied, and compelled them to worship me like an idol."

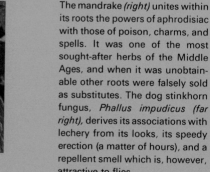

The mandrake *(right)* unites within its roots the powers of aphrodisiac with those of poison, charms, and spells. It was one of the most sought-after herbs of the Middle Ages, and when it was unobtainable other roots were falsely sold as substitutes. The dog stinkhorn fungus, *Phallus impudicus (far right)*, derives its associations with lechery from its looks, its speedy erection (a matter of hours), and a repellent smell which is, however, attractive to flies.

sembles a female navel, at least for those with eyes to see it. The dog stinkhorn fungus—*Phallus impudicus*—bears a resemblance to the source of its scientific name. They are all therefore prominent in the long list of aphrodisiacs.

Stimulation can come from plants in other ways, visual, aromatic, and tactile. Flagellation is an old and common means of arousal. It causes a rush of blood to the assaulted area—usually a close neighbor of the genital organs—and, according to a rich vein of literature, is quickly followed by intense desire. A particular case of this is when the beating is inflicted by means of nettles, a process solemnized by the name urtication. The acid of the stings effects what an ordinary whipping does—only more so. The Romans knew it, and so did Rabelais, who prescribed it for exciting a woman.

There are undoubtedly sub-

stances which, taken internally, can bring about similar results. For instance, drugs which act on the kidneys and bladder may indirectly stimulate the genital organs. They have been discreetly called Italian elixirs and *pastilles galantes* in the past. Indeed, simply eating too much is a useful formula, though it should not be repeated too often. But plants which were most widely used in ancient times and during the Renaissance were the ones also familiar as poisons. The sinister family of the Solanaceae again occurs. The constriction of blood vessels which they brought about could produce feelings of libido as a side effect. (It is often written, though difficult to confirm, that a man being hanged experiences a powerful orgasm—a tradition that incidentally led to the belief that mandrakes grew only on the site of a gallows.) Other considerations have established still more plants on the

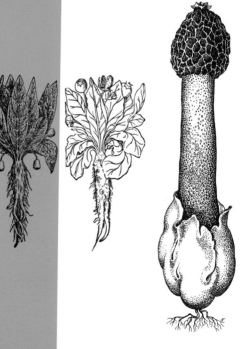

list. Rare and tasty foods like the truffle (which also, like the orchid, has visual associations) and asparagus have always been regarded as aphrodisiac. Their reputation, like that of the oyster or caviar, may be due to a general elevation of spirits rather than a particular arousal of flesh. It is hard, at this distance in time, to see why potatoes, tomatoes, and

cocoa were thought to stimulate desire for a century after their introduction to Europe if it was not because novelty itself can excite. Alcohol, on the other hand, has kept its reputation in spite of a long record of failure. Shakespeare's porter gave the

Preparation for the sabbat *(left)* depicted in an eighteenth-century engraving which, like many others, makes full symbolic use of the broomstick. Poisonous plants like henbane *(above)* were often ingredients of witches' potions.

Below: Witches provoking rain and thunder with an arcane brew.

wisest summary of its effects: "It provokes the desire, but it takes away the performance."

The connection between witches and erotic philters and practices is not as strong as it seems. To the mind of the male excluded from such rituals as the sabbat meeting, everything that was heard about it doubtless smacked of sexual orgy. The secrecy, the anointment of naked bodies, the abandon of intoxication, the reputed presence of the devil, the nocturnal assignations, spells, chantings—together they must have suggested a package of evil which the exclusion of the male

only intensified. And so, from time to time, the male pounced and persecuted. The accounts of those sabbat meetings which survive come from court cases, where male resentment no doubt exaggerated the proceedings, though there are less partisan accounts which corroborate some of the elements—the devil's roll call, the dancing and liturgies (some of which survive in children's traditional games), the parody of the Mass, the homage to and union with the devil. We shall never know for sure what took place on the Brocken (Blocksberg, in the Harz Mountains) or Sweden's Blokula or France's Puy-de-Dôme. Nor can we know how sure were the authorities, when they pressed pins into young women's bodies to find the giveaway patch of numbness, that those they accused were guilty of outlandish practices. And if they were, we cannot—because of the welter of contradiction in the subject—know their motives. Whatever their object, it was plants that helped them toward it, blotting out the consciousness of the workaday world and filling them with fantasies of release. In the end, too, it was plants which—with a double irony—claimed the guilty. Plants have always provided men with the means of punishment—the wood of the cross and gallows, the rope and the rod. It was wood too which, crackling into flame, finally consumed the pinioned malefactors.

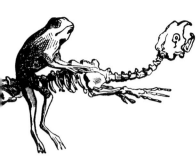

Toads, which do contain toxic substances, have many associations with witchcraft. A New England belief was that killing a toad induced rain.

The painter Goya enjoyed portraying the manic, ghoulish, sinister aspects of life, and several of his works deal with witchcraft and sorcery. Here he shows the devil in the characteristic guise of a goat, surrounded by witches under a crescent moon. The ivy draped around his horns is an age-old symbol of abandoned frenzy.

Some of the grotesque facets of witchcraft are seen in this engraving by the fifteenth-century German, Hans Baldung. Such depictions made it easier to apply the rigors of the law to those condemned for Satanic practices. It has been estimated that the bull of Pope Innocent VIII of 1484 against witchcraft led, over the centuries, to the execution (usually by burning) of over a million people.

And Helen daughter of Zeus
nepenthe, which gave
Those who drank of it
the whole day long
mother or father
though a beloved
killed before

Homer,

poured into the wine a d
forgetfulness of evil.
did not shed a tear
even though their
were dead, even
son had been
their eyes.

Iliad

"A man must take a rest from his memory," said a Guatemalan Indian, asked why he drank a narcotic brew. When Vincent van Gogh was asked why he painted with such intensity during his latter, insane years, he said: "The work distracts my mind, and I must have some distraction." The means for such distraction or withdrawal are plenty, and it seems that most human beings want or need to make use of them, even if only seldom and for short periods. The urge to escape is an instinct as strong, sometimes, as hunger.

Thus people lose themselves in art and music, in dancing and wild carnivals. They throw themselves into frenzies of evangelical religion. They fall in love. They give themselves to the rousing rhetoric of a demagogue or of a hell-fire preacher. One way or another, they break through the bonds imposed by reason and order, the pressing—and very often monotonous—demands of day-to-day life. Always and everywhere, there are plants to help them.
Numerous theories have been

advanced to account for the presence of narcotic, stimulant, intoxicant, and hallucinogenic substances in plants, and to explain why plant families like the Solanaceae contain so many more active drugs than most others or why certain areas of the world—particularly Mexico and tropical South America—are so abundantly, almost unfairly, endowed with plants that act powerfully on the human mind. No doubt science wll know one day, but it is far from doing so now. These things are the accidents and quirks of evolution. It

Left: Behind the figure of the Maya goddess Mayahuel is a flowering maguey plant. She, as the wife of a farmer, had discovered the drink named *pulque* made from the fermented juice of the plant. As a reward she was created a goddess.

Opposite page: Tie-dye cave, an attempt by the USCO group, in 1966, to reproduce the visual sensations of hallucination—the "psychedelic dream."

is important only that people recognized them early and made full use of them.
Mystery also surrounds the actual ways in which these natural substances act on the brain and nervous system; in particular, it is not known why some of them cause a dependence which it is almost impossible to get rid of, and others—while inducing the same or similar sensations—can be given up without any difficulty. Some drugs, of which morphine is a noted example, can never produce their

first pleasurable effects without an increase in the dose. So habitual use means a constant increase in the amount taken, until one day's intake would be enough to kill an initiate. Here, obviously, the drug has become as important to the body's routine functions as one of its own glandular products. The body has adapted to its regular dissemination through the bloodstream. To remove it would be a shock the body would adjust to only with difficulty. Yet, even while it is essential, it is destructive. Here lies the most appalling dilemma facing the addict.
The differences between individuals show that, even if the chemical procedures could be fully understood, there is no set of rules that applies to the whole human race. In the West, we see this clearly in the use of tobacco and alcohol. To some people a cigarette is anathema; some can smoke one or two a day, all their lives, with utter contentment. Others, if they smoke at all, must smoke fifty a day. The same applies to alcoholic drinks. It is not even possible always to know who is an addict. The compulsive drinker may imbibe no more than his fellows, and his addiction may only show if he is forced for some reason to renounce his daily quota.
It has been said that much of Western literature would not have been written were it not for tobacco, coffee, wine, and other

stimulants. Certainly a body of writing and art is owed directly to the influence of opium, cocaine, cannabis, and heroin. Even if a form of degeneracy can be imputed to writers who took these heavy drugs—Baudelaire, Verlaine, Poe, de Quincey—there are many more contentedly bourgeois authors who relied heavily on their caffeine or nicotine quotient. Benign Anthony Trollope puffed cigars as he wrote, and that monument of Victoria's reign, Tennyson, sang of love, nature, and the legends of old in the ever-thickening pipe-fog of his study. Yet Tolstoy could inveigh against tobacco, call its users men who had surrendered their will, and write some of the world's greatest novels with a bland indifference to the allure of the plant world.
To drug-plants we owe more than literature. They help people to live peacefully side by side. All over the world they are the accompaniments to social rituals, to expressions of joy, love, and religious convictions. Sometimes they embody religions, becoming the centers of cults and objects of worship. From opium, absorbed daily by millions of people, bringing them visions, ecstasy, dreams, distress, or despair, to the coffee, tea, and betel, which provide no more than a scarcely perceptible fillip in the day's mundane routine, these plants exercise our minds to an extent we are seldom aware of.

In this selection of the world's mind-affecting plant-drugs, many are mildly poisonous, some—in sufficient quantity—can be fatal. Those who take them regularly are familiar with their dangers. Those who do not should not try without expert guidance.

PLANT, PROVENANCE AND DESCRIPTION

PEYOTE (Lophophora williamsii)

This is a cactus which grows in Texas, the valley of the Rio Grande, and northern and central Mexico. It is small—seldom more than 4 centimeters high and 10 in diameter. Its surface is gray-green, and the flowers vary from white to pale pink. Above the carrot-shaped root, the crown grows bulbously outward, its surface divided into seven or more segments, like an orange that has been peeled. These crowns contain the active constituents which are much sought after. They are often known as "mescal buttons." *Peyotl* was the Aztec name. Confusingly, peyote is sometimes used to describe a hallucinogenic mushroom, while mescal can refer to a fermented liquor made from agave.

American Indians usually swallow the buttons (or crowns) raw, having simply softened them with their saliva. Depending partly on the consumer and partly on the occasion, they may take anything from four to thirty or more at a time. Sometimes the buttons are soaked in water for a period, then the water is drunk. Dried, the buttons keep indefinitely.

Nine alkaloids have been isolated from the cactus, but mescaline is the principal inducer of visions. The effects of the interaction of

OLOLIUQUI (Rivea corymbosa)

A climbing plant, *Rivea corymbosa* twines its way over surrounding herbs and shrubs and puts out trumpet-shaped flowers not unlike those of the familiar, pretty, but destructive garden weed convolvulus, to whose family it belongs. Rivea's flowers are white, and they grow in dense clusters, producing one large capsule-seed each. Although its use as a hallucinogen is mainly confined to Mexico, it grows throughout Central America, Florida, and the West Indies. For many years into this century its classification was a baffling matter, as the seeds used to produce its dramatic effects were usually mixed with those of other related and similar plants, mainly morning glories. Much that can be said about rivea applies equally to these others.

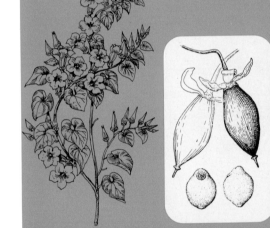

Fifty years ago few scientists suspected the true source of the drug ololiuqui, though much was known of its use among Mexican Indians. Indeed the whole morning glory family was excluded from the possibility of yielding potent alkaloids. It was not until 1955 that rivea's hidden powers were revealed to science, in spite of the fact that its use among Mexicans went back for centuries. Five years later, the same Albert Hofmann who had synthesized the active ingredients of ergot dis-

MANDRAGORA (Mandrax officinarum)

There are six known species of mandragora, growing in the area from southern Europe to the Himalayas. The most famous, the European mandrake of history and myth, is native to the Mediterranean and southern Europe. It is a member of the family Solanaceae, which includes the potato and the tomato as well as some of the world's most virulent poisons. It is a perennial plant with a thick, hard root which can reach down as far as a meter. Its habit of branching often gives it a remote likeness to the human figure. From this similarity many of its magical attributes derive. Leaves grow from the base of the plant, reaching between 15 and 20 centimeters in length. The bell-shaped flowers are white or pale purple, and the round, fleshy berry is deep yellow.

To make it ready for consumption, the root was either left to rot—for sixty days, according to some prescriptions, after which the green and stinking pulp was ready to eat as it was or in an elaborate gruel—or boiled. The leaves also were infused in boiling water to make a potent tea. One of the plant's main uses in medieval times was as a poison, and then the pulp or liquid was often concealed in tastier foods.

Among the contained alkaloids are scopolamine, atropine, hyos-

194

EFFECTS

USE AND ABUSE

these components are felt by those who eat the whole button, but not by people who take mescaline orally or by injection for psychiatric or other purposes. The plant and the extract are both strongly hallucinogenic.

Mescaline hallucinations have been described as "the saturnalia of the specific senses, and chiefly an orgy of vision." The most famous and eloquent account was that of Aldous Huxley in 1953: "I was seeing what Adam had seen on the morning of his creation—the miracle, moment by moment, of naked existence....Being, Awareness, Bliss—for the first time I understood... precisely and completely what those prodigious syllables referred to....I longed to be left alone with Eternity in a flower." The effects of eating the whole buttons seem to follow a general pattern: a period of euphoric calm with greatly heightened awareness leading to visions of amazing splendor—colors, geometric shapes, familiar scenes and objects thrown into weird and often grotesque associations.

The use of peyote goes back through the empire of the Aztecs to an age of legend and myth. Certainly the cactus has always had strong religious associations. It was both a god and a route to heaven. When the Spaniards conquered Mexico, they were quite unable to suppress the religious rituals which surrounded the plant, the January celebrations which led to days of intoxication, or the pilgrimages of whole tribes to areas where the peyote grew abundantly. So worship of the plant was merged with Christianity. In North America this century a group of Indians who formed the Native American Church had a long legal battle with the Supreme Court after their consumption of peyote as the center of their otherwise Christian services had been prohibited. They won.

covered that it was the same ergot alkaloids which gave rivea its hallucinogenic properties. The main constituent, in fact, is D-lysergic acid amine, otherwise known as ergine. The traditional means of taking the drug is to grind the seeds, soak them in water, and drink the filtered liquid.

Of the Aztec practice of consuming the seeds of ololiuqui, a seventeenth-century Franciscan priest wrote: "When priests and Indians communed with gods and wanted to ask for signs of the future, they took this plant to intoxicate themselves, and subsequently saw a thousand visions and a thousand demons." Physical effects of the plant include listlessness, apathy, and a soothing of pain. In contrast to this loss of bodily sensitivity, the awareness of the mind appears to heighten. Objects are seen more clearly, understood more easily. The visions that follow often include strange color combinations and the appearance of little people or other creatures. These and other recurring themes vary with the subject's cultural background.

Like peyote, ololiuqui has been important in American Indian rites since Mexico's prehistoric period. A god was supposed to reside in the seeds, and both the seeds and offerings to the contained deity would be left in places where divine blessing was sought, for instance among ancestor idols. The Aztec name of the plant connects it with snakes. When a sacrifice was to be performed, Aztec priests burned the seeds and mixed the ashes with extracts from other plants and with animals and insects, alive or dead. The mixture was then spread on their bodies, to render them fearless and inspired. In recent times in the United States closely related species of morning glory have been grown for their hallucinogenic properties. But potent species have been removed from the legal market.

camine, and mandragorine. Hyoscamine and atropine produce an initial excitement followed by torpor. To a lesser extent, this is the result also of the other alkaloids. The plant is dangerously toxic.

The many and to some extent unpredictable effects of mandrake, together with the myths and magic rites with which it has been associated, have led to a wide variety of attributes, including—through the application of the doctrine of signatures to its human-shaped roots—that of aphrodisiac. In fact it produces a short phase of excitement, including quickening of the heartbeat, raising of temperature, and dizziness. Large or repeated doses can follow these symptoms with delirium, coma, and death. Regulated small doses may simply lead to a long period of drowsiness. Dioscorides and later writers record its use as an anesthetic during operations. Its fruits were sometimes put under a patient's pillow to help him sleep.

The Book of Genesis strongly implies—in the story of Leah, Rachel, and Jacob—that mandrake was considered to induce fertility in women. It has certainly been used since the earliest times in connection with magic, lovemaking, and witchcraft. The emperor Rudolf II kept large numbers of the dried roots as dolls, dressed them in finery, and bathed them once a week. Witches used a mixture made of mandrake juice and other ingredients to rub on their bodies, after which their minds were supposed to depart on cosmic journeys—early examples of the "trip." A widespread medieval belief claimed that mandrakes grew under the gallows where men had been hanged. They were supposed to spring from the sperm emitted during the criminal's deaththroes.

195

TOBACCO *(Nicotiana tabacum)*

Another member of the Solanaceae family, *Nicotiana tabacum* is a tall annual with large green leaves, long trumpet-shaped flowers which may be white or purple, and large seed capsules. There are nowadays numerous varieties, and the species itself is supposed to be a hybrid of wild Brazilian plants. Other species of *Nicotiana* occur wild in Australia, Polynesia, and other warm temperate regions, but not all of them are suitable for tobacco making. The main producers of cultivated tobacco plants are today the United States, China, India, Russia, and Brazil, in that order. *Nicotiana rustica* is grown mainly in Turkey (though it originates from Mexico) and produces a tobacco containing more nicotine.

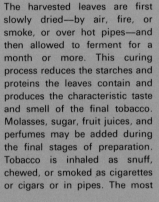

The harvested leaves are first slowly dried—by air, fire, or smoke, or over hot pipes—and then allowed to ferment for a month or more. This curing process reduces the starches and proteins the leaves contain and produces the characteristic taste and smell of the final tobacco. Molasses, sugar, fruit juices, and perfumes may be added during the final stages of preparation. Tobacco is inhaled as snuff, chewed, or smoked as cigarettes or cigars or in pipes. The most

COCA *(Erythroxylum coca)*

Distinguished by its red wood and the thick growth of its leaves, coca is a shrub native to the lush eastern slopes of the Andes and the source valleys of the Amazon, in Peru, Bolivia, and Ecuador. It is also cultivated in Indonesia and Ceylon, where other, less potent, species of Erythroxylum are native. Its flowers are small and white, its fruits red and fleshy. The leaves, which are the part most richly containing the active chemicals, grow to a length of 6 or 7 centimeters. Coca is the most common name, but it has others in different areas, among them *ipadu*. A newly planted tree will have full-size and usable leaves in about four years.

The most important alkaloid the leaves contain is cocaine, first isolated in 1885. (It was then believed by some that it would be a good way of getting addicts away from the morphine habit.)
This can be absorbed into the bloodstream by any means—drinking, smoking, as snuff, or rubbed into the gums or any other mucous membrane. The leaves themselves contain other alkaloids and related substances. Peruvian Indians and others simply chew the dried leaves, some-

BETEL NUT *(Areca catechu)*

The betel is a palm tree growing in the South Pacific archipelagoes, northern Australia, Malaysia, and India. In some parts of this region the Areca is replaced by other closely related species, which are exploited for the same purposes. The leaves are long, as in most palms, reaching a meter or more. The flowers hang down in complex clusters, and each if fertilized gives rise to a single nut, about 5 centimeters long and reddish orange. The name betel originally applied—and still applies—to a vine plant whose leaves are used to wrap the nut in. This is the *Piper betel*, which is found native to approximately the same areas as the Areca. Both plants, confusingly, may be referred to as betel.

The betel nut is shredded with a grater, then mixed with some chalk and spices and wrapped inside the leaf of the *Piper betel*. The whole is then chewed—all day long and by hundreds of millions of people in the Far East and southern Asia. Cardamom and turmeric are the spices most commonly used to garnish the preparation. Sometimes the fresh nut is used; sometimes it is first cured by boiling in water and drying in the sun. In this latter case it will contain less tannin and taste nicer.

active ingredient is nicotine, an alkaloid which interferes with the nervous system and in the long term may raise blood pressure, quicken the pulse, and impair digestion.

Compton Mackenzie said that if smoking were universally prohibited, world war would break out in a matter of days. Its addictive qualities obviously lie in its ability to tranquillize the nervous system rather than in its other physical effects, which are in the main detrimental to general health. Tobacco arouses strongly contrasted emotions. "A cigarette is the perfect type of pleasure," says Oscar Wilde's Dorian Gray; "it is exquisite, and it leaves one satisfied." Byron wrote of "sublime tobacco," and Lamb declared "For thy sake, Tobacco, I would do anything but die." On the other hand, King James I fulminated against it: "The black stinking fumes thereof nearest resembling the horrible Stygian smoke of the pit that is bottomless."

Indians of South and Central America have smoked tobacco immemorially, and still do. They use it in rituals to do with religion and healing. Accounts of its effects among them seem strangely exaggerated, and are probably due to the admixture of other drug-plants. It is usually taken as snuff, though the best-known ritual involves pipe-smoking—the pipe of peace. Columbus learned of the habit of smoking in Cuba in 1492, and within decades the habit had converted more Spaniards than Christianity had won over Indians. Sir Walter Raleigh is credited with its introduction to England from Virginia. Soon vast areas of American forest were being cleared to grow the plant, and slaves were sent over from Africa for its cultivation.

times making a pulp by mixing them with other leaves, or lime, in gourds. They are said to use an average of some two ounces of leaves a day.

The effects of cocaine are vastly greater and—unless used for medical purposes (anesthesia, etc.) under carefully regulated conditions—more damaging and addictive than those of chewing the leaves, which is an everyday habit among those who grow them. Cocaine acts like adrenaline. It causes a feeling of elation, often accompanied by hallucinations, followed by depression and listlessness. Repeated eating of cocaine not only constricts the arteries, straining the heart, it also causes acute mental disorders. The leaves, on the other hand, while increasing the pulse rate and sometimes causing palpitations, produce a feeling of vigor while suppressing the appetite. European travelers to the Andes also found that the leaves were of considerable help in coping with high altitudes.

Like most other drug-plants of this area of the world, coca has had a long record in the native religious habits and rituals. The arrival of Pizarro and the Spanish in Peru, and the development of gold mines, brought a fresh and sinister turn to its history. Slaves consigned to the gold mines were given a daily ration, which improved the quality of their work and also suppressed to some extent feelings of discontent. Similar use of the plant has been alleged in more recent times, as an opiate for underpaid workers. An excellent postal system in Peru, based on runners, was often said to owe its efficiency to coca leaves. Cocaine itself is now less used in medicine than it used to be, its addictive powers being second only to those of morphine.

The dried nut also stores better. The active alkaloid in the betel is arecoline, a comparatively mild chemical to enjoy such widespread popularity.

Betel is a mild stimulant. In the areas where it is chewed it is part of the way of life. The habit is started in infancy (it used to be said that nobody could speak Burmese properly until he could chew betel) and continues throughout life. It is addictive, but in a less captivating way than tobacco. A useful side effect is that the contained alkaloids destroy internal parasites in places where these are a common menace. In medicine, arecoline is used specifically to cure tapeworms, both in man and animals. Many people retain the nut in their mouths during sleep. In time the habit turns teeth brown and black. This defect has been turned into a virtue in some Pacific islands, where black teeth are considered a mark of high social standing.

In India the betel nut has been chewed for a great deal longer than two thousand years. Early Chinese and Sanskrit texts refer to it, and the Greek Theophrastus described it in the fourth century B.C. Before the Middle Ages it spread throughout the Arab lands, and a Persian record claims that in one town there were thirty thousand shops existing purely for the sale of betel. It figures in folklore and in historic accounts. Women ascending the funeral pyre after their husbands have died are comforted by a final chew. Lovers give betel to each other, though Louis Lewin, the great German pioneer of drug studies, said that love was one of the few forces which could—for a while at least—cure people of the habit.

AYAHUASCA *(Banisteriopsis caapi)*

This climbing plant is found in the rain forests of the north and east of South America, especially in the region of the Amazon and its tributaries in Peru, Ecuador, Colombia, and Brazil. It is a liana, draping itself over the trees of the forest and hoarding the sunlight in its long, broad leaves. Its flowers have pink petals and occur in irregular clusters. They develop when pollinated into samara nuts—in other words, they are winged like the fruit of maple or sycamore. Ayahuasca, caapi, and yajé are the names given to the tree or its bark in the Amazon basin, natéma and pinde in Ecuador and the west. They are also used to describe *Banisteriopsis inebrians,* an almost identical species with similar effects.

The fibrous bark of the vine is beaten in a gourd or mortar. Several other ingredients are added during this process. They differ from region to region, and it is thought that individual shamans have their own private (and jealously guarded) recipes. After the pounding, the mixture is thinned with water, sometimes sieved, and finally drunk. In some cases the additives undoubtedly have an extra effect, either narcotic or stimulant; but many of them still wait to be analyzed. No doubt

KAVA-KAVA *(Piper methysticum)*

A shrub which can grow as high as 4 meters, the kava-pepper is common throughout the islands and archipelagoes of the South Pacific. The drink prepared from its roots is known as kava-kava, kava, keu, ava, or yangona, depending on the language spoken. It has dense spikes of white flowers, each containing either male or female parts, but not both. Its leaves are rounded, with the base shaped like the top of a heart. The stubby root is the valued part. It used to be said that the plant only grows where the native population has a light skin, and theories as to its origin and spread were deduced from this. But more recent research has shown this to be untrue, leaving its first homeland in doubt. It is now widely cultivated.

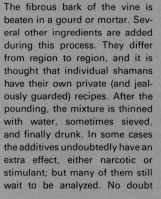

Preparation of the beverage involves, traditionally, long chewing by men and boys with good teeth. They do not swallow the root or the saliva it stimulates, but spit the whole gobbet into a bowl. Hot water is added, and the mixture is left to infuse. The advent of Western standards of hygiene caused some natives to prepare the drink by simply boiling the roots in water; but the result is said to differ from the masticated variety as champagne does from home-brewed wine. Whichever

COFFEE *(Coffea arabica)*

The successful spread of coffee round the tropical regions of the world has obscured its origins. However, it is generally considered (despite the implication in its Latin name) to have been native to Ethiopia, and to have been taken thence to Arabia (where Mocha became an important trading center for coffee). Nowadays much of the best coffee is grown in South America. Brazil is the largest producer. Claims for the production of the best-quality coffee are made for Jamaica, Kenya, Mysore in India, and some other countries. The plant is a shrub or small tree, reaching up to 4 meters if allowed to, but generally pruned to encourage intense growth and to make the beans more accessible to pickers. It produces sweet-smelling white flowers. These yield green berries, which ripen to a brownish red. Cultivation has created innumerable varieties.

Commercial preparation of the coffee beans varies according to area, variety, and quality. The outer skin of the berry is first removed, either by means of a pulping machine or by sun-drying. In the first case the beans are allowed to ferment for a time before they are dried. Most of the so-called instant coffees are prepared from a different species of plant—*Coffea canephora.* Beans of *C. arabica* need to be ground before they are infused in water; even then, boiling under pressure

none of them is without a distinct purpose. South American witch doctors—who also brew the elaborate variants of curare—are expert natural pharmacists. The alkaloids in ayahuasca include harmine and harmaline. They act on the nervous system to produce sensations of pleasure and hallucinations.

It is an unusual property of ayahuasca that it can enable the person who takes it to continue with the normal activities of daily life while experiencing to an extraordinary degree the enhancement of vision which the drug brings. An Indian under its influence has been seen to run through the forest, at night, without any danger of tripping or falling. At a more advanced stage, the *ayahuascero*—as the imbiber of the drug is known—has visions of color-plays, strange beasts and lands, all no doubt related in some way to his surroundings or folklore. The quantities needed to produce hallucinations will first cause unpleasant symptoms, such as vomiting and vertigo. The drug is related to erotic rituals and seems to have an aphrodisiac effect.

Ayahuasca has a long connection with magic and prophecy. A nineteenth-century traveler in Ecuador wrote that it enabled men "to tell the future and solve difficult questions...to decipher the enemy's plans and make appropriate provision for attack and defence; to find out what sorcerer has laid a spell of sickness on a relative, to establish friendly relations with men of other tribes or with guests; and to ensure the love of their women." There are no records of its early use, partly because of the illiteracy of its users, partly because when it was heard of by those on the outside, its identitiy was confused with those of the plants added to it. But it has certainly been used for centuries in magical rites.

way is employed, the infusion is followed by long stirring, and then it can be drunk. Marindin and dihydromethylsticin are the active components. The alkaline saliva of those who chew it is said to add to the effects of the drink.

Kava can produce an effect not unlike drunkenness— and it is sold in numerous shops which closely resemble in their practices the Western inn or public house. But in the quantities in which it is usually drunk— half a coconut bowl or so—it leads to a state of careless content, with perhaps a heightened awareness of sight and sound. At no stage are the mental or physical faculties impaired in an obvious way. A prolonged drinking session generally leads to a prolonged sleep.

Indeed the beverage is used medicinally as a sedative. Excessive doses can cause restlessness and pugnacity, however. Europeans have found that the sleep which follows moderate consumption often brings vivid, sometimes erotic dreams.

European missionaries arriving in the South Seas were quick to ban the use of kava-kava, where they had the power to do so, on the grounds that it was a dirty and debasing practice. Their compatriots brought at the same time alcohol and venereal disease, which were considered a poor exchange. In fact the drug survived, and on her jubilee visit to Samoa in 1977 Britain's Queen Elizabeth drank a draught in the island's King Kava ceremony.
Use of the plant is incorporated in many religious and magical ceremonies, and the knowledge of how kava is prepared is supposed in Samoa to have been the gift of a half mortal, Tagaloa Ui, whose father was the sun.

is necessary to extract the best value from them. Between 1 and 2 percent of the dry weight of each seed is the mild stimulant caffeine. Essential oils, glucose, and proteins are also present.

Normal or moderate consumption of coffee—and that can mean up to a hundred thousand cups in an average lifetime—seems to have mildly beneficial effects on the drinker's spirits, and no deleterious ones. Slight dilation of the blood vessels takes place, and there is an extra stimulation of the heart. In some people coffee can interfere with sleep, especially if taken late at night. But none of these effects is of itself worrying. On the positive side, the drink can help to rouse people from a drowsy state and make them feel more alert. Excessive consumption of course has harmful results, from stomach upsets to heart troubles. It has been quite wrongly claimed in the past to reduce libido and produce sterility.

It was probably in the sixth century that some coffee plants, imported from Ethiopia where they grow wild, were domesticated in Arabia. The drink elicited great praise from sultans and philosophers, and long eulogies were written about it. A thousand years later it became popular in the West. The Dutch established plantations in the Far East, and the English and French in India and the West Indies. In the middle of the nineteenth century a serious disease wiped out the important crop in Ceylon (Sri Lanka). Tea was substituted, and the island has since become famous for that. The introduction of coffee has always been opposed by some, while others have wildly exaggerated its blessings, claiming it as a potent aphrodisiac and panacea. It is now the most important single crop produced by tropical regions.

KHAT *(Catha edulis)*

Khat or qat is a shrub or tree that grows as high as 15 meters. Its leaves are dark green and waxy-looking, the flowers small, delicate, and yellow. The fruit is a capsule containing from one to three seeds. It grows in Ethiopia and Arabia, but above all it is a plant of the Yemen, where it is widely cultivated. Ethiopia is in fact its native land; it grows in the cool valleys at considerable heights. It was transported to Arabia before the sixth century A.D. and became thoroughly acclimatized. Soon associated with Islam, it has seldom had much appeal outside that community, lacking the universal appeal of its compatriot coffee.

Leaves and stems are eaten fresh, though in some parts of Arabia they are made into an infusion. Freshness is important, and dealers are at great pains to convey their merchandise from the hills to the towns as quickly as possible—often by an overnight service. In its native Ethiopia, the plant's leaves are used to flavor a local honey wine.

Among the leaf's active constituents are scopolamine (an alkaloid), dexedrine, and ephedrine. Scopolamine is similar in its

MAGIC MUSHROOM *(Psilocybe mexicana)*

The term "magic mushroom" is applied to several species growing in Mexico, all of which were shrouded in secrecy by the shamans who used them in religious rites. Most of them have now been identified. *P. mexicana* is one of the most important. It belongs to a family of some twenty-five species, several of which grow commonly in Europe and the United States. Only a few have strong or hallucinogenic components, and these are found in Mexico, Guatemala, Honduras, and Nicaragua. The one in question is small, seldom rising more than 2 centimeters. It has a pale pink mantle with gills underneath, and the stem or stipe is thin and spindly. It grows quite commonly in humid places and especially on limestone, up to an altitude of nearly 2000 meters.

No special praparation of the magic mushrooms is needed. They are eaten raw. However, this consumption is accompanied by complicated rituals among Mexican Indians who are taking the drug for religious reasons. One of the earliest observers of these rituals, Bernardino de Sahagun, wrote in the seventeenth century that the mushrooms were eaten with honey, after which participants in the rites would either dance and sing, or sit motionless and pensive. The main component of

FLY AGARIC *(Amanita muscaria)*

The form and color of the fly agaric are better known than those of any other fungus, having been publicized in many children's books and paintings, and not least in Walt Disney's film *Fantasia*. Richard Evans Schultes, one of the greatest practical researchers on hallucinogens, has written that fly agaric is "probably the oldest of the hallucinogenic plants and once perhaps the most widespread, insofar as man's utilization of it is concerned." It grows throughout the north of the Eurasian land mass, and also in North America, but there are chemical differences in the fungi of these regions, and those of America have never been used as drugs. The cap of the fly agaric is bright red, turning in time to brown; and it is flecked with white remnants of the veil which first covered the emerging body.

Fly agaric contains a highly toxic alkaloid called muscarine. It is very similar to acetylcholine, a substance occurring naturally in humans and animals which transmits impulses from one nerve fiber to the next. Muscarine therefore interferes with the nervous system to a considerable degree. The mushroom is eaten whole by those natives of Siberia and neighboring provinces of northern Russia, but it is always boiled first. Uncooked, the alkaloid is not absorbed into the bloodstream. In

effects to atrophine, derived from deadly nightshade. Though khat is often compared with tea and coffee for its effects, it is in fact much stronger, and equally more dangerous.

Khat is used medicinally as an anesthetic, and it was traditionally mixed with opium to be used in the operation which converted healthy young lads into trustworthy attendants of the harem. But it has other, more desirable effects. It can exhilarate, as caffeine plants do. And it can lessen sexual desire, which at many periods of Arab history has rendered it valuable to large numbers of the male population. In excess, however—and its addictive qualities mean that it often is taken in excess—it can lead to loss of appetite, serious insomnia, and cardiac problems. Nevertheless its popularity remains widespread, and it has been said that the inauguration of Ethiopian Airlines was in large part due to the need for daily exports from that country.

The Koran forbids the consumption of any intoxicating substances, and some have interpreted this law to cover khat. Others say that it is not only allowed but was specifically encouraged by Mohammed to compensate for the banning of alcohol. The plant is part of the social history of the Arabs. Facilitating work with a minimum of sleep, it has traditionally been supplied by hard employers to those who worked for them. As a sexual depressant, it has been of great service to those young men who found that laws of inheritance and the close guarding of nubile girls until a marriage contract was entered into were putting excessive strain on them. Khat is also a great social lubricant, and is communally chewed in the evenings.

P. mexicana is called psilocybin, and there is a less active compound psilocin. Both have a chemical structure which is very similar to that of mescaline, and both appear to act on the nervous system in an almost identical way.

Physical reactions to the magic mushrooms follow a distinct pattern. There is a relaxation of the muscles, then a difficulty in concentrating, with evidence of emotional disturbance—which might be loud laughter or mere giggling. Not all who take the mushrooms experience hallucinations, but those who do generally proceed into a phase of depression and exhaustion. The actual visions take many forms, but often involve a feeling of total separation from the body and surroundings of the patient. (It is this aspect which makes synthetic psilocybin of value in psychiatry.) Imaginary objects, color patterns, and scenes appear and are accompanied by sounds. Associations with time and place play a part in the determination of these hallucinations.

"I myself," wrote Robert Graves, "have eaten the hallucinogenic mushroom *psilocybe*, a divine ambrosia in immemorial use among the Mazatec Indians of Oaxaca Province, Mexico; heard the priestess invoke Tlaloc, the Mushroom-god, and have seen transcendental visions." The antiquity of this mushroom religion in Mexico is borne out by the survival of old frescoes and stone mushrooms which have been dated back to 1000 B.C. (For a long time these stones, in the shape of mushrooms, were assumed to be remnants of phallic worship; the theory told more about the anthropologists than about their subjects.) The conquistadores found the religion thriving but secret. Their attempts to suppress it led in places to a hybrid "mushroom Christianity" being practiced, and this still continues.

the past those who valued the mushroom would, in order to conserve limited supplies (or, as some claim, to get more immediate effects), drink the urine of people who had already consumed the mushroom.

The word berserk—meaning literally a bear's coat—was originally applied to Norse soldiers who fought their battles in a state of wild and fearless frenzy. Some assert that this state was induced by consumption of quantities of fly agaric. The first effects are generally felt within an hour of eating—the normal dose being between one and four mushrooms. These symptoms indicate a high state of nervousness, with shaking and convulsions. Sometime later there may be hallucinations, and this stage may be followed by wild and destructive behavior—called going berserk. Finally the subject falls exhausted into a deep sleep. The visions tend to increase the size of objects already seen. A crack becomes a chasm, a twig turns into a tree, and a man of modest stature grows into a menacing giant.

Recent theories have claimed *Amanita muscaria* as one of the most potent forces in Indo-European myth and religion. Up to this century use of the mushroom had been thought to be confined to the hardy tribes of northern Eurasia. It has now been suggested—and there is considerable opposition to the view—that fly agaric used to grow much more commonly in the world's temperate regions, and was in fact the divine ambrosia of the Mediterranean gods and the soma of Vedic ritual and religion. It was in fact the counterpart to the magic mushrooms of Central America. R. Gordon Wasson was the originator of this theory, and it has since been enthusiastically endorsed by Robert Graves. Recent silly extensions of the idea have tended to obscure its merits.

IBOGA *(Tabernanthe iboga)*

This is a shrub of delicate stems which grows up to 2 meters high. It is found in equatorial Africa, mainly in Gabon and the Congo, regions which unlike Central and South America have in general made little use of the stimulant and hallucinogenic plants growing in abundance. The leaves are long and thin and measure up to 14 centimeters. Small pink-spotted white flowers appear in loose clusters, and each produces a single fleshy seed. The yellowish roots, which provide the active substances, are thick and knotted. The family to which iboga belongs—the Apocynaceae—probably contains more alkaloids than any other. Most of them are not exploited, either because they are too toxic for primitive use or because their properties remain to be discovered by the native populations.

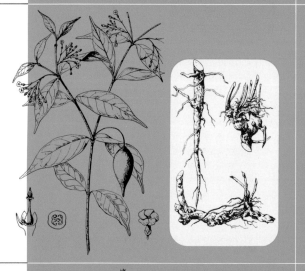

The most powerful constituent of the iboga root is the alkaloid ibogaine, though there are probably more than a dozen others. Preparation of the root brings in several other plants of the region, some of them with independent hallucinogenic properties. These are boiled together and the liquid drunk. The final mixture contains a rare variety of alkaloids, many of them used individually for other purposes, such as killing fish or treating internal parasites and external bites, stings, and

CHOCOLATE *(Theobroma cacao)*

The chocolate, or cacao, tree may grow up to 10 meters tall and can live as long as eighty years. It grows in the tropics only, having originated in Central and South America, and it is now widely grown in West Africa, the Far East, and some Pacific islands. High rainfall and a rich soil are necessary for the abundant production of the seeds from which cocoa is extracted. The pink flowers and subsequent yellow or red pods grow on the trunk of the tree, which is not only unusual but highly convenient for harvesting. The word cocoa was introduced into English by confusion with the coconut in the eighteenth century. Cacao is the Mexican name for the pod, and chocolate comes from the Mexican (and Spanish) term for the beverage ultimately brewed from its seeds.

The preparation of cocoa involves the shelling of the beans, after extraction from the shell and mucilage which surrounds them. They are then roasted and ground. The manufacture of cocoa powder requires the removal of over half their content, which is a fat known as cocoa butter. This extract is not wasted, but added to the powder being used to make chocolate. The drink cocoa is made by the addition of boiling water or milk, and sugar. Brillat-Savarin cloaked a culinary tip in exaggerated mys-

COLA *(Cola nitida)*

This is a tree growing to upwards of 20 meters, producing pale flowers with thin red stripes on them. These contain five carpels, each of which produces, if successfully pollinated, a follicle or kind of pod which may contain as many as eight seeds. The follicle has a rough and wrinkled skin and a characteristic smell. The natural home of the cola tree is the tropical rain forests of equatorial Africa, but it has spread through cultivation to India, the Far East, and the West Indies, due to the colossal demand of recent times. The nut has many different names according to the country and region, and the Arabs call it Sudan coffee. It is certainly prized by many Africans as coffee is by other races.

Many Africans and West Indians simply remove the nut from its pod and chew it for the slight stimulation provided. Alternatively it can be boiled and the resulting liquid drunk. As with coffee, the most active constituent is caffeine, to which is due the characteristic alertness of the consumer. There is also a smaller quantity of the alkaloid theobromine. Commercial growers, who form the vast majority, leave the nuts to dry in the sun before exporting them for manufacture into different growths. The draught is carefully regulated according to the ritual (which may be a trial by ordeal) and the age and health of those who are to consume it.

Iboga makes people feel more energetic than usual and allows them to go without sleep for longer periods. In heavy doses, it goes on to produce a trance-like state, or behavior similar to that of a sufferer from epilepsy. Nineteenth-century Belgian explorers of the Congo saw that ordinary quantities were given to soldiers and hunters who had to stay awake at night. Consuption of large quantities was mainly reserved for the rites connected with secret cults. Those being admitted to such rites for the first time are made to drink enormous quantities, which produce all kinds of alarming results and may well lead to death. This is taken as a judgment from the gods.

The iboga tree is central to the religion of the Bwiti and other tribes of Gabon and the Congo. It is supposed to have arisen originally from the separately buried parts of the ancestor of the Bwitis, and to allow communication with the world of the spirits. The rites were not seen or known about until the nineteenth century, and not described until the twentieth, but they presumably go back for countless generations. Knowledge of the effects of iboga is part of the armory of the local witch doctors, helping them to maintain their power and influence. It is clear also that, unlike other secret cults, the Bwiti is growing in popularity; it represents an entrenched resistance to Western and Christian influence.

tique when he wrote that the Mother Superior of the Convent of the Visitation at Bellay had confided her secret to him: "Make it the night before in a faience pot and leave it...it becomes concentrated and of greatly improved consistency." The beans contain both caffeine and theobromine, which are mild stimulants.

To those who like to end their day with a cup of milky cocoa, thus investing it with an innocent and domestic coziness, its past reputation can come as a surprise. The Spanish brought it from America in the sixteenth century, and it soon became known as a cure, a placebo, a stimulant, and an aphrodisiac. It was also thought to increase fertility. An eighteenth-century English doctor said that from dinking chocolate his wife "was brought to bed of twins —three times." Brillat-Savarin called it "one of the most effective restoratives," and Madame de Sévigné, by a rather curious association of ideas, wrote that a well-known marquise "took so much chocolate, being pregnant last year, that she was brought to bed of a little boy that was black as the devil."

The name given to cacao by Linnaeus—*Theobroma*— means "food of the gods." The Aztecs had certainly made it a standard tribute to kings. They used the beans as coins (a habit which continues unofficially in parts of Mexico), and city taxes took the form of chests full of beans, sent to the imperial treasury. In Europe the drink became the preserve of the rich and fashionable. Maria Theresa, the mother of Louis XIV, was addicted to it. She kept reserves on the sly, as a secret drinker might do now.

As late as the eigteenth century a French commentator wrote that "the great take it sometimes, the old often, the people never." The chocolate that we know today was the nineteenth-century invention of the Dutchman C. J. van Houten. With the help of the fat removed from cocoa powder, he made the first edible bars of chocolate.

kinds of soft drink. The drying not only hardens the nut but also renders it more bitter, so that it is never chewed in this state.

Cola has similar effects to those of coffee. It revives tired people, and is a great boon to the traveler and heavy laborer. It also reduces feelings of hunger, so that it is doubly useful to those who have to travel long distances at great speed. Its aftereffects are generally few or none. But, as is the case with most stimulants, a great deal depends on the metabolism of the consumer. Two nuts have been seen to cause a strong man to grow restless, tremble, and suffer prolonged insomnia. Although the main constituents are caffeine and theobromine, there are many other alkaloids which can act on different people in different ways. Like most stimulants, cola has been credited with aphrodisiac powers.

An African legend shows that among some races the cola has a significance not unlike that of the apple in the Garden of Eden. God, it is said, was once about his business in the normal way, when a particular task forced him to remove the cola nut he was chewing. When he had finished the work, he forgot for the time being about his nut, and went away. A man passed by, saw the nut, and—in spite of his wife's remonstrances— began to chew it. God returned and the man tried to swallow his trophy. But God seized him by the throat and forced him to disgorge. Adam's apple is the lasting mark of God's fingers on the throat.

The cola has always been popular in West Africa and has been used much as an object of barter and trade. But its use this century in mildly stimulant soft drinks has increased demand several thousand times.

The historians of China and India vied with each other to prove that tea originated in their own native land. According to the Chinese, the emperor Shen-nung was boiling a vat of water when some leaves from a nearby shrub blew down. The water took on a divine fragrance, and the emperor gave the recipe to his people. Indians say the drink had been known for thousands of years in Bengal before a Buddhist monk took plants to China in the sixth century A.D. The version is sometimes given more picturesque form. The monk existed before tea was known. While traveling to China (for other reasons), he swore to devote his whole life to meditation on God, never even allowing himself to sleep. Months and years of wakefulness passed; but one day fatigue got the better of him, and he dozed off. His horror on waking led him to prevent more lapses by cutting off his eyelids. Returning next day to the same spot, he saw each eyelid had taken root and grown into a shrub. Thus did India give China the gift of tea.

Science nowadays tends to support the Indians, for it seems that Assam grows more wild tea plants—close relatives of the camellia—than any other region. Today China produces more than her rival, but India supplies more countries. Already more tea is drunk than any other liquid except water. It is a favorite beverage of half the world's population, and demand continually grows. Its appeal is

explained by the leaves' subtle combination of tannin, caffeine, and essential oils. The great Japanese apologist of the tea ceremony, Kakuzo Okakura, put it in terms of other drinks. Tea, he said, "has not the arrogance of wine, the self-consciousness of

—even to a rose whose scent is reminiscent of it. A hundred years ago it brought into being the most elegant episode in the history of sailing, when the tall tea clippers raced their fresh cargoes from the Far East to Europe and America. A century

Above: Bodhidharma, the patron of the tea plant. According to Buddhist tradition, the secret of Buddhahood, or the way to complete self-realization, was passed down from patriarch to patriarch. The twenty-eighth of these, Bodhidharma, took the knowledge from India to China, as he did also, according to some accounts, the tea plant, *Camellia sinensis.*

Left: The Japanese tea ceremony is a long, slow process, taking place in an almost bare room so that attention can be focused on the minute particulars of the ritual and on the few objects and savors connected with the tea itself. Every detail is as it always has been—not the least part of the ceremony's motives being to maintain links with the past and with the spirits of one's ancestors.

coffee, nor the simpering innocence of cocoa." That quintessential Englishman, Samuel Johnson (whose countrymen were soon to be consuming more tea per head than any other nation) declared himself "a hardened and shameless tea-drinker.... who with tea amused the evening, with tea solaced the midnight, and with tea welcomed the morning." Tea's influence on the world can hardly be estimated. Through Russia, Europe, and North America, it marks the phases of the day and has given its name to mealtimes, porcelaine, cutlery, clothes, furniture

before that, it was a tax on tea—and the subsequent tipping of a consignment into the sea at Boston—which sparked the war that gave the United States independence. To an English army it would be unthinkable to fight a war without the constant brewing of tea in the background. Cha, they call it, using the variant of the Chinese word by which tea was known when it first came to England, or simply a "cuppa."

All the same this universal brew was unknown in the West four hundred years ago. The Dutch brought it from India about

1610, and it took the rest of the seventeenth century to establish irself in the daily lives of ordinary people. For most of its history tea has been the preserve of the East, and there it has been exalted to a position accorded no other drink. It was early seen that, in addition to its tonic and refrehing properties, it lent itself with peculiar aptness to the ritual and spirit of Taoism. Much was read into it that would not occur to Western minds. It became the "froth of the liquid jade," a "religion of the art of life"; and the tea ceremony grew up as a symbol of the Zen

Le Thé vert.
Thea viridis, Linn. Sp. Pl.
Angl. Thée v.

Left: The tea plant, *Camellia sinensis,* in flower. *Below:* Harvesting the tea near Darjeeling, one of the sources of good black tea; to prepare this, leaves are dried but not fermented, as they are for green tea.

concept, that universal truths lie in life's smallest and least significant activities.

The eighth-century Chinese poet Lu Wu wrote a book on the ceremony in which his imagery illustrates this cosmic harmony. Tea leaves, for instance, must have "creases like the leathern boots of Tartar horsemen, they must curl like the dewlap of a mighty bullock, unfold like a mist rising out of a ravine, gleam like a lake touched by a zephyr, and be wet and soft like fine earth newly swept by new rain." A far cry from the English cuppa. But this is only a beginning. He expatiates on the quality of celestial porcelain to be used, the twenty-four utensils—from bamboo stirrer to tripod brazier—used in the making of tea, categories of water, stages of boiling (the last "when the billows surge wildly in the kettle"). The final euphoria comes with the drinking, each cup increasing the intensity of corporeal sensation and cerebral response. As another poet, Lu T'ung, wrote, listing the effects of each successive cup: "At the fifth I am purified; the sixth calls me to the realms of the immortals. The seventh cup— ah, but I could take no more. I only feel the breath of cool wind rising in my sleeves. Where are the Isles of the Blessed, Horaisan? Let this sweet breeze waft me there."

The Mongol invasions of the thirteenth century robbed China of these herbal rites. Tea resumed the role of beverage, not pathway to Elysium. But Japan, having adopted the tea ceremony a century or more before, escaped the Mongol conquest. And in Japan the rites continue.

The West has ignored these subtleties. Not even the silver teapots, the Dresden porcelain, the genteel conversation, and the

thinly sliced cucumber sandwiches of the Victorian tea party approximated the spiritual involvement of Oriental ceremonies. Balzac invested his tea with an exotic aura when he claimed that it had been picked by virgins at sunrise in a garden kept by mandarins for the emperor of China. But the prevailing philistinism is more clearly seen in the practices of W. E. Gladstone, the British Prime Minister. The hot water bottle he took to his bed each night contained tea. When its surface had warmed his toes, he drank the contents for inner warmth.

WINE—THE RED AND THE WHITE

Left: Caravaggio's painting of Bacchus, the god of wine. He supposedly brought the vine from the Middle East to Greece and later Italy. Throughout the Classical period he was associated with physical pleasure, festivities, and drunken manias.

This detail from the church door at the castle of Valère, at Sion in Switzerland, symbolizes Christ's assertion that wine was his blood.

If wine is Europe's drink, with its sovereign grapes residing in France and Germany, it nevertheless owes its existence both to Persia—where the wine grape, *Vitis vinifera*, originated—and to the United States. America's

Vintage scene painted on an eighteenth-century-B.C. tomb at Thebes in Egypt.

was twenty years before a solution was seen. The maligned (but immune) American vine was sent over by the millions, and ever since each European vine is grafted, before planting, onto an American rootstock.

him that is ready to perish, and to him that hath grief of heart; let him drink that he forget his poverty, and remember his misery no more." True, in excess it numbs the faculties, clouds the vision, defies arithmetic by making two of one, and causes its consumer from time to time to lie insensible on the floor, pavement, gutter, or similar foundation. But its merits far outweigh these slight defects. That rotund Shakespearean, Falstaff, was never so eloquent as when he expatiated on the virtues—in this case of sherry—which he had such good reason to know: "A good sherris-sack hath a twofold operation in it; it ascends me into the brains; dries me there all the foolish, and dull, and crudy vapours which environ it, makes it apprehensive, quick, inventive, full of nimble, fiery, and delectable shape, which delivered o'er to the voice (the tongue) which is the birth, becomes excellent wit. The second property of your excellent sherris is, the warming of the blood...."

indigenous grape produces a quite unpalatable tipple, but its merit is in being immune to the ravages of another American native, the phylloxera beetle. When European settlers tried to introduce the European vine, it repeatedly fell victim to this pest. Then, a few horrific years following 1860, the beetle took ship to Europe and killed almost every vine on the Continent. It

Noah in a drunken stupor *(below)* was a popular theme in the Renaissance.

Europe once again supplies more wine than the rest of the world's total.

Wine inspires. It "cheereth God and men," as the Bible tells. It breaks social barriers, and is second only to death in putting kings on a par with peasants. Solomon (who came late to wine—the Egyptians were drinking it six thousand years ago) ordered that "wine be given to

208

Fill ev'ry glass, for wine inspires us,
and fires us
With courage, love, and joy.
Women and wine should life employ.
Is there on earth aught else desirous?

John Gay, *The Beggar's Opera*

In vino veritas—in wine is the truth.

Pliny the Elder

Come, thou monarch of the vine,
Plumpy Bacchus with pink eyne!
In thy vats our cares be drown'd,
With thy grapes our hairs be crown'd:
Cup us, till the world go round,
Cup us, till the world go round!

Shakespeare, *Antony and Cleopatra*

The poet Li Tai Pe *(above)* was one of the great celebrators of the vine and the delights of intoxication. *Left:* The bloom on grapes contains the yeasts which will react with water and sugar to produce alcohol.

BEER—
THE CELESTIAL GARGLE

Oh many a peer of England brews
Livelier liquor than the Muse,
And malt does more than Milton can
To justify God's ways to man.
Ale, man, ale's the stuff to drink
For fellows whom it hurts to think:
Look into the pewter pot
To see the world as the world's not.

The lines are Housman's, and they are an unusual tribute from the fraternity of poets to beer. It is neither the most convenient nor the most refined means of attaining a state of exaltation. It has a smack of Nordic roughness which is at odds with the vinous civilizations of the Mediterra-

Gambrinus, the royal patron saint of brewing and beer, in a sixteenth-century Dutch painting by an unknown artist. *Below left:* A German Renaissance manuscript shows the brewing of beer.

nean. If a certain snobbery has a part in this attitude (beer was always the poor man's drink, made from the wheat, oats, millet, or barley by which he was surrounded), it still remains true

that while many progress from beer to wine, the opposite process is rare.

Sprouted barley, or malt, is the main source. It is crushed, boiled, and mixed with yeast, then left for some days to ferment. The action of yeast on the malt's starch and water produces alcohol, exactly as it does with wines and spirits. (Grapes, however, attract their own yeasts; with their high content of sugar and water they can turn to wine while still on the plant, though fermentation will continue for months afterward.) Nowadays most beers have other plants added for flavor, above all hops. Old additives included mushrooms, sugar, bay leaves, and poppy seeds, but there was a time when nothing at all was added. Flavors were thought up in the Dark Ages monasteries of France and spread to England and Germany and Scandinavia in the centuries that followed. Purism

BREWING

The basis of beer is always a cereal crop, usually barley, an ear of which is seen above. The starch contained in the grain will not be affected by the brewing process unless it is first allowed to germinate. The chemical change during this process converts the starch into malt. Malting takes place on a dry wooden floor in a room kept at a steady temperature to encourage growth. The malt is subsequently crushed in a press and boiled in huge vats, as shown in this eighteenth-century engraving from a German treatise on brewing. After boiling it is left for several days to ferment. During this period heavy fumes are given off by the action of added yeasts on

the starch and the fumes can be intoxicating in themselves. Flavorings may be added later. The most common is hops, shown *(left)* in an edition of Bock's herbal of 1577. This has now become a standard ingredient of most beers, but for centuries it was regarded as an adulterant to the pure brew and was forbidden by law in some countries, including England. Alternative flavorings, which have never achieved the same popularity, include mushrooms, sugar, and poppy seeds.

Left: A friar drinking beer. Many monasteries have won high reputations for the quality of their brewed beer, as well as for wines and aromatic liqueurs.

Below: A distilling furnace, from Philipp Ulstadt's *Coelum Philosophorum*. Spirits are obtained by boiling off alcohol from wine and other liquids. This is made possible since the boiling point of alcohol is well below that of water.

or jingoism caused the English to prohibit hops until 1556—later than all the rest—and a rhyme which is faulty in its chronology but sure in its conviction of the old days being the good ones lamented that:

*Hops, reformation, bays and beer
Came into England all in one year.*

Like wine, beer was known to the Egyptians five or six thousand years ago. It spread through Europe and Asia and was common in the Roman Empire, though the Romans themselves thought it barbaric. "The people of the West get drunk on moldy grain," complained Pliny. The grain used has always depended on the crops that prosper in a given area. Rice is used in Japan, and the beer of the United States is often based on corn. Barley remains the European norm, its name and that of the drink sharing a common root.

To be sure there are great beers. Holland, Czechoslovakia, and Ireland are among their producers, and there is a bemusing subtlety about the queen of Irish beers, Guinness, which puts it on a par with good wines. Dark from the roasting of the malt, and topped with a froth that is more like cream, stout (or porter, as it is called) has certainly enslaved the minds of poets. It has killed a few, too. The observation that an Irishman would bypass ten naked houris to reach his jar of porter—a gargle, Brendan Behan always called it—tells more of the drink than it does of the Celt's sexual reticence.

It is to yeasts, plants of the most elemental kind, that the formation of alcohol is mainly due. They are therefore responsible, with man, for that other great category of intoxicating liquors, the spirits. They are also one of the newest additions to the roll of stimulants, for though the Greeks could distill, it was the Arabs who perfected the art in

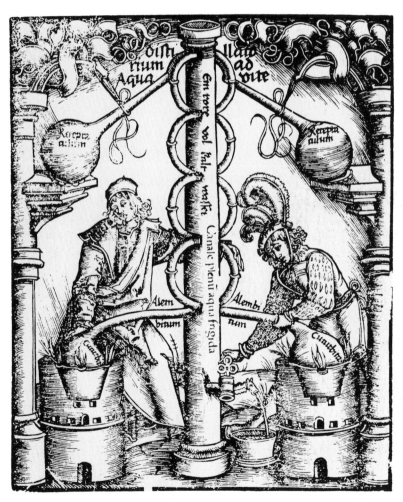

the Middle Ages. Distillation was effected most satisfactorily by heating a fermented liquor to a point between the boiling points of alcohol and water, so

that the alcohol alone vaporized, passed through a cooling coil, and was collected at the far end in a pure concentration. To the alchemists the process came close to their highest ambition, to distill gold from base metals. Alcohol, like gold, was a form of that fifth element—the *quinta essentia* or quintessence—which transcended earth, air, fire, and

water. Many today, devoted or addicted to their whisky, brandy, gin, rum, marc, or other *eau-de-vie,* would forcefully agree.

211

CANNABIS—HEMP, HASH, POT, BHANG

For some purposes the fibers made from the stems of hemp, or *Cannabis indica,* are better than those from flax and other plants. They resist water. They are good for sailcloths, caulking, and many more nautical functions. So wherever there are boats or navies or fishing fleets, the products of cannabis play—or played, until the general use of artificial fibers—an important part. If the climate allows, people who need it grow it themselves. In the time of Herodotus, about 500 B.C., cannabis had already spread from its south Siberian homeland to India, Asia Minor, northern Africa, and beyond.

During the last few hundred years—it is not known exactly when—it reached America. The climate of Central America, Mexico, and also the southern United States suited it ideally. It grew in plantations and thrived as a weed. For a while, in the eighteenth century, it was the most important agricultural crop of the Southern states. George Washington grew it on his estate at Mount Vernon. Authority smiled on it because of the service it did a growing maritime nation. But eventually the time came when authority could no longer overlook the plant's other roles.

What have become the more famous properties of cannabis belong to a resin exuded by the female flower. (Male and female flowers are borne on separate plants.) The best-quality *charas* or hashish, which is pure resin, is collected before the flower is fer-

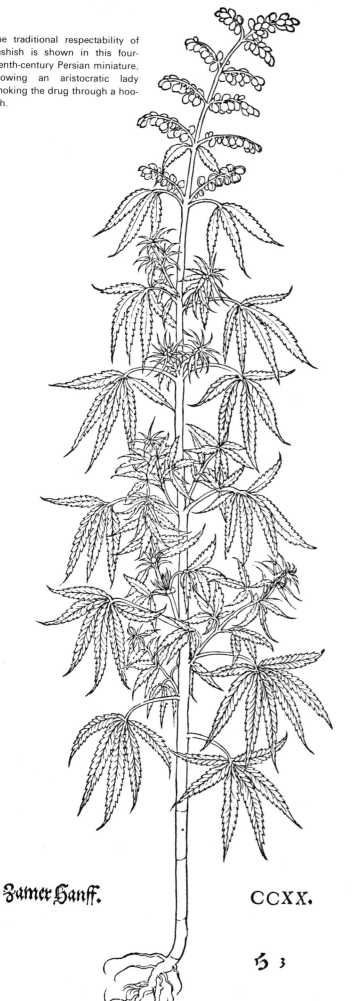

The traditional respectability of hashish is shown in this fourteenth-century Persian miniature, showing an aristocratic lady smoking the drug through a hookah.

Zamer Hanff.

CCXX.

Below: *Cannabis indica,* one of the oldest plants in cultivation. It is grown for its waterproof fibers, the oil of its seeds, and the drug known throughout the world. The woodcut *(left)* is from Fuchs's *Kreuterbuch* of 1543.

tilized. Marijuana is composed of the whole flowering head of wild plants. and it contains less resin and alkaloids than hashish. Marijuana is the Spanish-Mexican term for *bhang. Ganja* is similar to marijuana but comes from cultivated plants. There are several more names and synonyms—pot, grass, hemp, hash, and others—used in different countries and by different groups of people.

When governments began to adopt a new and censorious attitude to hashish, it was not because they had acquired new knowledge. The drug aspect of cannabis has certainly been known for as long as its capacity to make cordage. The Scythians described by Herodotus used to breathe in the fumes with the steam of their primitive sauna baths. The Chinese and Indians were smoking it at the same period, and probably had done for centuries. It was known to the accomplished black civilization of central Africa which built the huge fortress and monuments of Zimbabwe. Above all, perhaps, it was the opiate of the Moslem world, leaving its characteristic sickly-sweet smell about the bazaars and mosques and streets of their towns and villages. It appears constantly in Arabic literature: "Had an elephant smelt it he would have slept from night to night" is a common way, in the *Thousand and One Nights* and other tales, of describing a large and potent dose, sometimes altered from a matter of two nights to "from

year to year." The Arabs invented the elegant centerpiece of relaxed intercourse, the hookah, for smoking both hashish and opium. And it was a redoubtable fanatic of the same race, Al-

Hasan ibn-al-Sabbah, who gave his name both to the pure resin of the female flowers of hemp, hashish, and to a class of crime—assassination—which his followers practiced with zeal. Al-Hasan was not the brigand that legend

Then I understood the delight of the spirits
and angels when they traverse the heavens and
the skies according to their rank of perfection,
and how eternity might occupy one in paradise.

Théophile Gautier

has sometimes pictured. He was a devotee of Islam who believed that the decline of the Moslem strength, its moral lethargy, the fragmentation into sects, and the encroachments of Christian Crusaders had to be ended by a ruthless campaign of intimidation and purge. From the fastnesses of the Persian highlands, south of the Caspian Sea, his *hashishins* swooped on caliph and caravan, acquiring loot and killing those they regarded as enemies. For a hundred years his followers continued the terror, until toward the end of the thirteenth century Genghis Khan wiped out the total force of twelve thousand men.

The fury of the *hashishins* was provoked by cannabis (it is generally agreed, though rival assertions are made for opium). They would stop at nothing to obey their leader's commands, and risk of death was no deterrent. Rather it was the supreme reward, for the visions they experienced from the drug were explained to them by Al-Hasan as a foretaste of the Moslems' paradise, complete with its three orders of houris and uncountable orgasms.

If this was the most bloodthirsty episode in the history of cannabis, it has nevertheless often been associated with rebellion, dissent, nonconformism, and what calls itself the alternative society in our own times. In the Western world it achieved its peak in the artistic dissidence of the Parisian literary scene last century. There it became associated with minds

and thoughts which vastly inflated its reputation. In undeserved tribute to its powers, the club where those who took it gathered was called, in a spirit of artistic defiance, the *Club des Haschischins.* The tribute was undeserved, and the reputation inflated, because—as those who used it frequently pointed out—the quality of the visions and dreams it led to depended entirely on the minds of those who experienced them. There are other drugs which seem to contain within them the seeds of visions, of exciting hallucinations, of patterns and colors which recur constantly regardless of the imagination or intellectual ability of the subject. Not so with cannabis. A dullard sees dull visions. Those of Gautier and Baudelaire and their fellow members of the aforementioned club were conditioned by the creative abilities of their own minds.

A sad case illustrates this. A friend of Baudelaire, the artist Ernest Meissonier, took hashish, expecting to enter the dizzy, inspiring spheres he had heard described. Instead of the opulent anarchy of ideas and scenes he anticipated, he saw only sedate and symmetrical patterns. It was as if, he said, he was in a garden planned by Le Nôtre—"and I told myself: in this state of intoxication I shall never have Imagination." He was seeing only what could already be seen in hundreds of his decorative prints.

To Baudelaire, who in his *Les Paradis artificiels* has left a record of drug effects matched only by de Quincey's *Confessions of an Opium Eater,* the illusions fostered by hashish seemed to unite all branches of perception, all the senses, in a celestial marriage. Partly out of his experiences grew the doctrine of *correspondances,* which held that the perceptions of one sense had a direct relation to those of another, and could indeed be equated. Both, as it were, were different currencies, stated values of which were interchangeable. So a smell could be the artistic equivalent of a color, a musical note, or the savor of a wine. Baudelaire himself (influenced by the numeric theories of Pythagoras) equated musical and arithmetic sequences. Others found relations between, for instance, the color crimson, the odor of carnations, and the particular tones of a tenor clarinet. Gautier saw the notes emanating from a piano in terms of blue and red sparks. Later in the century the continued isolation of art from life, and from its established patrons the Church and the aristocracy, brought more outrageous—if less satisfying—correspondences.

A concert was once given in Paris at which, instead of notes being played, perfumes were released. A tonic scale from patchouli to bergamot was the basis. Not a sound was heard, save the impatient coughs and rustlings of the small audience.

It has been argued that theories of this kind were art going beyond itself, to fantasies which are ultimately sterile, and that cannabis may be blamed for leading good minds astray. Baudelaire himself wrote disparagingly of the drug, blaming it in later years for his physical and mental decline, though it is probable that opium, which occupied many more of his years than did cannabis, was chiefly responsible.

From this time on, the plant fell into mounting disfavor with established authority. A series of international conferences during the 1920s and 30s recommended the banning of both plant and use, and prohibition was introduced in the United States in 1937. But the habit was already widespread there, and there was little chance of the ban being applied thoroughly. Successive reports of research done on the toxic and addictive qualities of the drug suggest that moderate use carries no more risk to health or sanity than tobacco and alcohol, perhaps less.

Moreover it offers an increasing horizon of medical uses. General benefits known for years—its ability to lighten the psychological load of depressives, and to stimulate appetite—are being augmented by specific uses in pathology. This may prove to be a plant that wars with man and wins.

OPIUM—SOMBER AND SEDUCTIVE SPLENDORS

Left: A frieze from the palace of King Sargon II in Khorsabad shows a priest holding a poppy stem with three seed capsules. Egyptian doctors prescribed opium for calming upset children and for bringing relief to those in pain.

Opium is as old as medicine. It has probably healed and soothed more people and relieved more headaches, toothaches, bilious attacks, and hangovers than any other plant in the world's history. It has been a blessing to gods too. Demeter, the Greek earth

mother, miserably searching for her abducted daughter Persephone, came upon a field of opium poppies (*Papaver somnifera*), picked one, and swallowed some of its contained gum. Her sorrow was forgotten.

This was in late summer, when the fertilized, purple-and-white flowers had given place to substantial, hard-cased seed capsules. Demeter, like all who have followed her example, would have slit these capsules in several places, upon which a thick latex gushed out, then dried hard. In this condition it is easily peeled off. The seeds themselves, within the capsules, contain no opium but are rich in oil, which is used in making bread and curries as well as fuel in lamps.

The opium latex is rich in alkaloids, including morphine and codeine, laudanine, nicotine, and papaverine. Until comparatively recently, opium was administered with little processing for most painful or mentally disturbing illnesses, though it was often mixed with other ingredients to make patent medicines. Each in turn claimed thrilling new magic properties, but they were doing little but alter the taste of the opium, which was magic enough by itself. Real developments began in the early nineteenth century, when the German Friedrich Sertürner isolated the alkaloid morphine.

Further alkaloids were isolated during the century, and the effects of doses became stronger and much surer with the invention in 1851 of the hypodermic syringe, whereby liquids could be injected directly into the bloodstream. More recently this technique has been used for heroin, which, though based on opium, has synthetic additives. Codeine and morphine are both usually injected.

Opium latex or milk can be eaten, drunk, smoked, or simply sniffed while being burnt. Its strongest association is with the dens of the Middle and Far East, where seamen in port for a day or two dream out their tired fantasies on tightly packed bunks. Its role in the West has often been obscured by people's reluctance to admit dependence on a drug. Nevertheless it has been known and used on a considerable scale since Roman times. There have been campaigns to suppress it, including a prolonged one in eighteenth-century France, when a quite false belief that poppy seeds contained opium led to a series of enactments which alternately banned and reprieved them. The invention of an alcoholic tincture of opium has been attributed to Paracelsus, who gave his brainchild the name

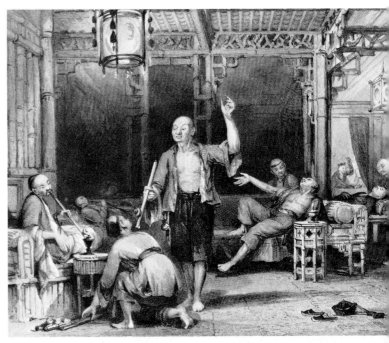

A chinese opium den *(above)* gives an impression of the squalor amid which addicts strove to return to the paradise their earliest experiences of the drug showed them. Sadly for them, its positive pleasures continually diminished as it took its toll of body and mind. The most they could hope for was to allay the misery of not taking it. In seaports, however, it also allowed a brief oblivion from the ardors of naval life.

More than once in the history of drugs, whole populations have been put at risk by the commercial policies of powerful states. The opium war waged by the British against China from 1839 to 1842 seems to have been one of the most cynical ever conducted. The debilitating effects of the drug, illustrated in the picture of Chinese workers below, caused the Chinese authorities to prohibit the drug. This meant a savage blow to the lucrative cultivation of the plant in Bengal, an important source of Britain's imperial wealth. In three years the British enforced a reversal of the Chinese decree. On the right, a campaign is shown in which the British fleet destroyed the junks defending the harbor of Canton in 1841. The Chinese opium trade revived for the rest of the nineteenth century, and a picture from the *Illustrated London News* of December 1883 *(above)* shows business being conducted on board an opium hulk at Shanghai in 1883. In Britain's defense it may be argued that the full effects of opium were not appreciated. Many respected members of the ruling class took the drug regularly—among them a pillar of society, William Wilberforce, champion of the emancipation of slaves. Others, however, were already demonstrating the worst effect of the drug.

laudanum. This was the most popular form of taking the drug until well into this century.

Victorian England, haven of moral rectitude, imported well over twenty tons of opium a year. It did not detract from the near saintly reputation of William Wilberforce, the prime emancipator of slaves, that he took daily doses of laudanum for the last forty-five years of his life. Jane Austen's mother took it against tiredness, and a little earlier Robert Clive—the military genius who managed to outwit both the Indians and the French in securing India for Britain—was a confessed addict, who finally killed himself with an overdose. George IV's doctors decided to wean him off alcohol by means of opium, though with misgivings about which of them was more likely to drive him along his father's road to madness. And up and down the country mothers were dosing their unruly infants with the stuff to calm them down, which they did, in thousands of cases throughout the Queen's reign, to the point of killing them—not intentionally, of course. The patent preparations they used were dressed up with names like Godfrey's Cordial, McMunn's Elixir, Mother Bailey's Quieting Syrup. But the manufacturers must have been well aware of the dangers, which had already been publicized by de Quincey.

Double standards also brought about one of the most repellent episodes in British colonial policy. Native to the Levant, Egypt, Turkey, and Persia, opium poppies had spread throughout the

COLERIDGE

Like many children of his time, Coleridge was probably given opium for some childish disorders in his early years. He continued to take it medicinally as a young man, but soon graduated to addiction. His two most famous poems, *Kubla Khan* and *The Ancient Mariner* were both inspired by what he called "the subtle and mighty power of opium." It was a power that caused him torments he was never able to escape.

DE QUINCEY

As an undergraduate, de Quincey bought a shilling's worth of laudanum at Oxford, and a short while later, in his lodgings, entered "an abyss of divine enjoyment." Perpetual ill health caused him to lean heavily on the anodyne qualities of the drug. He wrote the classic of opium addiction, *The Confessions of an Opium Eater,* in 1821 with the drug's support. Many attempts to give up failed. He died in a delirium, muttering about an invitation to "the great supper of Jesus Christ."

EDGAR ALLAN POE

The still-continuing debate about whether Poe was an addict or not is not helped by his unceasing lies about himself. The only reference he makes to taking it—an alleged suicide attempt—leaves the matter open. Certainly opium recurs often in his works. And Francis Thompson, who knew all about the drug, said Poe's was "the world of an opium-dream"—a world of gothic imaginings, sumptuous apartments draped with crimson hagings, despair, madness, and sin.

CHARLES BAUDELAIRE

Baudelaire had his first opium as a student at the Sorbonne. He later switched to hashish, reverted after a while, but often mixed the two. Though not often explicit about which drug was influencing him, he contrasts the harsher and more violent effect of hashish with the gentle and indulgent qualities of opium, with its "somber and seductive splendors." His *Rêve parisien* seems to have been written under the drug's influence; but some descriptions were borrowed from the works of de Quincy and Poe.

JEAN COCTEAU

Cocteau carried on the traditions of the nineteenth-century romantic movement, to the extent of repeating experiments with opium. Dreams, he claimed in his *Opium: Journal d'une désintoxication,* "can be a kind of education." Many of his writings and bizarre drawings reflect the dubious advantages of such education.

Below: A morphine addict in a painting by Grasset (1841–1917). The hypodermic needle, invented in 1851, made possible the direct insertion of chemicals into the bloodstream.

Moslem world as far as China, possibly as a result of Alexander the Great's campaigns. Bengal had been a major producer and China an important consumer for centuries, when the Chinese authorities imposed a ban. England, concerned more with the economy of her colony than the moral fabric of the Chinese, responded in 1839 with a three-year war. As a result, millions of Chinese remained addicts of what their government called the "foreign black mud" until 1906, when new edicts more successfully ended opium's hold on the country.

The worst aspect of opium addiction was that, having enslaved a person by the ecstasy of

early experiences, it provided ever-diminishing pleasure while strengthening its chains. The list of artistic luminaries it claimed is a formidable one. In England, Wordworth is the only romantic

poet not on record as having taken it. Not all who did were addicted—different metabolisms react in different ways, and it requires very strong doses to establish a real hold. Those who did fall under its spell often came to regard it as a divine influence, just as early man did, and just as contemporary primitives still regard their herbal drugs. Baudelaire, Verlaine, Francis Thompson, Coleridge all referred to it in religious contexts and made the smoking of it into something of a holy ritual. De Quincey, its most eloquent slave, regarded himself as the "Pope of the true church of opium." But, if it was akin to a god in the eyes of many, it was as jealous a god as the Old Testament Yahweh.

"O God, save me—save me from myself...driven up and down for seven dreadful Days by restless Pain, like a Leopard in a Den, yet the Anguish and Remorse of Mind was worse than the pain of the whole Body." This was Coleridge, trying to escape from one god through the intervention of another, in 1813. Yet since his day the number of addicts has grown dramatically, and it continues to grow by a Malthusian progression. De Quincey's *Confessions* encouraged more people than it deterred. The victory over China in the 1840s had repercussions in the West a century and more later when the illicit Chinese trade moved into Europe, backed by supplies which would not have existed except for that cynical war.

Far left: The opium poppy, *Papaver somniferum,* whose flowers yield the capsules *(left)* from which the latex or milk is spilt by regular vertical incisions. Drying quickly after it emerges, the latex is easily peeled off. *Below:* Cultivation of the poppy in Turkey, one of the main sources.

Claviceps purpurea, or ergot, is a parasitic fungus which usually completes its life cycle on or below a plant of rye, though certain other grasses can be its host. Its fruiting body develops on the ear of the rye, turning it into a

long, dark brown appendage. It is common in Russia, through central Europe, and as far west as Spain. Not very conspicuous, it was not realized to be a fungus until the end of the sixteenth century. Then it was linked, for the first time, with a disease which has periodically ravaged whole communities and inflicted unbearable suffering.

After that it attracted a good deal of attention from botanists and scientists, but it was not until this century that the poisonous alkaloids abundantly present in it were isolated. It was found to be a virtual chemical

factory, and several of its constituents (as is the way with poisons) were seen to have medical importance. In particular, ergotine was of use in narrowing the uterus after childbirth, and ergotamine was able to allay

some of the pain of migraine. Lysergic acid was also present, a close chemical relative of the other two.

In 1938 a distinguished scientist at the Sandoz chemical laboratories in Basel, Albert Hofmann, was attempting to use the molecular structures of these ergot derivatives to produce other useful medical substances. One of his experiments involved the addition of an unrelated chemical, diethylamide, to lysergic acid. He was neither looking for nor did he find, at the time, anything which would directly affect the state of consciousness

Above: Albert Hofmann, during the course of his research on ergot in the Sandoz Laboratories in Switzerland, synthesized LSD and in 1943 discovered its effect on the human psyche. Dr. Hofmann, shown here holding a molecular model of LSD, and his collaborators were also successful in isolating the hallucinogenic principles of the Mexican drugs teonanacatl and ololiuqui and in synthesizing the active fungus material psilocybin and psilocin.

Left: Timothy Leary was a lecturer in clinical psychology at Harvard until 1963, when his researches into the effect of psychedelic drugs, including LSD, mescaline, and psilocybin, led him into a storm of controversy. He believed that drugs can afford valuable insights into religious, philosophical, ethical, and aesthetic matters.

Right: A cat under LSD is terrified by a mouse.

Below: An early depiction of ergot on ears of rye.

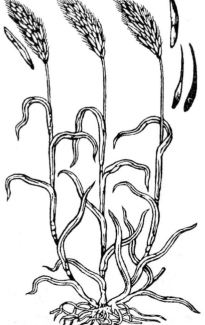

in the human mind. Indeed, it was not till five years later that he discovered what the combination of chemicals amounted to: the most powerful hallucinogen in the world's history, d-lysergic acid diethylamide, or LSD. The discovery was accidental. One day he felt peculiarly restless and dizzy after some hours in the laboratory. He went home, lay down, and had the first LSD trip in history. It took a careful process of elimination to discover why.

It was a synthetic additive which made ergots into the potent influence on medicine, psychiatry, art, painting, and cosmopolitan crime which they have since become. Lysergic acid by itself is not a hallucinogen. Nor are any of the other constituents of the fungus. But their appalling past effects, combined with the

mythology and imagination of those who suffered them, created remarkable delusions.

Ergots were never deliberately eaten, but before their connection with disease was established, and especially in times of shortage, they would sometimes be collected with the rye harvest and baked into the bread. Those who ate the bread would experience convulsions, electric sensations of tingling and crawling over the skin, and violent sickness. Constriction of the blood vessels—now a benefit in cases of difficult childbirth—then led to abortions, and in time to gangrene. Those who survived did not always survive intact. They might well have lost fingers or toes, arms or legs. In addition, while the disease raged, they felt a parched burning within them, which was so agonizing that it drove many mad.

In Christian times the obvious intermediary to invoke for this condition was St. Anthony. As a young man he had disowned the world and taken up residence in the Sinai desert. His most serious problem there was visions of naked and enticing girls and of wild animals. But he resisted both and lived to the ripe age of 105. It was this moral strength in resisting feverish delusions which particularly appealed to the victims of ergotism. Around the year 1100, when his son Gérin was stricken with the disease, a certain Gaston de Valloire promised St. Anthony in prayer to devote his life and wealth to other victims if his son's life was

spared. It was, and the Order of St. Anthony came into being.

Outbreaks continued all over Europe, but the saint responded generously to appeals for help. If a criticism could be leveled at him, it would be that he became almost over-officious in the execution of his responsibilities. For in addition to curing innocent victims, he readily inflicted the disease on the wicked. Soldiers who abused an image of him during the Reformation were immediately consumed by his fire. Those who called on him to witness their promises and afterward broke them would notice in due course a black stain on some part of their bodies. Accompanied by agonizing heat, it would gradually spread, leaving charred limbs to fall off in their time. With a curious. almost complacent brevity, a medieval chronicler tells of another case of saintly severity. The daughter of a noble family in the Dauphiné had stolen a silver vessel. "The servant-girl was accused," says the writer, "and badly treated, but her innocence caused them to question the daughter. She said that the fire of St. Anthony would burn her if it was she, and instantly the fire attacked her leg. The only remedy was to cut it off." The breathless narrative jumps forward in time without a gap. "Somebody married her and the husband was very surprised to see his wife put one of her legs on the table without bringing it to bed."

Ergots have been blamed by some for a strange phenomenon that still continues, from time to time, in Sicily and Calabria. This is more a madness than a disease, and it is traditional to blame the tarantula spider for it. The victim, after working in the fields, where the spider certainly exists, becomes fevered in mind and body. Again there is a burning heat, illusions, rantings. So common was the affliction, until as recently as the 1930s, that the churches of the area would hire a group of fiddlers to effect the conventional cure. The victims were assembled and began to dance to the music. This continued for hours on end—sometimes a whole night and day—until they fell in an exhausted coma to the ground. On waking they were cured. But, though the tarantula is blamed—and the dance is called the tarantella—it seems that the spider's bite is innocuous. A more likely cause is the parasite of rye.

Like bubonic plague, ergotism seems to have withdrawn almost entirely from Europe now.

Where the fungus still grows, milling techniques effectively separate it from the healthy grain, and the resultant bread is perfectly safe. There are areas where it is intentionally grown by pharmaceutical companies for medical products or for the manufacture of LSD; and the little brown growths can just be made out in the summer in Switzerland's rye fields.

Its future lies in doubt. Twenty or thirty years ago, the synthesis and trials of LSD led to an enthusiastic optimism about its potential in treating schizophrenia and other psychoses. Then the dangers came to light. Some estimates claim that half the conditions being treated in American psychiatric hospitals were themselves induced by drugs, not least by LSD. Many of the supplies shipped across from Europe find their way into the hands of crime syndicates, adding enormously to their powers and their purses. In some ways the intercession of a saint in heaven has never been more necessary.

on legends of the saint, partly on the horrors of the Thirty Years' War which the artist witnessed. In the bottom right-hand corner the aged ascetic bravely resists the terrors and temptations sent to test his pious resolves. His success made him patron of the sufferers of that other burning assault, ergotism.

223

All too often a person returning from a private world of vision and empathy finds himself frustratingly limited by his means of expression. He feels like Orpheus returning from Hades—the incomparable prize slips from him at the last minute. He is left, not with a memory, but with a reflection of that memory. His faculties of sight, speech, and imagination, being a legacy of the real, material world, are not fitted to conjure that foreign, exotic world which he has visited.

When Aldous Huxley describes his experiences under mescaline, there is a noticeable failing throughout all he has to say. He cannot escape from the conventions in which he was brought up—the Judaeo-Christian tradition—when he wants to convey the essence of universal religion. Artists, too, are constricted. Their paints and canvas are like feet of clay when wings are called for.

Nevertheless drugs do bring forth art that is enigmatically different from the art, be it representational or abstract, of real and palpable experience. So does religion. So do the nightmare perceptions of Hieronymus Bosch and the elder Pieter Brueghel, the intensified vision of van Gogh, or the diseased distortions of Edvard Münch. Again plants are the agent, the door through which perceptions of strange and occult realms are allowed to those who, for want of plant-drugs, would never have them.

Above: Detail from *Hide and Seek* painted by the Russian Pavel Tchelitchew about 1941. He may not have taken psychedelic drugs, but he penetrated an occult world deep in his own mind.

Left: Experience of the peyote cactus is reflected in *Peyote Meeting* by Stephen Mopope, 1930.

Right: Merging of figures into a visionary pattern in a 1955 drawing by Arthur Okamura.

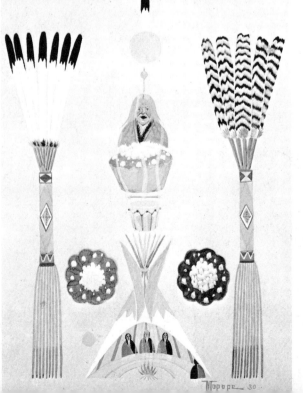

Above: Pen-drawing by Jacques Kaszemacher of 1965 shows a geometric mysticism based on psychedelic experiences.

Opposite page: Self-portrait at 55 East Division Street, a lithograph by Ivan Albright, 1947.

There are few people whose spirits are not lifted by the sight of flowers. Poets and artists look to flowers for symbols of happiness and beauty, love and pleasure. It is not only their appearance, colors, and scents that delight us. Like the sea, the kingdom of plants exercises an irresistible fascination upon our minds. In a landscape of trees—the "bare ruined choirs" of winter, the fresh and various greens of spring, the thickly matted foliage and lavishly splashed colors of high summer—lies the consistent and recurring pattern of the human environment. We know the seasons by the state of plants. A million years ago our gauche ancestors knew them even better. We emerged from a fostering blanket of plants, and our spirits and emotions, as well as bodies and minds, are fed and conditioned by them.

The gods of early man were plants, and our gods—Christian, Muslim, Hindu, Buddhist—are inseparable from plants still. At the dawn of each of the modern great religions a tree grows, the tree of the universe, of paradise, of the knowledge of good and evil. Woven into our worship, plants are part of our other spiritual rituals. They brighten festival and carnival, dances and parades, the celebrations of birthdays, marriages, victories. If plants are absent, we invent them. In prose and poetry, paint and stone, they continue to enhance our lives

power
over the spirit

in winter, at night, in the middle of asphalt cities. And when a young lover wants to express the most fervent, truthful passion he has ever felt in his life, he dispenses with dictionaries and learning, and the cunning arts of rhetoric, and says it with a rose.

Pages 228–229: Jan Brueghel's painting *Flora in the Flower Garden* shows the ancient Italians' goddess of flowers in a lavish Arcadian setting. Ovid tells how, after Zephyr had embraced her, flowers sprang from her breath and spread over the country.

This fresco *(right)* from Pompeii shows a maiden, symbolic of spring, gathering flowers for decoration.

For primitive man, before writing and exploration, before telescopes and microscopes and any remotely informed concept of the universe, before theories of evolution and the infinitesimal origins of all life, before any network of communication through which such theories could pass and grow, there was no possible understanding of a time scale: no centuries or millennia (none at least considered as such) to mark the rise and fall of different cultures or eras. Only the sun, moon, and seasons, death, birth, and imprecisely transmitted memories of ancestors, old cataclysms, romances, and migrations added a cloudy dimension of time to the visible, tangible present. Cause and purpose were enshrined in the palpable world. In the environment he could see man sought, for the most part, the sources of those powers that affected him, powers over his health and sickness, joy and despair, fear and courage, victory and defeat, life and death.

There, in what he could see, he found those powers. For him, they were enveloped in the objects of the sky and the components of climate like rain, storm, and wind; in the suggestive shapes of the landscape; in animals, and such artifacts as totems, cut stones, and idols; but above all in plants, the vast, varied, and constantly varying division of nature that carpets the land and the accessible floor of the sea, whose forms are seemingly infinite, and whose hold over the well-being of man is both indispensable and incalculable.

They fed him and cured his ills. They helped him kill both prey and enemies. They carried him to heights of ecstasy and into prolonged dreams. Some, simply by looking beautiful, delighted him. Others made him afraid—trees whose exposed roots or twisted branches looked in the twilight like maleficent beings, thorns that reached out to catch him as he ran, dark woods in which the unknown lurked. One way or another, plants exercised a constant power over his body, mind, and emotions. When he came to isolate and personify these separate powers, he peopled plants with spirits, kindly or malign, and proceeded to mollify them.

It must be a lonely, lowly plant that has never attracted the respect or worship of man. Every culture peopled the vegetation that surrounded it with a pantheon of gods and spirits, jinn and genie, goblins and demons, pixies and leprechauns, witches and trolls, elves, satyrs, centaurs, naiads, dryads, fauns, nymphs, and gnomes. Every national and regional folklore has its tales of forest demons, of the kind of spectral huntsman who in all countries from England to India rides through the woods which he personifies, spreading fear, sickness, and death; the female spirits whose beauty lures men to their graves; or those beneficent beings who offer sanctuary and refreshment under the shade of trees of which they are the incarnation. Every folklore has stories of plants with souls, plants which talked, plants in which the spirits of individual people were captive.

It was not as individuals alone that plants transcended reality. For in profounder and more mystical ways the annual cycle of plant life was intricately tangled in man's own destiny. In summer, nature burgeoned in a generous plenty. In winter, so it seemed, it died. Leaves dropped, flowers and fruits shriveled, and green became funereal brown.

Man knew little about the subterranean workings of root and corm, seed and bulb. For him, every spring, life emerged from death. To encourage it, he paid his respects to nature. He celebrated the spring, performed his own regenerative rites, and came to think of his own fertility as akin to that of nature. So the phallus and vulva and human copulation were involved in spring rituals to ensure the rebirth of plant life. And—by opposite association—plants were credited with powers over human procreation. All over the world, the celebration of May Day brings together the creation of both human and plant life.

Folklore is a mirror held up to the tangle of beliefs and practices of people long ago. It cannot present their gradual evolution, the way one idea was born of another. So it often appears like a collection of isolated legends and superstitions. Nevertheless scholars have traced some common themes, concepts which, once accepted, clung on tenaciously and have sometimes survived in a corrupted form to the present. At least some aspects of the Christian Virgin Mary stem from the concept of the Earth Mother, a goddess worshiped by the earliest cultivators to ensure that she bore them crops as their women bore them children. The Dasas of the Indus Valley, the Demeter of Greece, Ceres and Flora of the Romans, the Great Goddess Ninhursaga of Sumer—

The myths of Greece and Rome are full of such metamorphoses. Narcissus, seeing his lovely face for the first time as he leans over the reflecting waters of a stream, falls in love with himself and remains on the spot, pining away till his body dies and his spirit is transformed into the flower that still bears his name. Myrrha conceives a passion for her father, contrives to lie with him, and is chased away when he discovers her identity. Her miserable exile is at last relieved by the gods, who turn her into a myrrh tree:

Her solid bones convert
to solid wood,
To pith her marrow, and
to sap her blood....

As a tree she bears the son, Adonis, whom her father unknowingly caused her to conceive (see page 232). She continues to weep, but her tears are the precious resin which the Jews used to anoint the Ark and the Tabernacle, and which one of the Magi brought in homage to the infant Jesus.

Dante imprisons suicides within trees; lilies are supposed to grow from the graves of men wrongly executed; and from the tomb of Tristan grows an eglantine rose which, however often men cut it back, grows up again to entwine the image of Isolde.

Scraps of plant lore extend their powers and influence over men. There was an Irish belief that the fairies were thrown out of heaven, and flowers were sent on afterward to succor them. But the Devil, for his own purposes, sent harmful plants, resembling the heavenly ones, to confuse the fairies and spread grief among them, just as a poison berry or mushroom, that looks like a harmless one, does so on purpose to trick and kill. Other traditions tell of the clairvoyant powers contained in plants: tea leaves in whose patterns gypsies can see the future, flowers like pimpernel whose openings and closings foretell changes in the weather, groves of trees which endowed holy men with divining powers, sticks which Chaldean priests threw to make revealing patterns on the ground. In different places and ages primroses, branches of almond or hazel, and other magic wands have revealed the sites where treasure was concealed. It was a plant too—the sesame—which obeyed Ali Baba's command to admit him to the cave of gold. Indeed, in its shapes, colors, and changes, the whole plant kingdom has been a treasure-house and inspiration for the spirit and imagination of man.

all of these, and many more elsewhere, did embody the active female principle, the continual renewal both of vegetation and of the human race.

If Darwin's theory of evolution went against the Bible's account of creation, it was more acceptable to other systems. Several of them showed man's ancestry to lie in plants, if not in the lower animals. There are Middle Eastern legends of girls being impregnated by blades of grass. One of the mythical founders of China, Foh-hi, was born of a girl whose seed was activated by a flower she ate when she found it bending over her clothes after bathing. The same theme is restated in numerous variations. Tree spirits become fathers of men, plants change into people. And, contrariwise, people are always changing into plants.

In such green palaces the first kings reigned,
Slept in their shades, and angels entertained;
With such old counsellors they did advise,
And, by frequenting sacred groves, grew wise.

Edmund Waller

Above all plants, trees have commanded the respect and reverence of men. Their stature and longevity—"Generations pass while some trees stand, and old families last not three oaks," wrote Sir Thomas Browne—have raised them to the level of gods. The oak itself was sacred to Zeus, king of the gods, and in its prostrate state symbolizes the conquest of paganism by Christianity. Not that the latter excludes trees from its imagery and legend; the dependence of Christianity on trees and other plants is as great as that of any other religion (see pages 236 and 237).

For early man trees were of crucial importance. They sheltered him and gave him food, fibers, and the means of transporting his possessions. But their influence was not only material.

Changed into a myrrh tree after committing incest with her father, the princess Myrrha nevertheless gave birth to a son, Adonis, who emerged from the tree's trunk nine months after her crime and was cared for by the nurse Lucina and wood nymphs. The legend may have grown from an older fertility rite. Trees often symbolize female principles (and snakes sometimes the male). As such they were worshiped in Egypt, as shown in the fourteenth-century B.C. relief (top right) and in the Indian sculpture of a tree goddess (near right). The figure of an Indian goddess, Chulakoka (far right), standing beside a flowering tree, brings together two tree-themes from Indian myth. One is the elephant, whose trunk is coiled around the tree and on whom the goddess stands—an animal which, like the snake, is used as a symbol of the male. The other is the belief that a tree will flower when a beautiful woman touches it with her foot. (The sculpture is from the second century B.C.)

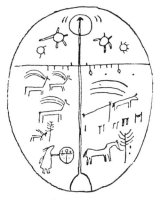

The forest's darkness concealed predatory animals, noises, elusive rustles and cracklings. Our fear of the dark may stem from an atavistic apprehension of the forest. Yet trees were beautiful too, and there are those who

The oil from the sacred sal-tree, *Shorea robusta*, is still used for incense in India. In earlier times it was closely twined with the life of Buddha. His mother bore him while holding a branch of the tree *(far left)*. In this Tibetan painting, the Buddha emerges from her right side after she had dreamed

hold that the Gothic cathedral is man's attempt to recreate the lofty dignity of tall boles surmounted by the sunlit tracery of leaves.

Their stature, their annual regeneration, and the unexplained (to those who first noticed it) power by which they drew sap to great heights through their stems led to worldwide beliefs in their divinity. They were peopled with spirits, credited with magic attributes, and in some cultures held to embody the whole structure of the cosmos.

that a white elephant came down from heaven and suffused her with his virility and wisdom. At the Buddha's death, two sal-trees formed a canopy above his body and, though it was winter, became covered with blossom from crown to foot. The shaman drawing *(top of page)* shows the mythical world tree that united earth and sky. The story of the metamorphosis of Daphne *(above left)* began when the girl's beauty aroused the ardor of Apollo. To escape his attentions she prayed to her father, a river god, who changed her into a laurel, or bay tree. The fifteenth-century Persian miniature *(above)* illustrates the legend of a talking tree which prophesied the early death, in a far distant country, of Alexander the Great.

233

Plants, according to the Veda, were created three ages before the gods. And certainly the Christian idea that God created human beings was preceded by beliefs that they sprang from trees. In the Iranian world picture the first man and woman were seen as a single tree, their fingers intertwined like twigs until two souls were breathed into them and they became separate beings. It is not hard to appreciate why, in pondering their origins, people saw in trees the archetype of growth, springing from the womb of the earth. To the primitive mind most things seem earth-born. Up to the last century English flint miners used to place stones upright in the ground in the hope that more would grow, and Robinson Crusoe planted the leg of a chicken with similar expectations. Long ago, people saw their ancestry in trees. But in these most massive of living creatures they saw more besides. In trees they traced the blueprint of the universe.

Yggdrasil was the world tree of the Norse. For them it brought a unity of pattern to all the living things they knew. The tree's roots were buried in the subterranean abyss from which all matter came. Its trunk rose through, and its lower branches supported, the disk of the earth. Its topmost branches sprayed out to form the heavens, whose clouds were its leaves and whose stars its buds. The four winds were four harts running across these branches, biting the buds. At the apex of the tree was an eagle, symbolizing the air. At its base was a serpent, gnawing at the roots and causing earthquakes and volcanoes on earth. Between the eagle and the serpent ran those perky and elusive pests, the squirrels, forever trying to stir discord between heaven and the dark abyss. From Yggdrasil's leaves dropped both rain and honeydew, the food of bees. So bees, which are people's souls, were fed by heaven. And thus, in a hundred picturesque details, the world picture was filled in on its arboreal background.

Hindus and Buddhists, Siberian shamans and Javanese holy men, Greeks and Romans all had their variants of the world tree. Common to them also is the concept of a tree of life, an epitome of paradise, whose fruits yield the divine ambrosia, blessing the lives of those who take it. When Zeus, the king of the gods, married Hera his sister, the goddess Earth brought as a wedding present an apple tree whose fruits were golden. By means either fair or foul (depending on which of several early sources you read), the tree came into the hands of the Hesperides, the daughters of the evening, who lived far out in the west, on the top of Mount Atlas. The west, in which the sun daily dies, was often seen as the realm of the dead, and it was probably in a symbolic conquest of death that Hercules came to steal the apples, in the last of his twelve labors. To do so he had to recruit Atlas himself, whose shoulders were bowed by the weight of the heavens, to kill the dragon which guarded the apples. While this was going on, Hercules took the weight of the heavens on himself, and narrowly escaped being left with them for ever. But he tricked Atlas back into supporting the load and went off with his plunder.

Apples and blessed gardens and immortality are themes found in other mythologies. Indeed, no other fruit enjoys the same exalted position. The Norse Edda tell of gods, when they feel old age coming on, eating an apple to restore their youth. ("An apple a day keeps the doctor away" is perhaps the most resilient snippet of herb lore.) The Arabian angel of death was able to destroy without harm to him-

self by holding an apple to his nostrils. And apples play a key part in the two seminal masterpieces of Western culture. It was for the reward of a golden apple that the three Olympian goddesses competed when Paris judged their beauty. To secure the prize Aphrodite offered Paris the most beautiful of mortal women—Helen—and in keeping her promise Aphrodite ignited the Trojan War, which is the subject of Homer's *Iliad*. And had Adam resisted the lure of the apple Eve offered him in Eden, there would have been no Bible, no Judeo-Christian world history other than the idyll of an immortal and obedient pair in Paradise.

To be fair, Adam's apple may have been Adam's apricot, Adam's quince, Adam's citron, or any of several other candidates. The actual meaning of the word, *tappuah*, that appears in the Old Testament is far from clear. Moreover, the native apple of Palestine is rather small and bitter—hardly appropriate for a central place in Paradise. These doubts have always left room for ingenious theories and exotic accounts, one of which was advanced by that credulous,

colorful traveler Sir John Mandeville. In Egypt, he reported, "men find long Apples to sell in their season and men call them Apples of Paradise and they be right sweet and of good savour and though ye cut them in never so many gobbets or parties overthwart or endlongs evermore ye shall find in the middles the figure of the holy cross of our Lord Jesu." To which he adds, for fear perhaps of being asked for evidence, "They will rot within VIII days."

Christianity in general made abundant use of the plant kingdom. Much of the power of its message derives from the symbolic use of trees. "Trees and woods," wrote the pious John Evelyn, "have twice saved the whole world: first by the Ark, then by the Cross; making full amends for the evil fruit of the tree in Paradise by that which was borne on the tree in Golgotha." Few of the properties of Christianity have vexed the minds of clerics, Crusaders, and scholars more than the nature of the true Cross. One claimant is the holm-oak or ilex, a tree which in other contexts is said nobly to take on itself the anger of the gods by attracting light-

ning. One story tells that before the Crucifixion all the trees of the forest agreed to shatter themselves in pieces rather than be instrumental in the Redeemer's death. When soldiers arrived to cut a tree down, they found all the trees except the ilex in tiny fragments. In some quarters the ilex is superstitiously avoided to this day.

Sir John Mandeville, true to form, recounts a more elaborate legend. The Cross, he has heard, was made from the wood of the Tree of Knowledge. When Adam was dying, he sent his son Seth to God for some oil of mercy from the seeds of this tree. Three seeds were sent, which, placed beneath his tongue, were buried with him. In time they grew into trees (one account has Noah's dove bringing back a sprig from them when the flood abated), and it was from these three trees that the Cross, according to Eastern Christians, was made. But Sir John disbelieves the story. The true Cross, he says, was made from four quite different trees: cypress, cedar, palm, and olive. Still other theories abound. One nominates the aspen, whose leaves ever since the Crucifixion have continued to tremble. And a curious account names the mistletoe, holding that it was once a fully fledged forest tree, but after its criminal role was condemned to be a creeping parasite. Whatever the truth is, there remain plenty of monasteries in Europe and else-

where whose claimed possession of part of the true Cross perpetuates the power of the tree in drawing worshipers from far and near.

The mistletoe's reduction in stature is a typical motif of mythology. The conquest of one people, creed, or religion by another often leads to the conquered race's gods being diminished to harmless insignificance. Fairies, leprechauns, and other little people of the supernatural realms are the midget descendants of full-sized gods. Today, without knowing why, people kiss under the mistletoe, and that is the beginning and end of their interest in it. Once, together with the oak on which it grew, it was the most sacred plant of the Druids, regarded as a panacea of all ills and celebrated with ritual sacrifices. But in Scandinavian myth it played a more sinister role, being the arrow with which Balder, the heroic son of Odin, was killed by the wicked spirit Loki. By agreement of the other gods, Balder was restored to life. The mistletoe, to be kept out of harm's way, was entrusted to Balder's mother Frig on condition that she never again let it touch the earth, which was the

empire of the evil Loki. So it remains atop the trees, and people who meet under it kiss in peace and love, in the assurance that the mistletoe can do no more harm.

In the dramas of myth and history plants play many roles. Perhaps the least acknowledged is that of moral preceptor to mankind. "Consider the lilies of the fields...." said Christ. Others have pointed to the undemanding patience with which they bring so much blessing and pleasure to the world. "We may draw matter at all times," wrote the herbalist John Parkinson, "not onely to magnifie the Creator that hath given them such diversities of forms, sents, and colours, that the most cunning workman cannot imitate, but many good instructions also to our selves; that as many herbs and flowers, with their fragrant sweet smels do comfort and as it were revive the spirits, and perfume a whole house, even so such men as live vertuously, labouring to do good, and profit the Church, God, and the common wealth by their pains or pen, do as it were send forth a pleasing savour of sweet instructions."

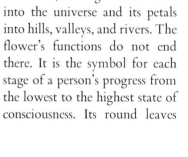

The plant world has its aristocrats: blooms whose form, structure, and perfume tower so remotely above those of other flowers that they seem to belong to other worlds. The very fabric of the petals of some of them—lotus, peony, tulip, rose, and

tamian empires, from whom it passed into the religion of the Jews, and later the Christians. Among them it attached itself to the Virgin Mary as a symbol of purity, particularly during the Annunciation, to emphasize her virginal innocence when she

When the Spanish conquistadores discovered the passion flower *(above)* in South America, they saw in its elaborate flowers the elements of the Crucifixion—whipping post, crown of thorns, spear, nails, bloodstains—which they took as a divine sign of their future success. *Left:* The Madon-

the world, turning the lotus itself into the universe and its petals into hills, valleys, and rivers. The flower's functions do not end there. It is the symbol for each stage of a person's progress from the lowest to the highest state of consciousness. Its round leaves

na lily, in photograph and in a detail from Simone Martini's *Annunciation. Above and right:* The lotus, in photograph and as it was believed to have conveyed the Buddha over the water.

lily—seems to be made of some unearthly substance, some kind of vibrant marble. Two of these above all—the lily and the lotus—are connected with spiritual things wherever they occur. The lily was a symbol of purity long before Christian times. The Greeks made its origin drops of milk spilled from Hera's breast when she was suckling the infant Hercules (the same liquid that splashed across the sky to form the Milky Way). It was sacred to the Assyrians and other Mesopo-

conceived Christ. One story tells that the doubter St. Thomas was absent when the Virgin died and would not believe that she had ascended to heaven. When her tomb was opened to convince him, it was found to be full of fragrant lilies and roses.
In the Hindu religion, the lotus is central. It is the cradle of the universe, having issued from God's navel and floated onto the waters of the flood which swept away creation. Within its flower sat Brahma, who was to recreate

represent the motion of intellect, and its ability to rise clean above the mud where it grows shows the dominance of divine wisdom. It stands for beauty, grace, and divinity, and there is no town or hamlet in India where its spreading tendrils and subtly simple flowers are not represented and revered.

The palm *(left),* symbol of victory, was carried during Christ's triumphant entry into Jerusalem.

BUDDHA

At the hour of his birth, an asvattha or peepul tree—
Ficus religiosa—sprang from the center of the universe.
He himself appeared floating on an enormous lotus
leaf. He is represented by the Chinese sitting under a
banyan tree, receiving homage from the god Brahma.
Under this same tree he attained his full dignity.

BRAHMA

The mulberry is the seed of Brahma, *Hemionitis cordifolia* is the leaf of Brahma, and from the munj tree,
Saccharum munja, comes the sacred girdle of his worshipers. He was born in the bosom of the lotus. Before
his birth there existed only Om, the supreme being,
and on the sea a lotus, which quickened into the sun.

CHRIST

The rose of Jericho, or rose of Mary, first blossomed
at Christ's birth. It closed its petals at the Crucifixion
and reopened them at the Resurrection. Cedar,
cypress, palm, and olive made up the Cross. The
crown of thorns was of holly and briar. The dwarf
birch was stunted because it formed the scourge of
Christ. But he blessed the palm for all time because it
once bent to offer its fruits to his mother.

APOLLO

The bay-laurel and palm were sacred to him. When
Zephyr killed the youth whom Apollo loved, he
caused the hyacinth to spring from the victim's
blood. The cornel cherry, *Cornus mascula,* was sacred
to him, and when the Greeks cut a plantation down
to build the wooden horse of Troy, he demanded
long expiation of the sacrilege. The Apollo of Lesbos
holds a tamarisk in his hand.

MOHAMMED

In the middle of the paradise of Mohammed stands
the mystical tooba tree, round which even the fastest
horseman could not ride in a hundred years. He
called henna, *Lawsonia inermis,* chief of the flowers
both of this world and the next. Legends tell that
both rice and the rose sprang from a drop of his sweat,
fallen from paradise.

TREES OF
TRAVELERS' TALES

There was a time when herbalists picked their healing plants only at certain times of day, during certain phases of the moon, or under the ascendancy of certain planets. Modern science was, for much of its life, skeptical and scoffing. A plant is a plant, it said, at any time of day, and carries the same ingredients. But increased knowledge made science itself wiser. Plants were found to contain as much as five times the amount of some chemicals at one period of the day as they did at another. Science coughed an acknowledgment, and reserved its scorn for moon and planet theories. Yet the belief that root plants grow best when planted while the moon is below the horizon, and fruits and leaf vegetables when the moon waxes, is still vigorously asserted by some champion vegetable growers. Even planet theories have their adherents. Perhaps, in time, the scientists will come round to these views too.

The trouble is, of course, that myths and folklore develop for different reasons. Arab traders spun exotic fables about their spice sources in order to frighten away competition. That branch of mythology is a pack of lies. No doubt too many travelers have had their credulity played on, like many modern journalists whose gullible enthusiasms inspire their subjects to fresh flights of fancy. Sailors, besides, are notorious for exaggerating, reckoning that weird tales raise their esteem in the minds of their hearers. Doubtless many a tall

The Scandinavian Yggdrasil, which represented the world, the underworld, and the heavens, in each of which lived animals whose conflicts were perpetually sharpened by scurrying squirrels.

tree or rainbow-colored bloom and many a man-eating shrub are the products of deck-dreams in a broad, monotonous sea.

Whether they are moonshine or hybrids of fact and fancy, these tales have color. From Ethiopia, that powerhouse of invention, came reports of a talking elm. According to Philostratus, two philosophers were engaged in heavy conversation under its shade. At one point a branch bent down to their level, and "with a distinct but high and shrill voice, like a woman's" it complimented the men on their wisdom and joined in the con-

versation. Other accounts tell of trees walking, a faculty exploited by anyone who could persuade, say, a fruitful olive (as Anastasius of Nice was supposed to do) to move from his neighbor's onto his own lands.

Plants are often said to have shown magnanimity to deserving humans. The fagots of wood piled up to burn a martyr would refuse to catch fire; and once a corporate gesture was made by the plants in the garden of Albertus Magnus. He was giving a banquet to persuade some men to help his monastery. It was a gray, wintry day, and the guests were cold and frugally fed. Suddenly the atmosphere changed. Trees burst into leaf and bore succulent fruit. Sweet-smelling grapes weighted the vine, and bright flowers radiated cheerfulness. (Even the birds came to sing.) The feast ended in great cordiality, the business was done, and when the last of the guests had departed, winter, snow, and drabness returned. But Albertus was happy.

There is very often collusion between animals and plants. The nightingale falls in love with the rose, cats travel miles to enjoy the delights of catnip. In Guadeloupe there is a legend of a tree that bears oysters. From the leaves of a magic tree in Chile come forth worms which grow into serpents. And when the leaves of a certain tree in the Moluccas drop to the ground, they are transformed into butterflies. Certain Chinese plants bring forth beautiful birds, but

in this context no plant has ever gained such a reputation as the barnacle tree, whose fruit was neither berry nor barnacle, but the barnacle goose.

During the Middle Ages there was a widespread belief that this goose (which in fact breeds in the Arctic, unseen by man) sprang from a tree. It could thereby be argued not to be meat but plant matter, and so perfectly acceptable food during times of fast. There are numerous versions of the legend. Gerard claimed that the actual fruit of the tree was a fish, from which spilled shells, "which shells, in time of maturity, do open, and out of them fall those little living things which, falling into the

A seal from Mohenjodaro (above) shows the sacred asvattha tree, from whose branches grow animal heads symbolizing fertility.

water, do become fowls." Giraldus Cambrensis, following the Norman conquest of twelfth-century Ireland, linked the bird with the barnacle that clings to wood or the hulls of ships. Within the shell, he claimed, was the

perfect miniature form of a goose, "and in the course of time, having put on a stout covering of feathers, they either slip into the water or take themselves in flight to the freedom of the air." He stressed nevertheless that the bird was of plant origin, the barnacles themselves being natural growths from the wood.

There is no limit to plants' mythic powers. Trees bleed in pity for the men hanged from their branches; flowers can open locks and unshoe horses. The smell alone of the apples of Pyban was enough to feed the

people—albeit pygmies—who lived near them. And in the *Arabian Nights* appears the musical tree which, whenever it breaks out into song, is accompanied by its leaves in consoling harmony.

While picking flowers in a meadow, the goddess Persephone, daughter of Demeter, was seen by the lord of the underworld, Hades, who swept her into his chariot and drove through a chasm to his dark kingdom. Demeter sued for her release and won, but because Persephone had eaten a seed from a pomegranate while there, she was compelled to return each year to her captor, dividing her time between her mother and the underworld. Winter is caused by Demeter's sorrowful neglect of the earth while her daughter is away.

The Mochicas created an empire along the coast of Peru between 400 and 1000 A.D. Before the Incas, they produced the finest ceramics of any culture in the subcontinent, and like other cultures they raised their staple, maize, to divine status. As this vessel shows, god and grain were one, at the same time the symbol and reality of fertility. Each year the god was petitioned by feast and sacrifice to grant a generous crop and to deter the god of rain.

Paradise was first of all a Persian word. It meant a garden or park. It also meant paradise in the sense we use the word. For the Persian—for the Moslem—there is no distinction between heaven and gardens, and there are many of other religions who would endorse the view. "God Almighty first planted a garden," wrote Bacon, "and indeed it is the purest of human pleasures. It is the greatest refreshment to the spirits of man." It is hard to think how any God, when archi-

tecting his heaven, could improve on some of the finest worldly gardens. And even humble gardens—mean patches constricted by boundary walls, ranks of utilitarian garden allotments, window boxes a meter long—are seen by their owners as corners of paradise. Every garden needs to be created. In every gardener there is a little bit of God.

"And the Lord God planted a garden eastward in Eden...."

Little is known about that most celebrated garden. "And out of the ground made the Lord God to grow every tree that is pleasant to the sight, and good for food; the tree of life also in the midst of the garden, and the tree of knowledge of good and evil. And a river went out of Eden to water the garden...." Nothing else is told, except some topographical details about the four branches of that river. Theories have multiplied over the centuries about where exactly the garden was sited, and fortunes, in pilgrim or tourist money, have been collected by rival custodians all over the Middle East and as far afield as Sri Lanka and Sweden. But the facts—if facts they be—are no more than those few lines in the second book of Genesis. For all the debate, they are enough to provide everybody with his private picture of the paradise garden.

As long as man was nomadic, gardens did not exist. So it is in the first centers of settlement that we find the earliest gardens, and in many cases the grandest. Nothing, by all accounts, has ever surpassed the massive ostentation of the Hanging Gardens of Babylon, a huge pyramid of pillars and terraces a hundred meters high, covered with trees and flowers, fountains and lakes, built to satisfy the whim of Nebuchadnezzar's wife, who was bored.

Babylon fell and Persia rose, and with it a different concept of gardens. There was a formality, of walls, canals, blue-tiled ponds,

and avenues of plane trees, to contain the sensual delights of color and scent. Gardens became a foretaste of the Moslem paradise, while the attention given to certain plants—roses, peaches, and other fruits—developed varieties which have since spread around the world.

Garden symbolism has always been strongest in the Far East. Chinese and Japanese gardens were conceived as microcosms of nature, busy with rockeries, streams, miniature bridges, pagodas, and islands of eternal youth or of unending happiness. They were stocked with exotic flowers and peacocks and pheasants strutted among the still sheets of water. From them grew the concept of the Zen garden of tranquility.

In the West, practicality marched with decorative qualities. The formal Roman garden, with its neat arrangements of juniper and laurel hedges, its long pergolas with their trellises of vines, its temples and statuary, made as much of medicinal plants as it did of ornamentals. So did the typical monastery garden, where every feature had its function: the pond for fish, hillock for rabbits, dovecote for a ready supply of winter food, and a neat geometry of herb beds that served as an outdoor medicine chest.

A garden allotment *(far left)* in Switzerland is a small strip of land rented by city dwellers who go out to it at every opportunity to work at Adam's profession, or perhaps to relax, enjoy their flowers, meet friends, and approximate their way of life as best they can to that of Eden.

A maple tree *(left)* at Matibo in Piedmont early in the nineteenth century shows an extreme case of the gardener's tampering with nature: a belvedere fashioned from the tree, with two eight-windowed rooms inside.

The inventive genius of Paul Klee (1879–1940) made a garden out of a motley of symbols and a motley of symbols out of a garden *(below)*. The flowers of his fantasy lean and leer in droll and curious contortions. Whimsy pervades the picture (Klee spoke of drawing as "taking a line for a walk"). But the prime inspiration of this *Cosmic Garden*—in which those who seek will find symbols sexual, religious, and mundane—is the world of plants, controlled by man's passion for order and organization.

Imagination can conjure nothing closer to paradise than a garden. Both the Bible and the twelfth-century Byzantine painting *(below)* show paradise as a garden, an Eden watered by four rivers, rich in fruitful trees, and inhabited by angels. In the illuminated Bible *(right),* designed for King Wenceslas a hundred years later, the link is maintained in the depiction of a heavenly bounty of fruits and flowers.

1 A fifteenth-century walled herb garden with monks at work cultivating the beds.

Into those twin functions of Eden and all gardens since—pleasure and produce—people have invested as much ingenuity as they possess. In the Renaissance garden, pleasure lay in contemplating the strict alignment of house, garden, and amenity. Nature was fairly severely subjugated to design, and she was to remain so until, if not freed, at least paroled by the English landscape gardeners of the eighteenth century. Nevertheless, within these defined limits there was room for a riot of invention. Natural objects were clipped into neat, quadrangular hedges, corseted around pergolas and arbors, interspersed with rocks and bricks, temples, busts, and colonnades. Terraces and flights of steps, parterres, and knot gardens extended the linear architecture of a house toward the countryside beyond the walls.

This imposed order became the setting for human entertainment and diversion. Along shaded walks people strolled conversing elegantly like the scholars of Academe, lovers bantered, and poets soliloquized. At feasts and masques, the music of cornet, lute, and sackbut wafted among the color and scent of flowers, pleasing three senses. The other two were not neglected. There would be peaches and oranges to divert the taste, and tactile pleasures came from baths, held without prudery in the open air. And there were games to play. Mazes and labyrinths trace a misty ancestry back to the chilling haunts of the Cretan Mino-

taur, but in Renaissance Italy, France, and England they became popular time-passers. Sometimes the sense of fun went beyond moderate tastes. At the sumptuous gardens of Philip the Good, Duke of Burgundy, at Hesdin, footsteps could release mechanisms which doused the unwary with water or feathers, or plunged them into ponds, while other devices could simulate thunder, lightning, or rain. In such settings plants were losing some of their hold on people, but it was not to be for long.

Seeds brought back from the Far East or the Americas revived an interest in individual plants which had anyway never been neglected in the monastery, botanic, and medicinal gardens of Europe. What those imports did was to provoke a spirit of flamboyance and competition among gardeners, a spirit which has never, before or since, surpassed the devotion of the Dutch to the tulip in the 1640s.

2 The medieval Mary-garden, surrounded by high walls, represented the Virgin birth; its flowers were symbolic of other Christian features.

3 A lover picks a rose in a sixteenth-century edition of The Romance of the Rose.

4 Visual and vocal arts are united in this Meistersinger's garden of 1645.

5 The labyrinth was always popular in the gardens of the rich, for it provided exercise, entertainment, and the perpetuation of an ancient symbolism.

The tulip had reached Europe from Persia (where it grows wild) a hundred years before, without exciting great notice. (An Antwerp merchant, not knowing what to do with the hundred bulbs he had been given, fried and ate them.) Suddenly tulips became the craze. Every Dutch painting of the period includes them; and merchants persuaded people that commission a Brueghel to paint a tulip than to buy the plant. When the bubble burst, hundreds of dealers went bankrupt, and many hanged themselves. There have been similar outbursts since with other flowers, but none has reached the heights of tulipomania.

The history of gardens contains innumerable excesses and deviations, numerous sharp switches

Water, important to any garden, has often been treated as the dominant feature, channeled through the flower beds to spring up in elaborate fountains or to fill huge baths. In warmer climates these were not merely decorative but were used, as the illumination at left from a fifteenth-century Lombard manuscript shows, for the bathing of both sexes.

A detail from the *Last Judgment* by Fra Angelico *(right)*. Depictions of heaven have always made use of the gardens and flowers familiar to the artist's environment. In paintings by the Italian and Flemish schools in particular, the detailed delineation enables exact identification of the most popular flowers: lilies, gillyflowers, marigolds, irises, roses, primroses, and others.

their gardens would be incomplete without them. Prices climbed, and for rare varieties they rocketed to the skies. Tulips, in a sense, became their own currency, the objects of market speculation. A miller parted with his mill for one bulb, others fetched thousands of florins, one a coach and pair, another five hundred kilos of cheese. It was cheaper to of style, fashion, and vogue. Gardens arouse passion, envy, and feuds. But for most people a garden remains what it always was: a lease during this life of a corner of the next. Voltaire's Candide, after all his adventures, sufferings, shipwrecks, and tortures, gives the age-old recipe for true contentment with his last words: "Let us cultivate our garden."

247

The greatest gardens of the Western world have often been shaped by the radical thought of one man. In the East, the evolution has been more gradual, the development of a concept to which individuals are subordinated. Vignola, Le Nôtre, Loudon, Capability Brown—who, when asked to design a garden in Ireland, replied tersely that he had not finished England yet—imposed their personal visions Farnese, the Villa Borghese, or the Villa Lante, of Versailles and Malmaison, or of Sheffield Park and Stourhead leave little to the imagination. The mind is too busy with appreciation to have time to reflect or imagine. Just as the oriental tearoom, setting of an ancient ritual, almost shocks the Western visitor accustomed to the jostled adornments of his cathedrals and dining-halls, so the Chinese or Japanese garden,

on a generation, and sometimes two or three. Not that any of them swept the past away; but they used it for their own aesthetic purposes.

There is another difference between West and East. The East suggests, the West says all there is to say. The splendors of the Villa with its sparse and studied symbolism, contrasts strongly with the often theatrical creations of the West.

But in the heights which, in their finest achievements, both cultures have reached, there is no room for objective grading, only for personal preference. Japanese

and Chinese gardens (in spite of widely different styles) express the intimacy of man with an idealized version of nature. Perfection is a goal much sought after, both in general effects and in individual plants and blooms. (A Chinese might well invite his friends to see a peony at peak.) And nowhere is perfection better expressed than in some of the famous Zen gardens, many of them little changed after five or six centuries.

There are shapes—of rock or wood—set in empty expanses to concentrate the attention. A lake may be in the form of the Japanese character for soul. Great trouble is taken to display every minute detail of nature: the play of sunlight through russet maple leaves, the subtle differences between fifty species of moss. The mind is concentrated and needs no company.

But the Western gardens lack something vital if they contain no people. Though the eighteenth century broke out of the formal restraints of the Renaissance, it continued to subject nature to art. Temples, belvederes, and bridges still catch the eye sooner than woodland, shrubs, and sweeps of lawn in the Palladian gardens that still enhance the landscape where the nineteenth century was respectful enough to leave them alone. Where it did, it could not have known what a service it was doing posterity. The age of great gardens is gone, and we must content ourselves with survivals from the past.

Laid out in the mid-eighteenth century, Stourhead *(far left)*, in Wiltshire, England, filled what had been a bleak valley with a studied asymmetry, surrounding an artificial lake with temples, grottoes, and—a fad of the times—a hermit's cottage, and woodlands that are now among the country's finest. Serenity is the keynote of the imperial Japanese garden at Shugakuin, outside Kyoto *(left)*. A detail *(above, top)* from the grounds of Versailles, and an engraving *(above, center)* of the gardens surrounding the Grand Trianon, a vista of magnificent formality designed by Le Nôtre. The gardens of the Villa Lante at Bagnaia *(above)* were Vignola's masterpiece, of which Montaigne wrote that "it takes the prize by a long way."

249

1 Detail from *Love Crowned* by Fragonard. Spring, flowers, and love are constantly woven together in myth and art.

2 One of the 60,000 plantings of liberty trees in France in 1790, after the Revolution.

3 Rich floral setting for the bride in the 1934 film *It Happened One Night*.

The worldwide celebrations of May Day trace their origins back to the Roman festival of the Floralia, to the Greeks, and on into the mists of prehistory. Their theme is love: universal love, brotherly love, young love.

And their inspiration in all the countries and continents which observe them (despite an incongruous annexation by communism in recent years) comes from the flowers of spring. Chaucer tells how every May Day the Court went out to the country "to fetch the floures fresh, and branch and blome":

And then rejoysen in their
great delite,
Eke each at other threw the
floures bright;
The Primrose, Violette,
and the Gold,
With garlands partly blue
and white.

For nothing better enshrines the emotional yearnings of man, or

provides a more congruous background for his celebrations and festivities, than flowers. Garlands, chaplets, wreaths, posies, bouquets, and nosegays still adorn bodies, rooms, churches, halls—and did much more in less prosaic times—whenever the occasion demands more than mere words can say. Tree plantings mark great events; a posy of daisies marks a child's impulsive delight in nature or affection for a parent. People give flowers at welcomes and at separations, on Christmas and birthdays, to lovers, mothers, brides, and patients confined to bed. Queen Victoria even gave a flower—the first buttonhole, as legend has it—to Prince Albert before their wedding, a gesture which caused that fastidious nobleman to cut a slit, instantly, in the lapel of his black morning-coat and insert the bloom.

A Martian might wonder if human happiness was entirely dependent on flowers. All over the world parades, pageants, and festivals attest that dependence, nowhere more so than on the subcontinent of India, where the rich aromas of tropical flowers pervade every moment of the day, while rituals demand the dedication of mountains of flowers at shrines and temples. In the past the Buddhist pagoda at Ruanwelle, nearly a hundred meters high, was so closely festooned with garlands that it seemed like a uniform pillar of flowers. The medieval regulations of the temple at Dambedenia in Ceylon demanded that

every day during the holy season a hundred thousand blossoms—and of a different kind every day—should be presented. Nevertheless, in terms of size alone, the greatest displays the world has seen belong to Flanders, which like its neighbor Holland never stints the vaunting displays of its native produce. In 1973 the great square at Ghent was filled by a floral pattern consisting of 1,800,000 begonias, covering

over 6000 square meters—the world's largest man-made flower arrangement.

One of the great flower festivals of Europe is held in Genzano, near Rome; it traces its ancestry to the riotous floral celebrations of classical times. Hans Andersen was astonished by its profusion of blooms, and the skill and industry which had gone into the making of floral mosaics—"richer in pomp of colouring than anything which Pompeii can show." Carpets woven of leaves and blooms hung from the

windows of houses, representing scenes from the Bible. "Roses formed the faces, the feet, and the arms; gilly-flowers and anemones their fluttering garments; and crowns were made of waterlilies, brought from Lake Nemi."

Certainly the love of ostentation is an emotion that makes full use of flowers. For the roses whose petals carpeted the floors and showered his guests at one banquet, Nero spent the price of a palace. Cleopatra caused a lake to be strewn with roses, and she had the floor of the room where

4 Girls in Bali decorate themselves with exotic flowers.

5 Two old women carry bouquets of flowers as symbols of mourning at a funeral.

6

6 Mask and spray of artificial flowers used in the Tyrol in the nineteenth century to drive away the winter spirits of darkness and cold.

7 Flowers by the billion deck the world's great pageants. Here women carry golden vases of flowers at the annual carnival in Rio de Janeiro.

7

8 A funeral mourner weighed down by flowers.

9 The wreath traditionally given to a victorious racing driver.

8

9

she entertained Mark Antony covered with them to a depth of half a meter. When the League of Nations was inaugurated at Geneva, the Aga Khan had 30,000 roses sent for the occasion. And in 1956, at his wedding to Grace Kelly, Prince Rainier of Monaco had the bay sprinkled with thousands of red and white carnations. In the face of all this opulence, it is perhaps a relief to recall the tasteful piety of the schoolgirls of Rouen, who every year, on the day Joan of Arc was burned, scatter flowers on that part of the Seine where the English threw her ashes.

Flowers accompany death as much as they do life. Amaranth and asphodel, myrtle and polyanthus, yew and cypress—of which Byron wrote, "Dark tree, still sad when other's grief is fled, the only constant mourner of the dead"—are denizens of the cemetery and guardians of the grave. With wreaths and bouquets we express our silent sadness for the dead. In death, as in life, flowers are the most eloquent orators.

The persistent influence of plants on our lives and thoughts is clearly shown in our languages. By simple association, simile, and curlicued metaphor, plant names have become names of people, families, states, and countries. They are used to describe qualities, achievements, emotions. The word "flower" itself shows this creeping conquest of our vocabulary as well as any other. The flower of a nation or of youth consists of the best, the

1250 took place in Apulia, at the Castel Fiorentino.

It was Palm Sunday—known in Spain as *Pascua Florida*—when Ponce de Leon disembarked beside the lush vegetation of the southeastern peninsula of North America; and Florida is the name he gave it. Several countries have used florins—coins stamped originally with the image of a lily. Fleurons are architectural ornaments inspired by flowers. Florid is, among oth-

were not slow to extract significance from the form and structure of plants. Leaves divided into three were used as emblems of the Trinity (and of other sacred trios before the advent of Christianity). So St. Patrick was able to teach the Irish the concept of the three-in-one and one-in-three by means of the shamrock, though in this case the symbol got divorced from the source. For when a survey was carried out in Ireland, around

eternal, is placed in antithesis to all other numerals. The figure four included the perfect ten, as one, two, three, and four togeth-

ROSE

VIOLET

DAISY

ANGELICA

MARGUERITE

IRIS

JASMINE

select. When matters go well, they flourish. Flower is a term of endearment:

Sweet flower, with flowers
thy bridal bed I strew

says the lovelorn Paris over the body of Juliet. It supplies numerous first names in several languages—Flora, Fleur, Florian, Florence—and several more surnames. Florence is the town of flowers. Emperor Frederick II avoided Florence whenever he could, to escape the outcome of a prophecy that he would die among flowers. But he was careless in his caution. His death in

er things, an alternative name for a whole style of architecture, the Decorated. And so the list goes on.

Since earliest times individual flowers have been symbols and synonyms for qualities and concepts. The bay, palm, olive, and laurel were all in their time given for, and symbolic of, victory. Flowers, because they promise fruit, can mean hope, and are often used as such in paintings, while the cypress and other funereal plants are often used in poetic language as euphemisms for death.

Schoolmen and philosophers

1900, to find which exact flower people meant by shamrock and wore in their buttonholes on St. Patrick's Day, there were about a dozen candidates. Lesser trefoil, *Trifolium minus,* led by a short head. But in a later rerun white clover, *Trifolium repens,* came home a clear winner, though none but its backers were convinced, and the debate continues to this day.

Five-petal plants also had magical significance, for reasons clearly explained by a nineteenth-century clergyman. "It is well known," he wrote, "that the numeral one, the undivided, the

er make ten. So four represents the All of the universe. Now if we put these together, four plus one will be the sign of the whole God-universe."

Most plants, however, kept clear of metaphysics, confining themselves to simple symbolism, names, and emblematic motifs. So Rose, Violet, Pansy, Daisy, Hyacinth, Daffodil, Daphne, and many more have all been popular first names for girls. Every language has its counterparts, though Chinese and Japanese present more vivid word-pictures—Little Peach Blossom, for example, and Lovely-lady-

The shamrock of Ireland is said to have been used by St. Patrick to explain the nature of the Trinity. But the identity of this national emblem is in dispute. Most claims are made for members of the clover family, *(from left to right) Trifolium repens, T. pratense, T. arvense.*

smelling-like-a-rose—in their tautly condensed names.

Like a fifth column, plants have infiltrated the terminology of color. For what better and more lasting standard could there be to describe shades of pink, rose, violet, mauve, indigo, peach, laven-

Many girls' names are taken from those of flowers. Peach and plum *(above)* are often incorporated in Chinese and Japanese names. Western favorites include those on the facing page.

der, orange, cherry, saffron? It was not color, however, but the sensual connotations of the rose that caused the prostitutes of Provence to be known as *roses* a hundred years ago, and that gave red-light districts such names as Rose Alley or Rose Street in several European countries. Indeed, in Solon's Athens it was decreed that prostitutes should wear flowery robes, to distinguish

them from the chaste whites of respectable ladies.

According to Shakespeare, when the heads of the houses of York and Lancaster swore their mutual enmity in London's Temple gardens, they plucked respectively a white and a red rose, which became heraldic symbols of the two families; they were finally united as a royal emblem at the end of the Wars of the Roses. Not all royal and national motifs are so simply explained, though the literature of heraldry is a rich one.

The royal name of Plantagenet, for instance, derives from the stubborn tenant of bleak hill and moorland, the yellow broom. A member of the pea family, it has pods which pop noisily to disperse their seeds; and legend tells that it was rebuked by the Virgin Mary for thus drawing attention to the infant Christ when she was hiding him from Herod's soldiers. Its penitence, and the fact that it was used for sweeping dirt from floors, gave it a reputation for humility; and as such it was picked by Geoffrey, prince of Anjou and Maine, to replace the haughty feather in his helmet when he went on a pilgrimage to the Holy Land. And so in time its Latin name, *Planta genista,* became that of Geoffrey's heirs, an English dynasty.

The most famous plant in heraldry is hedged about with confusion. For nobody can be sure whether the fleur-de-lis is a lily, as many old descriptions imply, or an iris, as its looks suggest. In the most convincing explanation

of its origins, it is an iris. According to this story, the king of the Franks, Clovis, whose emblem was three toads, was fighting off the invading Goths, somewhere near Cologne. Before the campaign he had promised his queen, Clotilde, that should he win he would become, as she was, a Christian. At one point he needed to cross the Rhine. Desperately looking for a place to ford it, he suddenly saw a patch of yellow irises growing on a bend in the river. Irises, he knew, grew in shallow water. He led his troops into the stream, crossed easily, and won his battle. Then, recognizing the irises as a divine sign, he joined his wife's religion and substituted irises for toads as his emblem. Later, when King Louis VII car-

The laurel, symbol of victory.

ried the flower as his banner emblem during the Crusades, it earned the name Fleur de Louis, or Fleur de Lis, and remained on the French royal arms—and indeed on the English until George III, some three centuries late, acknowledged that the English claim to France was forfeit to facts.

After the fall of the French monarchy, violets came to represent the Bonapartists—Josephine had thrown Napoleon a bunch of them at their first meeting, and he continued to prize them till his death. In matters of love, flowers have from time to time developed a language all their own. In Turkey, the grape hyacinth was a secret sign of acceptance, a floral yes. Rejection was, in the Middle East, covertly expressed by the wearing of an iris. It was indeed from Turkey, where cryptic signs were the only possible means of communication in the harem, that a whole code of floral signs invaded Europe in the eighteenth century. Soon an amorous youth could express with a bouquet all that his shyness made it difficult to put into words. "You are my inspiration," said the angelica. "I die if neglected," complained the laurustinus. "Flirt!" accused the bugloss, while the rose said simply, "I love you."

253

Plants inspire literature at all levels. Though the examples which spring most readily to mind are the work of poets—their conceits, similes, metaphors, morals, their exuberant joy at a bloom or a "host of golden daffodils," their ability to see, as Blake saw, "a heaven in a wild flower"—nevertheless, some of the finest writing has come from those who set out simply to describe the reality of what they saw. This is not so true nowadays as in the past. One does not riffle through the pages of *Scientific American* for the sweetness of its prose style. But in the seventeenth century Robert Hooke could still serve two masters—Science and Art—in his pioneering descriptions of objects seen through the microscope:

The Seeds of Purslane seem of very notable shapes, appearing through the Microscope shap'd somewhat like a nautilus or Porcelane shell. . . . cover'd over with abundance of little prominencies or buttons very orderly rang'd into Spiral rows, the shape of each of which seem'd much to resemble a Wart upon a mans hand. . . . Carret seeds are like a cleft of a Coco-Nut Husk; others are like Artificial things, as Succory seeds are like a Quiver full of Arrows, the seeds of Amaranthus are of an exceeding lovely shape, somewhat like an Eye: The skin of the black and shriveled Onyons and Leeks, are all over knobbed like a Seals skin.

Some of the herbalists too were masters of prose style. It would be hard for any modern botanist to write with a more pleasing, and at the same time explicit, clarity than Hooke's predecessor John Gerard, in his description of the woody nightshade:

The floures be small, and somewhat clustered together, consisting of five little leaves [i.e., petals] apiece of a perfect blew colour, with a certain pricke or pointel in the middle: which being past there do come in place faire berries more long than round, at the first green, but very red when they be ripe; of a sweet taste at the first, but after very unpleasant, of a strong savour, growing together in clusters like burnished coral.

From such language it is a short step to poetry, if indeed there is a boundary at all. Clarity is as necessary to poetry as meter and leaps of imagination, though there is, indeed, a strict meter in the characteristic form of *zen* poetry, the three-lined *haiku*:

*The peony has fallen.
A few scattered petals
Lie on one another.*

in which, while the description could hardly be terser, the effect is of total evocation.

Sooner or later, the imagination is set in motion by the contemplation of plants. Here too the effect can be seen in the botanist of former ages, when he is inspired to add motives, thoughts, and emotions to his subjects. Nature, wrote Pliny, seems to cry to the husbandman:

*Why do you look at the sky?
I have given you plants to tell you*
the time, and so that the sun should not make you turn your face away from the earth the heliotrope and the lupin follow it in its daily course.

Such conceits lead to the metaphors and morals that poets and philosophers delight in. The link between love and plants is one that has been evoked by poets since the first telling of the Eden story. And in the Song of Solomon (despite pious attempts to impose more theological interpretations) it reached headily sensual heights:

*I am my beloved's,
And his desire is toward me.
Come, my beloved, let us go
                    forth into the field;
Let us lodge in the villages.
Let us get up early to the vineyards;
Let us see if the vine flourish,
    whether the tender grape appear,
And the pomegranates bud forth:
There will I give thee my loves.
The mandrakes give a smell,
And at our gates are all manner
    of pleasant fruits, new and old,
Which I have laid up for thee,
                    O my beloved.*

Flowers, above all, are used to illustrate the evanescence of sensual pleasures. *Carpe diem*, wrote Horace, "believe in tomorrow as little as may be," and Ronsard took up the theme with a rose for his subject:

My love, let us go to see whether the rose, which this morning opened her purple robe to the sun, has not lost this evening the folds of her gown and grown pale, as you have done.

There! See how in a short time she has let her beauty fall upon the ground. Oh, truly hard hearted is nature, that such a flower lasts only from morning to evening.

In England, Robert Herrick, displaying what was soon to become almost an obsession with death, translated the idea into one of the most famous quatrains in the language:

*Gather ye rosebuds while ye may;
Old time is still a-flying.
And this same flower that
                    smiles today
Tomorrow will be dying.*

Elsewhere he used daffodils to show the same transience of mortal things:

*Fair daffodils, we weep to see
You haste away so soon:
As yet the early-rising sun
Has not attain'd his noon.
Stay, stay
Until the hasting day
Has run
But to the evensong,
And, having prayed together,
We will go with you along.*

Daffodils, like roses, have always been beloved by poets; as Shakespeare says in *The Winter's Tale*:

*When daffodils begin to peer,—
With hey! the doxy over
                    the dale,—
Why, then comes in the sweet
                    o' the year. . . .*

But in another consummate fragment from the same play he shows the dangerous ambivalence of that season:

世傳揚補之畫梅得蘂花如簇之妙徽宗題曰邨梅
丁野堂畫梅理宗變之野堂遂有江路野梅之對二者
皆蒙兩朝厪賞而品目之千古藝林侈爲美談今余東作
橫枝踈影之能何由入九重而供
御覽也畫畢戲言
穀原比部先生一笑己卯冬日七十三翁杭郡金農記

"The flowers on the paper will not fall and die as my friends have done," reads part of the inscription high up on the left of this painting *Branches of Blossoming Plum* (1759) by Chin Nung. The inscription was added in 1804 by a poet, Chu Hsiu-tu, who had been a friend of the artist when the painting was done. Another part of the poet's text reads, "Chin Nung's old brush brought forth spring colors; I wonder if because of my love it blossomed in a single night."

...*golden daffodils,*
That come before the swallow
                    dares, and take
The winds of March with beauty.

The old legend—told, among others, by Ovid—of the youth Narcissus pining away in devotion to his own image reflected in the water, and turning into the flower of the same name, has also given daffodils a prominent place in literature. But Wordsworth showed there was no need to gild the daffodils with extraneous association. He saw them:

Beside the lake, beneath the trees,
Flutt'ring and dancing in
                    the breeze.
Ten thousand saw I at a glance,
Tossing their heads in
                    sprightly dance....

And that sight remained with him forever:

For oft when on my couch I lie,
In vacant or in pensive mood,
They flash upon that inward eye,
Which is the bliss of solitude.
And then my heart with
                    pleasure fills,
And dances with the daffodils.

Milton's daffodils were unusual. In his lament for Lycidas he wrote:

Bid amaranthus all his beauty
                    shed,
And daffodillies fill their
                    cups with tears
To strew the laureat hearse
                    where Lycid lies.

But it would be beyond the powers of daffodils to fill their drooping trumpets with any-thing. In reflecting the influence of flowers, poets have often neglected details, their heads weighted with higher matters. Spenser wrote of "Sommer prowde with daffadillies dight" without bothering to think that daffodils begin and end with spring. Tennyson, who was not above describing two separate moons in the same scene, also began his poem *Mariana:* "With blackest moss," suggesting a case of melanism that might have excited a botanist. Matthew Arnold thought he saw "pale pink convolvulus in tendrils creep," though that sinuous flower never has tendrils. But some poets can be relied on to combine their thoughts with accuracy—Shakespeare, Herrick, Crabbe, Wordsworth, and John Clare, whose empathy with nature was perhaps greater than anyone's:

Aye, flowers! The very name
                    of flowers,
That bloom in wood and glen,
Brings spring to me in winter's
                    hours,
And childhood dreams again.
The primrose on the woodland's lee
Was more than gold and lands
                    to me.

The less natural, almost Venusian form and fabric of the tulip was caught by Humbert Wolfe:

Clean as a lady,
Cool as glass,
Fresh without fragrance
The tulip was.

The craftsman who carved her
Of metal, prayed:

"Live, oh thou lovely!"
Half metal she stayed.

Nevertheless the tulip has been a favorite subject of artists, and in literature it has the rare distinction of providing the theme of a novel: Dumas' *The Black Tulip.* It is not a great novel, but it is a lively description of that extraordinary mania which gripped Holland in the seventeenth century, inflating the value of tulips to that of whole castles and family fortunes. The story tells of the development of the black tulip (as elusive a prize as blue roses and green carnations) and the campaign by hostile interests to destroy it.

It was a novel by Dumas fils, later made into an opera by Verdi, which raised a flower to the level of a romantic vogue. *La Dame aux Camélias* was based on the story of a real girl, Alphonsine Plessis, whom both Liszt and Dumas loved, and who died when she was only twenty-two. It was her habit to wear white camellias, and it was these which filled her coffin and were placed on her grave in Montmartre. Soon after, camellias were the rage; and dealers were made or broken by speculation in new species. For while writings in all languages make it clear that love of plants is a constant emotion in man, it is also true that plants can, without resort to poison or intoxication, but simply by looking as they do, drive him to frenzied excesses otherwise associated only with drink, women, and money.

The expression on the face of an old man of Afghanistan as he smells a rose conveys the feelings of rarefied pleasure which the flower can arouse. According to Moslems, white roses sprang from beads of sweat dropped by Mohammed when he ascended to heaven.

No palace revolution could ever tumble the rose from her status as queen of the flowers. Roses are the source of wines, dyes, medicaments, oils perfume, pomanders, potpourris. In their season they are the most conspicuous ornaments of the gardens of five continents. Cascades of roses

diately love piniored him to the sky. For three days and nights he could not move, but continued to gaze on her, showering her with warm kisses. But the lord of the universe, seeing the ordered workings of the world threatened, turned the girl into a flower and ordered the sun on.

(Which is why you will notice that roses hang their heads and blush when the sun passes overhead.)

Sir John Mandeville had a different account. According to him, a girl of Bethlehem was to

there both kinds spread to the rest of the world.

The Greeks had a different explanation for the two prime colors of roses. In their account Aphrodite was hurrying toward the wounded Adonis when she stepped on a white rose, one of whose thorns pricked her. Her

The rose as symbol of the Rosicrucians, a semimystical group with their origins at least partly in medieval alchemy.

One theory derives the word Rosicrucian not from *rosa* but from *ros,* Latin for dew. Dew was thought to be capable of resuscitating a rose.

In *Jass,* a Swiss card game, the rose forms one of the suits. The flower in the design is six-petaled, rarer in single specimens than the five-petaled variety.

The coat of arms of the Swiss town of Rapperswil bears two roses *(above).* The flower is a widely used armorial charge. The Tudor rose *(right)* amalgamates the white and red roses of the families united by King Henry VII's marriage to Elizabeth of York.

have decorated the grandest feasts, the greatest scenes of sybaritic luxury. They have inspired innumerable poets. They have been symbols of love, virtue, trust, virginity, secrecy, the fall of man; emblems of countries, towns, and families. And the tales told of the rose are legion.

A Rumanian legend describes the origins of roses. A beautiful young princess—who else?—was bathing in the sea. The sun caught sight of her, and imme-

The role of the rose in wooing is shown in this miniature from a fifteenth-century translation of the works of Albucasis.

be burned for a crime she had not committed. She prayed to God to save her and proclaim her innocence; and as soon as she stepped on to the fire, it was extinguished. Her innocence was shown by the fact that all the sticks which had been burning became red roses, and those which had not been kindled became white roses. And from

blood dyed the rose red, and its descendants always remained that color.

Despite this grievous encounter, the rose was Aphrodite's symbol, and when the Christians began to assume the mantle of pagan mythology, the flower became the emblem of the Virgin Mary and of other Christian saints. Some time after the year 300 A.D., Dorothea, a girl of Caesarea, was to be burned for refusing to recant her belief in the new religion. On her way to the

In the classical world the rose was sacred to Venus, goddess of love. While its beauty and fragrance bespoke the perfection of love, its thorns stood for the wounds love can inflict. Christianity borrowed the flower as a symbol of the Virgin Mary, seen *(below)* in Stefan Lochner's fifteenth-century *Virgin in the Rose Bower*. The Virgin was called "the rose without thorns," referring to the time before Adam's fall when the plant itself was supposed to lack them.

The wild rose or dog rose (the root of which was supposed to cure mad dogs' bites)—ancestor of the infinite array of roses enjoyed today.

place of execution a man asked her sarcastically to send him roses from her heavenly bridegroom's garden. A little later, at the moment of her death, a child came to the man carrying a basket of roses. He recognized this as a sign from God and converted to Christianity—a move which later led to his own execution.

Despite its fragrance, a long time elapsed before the discovery was made that distilled roses yielded one of the finest scents. This was due, so legend has it, to a happy coincidence at the marriage feast of a Mogul's son at the palace of Lahore. A new canal had been dug for an aquatic procession, and the water was sprinkled with roses. In the heat of midday the bride and groom were lazing in a boat. She skimmed her fingers along the water's surface, and soon realized, from the aroma, that in the heat the water had extracted fragrance from the roses. The matter was turned over to the apothecaries, who were soon using their alembics and retorts to distill rose perfume. Later the custom spread west, picking up in Persia the words julep—rose water—and attar—perfume. Nowadays the world's best attar comes from the Kazanlik valley in Bulgaria.

In a good season one hectare of land will yield more than three tons of damask roses. But the attar distilled from them will fill no more than two liter bottles.

Most rose lore relates to three varieties of rose: the white, the French, and the damask. Today, after hectic years of hybridizing, the manifold forms and colors of floribundas and hybrid teas have elbowed those three from their former prominence, though

there are people who say that most subsequent varieties are too vulgar or contrived. Meanwhile the old wild rose— ancestor of them all—continues to flower, largely unsung.

A photographic montage of several varieties of rose, differing in form, color, and ancestry, but artificially united on a single stem.

257

Left: Children, no less than great masters, react to the aesthetic appeal of plants, making them one of the most popular themes of their drawings. *The Grey Tree,* by Piet Mondrian *(bottom of page),* is an example of how the visual impact of plants can be sublimated into abstract design. It is an interesting reflection on an artist best known for an

It is hard to say which came first, the pear shape or the pear; or whether man, early man, doodling with a stick in the sand or a lump of charcoal on his cave wall, would spontaneously have arrived at coils and spirals and the shapes of leaves and inflorescences if those same plant features had not first put the forms in his mind. Certainly the acknowledged debt of artists to nature is enormous, almost infinite. Even abstract designs, until recently, traced an easy and direct pedigree back to the shapes and arrangements of natural objects, and above all to plants.

Modern abstracts must perhaps remain an enigma. Behind many of them lies a determined effort to break free of the traditional repertoire of forms, to invoke concepts from some pure, unworldly, Platonic outside, and in rejecting the past to reject nature too. Yet even here a scrawl of lines, a constrained geometric pattern, or a riot of anarchic color can sometimes recall a tangle of vegetation, or the perfect ordering of a flower's parts, or the cross section of a stem, or the blurred daubs of a hedgerow in full flower, seen indirectly through the corner of the eye. And even if the inspiration is not so direct—if it comes from some long-neglected storehouse of the mind—it is impossible to say that plants and the other elemental ingredients of nature were not the first parents of the concept, an aesthetic Adam and Eve. For plants do not have to rely on their chemical or nutritious value to influence our lives. They can bypass the digestion and the bloodstream and go straight to the head, there to work spells by which artists can carry human achievement to its heights.

For the most part, plants' powers are not exercised obscurely. Indeed, for most of their history they were used in art with little attempt to elaborate. Formalized motifs recur in decoration of all kinds: the acanthus of Corinthian capitals, the pineapple finial, olive-leaf borders. Necklaces and brooches, plaster swathes and festoons, wrought-iron gates, cornices, balustrades, chair backs, and carpets often reflect or imitate with their contained designs leaves, flowers, trees, fruits, buds, creeping or pendant stems, pistils, and stamens.

Plants are the inspiration of two different groups of art which parallel closely their use in literature. First come the instructive illustrations—no less refined because they attempt to show, without added meaning or significance, what is there. The herbals of the Middle Ages and Renaissance are treasuries of floral art, and they established a noble tradition of conveying information by sensitive and realistic representation. Among the great names in this line are some who belong equally in botanical art and the more creative category which artists call real art and botanists *mere* art: Dürer and da Vinci, and some later Dutch masters. Sometimes the purpose of these realists was to explain plant structure to students of science, sometimes to bring home a true picture of exotic species seen on distant travels. The overwhelming lesson of all these pictures is how long it took artists to notice the full range of subtle intricacy which any plant possesses. In spite of their single-mindedness, the herbals of Brun-fels and Fuchs, and the later paintings by Johann Walter, Nicolas Robert, and Georg Dionysius Ehret—whom many consider the greatest flower painter of all time—can be faulted on grounds of accuracy. It was not till the nineteenth century that technique and observation—reflecting the advanced state of botanical knowledge—were perfectly married in the work of Gerard van Spaëndonck, Pierre-Joseph Redouté, and others.

Meanwhile the plant world never ceased to inspire more general artists. To the sprigs, nosegays, or individual blooms that the people they painted wore or hold, portraitists added floral backgrounds, garlands, and sometimes glimpses of gardens or whole pastoral scenes. Medici and d'Este princesses stand high in the foreground of Tuscan landscapes. Flemish Renaissance painters in particular, but also those of other schools, relished the accurate portrayal of identifiable flowers in their groups and allegorical paintings.

The Dutch with their timeless interiors, Watteau and Fragonard with their scenes of innocent (though sensual) and lively gaiety, the idealized Arcadian landscapes of Claude, Poussin, and David, all lean heavily on flowers for their effects. Flowers in these paintings convey moods and emotions in a way that no other subject save the human face and body can. But the stylization of the nineteenth century threatened to nullify these almost palpable im-

architectural, almost mathematical, approach to art that nature was among his explicit early influences. *Autumn (below)* is by Giuseppe Arcimboldo, a sixteenth-century Milanese whose bizarre amalgams are sometimes claimed as direct ancestors of the work of the surrealists. Most of his work—which was more highly rated in his own day, when he was much in demand, than it is now—incorporates weird and fantastic heads, a background landscape, and a cornucopia of fruits and flowers, all meticulously painted. While the more curious elements of his work were not seen again for a long time after his death, he belongs to a consistent tradition of still-life painters.

pressions. Just as the early Victorians seemed to miss the point of flowers in the heavy horticultural stress of their gardens, so painters were depriving flowers of body, scent, and life. But then the Impressionists arrived.

We cannot count the leaves of a water lily by Monet, or the number of petals in a rose by Renoir. Van Gogh's sunflowers can seem like a blur of contorted yellows, and the *pointillistes* made no attempt to scrutinize botanical data. The traditional roles of plants in painting—to represent the season of the year, or the myths of Flora, Narcissus, Hyacinth, or Anemone—were far from their minds as they set down with consummate skill not what the eye saw directly but what the mind saw through the eye. In the paintings of Botticelli, it is said, no less than thirty separate species of flower can be accurately identified; in the Impressionists, only a few.

Simply as background and decoration, plants have called forth all the skill and sensitivity of the artist. Detail *(left)* from the *Annunciation* by Fra Angelico, showing several easily recognized flower species. *Above and far right:* Various ornamental pictures of flowers drawn from oriental sources. The detail from a millefleurs tapestry of about 1500 *(right)* shows a unicorn protecting a tree—symbols respectively of chastity and a bride—in a sea of flowers. The comparatively crude medium of mosaic *(below)* can nevertheless produce beautifully stylized effects, as this fifth-century vase of fruits from Ravenna shows. Pregnant with meaning, flowers have been used constantly in oriental art. This painting of cherry blossoms *(below right),* from Kyoto, is on gold paper and was used as a wall panel about 1600.

THE PERPETUATION
OF SUMMER

Below: The tomb of the Fourth-Dynasty King Snefru, at Dashour in Egypt, has the ceiling decorated with grapevines. *Below right:* A floral design from the Golden Temple in Amritsar, India. Against a background of white marble and gold, the design is picked out in semiprecious stones. *Right:* La Sala delle Asse in the Sforza castle at Milan was decorated with frescoes by Leonardo da Vinci near the end of the fifteenth century. Almost eliminated by time, they were imaginatively restored in 1901. The huge design, with its arches created by trunks and branches, and the complex intertwinings of stems and creepers in which he delighted, shows also his attentive response to nature. Founded in a firm Gothic tradition of intricate and fantastic representations of plants, leaves, and espaliers, Leonardo's frescoes add a new dimension of lifelike reality to the details. His absorption in nature was to last his whole life.

When summer goes, and increasing cold confines people in their houses, the sad parting from their plants is alleviated by art (the same principle is evinced by those hunting men whose houses reproduce in print, ashtray, and table mat the scenes of the chase). At its extreme, this dependence on plants was shown by a legendary Chinese emperor whose craftsmen reproduced not only the plants, but a changing panorama of them to match the movements of the artificial sun across the ceiling of his palace.

The mural is the most convincing means of thus preserving nature's aspect, for it can fill the field of vision as outside scenes do. So vines of two dimensions can re-create the lush fruits of the autumn, and creepers and climbers in full flower can bring the suggestion of spring to bare, cold walls.

Art that depends on a brush held in a human hand can never tell the whole truth of a plant's appearance. The execution of any painting takes time, during which flower, light, and the artist's perception will change, if only in the minutest degree. A photograph captures the moment. It too may be wanting in truth. It may lack the dimensions of vision of which the human eye is capable. But, alone or in tandem with a microscopic lens, the camera can supplement human observation and reproduce nature's patterns with a stark immediacy.

Photography can also show the effects of time, and in a far more vivid way than the eye can see. Pictures of a single plant, taken at regular intervals and projected as motion pictures, can reveal the process of growth and decline, and other movements by the plant, in a way that was impossible before the invention of the camera. Similarly, the camera fitted with a microscope can record details of structure and behavior in plants which only increase our admiration of their powers. It can show, for instance, that the point of a cactus spine—

Soehrensia—is sharper than that of a precision sewing needle and rivaled only by that of a sapphire needle. And it can reveal structures and proportions which not only put us in awe of their artistry, but often instruct us in scientific technique.

Photographs of *(above, left to right)* wheat *(Triticum vulgare)*, seedear *(Beckmannia erucaefor-*

For if technology has opened up new worlds in the plant, plants have generously in return given us several sound technological principles. They were in fact doing so when the camera was in its infancy. When Sir Joseph Paxton was working on plans for the Crystal Palace to be erected for the London exhibition of 1851, he was at a loss for a way of combining hundreds of tons of glass with a framework that

mis), and naked barley *(Hordea trifurcatum)*. In the center are *(left to right)* scabious *(Scabiosa prolifera)*, passion flower *(Passiflora edulis)*, and dahlia *(D. rosea)*. The photographs below *(left to right)* are of teasel *(Dipsacus fullonum)*, yarrow *(Achillea millefolium)*, dogwood *(Cornus kousa)*, pincushion *(Cotula trubinata)*, centaury *(Centaurea kotschyana)*, and ragwort *(Senecio cineraria)*. On the opposite page are phacelia *(P. congesta)* and the guelder rose *(Viburnum opulus)*. At the far right is a seed capsule of *Blumenbachia hieronymi.*

must look light, airy, and insubstantial. And then he remembered *Victoria amazonica,* the royal water lily, a plant whose round and delicate leaves can reach a diameter of two meters without any intrusive show of support. The underside of the leaves gave Paxton his clue. Ribs radiated from the center, then branched and branched again into ever smaller struts which, meeting up with each other, provided a graceful but durable support for the leaf—and indeed for a person sitting on it. The principle was adopted, the Crystal Palace built, and a turning point reached, not only in structure but in the aesthetics of architecture as well.

Careful study of other plants—preferably through the impassive eye of the camera—has revealed other structural and aesthetic principles: the Fibonacci series, for example, which describes another pattern of branching, in

a progression from one to two to three to five to eight, and so on, or the so-called "golden ratio" (twenty-one to thirty-four) which artists, consciously or not, have adopted as the ideal since the Renaissance.

To plants themselves, photography has provided an unexpected benefit. A hundred—even fifty—years ago, it mattered little to a species that people on their excursions into the country picked armfuls of bluebells, primroses, daffodils—and many rarer flowers that were not rare to the point of extinction. True, they are still hazardously collected to provide a day or two of pleasure at the cost of the future of their kind. But fortunately, people are now more apt to take them home on film.

265

After he had been a novice in the Abbey of Cîteaux for about a year, it emerged that Bernard—later to be known as St. Bernard of Clairvaux—did not know whether the ceiling of the hall in which he spent most of his day was flat or vaulted. All his faculties were dedicated to God, and he took no notice his surroundings. Any decoration he regarded as the temptation of evil, as if it were a harlot on the road to heaven.

Great and saintly innovator that he was, it is a relief to the less ascetic among us that St. Bernard and those who agreed with

A Corinthian capital formed of stylized acanthus leaves.

him—and there have been puritans and iconoclasts in every age—did not always get their way. Churches no less than palaces and castles are the custodians of some of the finest decorative art. One artistic technique with which these structures are perpetually associated—for it is built into their very fabric—is relief sculpture, the forging from bare and lifeless rock of vital and realistic forms and images. Among those images, as in all other branches of art, plants have left copious tokens of their universal influence.

No plant has created more forests of stone than the acanthus, the stylized copies of which, gracing the tops of Corinthian pillars, have become almost synonymous with classical architecture. It is told that the idea for its use arose when a Corinthian nurse, mourning over the grave of her charge—a very young girl—put a basket containing her toys and trinkets nearby and covered it with a flat tile. It happened that an acanthus root was under the spot. In spring it grew up around the basket and its leaves opened into their elaborately scalloped shapes. But, reaching the overlap of the tile, they were turned back. An architect, Callimachus, saw this, was charmed with the effect, and used it in his next building. From there it spread around the world.

The lotus has had almost as much influence on stonework. Symbolizing the annual renewal of the crops through its religious association with Isis and Osiris, it was used in Egyptian buildings from the earliest times. Instead of capitals alone, whole columns were based on its design, its leaves decorating the foot—and an elaborated version of its flower the top—of a deeply fluted, stemlike pillar. From there it spread through the Middle East to India and China, where its associations with Buddha added to its ornamental roles.

Plants that lend themselves to a formal, repetitive design have always been favored as architectural motifs. The height of such stylization comes with the great rose windows of some Gothic cathedrals, notably Chartres, where daylight is allowed to illuminate the colored glass of symmetrical roundels, giving an impression of some other-world-

A stone motif from the sixth-century B.C. treasury at Delphi (above) shows a lotus set in a palm leaf. The perforated floral screen (opposite, above)—a feature much favored in India and Persia—is from the sixteenth-century Sidi Sayyid Mosque, at Ahmadabad, Bombay.

A seventeenth-century carving of the peepul, or bo-tree (left), from Bangkok. This tree is supposed to have sprung from the center of the earth at the moment of Buddha's nativity, and under it he received his enlightenment.

Romanesque reliefs (below) from the Museo del Duomo in Ferrara, Italy, show, with a sensitive naturalism, the fig harvest in August (left) and the grape harvest in September (right).

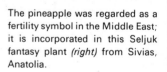

The pineapple was regarded as a fertility symbol in the Middle East; it is incorporated in this Seljuk fantasy plant (right) from Sivias, Anatolia.

An Art Nouveau table lamp from the Tiffany studios (far right) of 1904 shows an artistic development from plant shapes.

ly flower opening out of the sky. In the same context are the convoluted versions of the Tree of Jesse, which traces the ancestry of Christ back to David and to his father Jesse. The Book of Isaiah tells that "there shall come forth a rod out of the stem of Jesse, and a branch shall grow out of his roots." From the twelfth century on, the concept was incorporated in many church windows, stone stems representing the tree and window lights the members of this royal line. There is a fine example at Wells Cathedral in England.

But the use of stone does not end with this formalized representation. In buildings all over the world vines coil realistically round arches and balustrades, ivy climbs skyward in its marbled exuberance, and swathes of flowers, wreaths, and garlands bedeck and enliven the cold expanses of polished rock.

FLOWERS OF INNOCENCE

Grapes, by Séraphine Louis, painted about 1930. Living simply and alone in the French town of Senlis, she expressed a rapturous appreciation of nature in her glowing and fantastic bouquets.

In a vision of the new Jerusalem, a dreamlike glimpse of paradise, the poet Thomas Traherne saw a city where:

Things Native sweetly grew
Which there mine Ey did view,
Plain, simple, cheap, on either side
the street,
Which was exceeding fair and wide;
Sweet mansions there mine Eys
did meet;
Green Trees the shaded doors did hide:
My chiefest Joys
Were Girls and Boys
That in those streets still up and
down did play,
Which crown'd the Town with
constant Holiday.

Children and flowers are con-stantly linked in poetic perceptions of paradise, for children—rightly or wrongly—are taken to be as innocent as Adam and Eve before the Temptation. Plants make a special appeal to childish minds. Shorn of their functionalism, drained of their poisons and parasites, they seem to offer a world of simplicity and harmony not only to children, but to the minds of men and women who aspire to be children again. It is perhaps only in the most sophisticated and artificial civilizations that such minds stand out as extraordinary. Many of the painters who have been labeled primitive or naïve during the last century in Europe and

Rubén Dario's Poem "I",
Adela de Ycaza, 1968

Long Winter,
Ivan Lacković, 1966

My Village,
Milan Rašić, 1967

Eve with a Fish,
Josip Generalić, 1969

The Great Forest, Ivan Rabuzin, 1960

North America would seem less radical or exceptional in other ages and places. To the modern Western mind they present a refreshing contrast to professionalism and esoteric technique, tradition, or training. They react in the most direct and unspoiled way to the impact of plants on the human mind. Their tributes to plants have nothing to do with food, timber, or any of the other myriad uses to which people put the produce of field and forest. If any motive underlies their simple depiction of what lies around them, it is one of celebration and thankfulness.

But these are surely the urges which drive any artist, however rarefied his awareness, however lofty his intellect, to portray the plants he sees every day around him. A Leonardo may study, probe, and dissect before he prepares his brushes. A Botticelli may measure his subjects minutely, then instill them with a studio radiance that fails to ape the sun's. A Rubens may summon flowers from his mind, not from the field, and give them forms and colors they should not possess. A Constable may paint the same scene at morning, noon, and twilight to understand the inscrutable workings of light. A Turner may engulf his flowery pastures with a fiery brilliance of his own creation. A Monet may blur his blossoms in a lyrical luster. But all, in their separate ways, are acknowledging the power of the plant over the human spirit, and telling—as best they can—of their gladness.

Illustrations on the following pages:

Pages 270–1: The Wedding of the Deer, by Ivan Generalic (1914–).

Page 272: Still Life with Fruit, by Giovan Battista Ruoppolo (1620–1685).

Page 273: Bouquet of Flowers, by Jan Brueghel (1568–1625).

Page 274: A series of microscopic cross sections through the stems and cells of various plants.

Page 275: Cross section of a red cabbage.

The Old Oaken Bucket,
Grandma Moses, 1943

First Landscape with Circular Elements,
Ivan Rabuzin, 1959

The Flamingos,
Henri Rousseau, 1907

Virgin Forest at Sunset,
Henri Rousseau, 1910

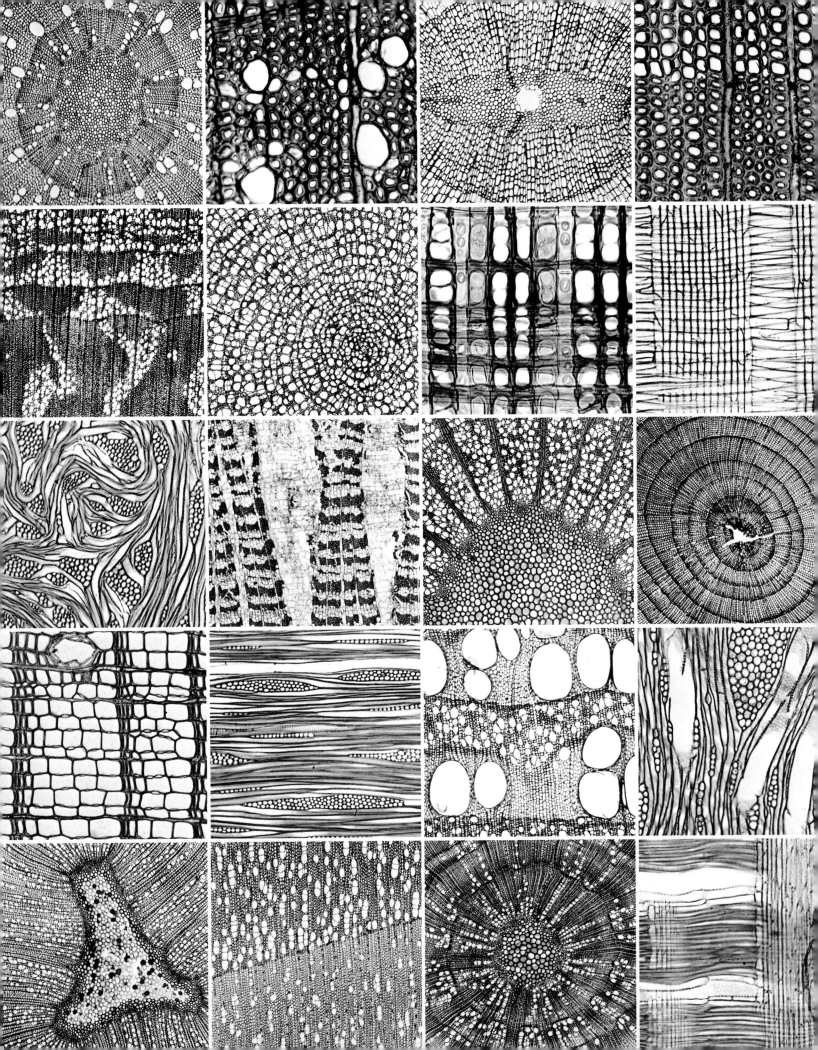

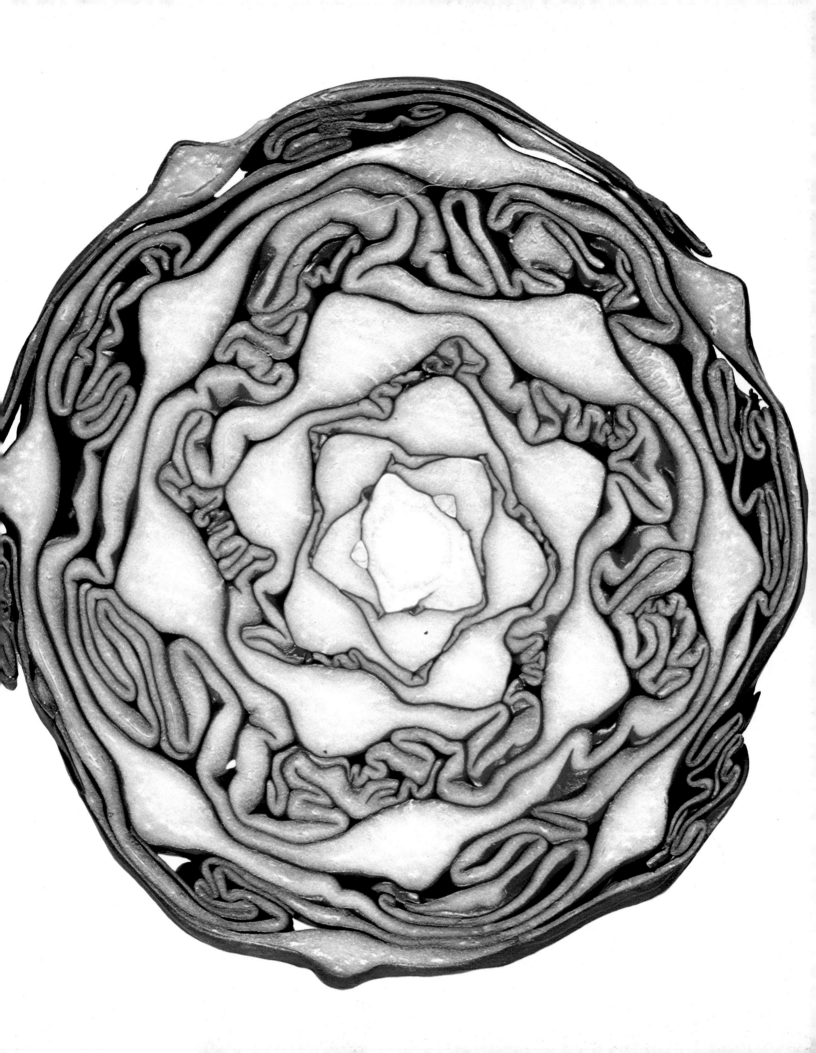

AFTERWORD

What greater delight is there than to behold the earth apparelled with plants, as with a robe of embroidered worke, set with Orient pearles and garnished with great diversitie of rare and costly jewels? . . .
But these delights are in the outward senses: the principal delight is in the mind, singularly enriched with the knowledge of these visible things, setting forth to us the invisible wisdome and admirable workmanship of Almighty God.

John Gerard, 1597

LIST OF PLANT NAMES

– ENGLISH–LATIN
– LATIN–ENGLISH

Where the English term is in parentheses, it means that there is no English equivalent for the Latin; the word in parentheses indicates the type of plant, such as (fungus).

Where the Latin name is simply one word followed by the letters "sp.," it means that reference is made in the book to the genus rather than (or in addition to) a particular species.

At times a single English name has been given two Latin equivalents—either because two Latin names are in common use, or because some distinct plants have the same English name.

A plant with two or more English names is listed as follows:
carnation/pink/gillyflower
    Dianthus caryophyllus

ENGLISH–LATIN

abaca *Musa textilis*
acanthus *Acanthus mollis*
acokanthera *Acokanthera venenata*
agrimony *Agrimonia sp.*
all-heal/valerian *Valeriana officinalis*
almond *Prunus amygdalus*
aloes *Aloe vera*
alpine rose *Rhododendron ferrugineum*
amaranth *Amaranthus retroflexus*
androsace *Androsace glacialis*
angelica *Angelica sylvestris*
angelica, garden *Angelica archangelica*
aniseed *Pimpinella anisum*
apple *Malus pumila*
archangel, yellow *Galeobdolon luteum*
arctic lupin *Lupinus arcticus*
arnica *Arnica montana*
arolla pine/Swiss stone pine *Pinus cembra*
arrowroot *Canna indica*
asarabica *Asarum europaeum*
ash *Fraxinus excelsior*
asparagus *Asparagus officinalis*
aspen *Populus tremula*
asphodel *Asphodelus sp.*
aster *Aster sp.*
asvattha/peepul tree/bo-tree
    Ficus religiosa
autumn gentian *Gentiana amarella*
avens *Geum sp.*
avocado pear *Persea americana*
ayahuasca *Banisteriopsis caapi*

balm *Melissa officinalis*
balsam *Impatiens noli-me-tangere*
barberry *Berberis vulgaris*
barley *Hordeum vulgare*
barley, two-rowed *Hordeum distichum*
barrel cactus *Echinocactus sp.*
basil *Ocimum basilicum*

bay *Laurus nobilis*
bergamot *Citrus bergamia*
betel nut *Areca catechu*
betony *Betonica officinalis*
big tree *Sequoia giganteum*
bindweed *Convolvulus arvensis*
birch *Betula sp.*
blackberry *Rubus fruticosus*
blackcurrant *Ribes nigrum*
black hellebore *Helleborus niger*
blackthorn *Prunus spinosa*
black truffle *Tuber melanosporum*
bladderwort *Utricularia vulgaris*
blueberry *Vaccinium corymbosum*
bogbean *Menyanthes trifoliata*
borage *Borago officinalis*
bo-tree *Ficus religiosa*
box *Buxus sempervirens*
bracken *Pteridium aquilinum*
Brazil nut *Bertholettia excelsa*
bread-wheat *Triticum aestivum*
briar/blackberry *Rubus fruticosus*
bristlecone pine *Pinus aristata*
broad bean *Vicia faba*
broom *Sarothamnus scoparius*
Brussels sprout
    Brassica oleracea var. gemmifera
burdock *Arctium pubens*
bryony, white *Bryonia dioica*
burnet saxifrage *Pimpinella saxifraga*
buttercup *Ranunculus arvensis*
butterwort *Pinguicula vulgaris*

cabbage, winter
    Brassica oleracea var. capitata
calabar bean *Physostigma venenosum*
camellia *Camellia japonica*
camphor *Cinnamonum camphora*
campion *Silene sp.*
cantaloupe *Cucumis melo*
Canterbury bell *Campanula medium*
capers *Capparis spinosa*
caper spurge *Euphorbia lathyrus*
caraway *Carum carvi*
carline thistle *Carlina vulgaris*
carnation/pink/gillyflower
    Dianthus caryophyllus
(carnivore) *Byblis gigantea*
(carnivore) *Drosophyllum lusitanicum*
carrot *Daucus carota*
cassava *Manihot esculenta*
cassia *Cassia acutifolia*
castor oil plant *Ricinus communis*
cauliflower *Brassica oleracea var. botrytis*
cayenne *Capsicum frutescens*
cedar of Lebanon *Cedrus libani*
ceiba tree *Ceiba pentandra*
celery *Apium graveolens*
centaury *Centaurea kotschyana*
centaury, common *Centaurea erythraea*
century plant *Agave americana*
chamomile *Anthemis nobilis*
chamomile, wild *Matricaria recutita*
chanterelle *Cantharellus cibarius*
Cherimoya *Annona cherimolia*
cherry, wild *Prunus avium*
cherry laurel *Prunus laurocerasus*
chervil *Chaerophyllum temulentum*
chestnut *Aesculus hippocastanum*
chicory, red *Cichorium intybus*
chicory, white Belgian *Cichorium intybus*
chili pepper *Capsicum frutescens*
chives *Allium schoenoprasum*
chocolate *Theobroma cacao*
cholla cactus *Opuntia fulgida*
cinnamon *Cinnamonum cassia*
clematis, wild *Clematis vitalba*
cloudberry *Rubus chamaemorus*
clove *Eugenia caryophyllata*
clover *Trifolium sp.*
clover, red *Trifolium pratense*

clover, white *Trifolium repens*
coast redwood *Sequoia sempervirens*
cobra plant *Darlingtonia californica*
coca *Erythroxylum coca*
cocklebur *Xanthium stramonium*
cocoa *Theobroma cacao*
coconut *Cocos nucifera*
coffee *Coffea arabica*
coir/coconut fiber *Cocos nucifera*
cola *Cola nitida*
colocynth *Citrullus colocynthis*
coltsfoot *Tussilago farfara*
columbine *Aquilegia vulgaris*
common centaury *Centaurea erythraea*
common rhododendron
    Rhododendron ponticum
common violet *Viola riviniana*
coriander *Coriandrum sativum*
cork oak *Quercus suber*
corn *Zea mays*
cornel cherry *Cornus mascula*
cornflower *Centaurea cyanus*
cotton plant *Gossypium herbaceum*
couchgrass *Agropyron repens*
cowbane *Cicuta virosa*
cowslip *Primula veris*
cranberry *Vaccinium oxycoccus*
cranesbill *Geranium sp.*
crocus *Crocus vernus*
cuckoopint *Arum maculatum*
cucumber *Cucumis sativus*
cumin *Cuminum cyminum*
curare poison nut *Strychnos toxifera*
cypress *Cupressus sempervirens*

daffodil *Narcissus sp.*
dahlia *Dahlia rosea*
daisy *Bellis perennis*
dandelion *Taraxacum officinale*
daphne *Daphne mezereon*
date-palm *Phoenix dactylifera*
deadly nightshade *Atropa belladonna*
deadnettle, white *Lamium album*
death cap *Amanita phalloides*
derris *Derris elliptica*
destroying angel *Amanita virosa*
dill *Anethum graveolens*
dittany *Dictamnus albus*
dog rose/wild rose *Rosa canina*
dog's mercury *Mercurialis perennis*
dogwood *Cornus kousa*
dwarf birch *Betula nana*

edelweiss *Leontopodium alpinum*
eglantine rose *Rosa eglanteria*
Egyptian bean *Nelumbium speciosum*
einkorn *Triticum monococcum*
elder *Sambucus nigra*
elecampine *Inula helenium*
elm *Ulmus procera*
emmer *Triticum dicoccum*
ephedra *Ephedra sinica*
ergot *Claviceps purpurea*
eritrichium *Eritrichium nanum*
esparto grass *Stipa tenacissima*
evening primrose *Oenochera biennis*

fennel *Foeniculum vulgare*
fig *Ficus carica*
flax *Linum usitatissimum*
fleabane *Pulicaria dysenterica*
Florence fennel *Foeniculum vulgare*
fly agaric *Amanita muscaria*
fool's mushroom *Amanita verna*
foxglove *Digitalis purpurea*
frankincense *Boswellia carteri*
French bean *Phaseolus vulgaris*
fumitory *Fumaria occidentalis*
(fungus) *Amanita rubescens*

(fungus) *Boletus aurantiacus*
(fungus) *Boletus aureus*
(fungus) *Clavaria formosa*
(fungus) *Clitocybe dealbata*
(fungus) *Daedalea quercina*
(fungus) *Entoloma lividum*
(fungus) *Gomphidius glutinosus*
(fungus) *Gyrometra esculenta*
(fungus) *Helvella gigas*
(fungus) *Inocybe patouillardii*
(fungus) *Lactarius blennius*
(fungus) *Lactarius volemus*
(fungus) *Panaeolus campanulatus*
(fungus) *Ramaria botrytis*
(fungus) *Rhodophyllus sinuatus*
(fungus) *Russula emetica*

gamboge *Garcinia morella*
garden angelica *Angelica archangelica*
gardenia *Gardenia florida*
garden marigold *Calendula officinalis*
garden pea *Pisum sativum*
garlic *Allium sativum*
gentian, autumn *Gentiana amarella*
gentian, yellow *Gentiana lutea*
giant bamboo *Dendrocalamus giganteus*
ginger *Zingiber officinale*
ginseng *Panax ginseng*
globe artichoke *Cynara scolymus*
golden rod *Solidago virgaurea*
gooseberry *Ribes grossularia*
goosegrass *Galium aparine*
gorse *Ulex sp.*
gourd *Lagenaria siceraria*
grape/vine *Vitis vinifera*
grape hyacinth *Muscari atlanticum*
ground ivy *Glechoma hederacea*
guelder rose *Viburnum opulus*

harmela *Peganum harmala*
hashish/marijuana *Cannabis indica*
Hazel *Corylus avellana*
heather *Erica sp.*
heliotrope *Petasites fragrans*
hellebore, black *Helleborus niger*
hemlock *Conium maculatum*
hemlock tree *Tsuga heterophylla*
hemp *Cannabis sativa*
hemp agrimony *Agrimonia eupatoria*
henbane *Hyoscyamus niger*
henna *Lawsonia inermis*
holly *Ilex aquifolium*
hollyhock *Althaea rosea*
holm oak/ilex *Quercus ilex*
honey fungus *Armillaria mellea*
honeysuckle *Lonicera caprifolium*
hop *Humulus lupulus*
horehound, white *Marrubium vulgare*
horseshoe vetch *Hippocrepis comosa*
horsetail *Equisetum arvense*
hound's tongue *Cynoglossum officinale*
houseleek *Sempervivum tectorum*
hyacinth *Hyacinthus orientalis*
hyssop *Hyssopus officinalis*

iboga *Tabernanthe iboga*
Iceland moss *Cetraria islandica*
ilex/holm oak *Quercus ilex*
(an Indian tree) *Hemionitis cordifolia*
indigo *Indigofera tinctoria*
inky cap *Coprinus atramentarius*
inocybe *Inocybe patouillardi*
iris *Iris sp.*
ivy *Hedera helix*
ivy *Rhus toxicodendron*

jasmine *Jasminum officinale*
Jeffrey pine *Pinus Jeffreyi*

jessamine, yellow *Gelsemium sempervirens*
Jesuit's bark *Cinchona officinalis*
jimsonweed/thorn-apple *Datura stramonium*
juniper *Juniperus communis*
jute *Corchorus capsularis*

kale *Brassica oleracea var. acephala*
kapok *Ceiba pentandra*
kava-kava *Piper methysticum*
khat *Catha edulis*
kiwi fruit *Actinidia chinensis*
kohlrabi *Brassica oleracea var. gongyloides*

laburnum, yellow *Laburnum anagyroides*
lady's bedstraw *Galium verum*
lady's mantle *Alchemilla mollis*
larch *Larix sp.*
laurestinus *Viburnum tinus*
lavender *Lavendula officinalis*
leek *Allium porrum*
lemon *Citrus limon*
lesser celandine *Ranunculus ficaria*
lesser trefoil *Trifolium minus*
lily *Lilium sp.*
lily-of-the-valley *Convallaria majalis*
ling *Calluna sp.*
linseed/flax *Linum usitatissimum*
loosestrife, purple *Lythrum salicaria*
lotus *Nelumbo nucifera*
love-in-idleness *Viola tricolor*
lucerne/alfalfa *Medicago sativa*
lungwort *Pulmonaria officinalis*
lupin *Lupinus nootkatensis*

mace *Myristica fragrans*
magic mushroom *Psilocybe mexicana*
maguey plant *Agave sp.*
mahogany *Swietenia mahagoni*
maidenhair fern *Adiantum capillus-veneris*
mallow *Malva sylvestris*
mandrake *Mandragora officinarum*
mango *Mangifera indica*
mangrove *Avicennia nitida*
maple *Acer sp.*
marguerite *Chrysanthemum frutescens*
marigold *Chrysanthemum sp.*
marigold, garden *Calendula officinalis*
marijuana *Cannabis indica*
marjoram *Origanum majorana*
marsh horsetail *Equisetum palustre*
martagon lily *Lilium martagon*
meadow rue *Thalictrum flavum*
meadow saffron *Colchicum autumnale*
melilot *Melilotus officinalis*
melon *Cucumis melo*
mescal buttons *Lophophora williamsii*
mesquite *Prosopis juliflora*
milkweed *Sonchus oleraceus*
millet *Eleusine coracana*
mimosa *Mimosa pudica*
mint *Mentha sp.*
mistletoe *Viscum album*
monkey pot *Lecythis sp.*
monkshood *Aconitum napellus*
morel *Morchella esculenta*
moss campion *Silene acaulis*
mountain ash *Sorbus aucuparia*
mugwort *Artemisia vulgaris*
mulberry *Morus nigra*
munj tree *Saccharum munja*
mustard *Brassica nigra*
myrrh *Commiphora myrrha*
myrtle *Nothofagus cunninghami*

naked barley *Hordea trifurcatum*
niger seed *Guizotia abyssinica*
night-scented stock *Matthiola bigornis*
nutmeg/mace *Myristica fragrans*

oak *Quercus sp.*
oak *Quercus robur*
oats *Avena sp.*
oil palm *Elaeis guineensis*
okra *Hibiscus esculentus*
old-man's-beard *Clematis alba*
oleander *Nerium oleandrum*
olive *Olea europaea*
ololiuqui *Rivea corymbosa*
onion *Allium cepa*
ophrys orchid *Ophrys sp.*
opium poppy *Papaver somniferum*
orange *Citrus sp.*
orange *Citrus sinensis*
(orchid) *Coryanthes albertinae*
oxeye daisy *Chrysanthemum leucanthemum*

paloverde *Cercidium torreyanum*
pansy *Viola tricolor*
panther cap *Amanita pantherina*
pariera *Chondodendron tomentosum*
parsley *Petroselinum crispum*
Pasqueflower *Pulsatilla vulgaris*
passion flower *Passiflora edulis*
patchouli *Pogostemon cablin*
pawpaw *Carica papaya*
pea, garden *Pisum sativum*
peach *Prunus persica*
peanut *Arachis hypogaea*
pear *Pyrus communis*
pecan *Carya pecan*
peepul tree *Ficus religiosa*
pennywort *Umbilicus rupestris*
peony *Paeonia mascula*
pepper *Piper nigrum*
peppermint *Mentha piperita*
peyote *Lophophora williamsii*
phacelia *Phacelia congesta*
pheasant's eye *Narcissus poeticus*
phormium *Phormium tenax*
pimiento/sweet pepper *Capsicum annuum*
pincushion *Cotula trubinata*
pineapple *Ananas comosus*
pink *Dianthus caryophyllus*
pistachio *Pistacia vera*
pitcher plant *Nepenthes hookeriana*
pitcher plant *Sarracenia purpurea*
polion germander *Teucrium polium*
pomegranate *Punica granatum*
poppy *Papaver somniferum*
potato *Solanum tuberosum*
prickly pear *Opuntia ficus-indica*
primrose *Primula vulgaris*
purple loosestrife *Lythrum salicaria*
purple saxifrage *Saxifraga oppositifolia*
purslane *Lythrum portula*
pygmy cedar *Peucephyllum schottii*
pyrethrum *Chrysanthemum cinerariifolium*

rafflesia *Rafflesia arnoldii*
ragwort *Senecio jacobaea*
ramie *Boehmeria nivea*
rape *Brassica napus*
raspberry *Rubus idaeus*
rattan *Calamus aquatilis*
rauwolfia/snakeroot *Rauwolfia serpentina*
red chicory *Cichorium intybus*
red clover *Trifolium pratense*
redcurrant *Ribes rubrum*
red valerian *Valeriana rubia*
rhododendron, common
    Rhododendron ponticum
rhubarb *Rheum rhaponticum*
ribwort plantain *Plantago lanceolata*
rice *Oryza sativa*
rose *Rosa sp.*
rosemary *Rosmarinus officinalis*
rowan/mountain ash *Sorbus aucuparia*
royal water lily *Victoria amazonica*
rubber *Hevea brasilicus*

rue *Ruta graveolens*
rye *Secale cereale*

safflower *Carthamus tinctoria*
saffron *Crocus sativus*
sage *Salvia horminoides*
saguaro cactus *Carnegiea gigantea*
St. John's-wort/tutsan *Hypericum pulchrum*
sal-tree *Shorea robusta*
sanders, yellow *Pterocarpus santalinus*
sassy bark *Erythrophleum guineense*
saxifrage *Saxifraga sp.*
saxifrage, purple *Saxifraga oppositifolia*
scabious *Scabiosa prolifera*
scarlet pimpernel *Anagallis arvensis*
sea-fennel *Peucedanum officinale*
sedge *Carex sp.*
seedear *Beckmannia erucaeformis*
sesame *Sesamum indicum*
shea butternut *Butryospermum parkii*
shepherd's purse *Capsella bursa-pastoris*
sisal *Agave sisalana*
sloe *Prunus spinosa*
snakeroot *Rauvolfia serpentina*
soldanella *Soldanella*
Solomon's seal *Polygonatum odoratum*
sorghum *Sorghum vulgare*
sorrel *Rumex sp.*
soybean *Glycine max*
Spanish chestnut *Castanea sativa*
speedwell *Veronica persica*
spotted deadnettle *Lamium maculatum*
squill *Urginea maritima*
stainer, yellow *Agaricus*
stemless thistle *Carlina acaulis*
stinging nettle *Urtica dioica*
stinkhorn fungus *Phallus impudicus*
storax *Styrax officinale*
strawberry *Fragaria vesca*
strophanthus *Strophanthus hispidus*
strychnine tree *Strychnos nux-vomica*
sugar *Saccharum officinale*
sugar beet *Beta vulgaris*
sugar maple *Acer saccharum*
sugar palm *Arenga sacchifera*
sundew *Drosera anglica*
sunflower *Helianthus annuus*
swamp cypress *Taxodium distichum*
sweet-flag *Calamus aromaticus*
sweet pepper *Capsicum annuum*
Swiss stone pine *Pinus cembra*
sycamore *Acer pseudoplatanus*

tamarisk *Tamarix gallica*
tansy *Chrysanthemum vulgare*
tarragon *Artemisia dracunculus*
tea *Camellia sinensis*
tea *Thea sinensis/Camellia sinensis*
teasel *Dipsacus fullonum*
thorn-apple *Datura stramonium*
thyme *Thymus vulgare*
thyme, wild *Thymus serpyllum*
tobacco *Nicotiana tabacum*
tomato *Lycopersicon esculentum*
tormentil *Potentilla erecta*
truffle *Tuber aestivum*
truffle, black *Tuber melanosporum*
tulip *Tulipa gesneriana*
turmeric *Cucuma longa*
two-rowed barley *Hordeum distichum*

upas *Antiaris toxica*

valerian *Valeriana officinalis*
valerian, red *Valeriana rubia*
venus's fly-trap *Dionaea muscipula*
vervain *Verbena officinalis*
vine *Vitis vinifera*

violet *Viola canina*
violet, common *Viola riviniana*
viper's bugloss *Echium vulgare*

walnut *Juglans regia*
water dropwort *Oenanthe crocata*
water hyacinth *Eichhornia crassipes*
water lily *Nymphaea alba*
watermelon *Citrullus lanatus*
water-trap plant *Aldrovanda vesiculosa*
wheat *Triticum sp.*
white Belgian chicory *Cichorium intybus*
white bryony *Bryonia dioica*
white clover *Trifolium repens*
white deadnettle *Lamium album*
white horehound *Marrubium vulgare*
wild chamomile *Matricaria recutita*
wild cherry/gean *Prunus avium*
wild clematis *Clematis vitalba*
wild thyme *Thymus serpyllum*
willow *Salix sp.*
window-plant *Fenestraria sp.*
winter cabbage
    Brassica oleracea var. capitata
winter heliotrope *Petasites fragrans*
wolf's-bane *Aconitum napellus*
wood anemone *Anemone nemorosa*
woodruff *Galium odoratum*
wood sorrel *Oxalis acetosella*
wormwood *Artemisia absinthium*
woundwort *Stachys arvensis*

yam *Dioscorea sp.*
yarrow *Achillea millefolium*
yellow archangel *Galeobdolon luteum*
yellow gentian *Gentiana lutea*
yellow jessamine *Gelsemium sempervirens*
yellos laburnum *Laburnum anagyroides*
yellow sanders *Pterocarpus santalinus*
yellow stainer *Agaricus xanthodermus*
yew *Taxus baccata*
yohimbe *Pausinystalia yohimba*
yucca *Yucca sp.*

zucchini *Cucurbita pepo*

LATIN–ENGLISH

Acanthus mollis acanthus
Acer sp. maple
Acer pseudoplatanus sycamore
Acer saccharum sugar maple
Achillea millefolium yarrow
Acokanthera venenata acokanthera
Aconitum napellus monkshood
Aconitum napellus wolf's-bane
Actinidia chinensis kiwi fruit
Adiantum capillus-veneris maidenhair fern
Aesculus hippocastanum chestnut
Agaricus xanthodermus yellow stainer
Agave sp. maguey plant
Agave americana century plant
Agave sisalana sisal
Agrimonia sp. agrimony
Agrimonia eupatoria hemp agrimony
Agropyron repens couchgrass
Alchemilla mollis lady's mantle
Aldrovanda vesiculosa water-trap plant
Allium cepa onion
Allium porrum leek
Allium sativum garlic
Allium schoenoprasum chives
Aloe vera aloes
Althaea rosea hollyhock
Amanita muscaria fly agaric
Amanita pantherina panther cap
Amanita phalloides death cap
Amanita rubescens (fungus)
Amanita verna fool's mushroom
Amanita virosa destroying angel
Amaranthus retroflexus amaranth
Anagallis arvensis scarlet pimpernel
Ananas comosus pineapple
Androsace glacialis androsace
Anemone nemorosa wood anemone
Anethum graveolens dill
Angelica archangelica garden angelica
Angelica sylvestris angelica
Annona cherimolia cherimoya
Anthemis nobilis chamomile
Antiaris toxica upas
Apium graveolens celery
Aquilegia vulgaris columbine
Arachis hypogaea peanut
Arctium pubens burdock
Areca catechu betel nut
Arenga sacchifera sugar palm
Armillaria mellea honey fungus
Arnica montana arnica
Artemisia absinthium wormwood
Artemisia dracunculus tarragon
Artemisia vulgaris mugwort
Arum maculatum cuckoopint
Asarum europaeum asarabica
Asparagus officinalis asparagus
Asphodelus sp. asphodel
Aster sp. aster
Atropa belladonna deadly nightshade
Avena sp. oats
Avicennia nitida mangrove

Banisteriopsis caapi ayahuasca
Beckmannia erucaeformis seedear
Bellis perennis daisy
Berberis vulgaris barberry
Bertholettia excelsa Brazil nut
Beta vulgaris sugar beet
Betonica officinalis betony
Betula sp. birch
Betula nana dwarf birch
Boehmeria nivea ramie
Boletus aurantiacus (fungus)
Boletus aureus (fungus)
Borago officinalis borage
Boswellia carteri frankincense
Brassica napus rape

Brassica nigra mustard
Brassica oleracea var. acephala kale
Brassica oleracea var. botrytis
    cauliflower
Brassica oleracea var. capitata
    winter cabbage
Brassica oleracea var. gemmifera
    Brussels sprout
Brassica oleracea var. gongyloides kohlrabi
Bryonia dioica white bryony
Butryospermum parkii shea butternut
Buxus sempervirens box
Byblis gigantea (carnivore)

Calamus aquatilis rattan
Calamus aromaticus sweet-flag
Calendula officinalis garden marigold
Calluna sp. ling
Camellia japonica camellia
Camellia sinensis tea
Campanula medium Canterbury bell
Cannabis indica hashish/marijuana
Cannabis sativa hemp
Canna indica arrowroot
Cantharellus cibarius chanterelle
Capparis spinosa capers
Capsella bursa-pastoris shepherd's purse
Capsicum annuum pimiento/sweet pepper
Capsicum frutescens cayenne
Capsicum frutescens chili pepper
Carex sp. sedge
Carica papaya pawpaw
Carlina acaulis stemless thistle
Carlina vulgaris carline thistle
Carnegiea gigantea saguaro cactus
Carthamus tinctoria safflower
Carum carvi caraway
Carya pecan pecan
Cassia acutifolia cassia
Castanea sativa Spanish chestnut
Catha edulis khat
Cedrus libani cedar of Lebanon
Ceiba pentandra ceiba tree
Ceiba pentandra kapok
Centaurea cyanus cornflower
Centaurea erythraea common centaury
Centaurea kotschyana centaury
Cercidium torreyanum paloverde
Cetraria islandica Iceland moss
Chaerophyllum temulentum chervil
Chondodendron tomentosum pariera
Chrysanthemum sp. marigold
Chrysanthemum cinerariifolium pyrethrum
Chrysanthemum frutescens marguerite
Chrysanthemum leucanthemum oxeye daisy
Chrysanthemum vulgare tansy
Cichorium intybus red chicory
Cichorium intybus white Belgian chicory
Cicuta virosa cowbane
Cinchona officinalis Jesuit's bark
Cinnamonum camphora camphor
Cinnamonum cassia cinnamon
Citrullus colocynthis colocynth
Citrullus lanatus watermelon
Citrus sp. orange
Citrus bergamia bergamot
Citrus limon lemon
Citrus sinensis orange
Clavaria formosa (fungus)
Claviceps purpurea ergot
Clematis alba old-man's-beard
Clematis vitalba wild clematis
Clitocybe dealbata (fungus)
Cocos nucifera coir/coconut fiber
Coffea arabica coffee
Cola nitida cola
Colchicum autumnale meadow saffron
Commiphora myrrha myrrh
Conium maculatum hemlock
Convallaria majalis lily-of-the-valley
Convolvulus arvensis bindweed

Coprinus atramentarius inky cap
Corchorus capsularis jute
Coriandrum sativum coriander
Cornus kousa dogwood
Cornus mascula cornel cherry
Coryanthes albertinae (orchid)
Corylus avellana hazel
Cotula trubinata pincushion
Crocus sativus saffron
Crocus vernus crocus
Cucuma longa turmeric
Cucumis melo cantaloupe, melon
Cucumis sativus cucumber
Cucurbita pepo zucchini
Cuminum cyminum cumin
Cupressus sempervirens cypress
Canara scolymus globe artichoke
Cynoglossum officinale hound's tongue

Daedalea quercina (fungus)
Dahlia rosea dahlia
Daphne mezereon daphne
Darlingtonia californica cobra plant
Datura stramonium jimsonweed
Datura stramonium thorn-apple
Daucus carota carrot
Dendrocalamus giganteus giant bamboo
Derris elliptica derris
Dianthus caryophyllus
    carnation/pink/gillyflower
Dictamnus albus dittany
Digitalis purpurea foxglove
Dionaea muscipula Venus's fly-trap
Dioscorea sp. yam
Dipsacus fullonum teasel
Drosera anglica sundew
Drosophyllum lusitanicum (carnivore)

Echinocactus sp. barrel cactus
Echium vulgare viper's bugloss
Eichhornia crassipes water hyacinth
Elaeis guineensis oil palm
Eleusine coracana millet
Entoloma lividum (fungus)
Ephedra sinica ephedra
Equisetum arvense horsetail
Equisetum palustre marsh horsetail
Erica sp. heather
Eritrichium nanum eritrichium
Erythrophleum guineense sassy bark
Erythroxylum coca coca
Eugenia caryophyllata clove
Euphorbia lathyrus caper spurge

Fenestraria sp. window-plant
Ficus carica fig
Ficus religiosa asvattha
Foeniculum vulgare fennel
Foeniculum vulgare Florence fennel
Fragaria vesca strawberry
Fraxinus excelsior ash
Fumaria occidentalis fumitory

Galeobdolon luteum yellow archangel
Galium aparine goosegrass
Galium odoratum woodruff
Galium verum lady's bedstraw
Garcinia morella gamboge
Gardenia florida gardenia
Gelsemium sempervirens yellow jessamine
Gentiana amarella autumn gentian
Gentiana lutea yellow gentian
Geranium sp. cranesbill
Geum sp. avens
Glechoma hederacea ground ivy
Glycine max soybean
Gomphidius glutinosus (fungus)
Gossypium herbaceum cotton plant

Guizotia abyssinica niger seed
Gyrometra esculenta (fungus)

Hedera helix ivy
Helianthus annuus sunflower
Helleborus niger black hellebore
Helvella gigas (fungus)
Hemionitis cordifolia (an Indian tree)
Hevea brasiliensis rubber
Hibiscus esculentus okra
Hippocrepis comosa horseshoe vetch
Hordea trifurcatum naked barley
Hordeum distichum two-rowed barley
Hordeum vulgare barley
Humulus lupulus hop
Hyacinthus orientalis hyacinth
Hyoscyamus niger henbane
Hypericum pulchrum St. John's-wort/tutsan
Hyssopus officinalis hyssop

Ilex aquifolium holly
Impatiens noli-me-tangere balsam
Indigofera tinctoria indigo
Inocybe patouillardii (fungus)
Inocybe patouillardi inocybe
Inula helenium elecampine
Iris sp. iris

Jasminum officinale jasmine
Juglans regia walnut
Juniperus communis juniper

Laburnum anagyroides yellow laburnum
Lactarius blennius (fungus)
Lactarius volemus (fungus)
Lagenaria siceraria gourd
Lamium album white deadnettle
Lamium maculatum spotted deadnettle
Larix sp. larch
Laurus nobilis bay
Lavendula officinalis lavender
Lawsonia inermis henna
Lecythis sp. monkey pot
Leontopodium alpinum edelweiss
Lilium sp. lily
Lilium martagon martagon lily
Linum usitatissimum linseed/flax
Lonicera caprifolium honeysuckle
Lophophora williamsii peyote/mescal buttons
Lupinus arcticus arctic lupin
Lupinus nootkatensis lupin
Lycopersion esculentum tomato
Lythrum portula purslane
Lythrum salicaria purple loosestrife

Malus pumila apple
Malva sylvestris mallow
Mandragora officinarum mandrake
Mangifera indica mango
Manihot esculenta cassava
Marrubium vulgare white horehound
Matricaria recutita wild chamomile
Matthiola bicornis night-scented stock
Medicago sativa lucerne/alfalfa
Melilotus officinalis melilot
Melissa officinalis balm
Mentha sp. mint
Mentha piperita peppermint
Menyanthes trifoliata bogbean
Mercurialis perennis dog's mercury
Mimosa pudica mimosa
Morchella esculenta morel
Morus nigra mulberry
Musa textilis abaca
Muscari atlanticum grape hyacinth
Myristica fragrans nutmeg/mace

Narcissus sp. daffodil
Narcissus poeticus pheasant's eye
Nelumbium speciosum Egyptian bean
Nelumbo nucifera lotus
Nepenthes hookeriana pitcher plant
Nerium oleandrum oleander
Nicotiana tabacum tobacco
Nothofagus cunninghami myrtle
Nymphaea alba water lily

Ocimum basilicum basil
Oenanthe crocata water dropwort
Oenochera biennis evening primrose
Olea europaea olive
Ophrys sp. ophrys orchid
Opuntia ficus-indica prickly pear
Opuntia fulgida cholla cactus
Origanum majorana marjoram
Oryza sativa rice
Oxalis acetosella wood sorrel

Paeonia mascula peony
Panaeolus campanulatus (fungus)
Panax ginseng ginseng
Papaver somniferum opium poppy
Papaver somniferum poppy
Passiflora edulis passion flower
Pausinystalia yohimba yohimbe
Peganum harmala harmela
Persea americana avocado pear
Petasites fragrans heliotrope
Petasites fragrans winter helitrope
Petroselinum crispum parsley
Peucedanum officinale sea-fennel
Peucephyllum schottii pygmy cedar
Phacelia congesta phacelia
Phallus impudicus stinkhorn fungus
Phaseolus vulgaris French bean
Phoenix dactylifera date-palm
Phormium tenax phormium
Physostigma venenosum calabar bean
Pimpinella anisum aniseed
Pimpinella saxifraga burnet saxifrage
Pinguicula vulgaris butterwort
Pinus aristata bristlecone pine
Pinus cembra arolla pine/Swiss stone pine
Pinus Jeffreyi Jeffrey pine
Piper methysticum kava-kava
Piper nigrum pepper
Pistacia vera pistachio
Pisum sativum garden pea
Plantago lanceolata ribwort plantain
Pogostemon cablin patchouli
Polygonatum odoratum Solomon's seal
Populus tremula aspen
Potentilla erecta tormentil
Primula veris cowslip
Primula vulgaris primrose
Prosopis juliflora mesquite
Prunus amygdalus almond
Prunus avium wild cherry/gean
Prunus laurocerasus cherry laurel
Prunus persica peach
Prunus spinosa blackthorn
Prunus spinosa sloe
Psilocybe mexicana magic mushroom
Pteridium aquilinum bracken
Pterocarpus santalinus yellow sanders
Pulicaria dysenterica fleabane
Pulmonaria officinalis lungwort
Pulsatilla vulgaris Pasqueflower
Punica granatum pomegranate
Pyrus communis pear

Quercus sp. oak
Quercus ilex holm oak/ilex
Quercus robur oak
Quercus suber cork oak

Rafflesia arnoldii rafflesia
Ramaria botrytis (fungus)
Ranunculus arvensis buttercup
Ranunculus ficaria lesser celandine
Rauvolfia serpentina snakeroot
Rauvolfia serpentina rauwolfia
Rheum rhaponticum rhubarb
Rhododendron ferrugineum alpine rose
Rhododendron ponticum
                  common rhododendron
Rhodophyllus sinuatus (fungus)
Rhus toxicodendron ivy
Ribes grossularia gooseberry
Ribes nigrum blackcurrant
Ribes rubrum redcurrant
Ricinus communis castor oil plant
Rivea corymbosa ololiuqui
Rosa sp. rose
Rosa canina dog rose/wild rose
Rosa eglanteria eglantine rose
Rosmarinus officinalis rosemary
Rubus chamaemorus cloudberry
Rubus fruticosus briar/blackberry
Rubus idaeus raspberry
Rumex sp. sorrel
Russula emetica (fungus)
Ruta graveolens rue

Saccharum munja munj tree
Saccharum officinale sugar
Salix sp. willow
Salvia horminoides sage
Sambucus nigra elder
Sarothamnus scoparius broom
Sarracenia purpurea pitcher plant
Saxifraga sp. saxifrage
Saxifraga oppositifolia purple saxifrage
Scabiosa prolifera scabious
Secale cereale rye
Sempervivum tectorum houseleek
Senecio jacobaea ragwort
Sequoia giganteum big tree
Sequoia sempervirens coast redwood
Sesamum indicum sesame
Shorea robusta sal-tree
Silene sp. campion
Silene acaulis moss campion
Solanum tuberosum potato
Soldanella soldanella
Solidago virgaurea golden rod
Sonchus oleraceus milkweed
Sorbus aucuparia rowan/mountain ash
Sorghum vulgare sorghum
Stachys arvensis woundwort
Stipa tenacissima esparto grass
Strophanthus gratus strophanthus
Strophanthus hispidus strophanthus
Strychnos nux-vomica strychnine tree
Strychnos toxifera curare poison nut
Styrax officinale storax
Swietenia mahagoni mahogany

Tabernanthe iboga iboga
Tamarix gallica tamarisk
Taraxacum officinale dandelion
Taxodium distichum swamp cypress
Taxus baccata yew
Teucrium polium polion germander
Thalictrum flavum meadow rue
Thea sinensis/Camellia sinensis tea
Theobroma cacao chocolate
Theobroma cacao cocoa
Thymus serpyllum wild thyme
Thymus vulgare thyme
Trifolium sp. clover
Trifolium minus lesser trefoil
Trifolium pratense red clover
Trifolium repens white clover
Triticum aestivum wheat
Triticum aestivum bread-wheat

Triticum dicoccum emmer
Triticum monococcum einkorn
Tsuga heterophylla hemlock tree
Tuber aestivum truffle
Tuber melanosporum black truffle
Tulipa gesneriana tulip
Tussilago farfara coltsfoot

Ulex sp. gorse
Ulmus procera elm
Umbilicus rupestris pennywort
Urginea maritima squill
Urtica dioica stinging nettle
Utricularia vulgaris bladderwort

Vaccinium corymbosum blueberry
Vaccinium oxycoccus cranberry
Valeriana officinalis all-heal/valerian
Valeriana rubia red valerian
Verbena officinalis vervain
Veronica persica speedwell
Viburnum opulus guelder rose
Viburnum tinus laurestinus
Vicia faba broad bean
Victoria amazonica royal water lily
Viola canina violet
Viola riviniana common violet
Viola tricolor love-in-idleness
Viola tricolor pansy
Viscum album mistletoe
Vitis vinifera grape/vine

Xanthium stramonium cocklebur

Yucca sp. yucca

Zea mays corn
Zingiber officinale ginger

SELECTED BIBLIOGRAPHY

GENERAL

Gerrard, John. *The Herball or General Historie of Plantes.* London, 1597, reprinted 1976.

Grigson, Geoffrey. *The Englishman's Flora.* London, 1958.

Hill, A. F. *Economic Botany.* New York, 1952.

Howes, F. N. *A Dictionary of Useful and Everyday Plants.* London, 1973.

Keble Martin, W. *The Concise British Flora in Color.* London, 1965.

Lundegardh, H. *Plant Physiology.* London, 1966.

Morley, B. D., and B. Everard. *Flowers of the World.* London, 1970.

Parkinson, John. *Paradisus in sole paradisi terrestris.* London, 1629.

Pliny the Elder. *Natural History.* Translated by H. Rackham. London, 1950.

Potter, S., and L. Sargent. *Pedigree: Words from Nature.* London, 1973.

Royal Horticultural Society. *Dictionary of Gardening.* Oxford, 1956– .

Smith, A. W., and W. T. Stearn. *A Gardener's Dictionary of Plant Names.* London, 1972.

Theophrastus. *History of Plants.* Edited by A. F. Hort. London, 1916.

Uphof, J. C. T. *Dictionary of Economic Plants.* London, 1968.

Usher, G. *A Dictionary of Plants Used by Man.* London, 1974.

Willis, J. C. *A Dictionary of the Flowering Plants and Ferns.* London, 1931 and 1966.

POWER TO SURVIVE

Bean, W. J. *Trees and Shrubs Hardy in the British Isles.* London, 1914–1933.

Brimble, L. J. F. *Intermediate Botany.* London, 1953.

Corner, E. J. H. *The Life of Plants.* London, 1964.

Fogg, G. E. *The Growth of Plants.* London, 1970.

Hymas, E. *Soil and Civilisation.* London, 1953.

James, W. O. *Background to Gardening.* London, 1957.

Johnson, H. *The International Book of Trees.* London, 1973.

King, R. *The World of Kew.* London, 1976.

Paturi, F. R. *Nature, Mother of Invention.* London, 1976.

Peattie, D. C. *Flowering Earth.* London, 1948.

Proctor, M., and P. Yeo. *The Pollination of Flowers.* London, 1973.

Ramsbottom, J. *Mushrooms and Toadstools.* London, 1953.

Reed, H. S. *A Short History of the Plant Sciences.* Waltham, Mass., 1942.

Russell, E. J., and E. W. Russell. *Soil Conditions and Plant Growth.* London, 1961.

Steward, F. C. *Plants at Work.* London, 1964.

POWER TO SUSTAIN

Anderson, E. *Plants, Man, and Life.* Los Angeles, 1971.

Braudel, F. *Capitalism and Material Life.* London, 1967.

Brothwell, D., and P. Brothwell. *Food in Antiquity.* London, 1969.

Carefoot, G. L., and E. R. Sprott. *Famine on the Wind: Plant Diseases and Human History.* New York, 1967.

Deerr, N. *The History of Sugar.* London, 1949.

Drummond, J. C., and A. Wilbraham. *The Englishman's Food.* London, 1964.

Elton, C. *The Ecology of Invasions by Animals and Plants.* New York, 1958.

Lemmon, K. *The Golden Age of Plant Hunters.* London, 1968.

Masefield, G. B., M. Wallis, and S. G. Harrison. *The Oxford Book of Food Plants.* London, 1969.

Moritz, L. A. *Grain-mills and Flour in Classical Antiquity.* Oxford, 1958.

Okakura, K. *The Book of Tea.* New York, 1964.

Rhind, W. *A History of the Vegetable Kingdom.* London, 1872.

Salaman, R. N. *The History and Social Influence of the Potato.* Cambridge, England, 1949.

Scott, J. M. *The Tea Story.* London, 1964.

Stobart, T. *Herbs, Spices, and Flavorings.* London, 1970.

Younger, W. *Gods, Men, and Wine.* London, 1966.

POWER TO HEAL AND KILL

Arber, Agnes. *Herbals, Their Origin and Evolution.* London, 1938.

Castiglioni, A. *A History of Medicine.* New York, 1947.

Darwin, C. *Insectivorous Plants.* London, 1900.

De Baïracli Levy, J. *The Illustrated Herbal Handbook.* London, 1974.

Forsyth, A. A. *British Poisonous Plants.* London, 1954.

Graham, J. D. P. *The Diagnosis and Treatment of Acute Poisoning.* New York, 1962.

Grieve, M. *A Modern Herbal.* New York, 1959.

Henrey, Blanche. *British Botanical and Horticultural Literature before 1800.* London, 1976.

Kingsbury, J. M. *Poisonous Plants of the U.S. and Canada.* New York, 1964.

Kreig, M. B. *Green Medicine.* New York, 1964.

Larousse des Plantes qui Guérissent. Paris, 1974.

Loomis, T. A. *Essentials of Toxicology.* Philadelphia, 1968.

Rohde, E. S. *Garden of Herbs.* London, 1920.

Schenk, G. *Book of Poisons.* London, 1962.

Scott, J. *The Mandrake Root.* London, 1946.

Taylor, N. E. *Plant Drugs That Changed the World.* London, 1966.

Thomas, B. *Curare: Its History and Usage.* London, 1964.

Thompson, C. J. S. *Poisons and Poisoners.* London, 1931.

Thompson, W. R. *Herbs That Heal.* London, 1976.

Trease, G. E. *A Textbook of Pharmacognosy.* London, 1961.

Wootton, A. C. *Chronicles of Pharmacy.* London, 1910.

Wren, R. C., and R. W. Wren. *Potter's New Cyclopedia of Botanical Drugs and Preparations.* London, 1968.

POWER TO ALTER CONSCIOUSNESS

Abrams, M. H. *The Milk of Paradise.* Boston, 1934.

Castaneda, C. *The Teachings of Don Juan: A Yaqui Way of Knowledge.* California, 1968.

Cohen, S. *Drugs of Hallucination.* London, 1965.

Davenport, J. *Aphrodisiacs and Love Stimulants.* London, 1965.

De Félice, Philippe. *Poisons Sacrés, Ivresses Divines.* Paris, 1936.

De Quincey, T. *Confessions of an English Opium Eater.* London, 1956.

De Ropp, R. S. *Drugs and the Mind.* London, 1958.

Emboden, W. *Narcotic Plants.* London, 1972.

Hayter, A. *Opium and the Romantic Imagination.* London, 1968.

Heim, R. *Les Champignons Toxiques et Hallucinogènes.* Paris, 1963.

Huxley, A. *The Doors of Perception, and Heaven and Hell.* London, 1959.

Laurie, P. *Drugs.* London, 1972.

Lewin, L. *Phantastica.* London, 1931.

Pelt, J.-M. *Drogues et Plantes Magiques.* Paris, 1971.

Schneider, E. *Coleridge, Opium, and "Kubla Khan."* Chicago, 1953.

Schultes, R. E., and A. Hofmann. *The Botany and Chemistry of Hallucinogens.* Springfield, Ill., 1973.

Solomon, D., ed. *Drugs and Sexuality.* London, 1973.

Solomon, D., ed. *The Marijuana Papers.* London, 1969.

Wasson, R. G. *Soma: Divine Mushroom of Immortality.* New York, 1969.

POWER OVER THE SPIRIT

Blunt, W. *The Art of Botanical Illustration.* London, 1950.

Blunt, W. *Tulipomania.* London, 1950.

Crisp, F. *Medieval Gardens.* London, 1924.

Folkard, R. *Plant Lore, Legends, and Lyrics.* London, 1892.

Grigson, G. *Gardenage.* London, 1952.

Hay, R., and P. M. Synge. *The Dictionary of Garden Plants in Colour.* London, 1969.

Hyams, E., and W. McQuitty. *Great Botanical Gardens of the World.* London, 1969.

Moldenke, H. N., and A. L. Moldenke. *Plants of the Bible.* New York, 1952.

Phythion, J. E. *Trees in Nature, Myth, and Art.* London, 1907.

Skinner, C. W. *Myths and Legends of Flowers, Trees, Fruits, and Plants.* New York, 1925.

Steele, F. *Gardens and People.* New York, 1964.

Thistleton-Dyer, T. F. *Folklore of Plants.* London, 1889.

Young, A. *The Poet and the Landscape.* London, 1962.

Young, A. *A Retrospect of Flowers.* London, 1950.

PICTURE CREDITS

A. A. A. Photo, Paris: 201 (top)

Academisch Historisch Museum, Leiden: 155 (top)

Agence TOP, Paris/Édouard Boubat: 250 (bottom)

Agenzia Fotografica Luisa Ricciarini, Milan/Nino Cirani: 68 (top left); 120 (top)

Alinari, Florence: 112 (top, right); 135 (left); 249 (right bottom)

American Museum of Natural History, New York: 35

William H. Amos, Middletown: 27 (top)

Annan Photo Features, Miami: 60

Archaeological Survey of India, India Office, London: 232 (bottom right)

Archive Photographique, Paris: 158 (bottom, first from left); 216 (top); 239 (right)

The Art Institute of Chicago: 225

Asian Art Museum of San Francisco: 62 (top left)

Aspect Picture Library, London/J. Alex Langley: 138/139 (top)

A–Z Botanical Collection, London: 25 (right); 118 (left, first and third from top; center, third from left; top right); 119 (top, first and third from left; second row, second from left; bottom right); 140 (No. 5)

Bayerische Staatsbibliothek, Munich: 163 (center right; bottom left)

Bayerische Staatsgemäldesammlung, Munich: 189 (top right); 228/229

S. Beaufoy, Ipswich: 56 (third row, first and second from right)

Max Berger, Bern: 42 (second from top)

Courtesy of the Berry-Hill Galleries, New York: 204/205

Biblioteca Apostolica Vaticano: 156 (bottom right)

Bibliothèque Nationale, Paris: 12 (center); 13 (third from left); 16 (top right); 113 (top and bottom left); 168 (right); 169 (first and third from left); 190 (left); 207 (left); 244; 256 (bottom)

Bildarchiv Foto Marburg: 266 (bottom left)

Bildarchiv Preussischer Kulturbesitz, Berlin: 149 (bottom right)

Black Star, New York/Archie Liebermann: 181 (bottom right)

Bodleian Library, Oxford: 15 (center right); 151 (center left); 162; 163 (top left and top center; bottom center); 190 (top); 192 (left); 230 (top); 231 (bottom and top right); 233 (center right); 234/235; 253 (right)

Anne Bolt, London: 96 (No. 2); 119 (bottom, second from left)

Botany School, Cambridge: 156 (bottom, second from left); 157 (center, third from right); 158 (bottom, second from left)

Brian Brake, Auckland: 68 (bottom left); 262 (left)

British Library, London: 24 (left); 34 (second from top); 92 (center, second from bottom); 112 (top); 150 (center right); 152 (center)

British Museum, London: 14 (right); 15 (top, Photo Hamlyn); 32 (left); 33 (center, first and second from right); 94 (center left); 156 (bottom left); 157 (center, first and second from right); 209 (right); 241

C. J. Bucher, Lucerne: 31 (bottom right); 87 (right); 119 (third row from top, right); 200 (right row, bottom); 215 (top right); 242 (left); 251 (bottom right)

Bührer, Lucerne: 13 (second from left); 20 (top); 42 (bottom); 46 (top); 47; 48 (right); 49 (top); 69; 92 (center, far left); 96 (No. 1, 8); 99; 101; 102; 103; 104; 105; 108; 109; 110; 118 (top; left, second from top); 119 (third row from top, second from right); 196 (top right); 257 (second from left); 275

Bulloz, Paris: 9 (right); 214

Burgerbibliothek, Bern: 159 (bottom, second from left)

California Historical Society Library, San Francisco: 41

Camera Press, London: 218 (bottom right)

Hans Carl Verlag, Nuremberg: 210 (bottom left)

Certosa di S. Martino, Naples; Photo: Rocco Pedicini: 272

Chishakuin, Kyoto; Photo: Benrido Company: 261 (bottom right)

Bruce Coleman Collection, Uxbridge: 22 (right, third from top, Jane Burton); 22 (right, second from bottom, Leonard Lee Rue III); 22 (right, bottom, M. P. L. Fodgen); 23 (left, third from top, Jane Burton); 23 (left, second from bottom, James Simon); 23 (left bottom, M. P. L. Fodgen); 23 (right, second from bottom, Joe van Wormer); 23 (right bottom, Clara Calhoun); 24 (bottom right, Gene Cox); 31 (top right, Prato); 38 (top, Norman Tomalin); 54 (bottom left, S. C. Bisserot); 126 (No. 9, S. C. Porter); 213 (right, Dr. Janus)

Collection of John M. Crawford, New York; Photo: Asian Art Photographic Distribution, Ann Arbor: 255

Columbia University, New York: 156 (top)

Cooper-Bridgeman Library, London: 169 (second from left); 177 (second from right)

Cosmopress, Geneva; Photo: DuMont Schauberg, Cologne: 268 (top)

Courtauld Institute of Art, London, Lee Collection: 226 (top left)

Othmar Danesch, Büttels: 40 (center); 42 (top)

Deutscher Brauer-Bund, Bonn-Bad Godesberg: 210 (top); 211 (top and bottom left)

Hans Dossenbach, Oberschlatt: 45 (left)

Ecole Française d'Archéologie, Athens: 266 (top right)

Eidgenössische Anstalt für das forstliche Versuchswesen, Birmensdorf: 54 (No. 3); 274

Eidgenössische landwirtschaftliche Versuchsanstalt, Reckenholz: 96 (No. 10)

Fritz-Martin Engel, Ansbach: 126 (No. 1, 2); 127 (No. 11); 188 (bottom, first and third from right); 189 (bottom right); 221

Friedrich Engesser, Küsnacht: 73 (bottom left); 80

Europäisches Brotmuseum, Mollefelde: 88 (center, first, second, and third from left; top right); 89 (left)

French Government Tourist Office, London: 249 (top right)

Frick Collection, New York: 250 (top)

Josip Generalić, Zagreb: 268 (bottom right)

Geologische Sammlung der Bergingenieurschule, Saarbrücken: 33 (center left)

Georg Gerster, Zumikon: 26 (right); 49 (left); 75; 78; 81; 82; 83; 84; 176 (right)

Giraudon, Paris: 13 (bottom left); 16 (bottom, second from right); 34 (third from bottom, avec l'autorisation spéciale de la ville de Bayeux); 95 (bottom right); 113 (top, second from right); 136 (bottom and right); 223 (right); 249 (right, second from top)

Gletschergarten, Lucerne: 74

Grandma Moses Properties, Inc., New York: 269 (bottom left, Detail from the painting "The Old Oaken Bucket," 1943 Private Collection USA)

Graphische Sammlung Albertina, Vienna: 167 (right)

Haags Gemeentemuseum, The Hague: 258 (bottom)

Claus Hansmann, Munich: 150 (bottom right); 151 (bottom, second and third from left; top right)

Hassia, Paris: 208 (center left)

Ernst A. Heiniger, Zurich: 6/7; 42 (third from top); 44 (bottom, second from right)

A. Heitmann, Stabio: 43 (bottom right)

André Held, Ecublens: 15 (center); 52 (right); 66/67

Prof. J. Arthur Herrick, Kent State University: 58 (top)

Hirmer Bildarchiv, Munich: 135 (top right)

Dr. Albert Hofmann, Burg im Leimental: 220 (top)

Frau Dr. Homburger, Zurich: 22 (right, third from bottom)

Horniman Museum, London: 13 (top, photo: Hamlyn Picture Library)

Horyu-Ji Temple, Nara; Photo: Tasaburo Yoneda: 226 (bottom left)

Illustrated London News: 137 (bottom left)

Walter Imber, Laufen: 30 (top and bottom right); 31 (center, top and bottom); 39 (left); 55 (No. 22); 61 (right); 86/87; 91 (top left); 94/95 (bottom); 96 (No. 3); 97 (No. 11); 118 (bottom, first and second from left); 172; 207 (right); 236 (center row, second from right)

Indian Office Library, London: 267 (top)

Institut Géographique National, Paris: 76

Israel Government Press Office: 73 (bottom right)

Jacana, Paris: 96 (No. 9, J. P. Hervey); 127 (No. 12, R. König); 139 (center, first and second from right)

Monique Jacot, Epesses: 251 (bottom left)

Jünger Verlag, Frankfurt: 44 (top, second from right); 55 (No. 17)

Keller, Emmenbrücke: 44 (bottom, third from right)

Kestner Museum, Hanover; Photo: Eidenbenz, Basel: 232 (top right)

Keystone Press, London: 137 (top right)

Ernst Klett Verlag, Stuttgart: 94 (top, bottom right)

Alfred Kümin, Freienbach: 209 (left)

Kunsthistorisches Museum, Vienna: 181 (top right); 273

Kunstmuseum Basel; Photo: Hinz: 269 (bottom right)

Kunstmuseum Bern: 243

Laboratory of Plant Taxonomy, University for Agriculture, Wageningen: 44 (top left); 97 (No. 14); 139 (bottom row, first from left); 200 (right row, top)

Laboratory of Tree-Ring Research, University of Arizona: 36

Landesmuseum für Vorgeschichte, Halle/Salle: 64 (top, second from right)

Frank W. Lane, Pinner: 27 (bottom)

Larousse, Paris: 168 (center, right and bottom); 183 (top right)

Lauros-Giraudon, Paris: 13 (second from right); 18/19

Hans Leuenberger, Yverdon: 138 (center)

The Lady Lever Art Gallery, Port Sunlight: 188 (top right)

Library of Congress, Washington: 218 (right, third from top)

Franz Karl Frh. von Linden, Waldsee: 26 (left)

Lindley Library of the Royal Horticultural Society: 169 (first and second from right); 257 (bottom right, Photo Cooper-Bridgeman)

Walter Linsenmaier, Ebikon: 23 (top left); 23 (right, second from top); 50; 51; 53 (center left); 54 (No. 12); 55 (No. 14

and 21); 56 (top row, first, second and last from left; second row; third row, first and second from left); 57 (No. 1–8, 10–12)

Louvre, Paris: 15 (middle left, Photo Réunion des Musées Nationaux); 148 (top, second from left, Photo Giraudon); 148 (bottom, second from right; Photo Réunion des Musées Nationaux); 199 (Réunion des Musées Nationaux)

William Macquitty: 248 (right)

Magnum, Paris: 85 (Henri Cartier-Bresson); 226 (top right, Henri Cartier-Bresson); 250 (center right)

Mansell Collection, London: 12 (right); 34 (top and center); 38 (center); 96 (No. 4); 113 (top, third from left); 119 (bottom, third from left); 148 (bottom left); 158 (bottom, first and second from right); 159 (bottom, first and third from left); 167 (bottom right); 178 (bottom and right); 182 (third from left); 187 (right); 191 (right); 192 (top); 216 (left and bottom right); 217 (top); 218 (right, second from bottom); 246 (bottom)

Leonard von Matt, Buochs: 132 (third and fourth from left); 134 (top); 136 (top)

Medizinhistorisches Institut der Universität Zurich: 218 (left)

Merseyside County Museum, Liverpool: 92 (center, third from top)

Metropolitan Museum of Art, New York: 68 (top right); 89 (right); 113 (top, second from left); 261 (center)

Mrs. Middleton, Amado; Photo: Katrina Thomas, New York: 269 (bottom, second from right)

Gale Monson, Tuscon: 46 (bottom)

Ann Münchow, Aachen: 34 (third from top)

Musée Guimet, Paris: 233 (left, Réunion des Musées Nationaux)

Musée National d'Histoire Naturelle, Paris: 2 (center and bottom); 16 (top left); 168 (center, second from left); 186 (bottom, second from left); 194 (bottom right)

Musées Cantonaux du Valais, Sion: 208 (top right)

Museo Lazaro Galdiano; Photo: Giraudon: 190 (bottom left)

Museum für Bildende Künste, Leipzig; Photo: Gerhard Reinhold, Leipzig-Mölkau: 187 (left)

The Museum of Modern Art, New York, Mrs. Simon Guggenheim Fund: 224 (top left)

Courtesy of Museum of the American Indian, New York, Heye Foundation: 224 (bottom left)

Museum Rietberg, Zurich: 8 (bottom); 182 (bottom right)

National Archives, Washington: 70/71 (top)

National Library of Medicine, Bethesda: 212

National Maritime Museum, London: 157 (center row, first from left; bottom); 217 (center right)

Nationalmuseet, Copenhagen: 64 (top center)

Courtesy of the National Park Service: 37

Natural History Photographic Agency, Westerham: 22 (left row, third from top, Stephan Dalton; bottom); 56 (third row, center); 118 (center right, John Topham); 127 (No. 5, Brian Hawkes; No. 17, K. G. Preston-Mafham); 182 (bottom left, K. G. Preston-Mafham); 188 (bottom left, Markhan)

Natural Science Photos, Watford: 20 (bottom, A. G. Leutscher); 39 (bottom left, Gil Montalverne); 39 (bottom right, P. J. K. Burton); 52 (left, P. A. Bowman); 54 (center, P. H. Ward); 111 (No. 11, Eric Crichton; No. 12, G. Matthews; No. 15, 18, Eric Crichton; No. 20, A. Leutscher)

Naturhistorisches Museum, Bern; Photo: Max Berger: 55 (No. 24)

Ny Carlsberg Glyptotek, Copenhagen: 98 (center right)

Oesterreichische Nationalbibliothek: 161; 245

Okapia, Frankfurt: 23 (right, third from bottom); 53 (center); 54 (top)

Orion Press, Tokyo: 148 (top right, Photo Hamlyn Picture Library)

Oronoz, Madrid: 9

Paläontologisches Institut, Zurich: 32 (left); 33 (top)

Photoworld Div. New York/Bob Taylor: 70/71 (bottom)

Pierpont Morgan Library, New York: 34 (second from bottom)

Publisher's Archives: 10; 11 (top and bottom); 16 (bottom right, from a serigraph by P. Mazonowicz); 21; 25 (left and bottom); 30 (top and bottom left); 31 (top and bottom left); 38/39; 43; 48 (bottom right); 53 (left and top); 54 (No. 4, 6, 7, 9, 10, 11); 55 (No. 15, 16, 18, 19, 23, 25); 56 (top and bottom, second from right); 57 (right); 58/59 (bottom); 65; 72; 86 (top); 87 (top); 88 (bottom, first and second from right); 90 (bottom right); 91 (top right); 92 (top); 93 (top right); 94/95 (top center); 94 (bottom left); 95 (top right); 111 (No. 9, 10, 13, 16, 17, 22); 122 (bottom); 127 (No. 6); 130 (top row; second row from bottom, right); 138 (top row; bottom right); 141 (No. 12, 13); 144 (top); 145 (top right); 147 (top left); 151 (bottom right); 173; 182 (bottom, second from left); 183 (bottom right); 188 (top left); 189 (bottom right); 194 (left row; right row, second from top); 195; 196 (left row); 197; 198 (left row and right row, first and second from top); 199; 200 (left row); 201 (left); 202 (left row; right row top); 219 (top right); 220 (right); 223 (top); 226 (bottom right); 252 (top left); 258 (top)

Radio Times Hulton Picture Library, London: 113 (top right); 119 (bottom left); 184 (bottom); 190 (bottom); 218 (right, first and second from top); 246 (top)

Rapho, Paris/Roland Michaud: 163 (bottom right); 168 (top); 239 (left); 256 (top)

Rathaus, Rapperswil: 256 (center, second from right)

Prof. Dr. W. Rauh, Institut für Systematische Botanik und Pflanzengeographie der Universität Heidelberg: 11 (center); 20 (top left); 30 (center bottom); 38 (bottom); 39 (top); 44 (bottom, three from left); 55 (No. 13); 86 (center); 91 (bottom left); 95 (center left); 96 (No. 5, 6); 97 (No. 12, 13); 118 (bottom, second from left); 119 (top, second from left; second row from top, first and third from right); 122 (right); 124; 126 (No. 7); 127 (No. 4); 129 (first and third row); 130 (second row from top; bottom row); 131 (center, top and bottom); 140 (No. 1, 2, 4, 6, 7, 8, 9, 10); 141 (No. 11, 14, 15, 16, 17, 18); 143; 145 (top left); 146 (left row; right row, four from top); 147 (left row, four from bottom; right row, first three from top and last); 176 (left); 177 (first and third row); 186 (bottom right); 194 (top right); 196 (right, first and second from bottom); 198 (right row, bottom); 202 (right row, first and second from bottom); 219 (top left)

J. N. Reichel/Top, Paris: 13 (bottom right)

Rheinisches Landesmuseum, Bonn; Photo: Edita SA Lausanne: 68/69

Roger-Viollet, Paris: 112 (bottom left)

Vulvio Roiter, Venice: 219 (bottom); 251 (center)

Royal Library Windsor: 166 (top left)

Scala, Antella: 132 (left); 167 (top left); 208 (top and bottom left); 230 (top left); 236 (center row, second from left); 236 (bottom); 237; 240; 247; 259; 260; 261 (bottom left); 266 (bottom right)

Oskar Schmid, Amriswil: 22 (left row, second and fourth from top; right row, first and second from top); 23 (left row, second and fourth from top; right row, first and third from top); 56 (first row, third from left)

Schuh, Zurich-Küsnacht: 60/61

Emil Schulthess, Zurich: 90 (bottom left); 91 (bottom right); 106/107

Schweizerische Landesbibliothek, Bern: 158 (bottom, third from left)

Seaphot: 28 (Colin Doeg); 29 (Warren Williams)

Sforza Castle, Milan/Photo Sinigalia: 263

Shogakukan Publishing Co. Ltd., Tokyo: 206 (center)

Rolf Siebrasse, Bielefeld: 125

Len Sirmann Press, Geneva: 180; 217 (bottom)

Harry Smith Horticultural Photographic Collection, Rettendon-Chelmsford: 248 (left)

Bob & Ira Spring, Edmonds: 40 (top)

Staatliches Museum für Naturkunde, Stuttgart: 30 (bottom right)

Staatliches Museum für Völkerkunde, Munich: 183 (top left)

Staatsarchiv, Fribourg/Photo Rast: 252 (top right)

Städelsches Kunstinstitut, Frankfurt: 133

Erwin R. Stalder, Meggen: 257 (top left)

State Historical Society of Wisconsin: 70 (left)

Dr. Franz Stoedtner, Düsseldorf: 64 (top, far right)

Thames and Hudson, London: 14 (left); 148 (bottom right); 233 (top right)

Franz Thorbecke, Lindau: 73 (top)

Time Life, New York/Yale Joe: 193

Tiroler Volkskunstmuseum, Innsbruck: 251 (top)

Robert Tobler, Lucerne: 42 (second from bottom); 62 (center); 131 (right); 140 (No. 3); 222 (top); 236 (center row, left); 261 (top, left and right)

John Topham Picture Library, Edenbridge: 56 (bottom right, R. G. Foord); 126 (No. 10, R. G. Foord); 127 (No. 3, Leonard Lee Rue III; No. 14, Windridge; No. 16, Ron+Christine Foord); 146 (right row, bottom); 191 (top left)

Tropenmuseum, Basel: 96 (No. 7)

Ullstein Bilderdienst, Berlin: 159 (bottom, first and second from right)

Universitätsbibliothek Tübingen: 149 (bottom, second from right)

University Library, Copenhagen: 238 (left)

University Museum, Philadelphia: 149 (bottom left)

U.S. Department of Agriculture, Salt Lake City: 77

Victoria and Albert Museum, London: 90 (top, Courtesy of Aldus Books Ltd.); 232 (center left, Courtesy Thames and Hudson)

Fred Waldvogel, Uetikon am See: 126 (No. 8); 127 (No. 13, 15)

Wallraf-Richartz-Museum, Cologne: 257 (top right)

By Courtesy of the Wellcome Trustees, London: 186 (top)

Eduard Widmer, Zurich: 267 (bottom left)

Galerie Wilde, Cologne: 227; 264; 265

Douglas P. Wilson: 27 (left, first and second from top)

Gordon Winter at Country Life: 68 (bottom right)

Max Wyss, Lucerne: 93 (left)

Zoologisches Museum, Zurich: 22 (top left)

PICTURE CREDITS:
FROM PUBLISHED WORKS

Adrian, Walther: *So wurde Brot aus Halm und Glut.* Ceres-Verlag GmbH, Bielefeld, 1951: 64 (top, first and second from left; bottom left)

Anderson, Suzanne: *Song of the Earth Spirit.* Friends of the Earth, San Francisco: 92 (bottom right)

Angé, Claude: *Larousse universel.* Vol. 2, Librairie Larousse, Paris, 1923: 63

Arber, Agnes: *Herbals, Their Origin and Evolution.* Cambridge University Press, 1953: 155 (bottom, second from right); 156 (bottom, third from left); 158 (top); 160 (left)

Arnau, Frank: *Rauschgift.* Verlag C. J. Bucher, 1967: 97 (No. 15); 180 (left, top and bottom)

Biedermann, Hans: *Medicina Magica.* Akademische Druck- und Verlagsanstalt, Graz, 1972: 2 (top); 4; 8 (top); 16 (bottom, second from left); 148 (top left); 150 (top center; bottom left); 151 (center, second from left); 155 (bottom, second from left)

Bihalji-Merin, Oto: *Masters of Naive Art.* McGraw-Hill Book Company, New York: 268 (bottom, first three from left); 269 (top; bottom, third from right); 270/271

Bock, Hironymus: *Kreuterbuch 1577.* Reprint 1964 by Verlag Konrad Kölbl, Grünwald b. Munich: 155 (bottom, third from left); 186 (bottom, first and third from left); 188 (bottom, third from left); 189 (bottom, second and third from right); 210 (right)

Brosse, Jacques: *L'Arbre.* Robert Delpire, Paris, 1962: 1 (right); 121; 233 (center, second from right)

Campbell, Joseph: *The Mythic Image,* Princeton University Press, New Jersey, 1974: 236 (center row, right)

Canby, Courtlandt: *Histoire de l'aéronautique.* Editions Rencontre, Lausanne and Erik Nitsche International, 1962: 34

Clarkson, Rosetta: *The Golden Age of Herbs & Herbalists.* Dover Publications, New York, 1972: 135 (right)

Cocteau, Jean: *Opium, Journal d'une désintoxication.* Editions Stock, Paris, 1930: 178 (top)

Conway, David: *The Magic of Herbs.* Mayflower Books, London, 1975: 151 (center, second from right)

Cook, Roger: *The Tree of Life.* Avon Books, New York, 1974: 184 (top left); 238 (right)

Debuigne, Gérard: *Larousse des plantes qui guérissent.* Librairie Larousse, Paris, 1974: 203 (bottom)

Dimier, Louis: *Histoire de la peinture de portrait en France au XVIe siècle.* Librairie Nationale d'Art et d'Histoire, Paris, 1924: 136 (center left)

Dossenbach, Hans D.: *The Family Life of Birds.* McGraw-Hill Book Company, New York, 1971: 246 (left)

Edlin, H. L.: *Mensch und Pflanzen.* F. A. Brockhaus, Wiesbaden, 1969: 98 (bottom); 120 (bottom)

Engel, Fritz-Martin: *Giftküche der Natur.* Landbuch Verlag, Hanover, 1972: 128 (top); 137 (bottom right and top left)

Folkard, Richard: *Plant Lore, Legends and Lyrics.* London, 1886: 15 (bottom)

Freitag, Helmut: *Wiesenblumen und Ackerblumen.* Belser Verlag, Stuttgart, 1966: 44 (top, second from left; bottom, first from right)

Fuchs, Leonard: *New Kreuterbuch. 1543.* Reprint 1964 by Verlag Konrad Kölbl, Munich: 144 (bottom right); 155 (bottom right); 160 (right); 212 (right); 213 (left)

Golowin, Sergius: *Die Magie der verbotenen Märchen.* Merlin Verlag, Hamburg, 1973: 188 (center left); 215 (top left); 230 (bottom)

Grimal, Pierre: *Larousse World Mythology.* The Hamlyn Publishing Group, London, 1965: 181 (left)

Hansmann, Lisclotte, and Lenz Kriss-Rettenbeck: *Amulett und Talismann.* Verlag Georg D. W. Callwey, Munich, 1966: 12 (top and bottom); 236 (top)

Hausammann, Suzanne: *Farbiges Indien.* Verlag C. J. Bucher, Lucerne, 1965, 2nd ed., 1968: 262 (right)

Heilmann, Karl Eugen: *Kräuterbücher in Bild und Geschichte.* Verlag Konrad Kölbl, Munich, 1966: 134 (bottom); 142 (top); 150 (bottom left); 159 (top); 166 (bottom, second and third from left); 167 (bottom left); 211 (bottom right)

Hyams, Edward: *A History of Gardens and Gardening.* J. M. Dent & Sons, London, 1971: 246 (center 3 ill.)

—: *Plants in the Service of Man.* J. M. Dent & Sons, London, 1971: 112 (bottom right)

Knight, Max: *Return to the Alps.* Friends of the Earth, San Francisco: 42 (third from bottom)

Kräusel, Richard: *Mitteleuropäische Pflanzenwelt.* Kronen Verlag Erich Cramer, Hamburg: 175

Künzle, Pfarrer: *Das grosse Kräuterheilbuch.* Walter Verlag, Olten, 24th rev. ed., 1974: 174

Law, Donald: *The Concise Herbal Encyclopedia.* Saint Martin's Press, New York, 1973: 2 (right)

Lawton, Richard: *Grand Illusions.* McGraw-Hill Book Company, New York, 1973: 250 (center, second from right)

Lehner, E. and J.: *Folklore and Odysseys of Food and Medical Plants.* Harrap, London, 1973: 206 (top)

Leuenberger, Hans: *Zauberdrogen.* Henry Goverts Verlag, Stuttgart, 1969: 220 (center left and right)

Linsenmaier, Walter: *Insects of the World.* McGraw-Hill Book Company, New York, 1972: 54 (Nos. 5, 8); 55 (No. 20)

Lonicero, Adamo: *Kreuterbuch 1679.* Reprint 1962 by Verlag Konrad Kölbl, Munich: 114/115; 253 (bottom)

Masselman, George: *The Money Trees, The Spice Trade.* McGraw-Hill Book Company, New York, 1967: 113 (bottom)

Masters, Robert E. L., and Jean Houston: *Psychedelic Kunst.* Droemersche Verlagsanstalt, Munich, 1969: 224 (right and bottom right)

Newall, Venetia: *The Encyclopedia of Witchcraft and Magic.* The Hamlyn Publishing Group, London, 1974: 184 (top right)

Pelt, Jean-Marie: *Drogue et plantes magiques.* Horizons de France, 1971: 200 (right row, second from top)

Porta, J. B.: *Phytognomica octo libris contenta.* Naples, 1558: 152 (left); 153 (top and center)

Roedelberger, A. Franz, and Vera I. Groschoff: *Ernte im Garten Eden.* Buchverlag Verbandsdruckerei, Bern: 22 (left, second from right)

Runes, Dagobert D.: *Illustrierte Geschichte der Philosophie.* Nagel Verlag, Geneva, 1962: 122 (top left)

Rytz, Walther: *Pflanzenaquarelle des Hans Weiditz aus dem Jahre 1529.* Verlag Paul Haupt, Bern, 1936: 166 (right)

Schubert, G. H. von: *Naturgeschichte des Pflanzenreichs in Bildern.* Stuttgart and Esslinge, 1853: 98 (top left); 128 (bottom); 129 (second and fourth row); 130 (second row from bottom, left); 131 (first and second from top, left); 132 (second from left; last from right); 134 (center); 135 (top left); 144 (left); 145 (left); 170; 177 (left); 252 (bottom); 253 (bottom)

Schulthess, Emil: *Amazonas.* Artemis Verlag, Zurich, 1962: 138 (left)

—: *China.* Artemis Verlag, Zurich, 1966: 79

Seligmann, Kurt: *Das Weltreich der Magie.* R. Löwit, Wiesbaden, 1948: 256 (center, first and second from left)

Stehli, Georg: *Pflanzen auf Insektenfang.* Kosmos Gesellschaft der Naturfreunde, Stuttgart, 1934: 124 (top)

Sutton, Anne and Myron: *The Life of the Desert.* McGraw-Hill Book Company, New York, 1966: 48 (top and bottom left); 49 (bottom)

Thorwald, Jürgen: *Macht und Geheimnis der frühen Ärzte.* Droemersche Verlagsanstalt, Munich, 1962: 148 (bottom, second from right); 149 (top; bottom, second from right); 163 (left, second from top)

Weigel, Christoph: *Abbildung der Gemein-Nützlichen Haupt-Stände.* Regensburg, 1698: 88 (top)

Dizionario della Natura. Vol. 2. Arnoldo Mondadori Editore, Milan, 1976: 119 (bottom, second from right)

DU, June 1971: 267 (bottom right)

Encyclopedia of Magic and Superstition. Octopus Books, London, 1974: 182 (top)

Le Magasin Pittoresque. Vol. 9, 1841: 242 (top)

Mon médecin: 100

Les Plantes médicinales: 171

Weltgeschichte in Bildern. Vol. 17, *Das Zeitalter der Revolution: von Washington bis Bonaparte.* Editions Rencontre, Lausanne: 250 (left)

Vollständige Faksimileausgabe des Codex Vindobonensis 93 der Österreichischen Nationalbibliothek, Medicina Antiqua. Akademische Druck- und Verlagsanstalt, Graz, 1971: 151 (top left); 154

Vollständige Faksimileausgabe des Tacuinum Sanitatis in Medicina (Cod. Vindobonensis S.N. 2644 der Österreichischen Nationalbibliothek). Adademische Druck- und Verlagsanstalt, Graz, 1966: 150 (top right); 155 (bottom left)

Vollständige Faksimileausgabe des Wiener Dioskurides (Codex Vindobonensis Medicina gr. 1.). Akademische Druck- und Verlagsanstalt, Graz, 1965–1970: 3; 16 (bottom left); 17; 152 (right); 153 (bottom); 164; 165

INDEX

286

287